EUROPEAN CONTRACT LAW IN A CHANGED BANKING AND FINANCIAL ARCHITECTURE

EUCOLATH
European Contract Law and Theory Series

European Contract Law and Theory Series, Volume 4

EUROPEAN CONTRACT LAW IN A CHANGED BANKING AND FINANCIAL ARCHITECTURE

Stability Design, the Common Good, and Private Party Participation

Edited by
Stefan GRUNDMANN
Pietro SIRENA

INTERSENTIA

Intersentia
Lefebvre Sarrut Belgium SA
Rue Haute, 139/6
1000 Bruxelles
Belgium

Distribution for the UK and
Rest of the World (incl. Eastern Europe)
Ingram Publisher Services UK
1 Deltic Avenue, Rooksley
Milton Keynes MK13 8LD
United Kingdom
Tel: +44 1752 202 301 | Fax: +44 1752 202 331
Email: orders@nbninternational.com

Distribution for France and other countries
Interforum Editis
92 avenue de France
75013 Paris
France

Distribution for the USA and Canada
Independent Publishers Group
Order Department
814 North Franklin Street
Chicago, IL 60610
USA
Tel: +1 800 888 4741 (toll free) | Fax: +1 312 337 5985
Email: orders@ipgbook.com

European Contract Law in a Changed Banking and Financial Architecture. Stability Design, the Common Good, and Private Party Participation

Artwork on cover: Lady in Abstract (ca. 1921) - Jay Van Everen (1875 – 1947) / Artvee

ISBN 978-1-78068-662-2
D/2024/7849/112
NUR 822

British Library Cataloguing in Publication Data. A catalogue record for this book is available from the British Library.

CONTENTS

LIST OF CASES

SUPRANATIONAL

EUROPEAN COURT OF JUSTICE

NATIONAL

AUSTRIA

The Austrian Federal Court of Justice (OGH), judgement of

FRANCE

GERMANY

Federal Court of Justice

IRELAND

NETHERLANDS

UK

USA

LIST OF AUTHORS

Esther Arroyo Amayuelas
Full professor of Civil Law at the Departament of Private Law, Universitat de Barcelona, Spain.

Nikolai Badenhoop
Head of Research Group, Leibniz Institute for Financial Research SAFE, Frankfurt, Germany. Postdoctoral Fellow, Leibniz Institute for Financial Research SAFE, Frankfurt; Max-Weber Postdoctoral Fellow, European University Institute (2021–22); PhD in Law from Humboldt University Berlin (2019). Expert for the European Parliament's ECON Committee in the legislative process on the Regulation on European green bonds, the 'EU Green Bond Standard' (2022).

Ewa Bagińska
Professor of Private Law, Gdańsk University, Poland.

François Barrière
Professor at Université Lumière Lyon 2, France.

Alessandra de Aldisio
Senior advisor at the Financial Supervision and Regulation Directorate of the Bank of Italy – Regulation and Macroprudential Analysis.

Stefan Grundmann
Professor of Private and Business Law, Humboldt University Berlin, Germany, and Professor of Transnational Law and Theory, European University Institute (EUI), Florence (part-time, alumnus).

Carlo Lanfranchi
Advisor at the Financial Supervision and Regulation Directorate of the Bank of Italy – Regulation and Macroprudential Analysis (Head of the Crisis management team), Phd in Law from Cattolica University, Milan, Italy (2018).

Moritz Renner
Professor of Civil Law, International and European Commercial Law, University of Mannheim, Germany.

Michael Anderson Schillig
Professor of Law, The Dickson Poon School of Law, King's College London, United Kingdom.

Pietro Sirena
Professor of Civil Law, Comparative Private Law, and Banking Law, Bocconi University, Milan, Italy.

Piotr Tereszkiewicz
Professor of Private Law, Jagellonian University, Kraków, Poland; Adjunct Professor, Cornell Law School, Ithaca, United States.

PART I
Architecture

CHAPTER 1

EUROPEAN CONTRACT LAW AND THE COMMON GOOD PLUS PRIVATE PARTY PARTICIPATION IN THE EU BANKING UNION

The Overall Challenge

Stefan GRUNDMANN

1. INTRODUCTION AND OVERALL THEME

European Contract Law has been affected by mega-developments in society of the last decade in multiple ways. These range from the digital revolution that led to a host of EU legislation, both regulation of individual contractual relationships and of markets and platforms,[1] to a similar revolution with

[1] For contracts on digital contents and services for sales of goods with digital components, see Directive (EU) 2019/770 of the European Parliament and of the Council of 20 May 2019 on certain aspects concerning contracts for the supply of digital content and digital

respect to sustainability, which, again with EU legislation as the dominant layer, has led deep into contract and adjoining company and capital markets law as well.[2] Many authors consider these two as the mega-trends of today's law of the enterprise – with the particular characteristic that regulation, company law and banking law are intertwined in particularly dense ways with contract

---

services, [2019] OJ L 136/1; Directive (EU) 2019/771 of the European Parliament and of the Council of 20 May 2019 on certain aspects concerning contracts for the sale of goods, amending Regulation (EU) 2017/2394 and Directive 2009/22/EC, and repealing Directive 1999/44/EC, [2019] OJ L 136/28. For the regulation of the responsibility of service providers, namely platforms, for illegal content and disinformation, see Regulation (EU) 2022/2065 of the European Parliament and of the Council of 19 October 2022 on a Single Market for Digital Services and amending Directive 2000/31/EC (Digital Services Act), [2022] OJ L 277/1. For the regulation of a fair and reliable functioning of digital markets and platforms: Regulation (EU) 2022/1925 of the European Parliament and of the Council of 14 September 2022 on contestable and fair markets in the digital sector and amending Directives (EU) 2019/1937 and (EU) 2020/1828 (Digital Markets Act), [2022] OJ L 265/1. For the regulation of core risks stemming from Artificial Intelligence (AI), see Proposal (of 21.4.2021) for a Regulation of the European Parliament and of the Council laying down harmonised rules on artificial intelligence (Artificial Intelligence Act) and amending certain Union Legislative Acts, COM/021/206 final; close to adoption, see European Parliament legislative resolution of 13 March 2024 on the proposal for a regulation of the European Parliament and of the Council on laying down harmonised rules on Artificial Intelligence (Artificial Intelligence Act) and amending certain Union Legislative Acts (COM(2021)0206 – C9-0146/2021 – 2021/0106(COD)). For an early broad analysis, see S. Grundmann and Ph. Hacker, 'Digital Technology as a Challenge to European Contract Law. From the Existing to the Future Architecture' (2017) 13 *European Review of Contract Law (ERCL)* 255; A. De Franceschi (ed.), *European Contract Law and the Digital Single Market: the Implications of the Digital Revolution*, Intersentia, Cambridge 2016; S. Grundmann (ed.), *European Contract Law in the Digital Age*, Intersentia, Cambridge 2018.

2 With respect to contract law, see Directive (EU) 2019/771 (above n. 1). With respect to reporting/company law, see Directive 2014/95/EU of the European Parliament and of the Council of 22 October 2014 amending Directive 2013/34/EU as regards disclosure of non-financial and diversity information by certain large undertakings and groups, [2014] OJ L 330/1, with reform agenda on due diligence, see European Commission Proposal of 23 February 2022 for a Directive of the European Parliament and of the Council on Corporate Sustainability Due Diligence and amending Directive (EU) 2019/1937, COM(2022) 71 final; close to adoption, see European Parliament legislative resolution of 24 April 2024 on the proposal for a directive of the European Parliament and of the Council on Corporate Sustainability Due Diligence and amending Directive (EU) 2019/1937 (COM(2022)0071 – C9-0050/2022 – 2022/0051(COD)). With respect to capital market law ('taxonomy'), see Regulation (EU) 2020/852 of the European Parliament and of the Council of 18 June 2020 on the establishment of a framework to facilitate sustainable investment, and amending Regulation (EU) 2019/2088, [2020] OJ L 198/13; and related to it, Regulation (EU) 2019/2088 of the European Parliament and of the Council of 27 November 2019 on sustainability related disclosures in the financial services sector, [2019] OJ L 317/1. On the new sales law's sustainability dimension, see S. Grundmann and Y. Atamer (eds.), *Sale of Goods Law in the 21st Century: Challenges Ahead*, Intersentia, Cambridge 2023, namely their introduction p. 1 et seqq. On company and capital market law and sustainability, see S. Grundmann, *European Company Law in Transformation – Strive for Participation and Sustainability* (2023) 42 *Yearbook of European Law* 210 (2024), section III.; A. Häsli and R. Weber, 'Climate Change Reporting and Due Diligence' (2021) 18 *European Company & Finnacial Law Review (ECFR)* 948; A. Hellgardt and V. Jouannaud, 'Nachhaltigkeitsziele

law in these new mega-topics.[3] Much less central in the apprehension of a larger contract law public in Europe is a development that had been triggered by the first mega-crisis in Europe in this decade, the Global Financial Crisis (followed by a whole series of mega-crises in Europe). This development, however, can well be seen as being just as important and indeed pointing in a similar direction. Moreover, it may even predate the other developments named. It may well be that the European Banking Union – created as a response to the global financial crisis (in 2008) and to the Euro sovereign debt crisis (in 2010) – constitutes the first instance of a decidedly common (public) good oriented reform.[4] In other words: this may well be the first instance of a public good trend in the areas where autonomous party decisions typically reigned supreme, a trend that can be seen as a fundamentally new '*green box* approach'.[5]

Indeed, the European Banking Union constitutes a stability regime that is characterised by greatly increased 'own funds' regulatory standards, a completely new recovery and resolution regime, and additional guarantees to clients whose enforcement is primarily entrusted to the European Central Bank (for Eurozone banks). Hence, the increased robustness, the very great attention paid to prevention with the foreseeing and planning of crises and the (highly exceptional) transfer of competences to the EU level characterise the regime in which long-termism is to play a much more prominent role.[6] All this for preserving a common (public) good as will appear from the following. The core question raised in this volume is how the European Banking Union regime relates to private parties. Both the development of the European

und Privatrecht' (2022) 222(2) *Archiv für die civilistische Praxis (AcP)* 163; E. Macchiavello and M. Siri, 'Sustainable Finance and Fintech' (2022) 19 *ECFR* 128; H. Fleischer, 'Klimaschutz im Gesellschafts, Bilanz- und Kapitalmarktrecht' (2022) *Der Betrieb (DB)* 37.

3 For an explanation of how company law and contract law form the core of private law more generally – the two united by the core role that autonomy plays, but also regulation as its counterpart – see S. Grundmann, 'Welche Einheit des Privatrechts? – Von einer formalen zu einer gestaltungsorientierten Konzeption des Privatrechts' in *Festschrift für Klaus Hopt zum 70. Geburtstag am 24 August 2010*, De Gruyter, Berlin 2010, pp. 61-91 and S. Grundmann, 'On the Unity of Private Law – From a Formal to a Substance Based Concept of Private Law' (2010) 18 *ERPL* 1055. Banking law is already traditionally characterised as an interplay between organisation (such as in company law) and contract law – and this constitutes the main structural dimension as well of *my* overall commentary on the field, quoted below n. 9.

4 See in this sense, S. Grundmann (above n. 2), section III.; but also J.-H. Binder, 'Vorstandshandeln zwischen öffentlichem und Verbandsinteresse' (2013) 42 *Zeitschrift für Unternehmens- und Gesellschaftsrecht (ZGR)* 760.

5 For an analysis of this concept, see S. Grundmann (above n. 2), section III (contrasting it with a phase in which an internal market rationale was the primary aim of EU company law ['*black-box* approach'] and a phase in which empowering multi-stakeholder participation became increasingly important ['*red-box* approach']. On the intersections between *green-box* and *red-box* approaches, see Grundmann (above n. 2) and also below in the text.

6 On this part of the topic, see below section 2. in this contribution and Part. II. of the volume.

Banking Union and this core question can be viewed in relation to the overall development of European Company, Business and Market Law of the 2010s and – in more detail – in the narrower context of the European Banking Union and private party claims and participation. While this contribution – on the overall architecture – focuses more on the broader view and tries to depict and analyse that architecture, the specific contributions in this volume as a whole try to cover both perspectives. These are the broader view (with some characteristic examples of common good and participation also beyond the EU Banking Union) and the more focused one (the majority of contributions).[7] All contributions, however, in conjunction paint a picture of the stability regime of the European Banking Union, how it has been introduced with a particular view to furthering the public good, including increasing solidarity (sharing this impetus with other outstanding instances of European Economic Law development), and how private participation has been designed and enlarged.

The second decade of the 2000s has certainly been characterised by crises – from financial to sovereign debt crises, via refugee and Covid crises back to rule of law, attack on democracy and again refugee crises – and, at least in part, by regulatory or legislative answers to them. The answer to the first and second crises named was – on the side of stability of the banking system – the establishment of the European Banking Union.[8] The main thrust was to establish a more robust banking supervision regime, with a view to repelling privatisation of gains coupled with socialisation of risks and losses (at the expense of taxpayers). This book is, firstly, about the interpretation of this development as a quintessential turn toward more public good oriented legislative strategies

---

7 On common good orientation and increased private party participation as the two cornerstones of the development (in EU banking and contract, but company and capital market law too), see below sections 3 and 4 in this contribution and Part III. in the volume.

8 On the side of sovereign debt stability, i.e., for the Member States, the parallel system consists of (1) a set of preventive measures, such as debt breaks, which were meant to be incorporated into the Member States' constitutions, or the European Calendar, according to which budget data have to be communicated to the EU Commission on certain dates, and (2) the so-called European Stability Mechanism (ESM) as a backstop for Eurozone Member States in distress. The ESM was set up on 8 October 2012 (a successor to the European Financial Stability Facility (EFSF)) as the permanent solution for a problem that arose early in the sovereign debt crisis: namely, the lack of a backstop for Euro area countries no longer able to raise capital on markets. For an account of these two core components, especially with the Fiscal Compact (so-called Six-Pack) and with the rescue fund in the form of the ESM, see F. Martucci, 'Non-EU Legal Instruments (EFSF, ESM, AND Fiscal Compact)' in F. Amtenbrink, C. Herrmann and R. Repasi (eds.), *The EU Law of Economic and Monetary Union*, Oxford Academic, New York 2020; online ed.; R. Cisotta, 'What Role for the European Commission in the New Governance of the Economic and Monetary Union?' (07/2013) *Istituto Affari Internazionali Working Papers* 13, J. Creel, P. Hubert and F. Saraceno, 'The European Fiscal Compact: A Counterfactual Assessment' (2012) 27 *Journal of Economic Integration* 537.

in EU contract, capital markets and enterprise law (quintessential common good orientation) and, secondly, about the empowering of private parties in participating in and profiting from this turn (increased empowerment and participation).

2. STABILITY REGIME OF THE EU BANKING UNION

2.1. EU BANKING UNION AND STABILITY – SURVEY

The EU Banking Union and the EU banking supervision architecture (revised under this term) were established and enacted in 2013/14 and have thoroughly been discussed as such and commented upon[9] – while the discussion of particular dimensions and namely of repercussions is still in flux. The reformed, and in large part completely new EU regulatory framework (2013/14) – relating to credit institutions – is divided into two parts.[10]

Already incomparably more robust (than before 2013/14) is the current banking supervision,[11] which since 2014 has increasingly come under the

9 J.-H. Binder and C. Gortsos (eds.), *The European Banking Union – A Compendium*, Nomos, Baden-Baden 2016; J.-H. Binder, C. Gortsos, K. Lackhoff and C. Ohler (eds.), *European Banking Union – Brussels Commentary*, C.H. Beck, Munich 2022; J.-H Binder, A. Glos and J. Riepe (eds.), *Handbuch Bankenaufsichtsrecht*, RWS Verlag, Cologne 2018; see also, much more condensed: S. Grundmann, *Bankvertragsrecht*, 2 vols., de Gruyter, Berlin, 2020-21 (GroßkommHGB Bde. 10+11), part 1 paras. 31-106; for the constitutional dimensions, see mainly S. Grundmann and H.-W. Micklitz (eds.), *The European Banking Union and Constitution*, Bloomsbury, London 2019.

10 In addition to the two genuinely European pillars (with European funds and institutions), there is a third pillar still 'only harmonised', as many Member States complain: the regulation of the deposit guarantee system, which is of course closely related to EU supervisory law in the crisis: S. Grundmann (above n. 9), part 1, para. 42. See Directive 2014/49/EU of the European Parliament and of the Council of 16 April 2014 on deposit guarantee schemes, [2014] OJ L 173/149. For the proposals for a genuinely European Scheme (EU deposit guarantee fund), see Proposal for a Regulation of the European Parliament and of the Council amending Regulation (EU) 806/2014 in order to establish a European Deposit Insurance Scheme COM/2015/0586 final – 2015/0270 (COD); and below Chapter 4 of this volume.

11 The central legal acts were Directive 2013/36/EU of the European Parliament and of the Council of 26 June 2013 on access to the activity of credit institutions and the prudential supervision of credit institutions and investment firms, amending Directive 2002/87/EC and repealing Directives 2006/48/EC and 2006/49/EC, [2013] OJ L 176/338 (CRD-IV); Regulation (EU) No. 575/2013 of the European Parliament and of the Council of 26 June 2013 on prudential requirements for credit institutions and investment firms and amending Regulation (EU) No. 648/2012, [2013] OJ L 176/1 (CRR); and (SSM) Council Regulation (EU) 1024/2013 of 15 October 2013 conferring specific tasks on the European Central Bank concerning policies relating to the prudential supervision of credit institutions, [2013] OJ L 287/63 (Single Supervisory Mechanism). On the main innovations see the next notes and above n. 9.

single umbrella of the European Central Bank (this last issue to be taken-up at the end of this section, 'a second word on the stability objective').[12] The size of valuable capital components and the solidity of each single component (as required by the regulation) was already considerably increased – but moreover is now broadly supplemented by further risk buffers, especially for those institutions and models where systemic risk, namely 'too-big-to-fail', seem more important.[13] In other words, complexity, lack of transparency of the structures and larger size, but also certain cycles of risk have become elements of increased 'own funds' requirements – and thus also of increased costs. At the same time, the number of supervisors has risen, namely with respect to crisis prevention, which already has to be meticulously planned on a continuous basis in the current supervision regime of the going concern, and hence in many cases and phases before signs of crisis are even showing (see below section 2.). Hence, one cannot speak of an entirely new *ongoing* banking supervision regime, but of one that is completely new only in respect of this core function (namely concrete crisis *prevention*).

Completely new, on the other hand, is the supervisory regime of the phase of the crisis itself, for systemically relevant crises/insolvencies (reorganisation, resolution). It will therefore be taken up in detail in section 2.2. and by several contributions in this volume (Chapters 2 and 3).

One word on the aforementioned stability objective is needed before this already. For decades, currency stability concerns have been in the spotlight, even more so with the introduction of the euro[14] – concerns that, by their very nature, are of macroeconomic kind. However, the first global crisis, which came close to that of the 1920s, then affected concrete

---

12 On the concentration of supervision in the ECB (institutional): J. Gren, 'The Politics of Delegation in European Banking Union: Building the ECB supervisory oversight capacity', (2017) 13 *Journal of Contemporary European Research* 1109; S. Grundmann and H.-W. Micklitz (above n. 9); and brief summary in S. Grundmann (above n. 9), part 1, paras. 54-56.

13 On the significant tightening of capital adequacy per se and through additional buffers, see T. Fischer and M. Boegl in J. Ellenberger and H.-J. Bunte (eds.), *Bankrechtshandbuch*, 6th ed., C.H. Beck, Munich 2022, § 110 paras. 103-114; S. Grundmann (above n. 9), part 1, paras. 42, 106. Frequently quoted the continued harsh criticism by A. Admati and M. Hellwig, *The Banker's New Clothes*, Princeton University Press, Princeton NJ 2014 (requiring capital adequacy of approx. 20 % of the risk; see also R. Greenwood, S. Hanson, J. Stein and A. Sunderam, 'Strengthening and Streamlining Bank Capital Regulation' (2017) *Brookings Papers on Economic Activity* 479-544; E. Posner, 'How Do Bank Regulators Determine Capital-Adequacy Requirements?' (2015) 82 *The University of Chicago Law Review* 1853; A.D. Morrison and L. White, 'Crises and Capital Requirements in Banking' (2005) 95 *The American Economic Review* 1548.

14 E.g., B.S. Bernanke and I. Mihov, 'Measuring Monetary Policy' (1998) 113 *The Quarterly Journal of Economics* 869; R. Clarida, J. Gali and M. Gertler, 'Monetary Policy Rules and Macroeconomic Stability: Evidence and Some Theory' (2000) 115 *The Quarterly Journal of Economics* 147; F.-C. Zeitler, 'Die Europäische Währungsunion als Stabilitätsgemeinschaft' (1995) *Wertpapier-Mitteilungen (WM)* 1609.

institutions, with legal personality, especially credit institutions. Supervision of these institutions had previously focused on the individual institution (with microeconomic tools), although regulation was of course intended to prevent the 'run risk', a risk of a macroeconomic nature. Since the global financial crisis, which was fuelled by massive contagion risks (due to tightly woven interbank links and the proven unforeseeability of imminent bank insolvencies such as Lehman Brothers),[15] the idea of preventing systemic – macroeconomic – risks has also become central to banking supervision law,[16] in addition to (continuing) micro-prudential supervision of individual institutions. With the perception of individual players – banks – as the source of key macro-prudential risks – and no longer only of reliability of currencies as an instrument to which liability claims cannot be attached in a meaningful way – one question arose, the question core to this volume. The question is what private law involvement and claims arise if single actors and institutions do not meet the standards, which the European Banking Union regime imposes.

A second word on the stability objective should be added, now on its institutional side, a true revolution. Beginning in 2014 and with its last step taken in 2021, the ECB assumed the lead in complete Eurozone banking supervision in the EU. This revolutionary step for Europe – with the competence of single-case administration shifted to the *EU level* – was taken due to the truly dramatic consequences, which the system of *national* bank supervisory authorities had led to. The main causes of the global financial crisis are (unanimously) viewed as supervisory failures today, including in Europe, while sub-prime lending (too extensive default risks that had the structure of cluster risks) and faulty structuring and incentives in securitisation in the United States were the starting point. With a view to avoiding similar scenarios in Europe in the future, namely banking supervision was to be (radically) changed and enhanced. The main systemic weaknesses in the global and European financial systems – with

---

15 Even in May 2008, Moody's affirmed the AAA rating assigned to Lehman Brothers Enhanced LIBOR Fund (and only placed on the watch-list its market risk rating), https://www.moodys.com/research/Moodys-affirms-Aaa-rating-assigned-to-Lehman-Brothers-Enhanced-LIBOR--PR_154761. On the dramatic succession of events, see L. Bell, 'The Fed and Lehman Brothers' (July 2016) *Working Paper for the National Bank of Economic Research* 29 et seqq.

16 On this issue, see T. Engel, *Systemrisikovorsorge durch Bankaufsicht, Bankgesellschaft und Bankvorstand*, Mohr Siebeck, Tübingen 2020; L. Chen, H. Liu, F. Liu and Y. Zhou, 'Bank regulation and systemic risk: cross country evidence' (2021) 57 *Review of Quantitative Finance and Accounting* 353; J. de Haan, Z. Jin and C. Zhou, 'Micro-prudential regulation and banks' systemic risk' (10/2019) *DNB Working Paper No. 656*; M. Schüler, 'How Do Banking Supervisors Deal with Europe-wide Systemic Risk?' *ZEW Discussion Paper No. 03-03*; S. Grundmann (above n. 9), part 1, para. 102; I. Freis-Janik, in S. Kümpel, P.O. Mülbert, A. Früh and T. Seyfried (eds.), *Bank- und Kapitalmarktrecht*, 5th ed., Otto Schmidt, Cologne 2019, paras. 2.313 and 2.316.

contagion risks that could not be contained nationally – are in fact twofold. On the one hand, the relevant rating agencies were too few (oligopoly), were subject to massive misaligned incentives (so-called confirmation bias and exorbitant conflicts of interest – profit interests detrimental to the public good), and were practically unregulated (all this is not a topic for discussion here).[17] On the other hand, there was massive failure of the national supervisory authorities (now primarily in the EU), which did not want to demand stricter risk provisioning efforts from domestic credit institutions than were asked from their competitors in (EU) foreign countries[18] – even where the risks had been recognised.[19]

Hence, this formed a classical type of regulatory capture[20] – and the main objective of establishing the EU Banking Union was to combat it by raising the competence to the EU level and by installing a regime of independence. Indeed one pillar of the response to the crisis was immunisation of banking supervision against political influence. The national banking supervisors were replaced by the unified system of EU banking supervision with two core characteristics: the ECB's direct supervision of the so-called Systemically Important Financial Institutions (SIFIs) and final decision-making powers on all others (so-called Single Supervisory Mechanism, SSM); and immunisation against political influence (independence).[21] Without discussing the system in detail, the enormity of the step becomes clear from the following. Only twice in the history of the EEC/EC/EU, at

---

17 On these issues, see with more references (also on the regulation existing today) S. Egidy, *Finanzkrise und Verfassung*, Mohr Siebeck, Tübingen 2019, pp. 26-58.

18 See for example S. Egidy, *Finanzkrise und Verfassung*, Mohr Siebeck, Tübingen 2019, p. 49; G. Tabellini, 'Why did bank supervision fail?' in A. Felton and C. Reinhart (eds.), *The First Global Financial Crisis of the 21st Century*, VoxEU and Centre for Economic Policy Research, London 2008, pp. 45-49; J.A. Kämmerer in M.A. Dauses and M. Ludwigs (eds.), *Handbuch des EU-Wirtschaftsrechts*, C.H. Beck Munich 7/2021, F.I. para. 23.

19 The cluster risk, which was generally well addressed in (EU) banking supervision law (for large exposures) and which in the sub-prime debt market lay in the fact that the only collateral of value (for sub-prime borrowers as a whole) was in real estate (specifically, the steady value of the US real estate market), cannot be analysed here in more detail. It was, however, quite recognisable despite (unjustified) AAA ratings given to the securities based on them. As a failure, it is then central that institutions and supervisory authorities – also with reference to the ratings – entered into/allowed investments burdened with cluster risk far beyond the level at which the risk is (statistically) bearable and above which it is (in the large loan sector) impermissible for reasons of leverage control. The central factor that 'justified' (and triggered) massive violation and breach of this sound cluster risk rationale was the (international) competitive pressure felt by the credit institutions of each country, which they in turn brought to bear on the supervisory authorities via their political authorities (such as finance ministries). See references in the previous two footnotes.

20 On this concept, G.J. Stigler, 'The theory of economic regulation' (1971) 2 *Bell Journal of Economics & Management Science* 3; more references: S. Grundmann (above n. 9) part 1 para. 58.

21 Technical-legal description and legal-political evaluation (with constitutional principles) see references above n. 9.

distinctive moments in time, was a comparable step taken (outside isolated sectors such as agriculture), the transfer of the entire implementation of a policy field to an EU institution (i.e. withdrawing implementation power from Member States). This was in 1958, upon the handover of a competition union to the EU Commission;[22] and, in 1992/1999/2002, when entering a (more) political Union, upon the transfer of Euro monetary supervision (as a flagship of this change) to the ECB (Maastricht Treaty). A radical amendment of this same magnitude (a true revolution) was apparently considered to be imperative ('without alternative') for the financial architecture, decided unanimously(!). This was so important to public opinion that even the entry into force of the EU Charter of Fundamental Rights in the same year was almost ignored.

2.2. RECOVERY AND RESOLUTION IN PARTICULAR

Completely new, as already stated, was the supervisory regime for bank crises, namely for systemic insolvency (reorganisation, resolution), a tailor-made regime for each mega-case, under the aegis of the Single Resolution Board (SRB) (Brussels).[23] The core legal acts to achieve this were – for the first time – the EU Bank Recovery and Resolution Directive (BRRD) and the so-called Single Resolution Mechanism (SRM Regulation).[24] Central to this section of

---

22 On this concept, in which EU competition law forms (only) a part, albeit a central one: E.-J. Mestmäcker, 'Auf dem Wege zu einer Ordnungspolitik für Europa' in *Eine Ordnungspolitik für Europa: Festschrift für Hans von der Groeben zu seinem 80. Geburtstag*, Nomos, Baden-Baden 1987, pp. 9-51; P. Behrens, *Europäisches Marktöffnungs- und Wettbewerbsrecht*, C.F. Müller, Karlsruhe 2017; see also S. Grundmann, 'The Concept of the Private Law Society after 50 Years of European and European Business Law' (2008) 16 *European Review of Private Law* 553.

23 See on this agency (and the other decision-makers in this part of the supervisory regime, which has been operational since 2016), N. Moloney, 'European Banking Union: Assessing its Risks and Resilience' (2014) 51 *Common Market Law Review* 1609, 1638 et seqq.; D. Zagouras, in J. Ellenberger and H.-J. Bunte (eds.), *Bankrechtshandbuch*, § 124b paras. 71-94; S. Grundmann (above n. 9), part 1, paras. 50, 60-64; and more references above n. 9.

24 Directive 2014/59/EU of the European Parliament and of the Council of 15 May 2014 establishing a framework for the recovery and resolution of credit institutions and investment firms and amending Council Directive 82/891/EEC, and Directives 2001/24/EC, 2002/47/EC, 2004/25/EC, 2005/56/EC, 2007/36/EC, 2011/35/EU, 2012/30/EU and 2013/36/EU, and Regulations (EU) No. 1093/2010 and (EU) No. 648/2012, of the European Parliament and of the Council, [2014] OJ L 173/190 (BRRD); Regulation (EU) No. 806/2014 of the European Parliament and of the Council of 15 July 2014 establishing uniform rules and a uniform procedure for the resolution of credit institutions and certain investment firms in the framework of a Single Resolution Mechanism and a Single Resolution Fund and amending Regulation (EU) No. 1093/2010, [2014] OJ L 225/1 (SRM). See more specifically on both legal acts: J. Goddard, P. Molyneux and J.O.S. Wilson, 'Banking in Europe: Integration, Reform, and the Road to a Banking Union' in A. Berger, P. Molyneux and

the chapter are four components primarily. First is the focus on planning the *recovery regime* already while the bank acts as a going concern (namely ongoing supervision as described in section 2.1). Secondly, institutionally, is the mutual cooperation and collaborative actions between supervisory authority and credit institution in *recovery planning*. Thirdly is the increase in *responsibility* for recovery burdens on (certain) creditors and shareholders. Finally and more generally, it is worth stressing at this point already that there is an unconditional commitment to the *stability aim*, which plays out also in the duties to which the banks' management (as the main private law actors) are subject. These four characteristics are shortly addressed in turn in this contribution (the first two of them are intertwined; the last one is dealt with below in section 3.2.).

The first two dimensions relate to an increased responsibility for stability (and early prevention of crises) both on the credit institutes and on the competent supervisory authorities, in cooperation with which the banks have to develop their recovery plans and who have to take an active role themselves. This overall description has two dimensions: early prevention ('early prevention principle') and multiple responsibilities on both sides to collaborate in risk prevention ('four eyes principle'). The goal is to establish a calendar of preventive steps, with (joint) responsibilities distributed among a number of obligated parties. The main tool are so-called 'living wills' developed even before the crisis. These are prophylactic recovery plans elaborated within the current (going-concern) banking supervision, based on the data made available in such supervision (temporal and factual interlocking), and grounded in responsibility both of the credit institution and of the supervisor to develop the plans independently, i.e., to participate more actively in the provisioning process (personal interlocking).[25] In all of this, maximum emphasis is placed on the independence of the supervisor from political influence potentially exercised at the instance of banks (avoidance of 'regulatory capture'). *Chapter 2* gives a survey of these and other crisis prevention tools and elements of the recovery/resolution framework from the perspective of supervisory practice.[26] While the regime constitutes a huge step in prevention, shortcomings are still seen. Namely, the weak basis for negotiated (and tailor-made) solutions is deplored, but also the lack of particular funding schemes for recovery, which have not been the object of

J.O.S. Wilson (eds.), *The Oxford Handbook of Banking*, 3rd ed., OUP, Oxford 2019, pp. 1000-1032; S. Grundmann (above n. 9), Part 1, paras. 39 and 60-64; and more references above n. 9.

25 E.g., J. Carmassi and R. Herring, 'Living Wills and Cross-Border Resolution of Systemically Important Banks' (2013) 5 *Journal of Financial Economic Policy* 361; see also compact description in S. Grundmann (above n. 9) part 1, paras. 41, 59, 62, 102.

26 A. de Aldisio and C. Lanfranchi, 'Pre-Insolvency in the BRRD – How to Enhance Recovery Measures', below Chapter 2 of this volume.

harmonisation in the BRRD and which might still contribute more intensely to the aim of early prevention and to push-back possibilities of obstruction (including rules on claw-back actions). This chapter pleads for a special type of financial instrument (mandatory convertible bonds) to incentivise capital injections into banks in financial distress – with a view to overcoming possible collective action problems.

This brings us to the third core feature named above. Increased responsibility for recovery burdens on (certain) creditors and shareholders is realised primarily by the 'bail-in' instrument. This instrument mainly aims to promote greater awareness of the goal of stability among shareholders and creditors (investors), i.e., awareness of the overriding objective of the regulation. These considerations raise the fundamental question of whether a stability culture in the European Banking Union regime does not need to be seen as a question also of justice or 'fairness' between affected groups of private law parties – hence strongly related to the common good (an idea taken up more broadly in section 3). With extensive bank bail-outs through (tax-financed) state aids, losses had been massively 'socialised' during the global financial crisis, while the profits previously made through speculative investment remained with the investors (hence were 'privatised').[27] With the requirement to have bail-in instruments, probably the most controversial measure in the new EU banking supervision, shareholders and such creditors whose bonds are previously flagged out to serve as such subordinate instruments (bail-in instruments) participate in the losses up to 100 per cent (and blockade by the exercise of voting rights is prevented). Each institution must include such instruments in its financing mix to a specified extent.[28] This is intended to create risk awareness (responsibility) among the 'principals' who determine business policy. The criticism that the taxpayer would not be totally relieved of the risk of bank insolvency because there would still be institutions like Deutsche Bank whose liquidation would trigger systemic shocks ('too-big-to-fail') is correct,[29] but conceals two things. At the same time, an additional industry-wide rescue fund is

---

27 On this oft addressed scandal, see for example: M. Mazzucato, 'We Socialize Bailouts. We Should Socialize Successes, Too', 01/07/2020, *The New York Times*; A. Schmitz, 'Finanzmarktkrise und Reorganisation von Banken' (2010) 24 *Zeitschrift für Wirtschaftsrecht (ZIP)* 1199; R. Hank and W. von Petersdorff-Campen, *Frankfurter Allgemeine Zeitung (FAZ)* (22/12/2013).

28 On the bail-in regime (Arts. 43-58 BRRD, above n. 24), see monographs by A. Kowolik, *Das Bail-in-Instrument*, Mohr Siebeck, Tübingen 2018, passim; I. Triantafyllakis, *Haftung nach dem Bail-in-Instrument*, De Gruyter, Berlin 2022; and also K.-P. Wojcik, 'Bail-In in the Banking Union' (2016) 53 *Common Market Law Review* 91; and short description in e.g., S. Grundmann (above n. 9), part 1, para. 105.

29 Sceptical in this respect, for instance: K. Alexander, 'European Banking Union: A Legal and Institutional Analysis of the Single Supervisory Mechanism and the Single Resolution Mechanism' (2015) 40 *European Law Review* 154, 185 et seq.

being built up from bank profits, which is also to be used prior to resorting to state aids (the so-called Single Resolution Fund – SRF).[30] Furthermore, the goal is not absolute security against systemic bank insolvencies (without regard to costs and strategic losses), but rather to significantly increase the risk responsibility of the main participants – and this applies as well to the bail-in instruments of SIFIs, where a 'too-big-to-fail' is conceivable (also according to the legislator). Therefore, all this (the bail-in plus a rescue fund) constitutes a significant step towards/in returning to the basic and fair principle that losses should be incurred where profits are made (and vice versa).[31]

In this completely novel kind of instrument, all depends, of course, on the concrete design of the bundle of property rights investors (still) have in such bail-in-able instruments. *Chapter 3*,[32] in its main and theoretical part, creates a conceptual framework for understanding the changes effected by such instruments (their bundle of property rights), both with respect to changes in procedure (for instance of voting) that can be observed and with respect to substantive inroads into the property rights (like total loss). Building upon this, Chapter 3 then continues with forecasts on the question in what respects these instruments may prove effective, and in what respect there may be risks of adverse and unforeseen effects of the design of bail-in-able instruments, but also the bank resolution framework as such. Concerns are expressed with respect to medium-size and smaller credit institutions that might not be able to bear the costs – the consequence being just the contrary of what was intended: namely reducing the share of SIFIs in the overall market with a view to lowering the risk of 'too-big-to-fail'.

2.3. IN PARTICULAR: PRIVATE CLAIMS WITHIN THE SUPERVISORY SCHEME

One core pillar in this volume and of this contribution on the overall architecture too, is private party participation in the changed banking and

---

30 Based on Arts. 67-78 SRM (Regulation (EU) No. 806/2014, above n. 24). K.-P. Wojcik (above n. 28), pp. 102 et seqq.; A. Kowolik (above n. 28), pp. 27 et seqq., 152 et seqq.; I. Triantafyllakis (above n. 28), pp. 224 et seqq.; short summary in S. Grundmann (above n. 9), part 1, paras. 50, 105.

31 See on the principle, its economic and ethical justifications: G.H. Stern and R.J. Feldmann, *Too Big to Fail: The Hazards of Bank Bailouts*, Brookings Institution Press, Washington DC 2004, pp. 23 et seqq.; A. Kowolik (above n. 28), pp. 1 et seq. On the outstanding importance of the liability principle in a market-based competitive order: W. Eucken, *Grundsätze der Wirtschaftspolitik*, 6th ed., UTB, Stuttgart 1990, pp. 280 et seq.

32 M. Schillig, 'The Transformation of Property Rights in Corporate Insolvency and Bank Resolution', below Chapter 3 of this volume.

financial supervision architecture. To put it differently, the question is which instruments, claims and design power are in the hands of private law parties within the private law arena, among private parties (see section 4 below and Part III of the volume) – despite the fact that the supervision regime as such is aimed at systemic and institutional stability. The latter would seem to constitute primarily a common/public good after all (see section 3 below and Part III of the volume).

Two contributions are about the claims of private parties, but not in this abovementioned private law arena, where the main focus of this volume certainly lies (Part III); rather *inside* the banking supervision system. Thus, while these are claims of private parties, they are still of a completely different kind. They are located inside the banking supervision system, directed against a (deposit) guarantee fund established within the system for particular stability purposes, or directed against the system (the supervisory authorities) in case of failure to take the legal measures aimed at stability. In the first instance, such claims are even explicitly foreseen by the system, in the second case, they are disputed, but still part of the functioning of the system itself. Hence, these two questions on private party participation – probably the two most intriguing ones directly linked to the supervisory system – are approached within the Part dealing with supervision (and its stability) itself.

Chapter 4 tackles the landscape of deposit guarantee schemes.[33] While undisputed in principle, deposit guarantee schemes as such are subject of one of the most fundamental disputes (and for some authors: *lacunae*) still present in the EU Banking Union regime. This is the dispute about whether and how the deposit guarantee scheme should be established at EU level ('EDIS') in a manner parallel to the Single Supervisory Mechanism (SSM) and the Single Resolution Mechanism (SRM) – which, however, would imply a huge shift.[34] Deposits now guaranteed within one jurisdiction by a fund established under that jurisdiction and funded by the financial industry of that country would then be guaranteed by a joint scheme – broadening both the pool of deposit-holders and of funds guaranteeing such deposits, and thereby affecting the level of reliability. Chapter 4 starts from this status quo and analyses deposit schemes from the perspective of harmonisation (EU law), including the prospects for further Europeanisation, their chances, details and risks. The contribution proposes an EU-wide re-insurance scheme as an intermediate step. Moreover, Chapter 4 analyses the perspective of a (harmonised) national law, French law – in the absence of a unitary European regime parallel to SSM or SRM. The contribution analyses in particular the practical application in concrete cases

---

33 F. Barrière, 'Deposit Guarantee Schemes: Towards a Harmonization Through the EU?', below Chapter 4 of this volume.

34 See references above n. 10.

of bank recovery and resolution proceedings under the new regime following the crisis, and does so for other Member States such as Italy and Spain as well.

Chapter 5 tackles the issue of liability of supervisory authorities for failure in prudent supervision.[35] While the focus is on failure in national supervisory authorities – more important for non-Eurozone jurisdictions such as Poland and other Central European States –, most questions discussed also arise in similar ways in the European system of supervisory authorities, namely within the European Central Bank system, and here too national law plays a significant role. The chapter, indeed, takes a broad comparative law stance and includes several national systems, but with a view to finding common denominators. In a broader general section on the basics of liability, it mainly points to the fact that these are claims not in contract, but in tort, and that tort claims, by the contrast, are structured rather similarly in the comparison of different jurisdictions. Typically, liability per se, damages and causation are distinguished. A number of Member States, for budget reasons or reasons of institutional independence, have in principle exclusions or restrictions of liability on the part of state agencies. For civil servants themselves (not often sued directly, anyhow), additional restrictions are currently in place for social reasons. Based on these more general foundations, the author then addresses the questions of (proof of) damage and causation based on common denominators that can be found in Member States' legal practice.

3. THE COMMON GOOD IN BANKING AND IN COMPANY AND CONTRACT LAW

3.1. COMMON GOOD AS THE CORE THRUST OF RECENT EU COMPANY LAW

This is not a volume on *company law* dealing with non-financial reporting and due diligence standards aimed at sustainability standards. Nor is it one on *value chains* and their corporate social responsibility dimensions and sustainability. Yet, when one speaks of common good, these are the areas that so much dominate the discourse today that any discussion of sustainability and common good issues must be embedded in at least a short survey of these company and value chain developments. This applies also to EU banking and contract law, our main topic in the volume and below in section 3.2.

In *European Company Law*, a key element of the common good is defined as a corporate social responsibility of large companies in Europe for

[35] E. Bagińska, 'Civil Liability of national Financial Supervisory Authorities', below Chapter 5 of this volume.

their value and supply chains worldwide, in particular with respect to their impact on environmental (namely, climate change) issues, and with respect to their impact on human rights. Four main threads of measures can be distinguished, which, in combination, form the basis for what can be called a '*green-box* approach', which dominated the last 5-10 years of EU Company and Capital Market Law development.[36] These four threads can be associated with the approaches of reporting, caring, abstaining, and signalling. The first pillar, *reporting*, is dominant and is the best known today, with Directive 2014/95/EU ('Corporate Social Responsibility [Reporting]' or 'Non-Financial Reporting').[37] The approach is to prescribe reporting for companies of a certain size (today some 12,000 in Europe) on key issues irrespective of their financial impact on the company, exclusively because of the importance of the issues for the public. The two main objects of reporting are those named above (environmental and human rights – ecological and social sustainability), and the rationale is that the dominant company in the group is obliged to report on the strategy it adopts with respect to the activities of its supply and value chains and their impact on the areas named. The most prominent criticisms of the reporting instrument in substance relate to the fact that not all the production chain is covered, but only the foremost and most direct partners in the chain, and that the accuracy of the non-financial reporting is not sanctioned in any way.[38] Just as important is the concern that the reporting remains vague, not precise and standardised, and that the

---

36 See the more extensive (but still comprehensive) survey in: S. Grundmann (above n. 2) section III. on which this section is based.

37 Directive 2014/95/EU of the European Parliament and of the Council of 22 October 2014 amending Directive 2013/34/EU as regards disclosure of non-financial and diversity information by certain large undertakings and groups, [2014] OJ L 330/1 (the NFRD); from the abundant literature see, namely, A. Häsli and R. Weber, 'Climate Change Reporting and Due Diligence' (2021) 18 *ECFR* 948; A. Hellgardt and V. Jouannaud, 'Nachhaltigkeitsziele und Privatrecht' (2022) 222 *AcP* 163, pp. 207 et seqq.; E. Macchiavello and M. Siri, 'Sustainable Finance and Fintech' (2022) 19 *ECFR* 128. See recent reform on the strengthening of auditing and liability for incorrect reporting, Directive (EU) 2022/2464 of the European Parliament and of the Council of 14.12.2022 amending Regulation (EU) No. 537/2014, Directive 2004/109/EC, Directive 2006/43/EC and Directive 2013/34/EU, as regards corporate sustainability reporting, (CSRD), [2022] OJ L 322/15, based on Proposal COM(2021) 189 final (the CSRD). From the literature (in part still for the proposal) see, namely, H. Fleischer, 'Klimaschutz im Gesellschafts-, Bilanz- und Kapitalmarktrecht' (2022) *DB* 37, 40; M. Nietsch, 'Von der nichtfinanziellen Berichterstattung zur Nachhaltigkeitsberichterstattung – Eine Momentaufnahme zum Vorschlag der Corporate Sustainability Reporting Directive' (2022) 43(10) *ZIP* 449.

38 On the criticism relating to the extent of reporting duties, see M. Kolter, 'Das Unternehmen als Subjekt und Objekt nichtfinanzieller Berichterstattung' (2019) *RW* 50; W. Schön, 'Nachhaltigkeit in der Unternehmensberichterstattung' (2022) *ZfPW*, 207, 245 et seqq. On the criticism relating to sanctioning the accuracy, see M. Renner, 'Menschenrechts- und umweltbezogene Unternehmensverantwortung zwischen Kapitalmarkt und Lieferkette' (2022) *ZeuP* 782, 803 et seqq.

addressees of the reporting are not clarified, namely it is unclear who should react to the reporting and why.[39] While these are important concerns, the recent reform quoted tries to tackle them, and this is not the place to discuss more deeply. One aspect should, however, be emphasised. As reports by firms of the size covered are public in multiple ways (reporting, included in prospectuses or periodical disclosure), they reach not only shareholders (who might, at least in part, be inclined to put returns above common interest concerns), but also public authorities, clients, investors, NGOs. To allege deficiency in such reporting with respect to addressees and their incentive structure would seem to underestimate the range of addressees and their multiple possibilities of reaction.

The second pillar is about '*caring*' – reaching beyond mere reporting on strategies adopted. The core duty (at board level!) is to exercise 'due diligence' in detecting human rights and environmental risks in the company's value chains, with a view to taking those steps that can be regarded as reasonable, and liability may potentially be incurred for not doing so or not acting appropriately with respect to the facts found. All this is enshrined in the current Proposal for a New/Amended Directive on Corporate Social Responsibility (CSRD) (2022), adopted in the European Parliament in April 2024 (as CSDDD).[40] The third pillar is about *abstaining*. This targets those endeavours and activities which after a prescribed due diligence assessment are shown to carry the substantial risk of massive violation of sustainability standards. These take the form, most directly, of gross inroads into human rights standards (life and health) because of modes of extraction or, in zones of conflict and war, activities which potentially even fuel such conflict. This aim is targeted by the so-called 'Conflict Minerals' regime, however only for very limited segments.[41] The

---

[39] On the criticism of vagueness and non-conclusiveness of the key addressees of the reporting duties, see M. Kolter, *Nachhaltigkeit durch Transparenz – Berichtspflichten als Instrument der Unternehmensregulierung*, Mohr Siebeck, Tübingen 2023; M. Renner (previous Fn.), pp. 791 et seqq.

[40] European Commission Proposal of 23 February 2022 for a Directive of the European Parliament and of the Council on Corporate Sustainability Due Diligence and amending Directive (EU) 2019/1937, COM(2022) 71 final; with Annex, same date, COM(2022) 71 final; close to adoption, see above n. 2; see namely summary in the Explanatory Memorandum, p. 3, 'closely interrelated' with the NFRD/CSRD (above n. 37), p. 4; from the abundant literature, see L. Hübner, V. Habrich and M.-Ph. Weller, 'Corporate Sustainability Due Diligence' (2022) *Neue Zeitschrift für Gesellschaftsrecht (NZG)* 644; C. Patz, 'The EU's Draft Corporate Sustainability Due Diligence Directive: A First Assessment' (2022) 7 *Business and Human Rights Journal* 291; M.-Ph. Weller and N. Benz, 'Klimaschutz und Corporate Covernance' (2022) 51 *ZGR* 563, 574 et seq., 582 et seq.

[41] Regulation (EU) 2017/821 of the European Parliament and of the Council of 17 May 2017 laying down supply chain due diligence obligations for Union importers of tin, tantalum and tungsten, their ores, and gold originating from conflict-affected and high-risk areas, [2017] OJ L 130/1 (called the Conflict Minerals Regulation); from the literature, see M.-L. Fehse

last pillar is about *signalling*, within the CSR agenda of those endeavours and investments that – by autonomous corporate decision-making and via external certification instruments or (other) intermediary involvement – can reliably be characterised as satisfying particularly high (and explicitly defined) standards and criteria of sustainability in their activities. This signalling relates both to the financial intermediaries and their reporting on such investments and to reliable certification instruments and potential criteria – in two EU Regulations closely intertwined, the so-called taxonomy regulatory setting.[42] This is the setting designed to empower a segment above the market standard with respect to sustainability.[43]

One key characteristic of the development of the regime is how closely company and contract law are intertwined: the responsibility for the *value or supply chain* is to be organised within company structures at the level of the lead enterprise (e.g., in Europe), the covenants and their monitoring, however, are to be organised down (or up) the chain of contracts. While national laws, for instance in France and in Germany, had already strongly embarked on a route to regulate the standards that have to be integrated into this (supply)

and F. Markmann, 'Die Konfliktmineralienverordnung der Europäischen Union' (2022) *Europäische Zeitschrift für Wirtschaftsrecht (EuZW)* 113; T. Teicke and M. Rust, 'Gesetzliche Vorgaben für Supply Chain Compliance – Die neue Konfliktmineralien-Verordnung' (2018) *Corporate Compliance Zeitschrift* 39; T. Voland and S. Daly, 'The EU Regulation on Conflict Minerals: The Way Out of a Vicious Cycle?' (2018) 52 *Journal of World Trade* 37.

42 Regulation (EU) 2019/2088 of the European Parliament and of the Council of 27 November 2019 on sustainability related disclosures in the financial services sector, [2019] OJ L 317/1 (called Sustainable Finance Disclosure Regulation, SFDR); Regulation (EU) 2020/852 of the European Parliament and of the Council of 18 June 2020 on the establishment of a framework to facilitate sustainable investment, and amending Regulation (EU) 2019/2088, [2020] OJ L 198/131 (called the Taxonomy Regulation).

43 From the literature, see I. H-Y Chiu, 'Building a Single Market for Sustainable Finance in the EU – Mixed Implications and the Missing Link of Digitalisation' in E. Avgouleas and H. Marjosola (eds.), *Digital Finance in Europe: Law, Regulation, and Governance*, ECFR Special Volume 5, De Gruyter, Berlin/Boston MA 2022, p. 181; E. Macchiavello and M. Siri, 'Sustainable Finance and Fintech' (2022) 19 *ECFR* 128, 136 et seqq.; S. Nagel, L. Lorenz and J. El-Qalqili, 'Nachhaltige Investitionen im System der Offenlegungs-VO und Taxonomie-VO' (2022) *Zeitschrift für Bank- und Kapitalmarktrecht (BKR)* 360; M. Habersack, 'Corporate Purpose' in G. Bachmann, S. Grundmann, A. Mengel und K. Krolop, *Festschrift für Christine Windbichler zum 70. Geburtstag am 8 Dezember 2020*, De Gruyter, Berlin 2020, p. 705. Ground-breaking on Signalling as a core device in an information model (and with particular emphasis on above market standards) is M. Spence, 'Job Market Signaling' (1973) 83 *Quarterly Journal of Economics* 355; for a contextualisation within the information model, see S. Grundmann, in S. Grundmann, M. Renner, H.-W. Micklitz, *New Private Law Theory – A Pluralist Approach*, Cambridge University Press, Cambridge 2021, ch. 12.

chain of contracts too,[44] Europe is following only now with its Proposal (recently adopted) on Due Diligence.[45]

3.2. COMMON GOOD AND ITS IMPORTANCE IN EU BANKING AND CONTRACT LAW

The focus in the measures discussed so far – in company law and for the supply chains linked to the lead firm or group – was primarily on ecological sustainability and the common/public good. However, there was also a second branch of protective dimensions concerning human rights at which these measures were aimed. Indeed, the foundational policy paper on sustainability at global level, the UN report on sustainability of 2008 (the so-called Ruggie report) conceptualises sustainability much more broadly, namely including *social sustainability* as a *second major pillar* of sustainability (as a common/public good) – ecological and social sustainability having a strong mutual influence on each other.[46] Looking now at banking law (outside taxonomy issues) and contract law (outside supply chains), social sustainability even

---

44 For France (*loi sur la vigilance*), Art. L225-102-5 Code de Commerce, see E. Savourey and S. Brabant, 'The French Law on the Duty of Vigilance: Theoretical and Practical Challenges Since its Adoption' (2021) 6 *Business and Human Rights Journal* 141; L. Nasse, *Loi de vigilance: das französische Lieferkettengesetz*, Mohr Siebeck, Tübingen 2022; P. Lequet, 'Loi "devoir de vigilance": de l'intérêt des normes de management des risques' (2017) 42 *Revue juridique de l'environnement* 705. For Germany (*Lieferkettensorgfaltsgesetz*), Act on Corporate Due Diligence in Supply Chains (short LkSG) from 16.07.2021, BGBl. I 2021, p. 2959; see M. Kaltenborn, M. Krajewski, G Rühl and M. Saage-Maass (eds.), *Lieferkettensorgfaltspflichtenrecht – LkGS, GwB, EU-HolzhandelsVO, EU-KonfliktmineralienVO, BetrVG, WRegG, CSR-RL-UmsG*, C.H. Beck, Munich 2023; A.-C. Mittwoch and F. Bremenkamp, 'The German Supply Chain Act – A Sustainable Regulatory Framework for Internationally Active Market Players?' in C. Tietje, G. Kraft and A. Mittwoch (eds.), (2022) 182 *Beiträge zum Transnationalen Wirtschaftsrecht*, https://omp.bibliothek.uni-halle.de/iwr/catalog/book/294; M. Renner, 'Menschenrechts- und umweltbezogene Unternehmensverantwortung zwischen Kapitalmarkt und Lieferkette' (2022) *Zeitschrift für Europäisches Privatrecht (ZEuP)* 782; G. Spindler, 'Verantwortlichkeit und Haftung in Lieferantenketten – das Lieferkettensorgfaltspflichtengesetz aus nationaler und europäischer Perspektive' (2022) 186 *Zeitschrift für das gesamte Handels- und Wirtschaftsrecht (ZHR)* 67.

45 See Proposal for a Directive of the European Parliament and the Council on Corporate Sustainability Due Diligence and amending Directive (EU) 2019/1937, COM(2022) 71 final of 23 February 2022 (Commission Proposal), close to adoption, see above . 2; on this for instance, see C. Patz, 'The EU's Draft Corporate Sustainability Due Diligence Directive: A First Assessment' (2022) 7 *Business and Human Rights Journal* 291.

46 See Human Rights Council, 'Promotion and Protection of All Human Rights, Civil, Political, Economic, Social and Cultural Rights, Including the Right to Development – Protect, Respect and Remedy: a Framework for Business and Human Rights' ('Ruggie Report'), A/HRC/8/5 (07.04.15); this report, namely the broad concept it proposes, is analysed by S. Ariel Aaronson and I. Higham, '"Re-righting business": John Ruggie and the Struggle to Develop International Human Rights Standards for Transnational Firms' (2013) 35 *Human*

becomes the core issue. Considering all of the sustainability branches, it was arguably social sustainability in particular that was the trigger for that broad flow of sustainability-related EU legislation in the second decade of the 2000s.

The new bank recovery and resolution regime (above section 2.2.) – together, of course, with the rest of the European Banking Union regime – is quintessential in this. More than any other single act – including those in banking contract law such as the consumer credit directives of 2008 and 2014 (see below) – it embodies the core idea of one foundational principle. Making (large-scale) private gains that produce (large-scale) social costs and do so systematically, i.e., because of the very structure of the (sets of) transactions, runs counter to the public/common good and should to the largest possible extent be prevented/forbidden.[47] Hence, the UN report on sustainability and the triggering event for an increased sustainability trend in company, banking and also contract law substantially coincided (around 2008) – and the European Banking Union constituted the most powerful and fully-fledged early social sustainability package in EU legislation. This package was then followed by the company law developments mentioned above and – in (banking) contract law proper – by the introduction of a fully-fledged regime on the duty of responsible lending (see below).

The contention that the European Banking Union regime constituted the real trigger for a decade where the 'common good' was to play a highly increased role in European contract, company and business law may sound astonishing at first sight – and has rarely been formulated, if at all. This contention does seem warranted, however, if one looks at the role of credit institutions in societies and public economies. They are the main stewards of a key resource in Western-style market economies: capital. All businesses need it and, therefore, these institutions do as well (including private individuals for large consumer expenditures and investments). Two roles are dominant, the provision of credit and the support of enterprises in raising capital directly on the investment market (issuing agents and intermediaries in secondary markets).[48] Without these two functions, there would be no market economy.

Rights Quarterly 333; rather critical is L. Catá Backer, 'On the Evolution of the United Nations' "Protect-Respect-Remedy" Project' (2010) 9 *Santa Clara Journal of International Law* 101.

47 See references above n. 27; and in particular for this principle, M. Mazzucato, 'We Socialize Bailouts. We Should Socialize Successes, Too' (01/07/2020) *The New York Times*; V. Neves, 'Social Costs: Where Does the Market End?' (2012) *RCCS Annual Review* 129; and groundbreaking was R.H. Coase, 'The Problem of Social Cost' (1960) 3 *The Journal of Law & Economics* 1.

48 On these two roles, which also constitute the two main forms of corporate financing (at least insofar as not primarily from assets of the management or company owners themselves, i.e., in almost all large companies), see P. Davies, S. Worthington and C. Hare, *Gower Principles of Modern Company Law*, 1st ed., Sweet & Maxwell, London 2021, para. 31-002; S. Grundmann (above n. 9), part 1, paras. 7-13 and part 5, para. 7.

For a functioning market economy, the difference between financing a business landscape more by bank loans or by capital markets is, however, peripheral – even though this difference is, of course, of high importance as such.[49] Other ways in which banks are influential – such as their sheer market shares in the production of GDP and such as 'depositary voting' for shareholders whose shares they hold in deposit – need not be discussed in addition. The core contention here is clear: credit institutions, while only forming part of the economy, form such an important and indeed indispensable part of it, that any legislative development and rationale that directly relates to them is highly significant for the development of economic law at large. And this has been the case since the establishment of the EU Banking Union for both the main players in stock corporations in the credit industry – the management board and shareholders (and creditors). As external evidence of this, since then, the global literature on corporate governance has split: into literature on corporate governance in general and literature on bank corporate governance in particular.[50]

The radical change towards responsibility for the public good, which the new regime brought for shareholders and investors, has been evidenced by the bail-in instrument's introduction as a mandatory part of 'own funds' finance of credit institutions under the new regime (above section 2.2.). Equally significant, perhaps even more far-reaching and 'general' is the change with respect to management. Traditionally, its role has been seen as being twofold. The first role is that of managing the company in a sufficiently profitable and stable manner (in the long term), and therefore also with a willingness to innovate and take risks, which is why management is, increasingly, granted discretionary powers (business judgement) in all stock corporation laws in market economies (entrepreneurial management).[51] The second role is that

49 As is well known, the second is predominant in Anglo-American countries; in continental European countries it is most likely to be found in France: see on the distribution only T. Didier, R. Levine and S.-L. Schmukler, 'Capital market financing, firm growth, and firm size distribution', European Systemic Risk Board, *Working Paper No. 4/2016*, March 2016, especially the quantitative overviews in Tables 8 and 9; also E. Wymeersch, Aktiengesellschaft (AG) 1995, 299, 309-315.

50 For example: K.J. Hopt and G. Wohlmannstetter, then K.J. Hopt, J.-H. Binder and H.-J. Böcking (eds.), *Handbuch Corporate Governance von Banken (und Versicherungen)*, 2nd ed., C.H. Beck/Vahlen, Munich 2020; I. H.-Y Chiu (eds.), *The Law on Corporate Governance in Banks*, Edward Elgar, Cheltenham 2015; on the likewise strongly divergent group law of banks (also comparative law) see M. Renner, *Bankkonzernrecht*, Mohr Siebeck, Tübingen 2019, esp. pp. 257-312; D. Negenborn, *Bankgesellschaftsrecht und Sonderkonzernrecht*, Mohr Siebeck, Tübingen 2019, pp. 13-182.

51 In essence, the rule states that the board of directors is not liable for business decisions if it complies with the law, has consulted sufficient information (procedural component) and the decision *ex ante* still appears justifiable from a commercial point of view: see the comparative survey in K.J. Hopt, 'Comparative Corporate Governance – The State of the Art and International Regulation' (2011) 59 *American Journal of Comparative Law* 1, 39 et

of finding a compromise – in line with the guiding principles of corporate law – between the interests of affected groups (entrepreneurial balance).[52] The amended *European* (!) banking supervision law breaks with this scheme radically. The primary objective of bank management boards – above all others – is to guarantee the short- and long-term stability of their own institutions (see e.g., Articles 88(1) and 92 CRD IV).[53] This guiding objective – at European level and therefore with prevalence over national (corporate) law – is nowadays understood, wherever this question is raised, to be binding for national corporate law.[54] The ultimate goal is no longer profit maximisation or the optimisation of said balance of interests and this raises the question whether this does not mutate credit institutions to companies for the public good (public utilities).[55] This regulatory framework no longer seems to support an announcement once made by CEO Joseph Ackermann who declared that he was aiming for annual returns of 25 per cent for *Deutsche Bank* (and declared that he also wanted to be held to this).[56] Today this, the largest credit institution of the economically strongest EU Member State (though not the largest in the EU) has returned from a business model strongly focusing on investment banking with high-risk potentials – albeit not only for regulatory reasons – to a more conservative business policy tailored more strongly to private and corporate clients.[57]

In one contribution to this volume, the – rather related – question has been asked whether the European Banking Union cannot only be seen as striving for

seq. Continental European jurisdictions, for instance German law, adhered to this rule too (see, for instance, s. 93 para. 1 phrase 2 German Stock Corporation Act – *Aktiengesetz*) – albeit rather late. See for example: G. Spindler in *Münchner Kommentar zum Aktiengesetz*, C.H. Beck, Munich, § 93 paras. 43 et seqq.; comparative law (US rule disseminated) and economic rationale also discussed by H. Fleischer, 'Die "Business Judgment Rule" im Spiegel der Rechtsvergleichung und Rechtsökonomie' in R. Wank, H Hirte and K. Frey (eds.), *Festschrift für Herbert Wiedemann zum 70. Geburtstag*, C.H. Beck, Munich 2002, p. 827.

52 See only: C. Schubert, *Das Unternehmensinteresse – Maßstab für die Organwalter der Aktiengesellschaft*, Nomos, Baden-Baden 2020, pp. 20-22 et passim.

53 More on this in detail: T. Engel, *Systemrisikovorsorge*, Mohr Siebeck, Tübingen 2020, pp. 151 et seqq.

54 Namely: J.-H Binder, 'Vorstandshandeln zwischen öffentlichem und Verbandsinteresse' (2013) 42 *ZGR* 760; M. Renner, *Bankkonzernrecht*, Mohr Siebeck, Tübingen 2019, pp. 262-272; S. Grundmann (above n. 9), part 1, para. 85; S. Grundmann, 'The Banking Union Translated into (Private Law) Duties – Infrastructure and Rulebook' (2015) 16 *EBOR* 357, 370-372.

55 J. Schiff, 'Is Basel turning Banks into Public Utilities?' (2015) 3 *Journal of Financial Perspectives* 4; see also I. Walter and A. Saunders, 'Reworking the Global Financial Architecture: Is Universal Banking the Best Way Forward?' (2013) 1 *Journal of Financial Perspectives* 7.

56 See only R. von Heusinger, 'Das magische Viertel' *Zeit Online*, 03/02/2005, <https://bit.ly/3czaEtp>); T. Kanning, 'Sind 25 Prozent zu gierig?' *FAZ online*, 30/04/2009 (<https://bit.ly/3cz19u6>).

57 Deutsche Bank, 'Geschäftsbericht 2020', Comments on 'Strategy' on pp. XVII et seqq. (<https://bit.ly/3kY0cA4>).

a common good, but also for solidarity within the Union, one of those 'new' principles to be found in the foundational Article 2 TEU on Union principles (like pluralism, tolerance, and ... solidarity). Three main findings emerge – albeit rather sketchily. First, an (affirmative) answer would be simple if deposit insurance had also been unified at the European level. A Europeanised deposit guarantee ('EDIS') scheme would constitute an EU-wide solidarity pact between the (industry-wide) bank funds held for deposit insurance. However, secondly, even without such Europeanisation of the deposit guarantee scheme, there is a scheme already existing today, which can be used for distressed credit institutions in specific circumstances upon application by their Member State, and which is indeed based on the principle of solidarity. This the European Stability Mechanism (ESM), the main instrument in solving the Euro sovereign debt crisis – and this was indeed about giving Member States in distress reasonable access to capital markets once again and using the creditworthiness of the others to this end.[58] In this case, other Member States (and their taxpayers) then provide better credit standing and assume the default risk for bank recovery in the Member State in question[59] (i.e. indirect, subsidiary solidarity of the EU population for credit institutions in crisis in other Member States). Third, the core mechanism of the EU Banking Union itself is also relevant to solidarity – or, more precisely, the repression of behaviour where solidarity is disregarded. It suppresses not only behaviour that does not display solidarity, but also speculative behaviour of investors that is directed against the population as a whole, i.e., which was/is based on the socialisation of losses and privatisation of profits (above sections 2.1. and 2.2.).

Coming to *banking contract law proper* public good plays an important role as well. In this field, at the core of genuine private law, the regime, which most directly has strong public good implications, may be that of a duty of responsible lending, now contained in two EU directives. *Chapter 6* tackles this issue.[60] Responsible lending – as a remedy for subprime lending – has a macro-

---

[58] On the ESM and its legal regime (based on public international law treaties), see C. Ohler, 'The European Stability Mechanism: The Long Road to Financial Stability in the Euro Area' (2011) 54 *German Yearbook of International Law* 47; S. Pilz, *Der Europäische Stabilitätsmechanismus*, Mohr Siebeck, Tübingen 2016; S. Röger, *Finanzhilfemechanismen für die Eurozone*, Duncker & Humblot, Berlin 2018. Interest rates for the borrower states were dramatically reduced for decades (from up to 30 % in the case of Greek government bonds during the crisis to an average of 0.54 % in the ESM), which over decades typically is equivalent to a debt cut of well over 50 %. For the interest rate figures before and under the ESM, see EFSF/ESM Financial Assistance, Evaluation Report, 2017, https://www.esm.europa.eu/system/files/document/ti_pubpdf_dw0616055enn_pdfweb_20170607111409_1.pdf, pp. 45 et seqq.

[59] On this form of use of the ESM see: Deutscher Bundestag, 'Fragen zur direkten Bankenrekapitalisierung durch den ESM', PE 6 - 3000 - 195/14; and C. Schoenfleisch and C. Calliess, 'Die Bankenunion, der ESM und die Rekapitalisierung von Banken: Europa- und verfassungsrechtliche Fragen' (2015) 70(3) *Juristenzeitung* 113.

[60] E. Arroyo Amayuelas, 'Responsible Lending', below Chapter 6 of this volume.

economic side (and a public good side to be discussed below). The macro-economic side, stemming from the sheer volume of sub-prime debt loans, is associated with the cluster risks pointed out as a main triggering event of the global financial crisis (above section 2.1.). The duty of responsible lending has, of course, an individual side too. It constitutes a contractual duty, in an *individual* contractual relationship, which, however, is linked to a *public* good consideration. This is the protection of the individual sub-prime borrower. Overall, the rationale of a duty of responsible lending is that the professional (lender) – with more professional long-term expertise and insight – acts in the interest of the consumer (borrower) too when it refuses to give credit in circumstances where restitution and payment of interest is not reasonably to be expected. This still constitutes a refusal of a demand for a loan, but as such refusal is also prescribed by law, the most plausible reading would seem to be that the refusal of a loan under these circumstances is considered to be for the protection of the long-term interest of the consumer not to go into insolvency. Not having the means for consumption now is seen as a solution superior to that of having such spending-power now at a high-risk of future insolvency, meaning destruction of one's economic existence, albeit (in consumer insolvencies) only for a certain number of years. This in turn can perhaps best be conceptualised as an emanation of the right to protection of human dignity (also protection against the borrower's own over-optimism as to future developments),[61] which is among the most fundamental human rights. Given this characterisation, the '*green-box* approach' (including protection of human rights as a public concern) would seem to imply that a duty of responsible lending constitutes a question also of public concern, and hence of the public/common good – as seen in the CSR agenda. Chapter 6 largely shares this view of the strong constitutional and public good dimension (namely in section 3.1.), even though it primarily focuses on the private and contract law side, the individual relationship, with strong emphasis on bringing together details and overarching rationale. For this purpose, the contribution concentrates on two phases: general consumer credit (Directive 2008/48/EU) and mortgage credit (Directive 2014/17/EU). While the first directive did not yet contain a specific rule on responsible lending, and the focus therefore is on seeing whether it still can be found in some inchoate form in the general traits of that directive, Directive 2014/17/EU today forms the point of reference. It contains a fully-fledged rule on responsible lending, including also (to a lesser extent) the legal consequences of any violation of the duty. While one might argue that this responsible lending duty is more important still in mortgage loans (because of their complexity, size and duration), and hence the 2014

61 See S. Grundmann, in S. Grundmann, M. Renner and H.-W. Micklitz (above n. 43), chapter 11.

directive just tackles a different subject-matter, the development of the legal measures considered until now would seem to suggest that times had also changed. The European Union was now indeed decidedly willing to introduce such a duty – which it had taken out of the proposal preceding the 2008 directive. Chapter 6 highlights the ongoing duty during the whole duration of the lending relationship, on the one hand the reasonable creditworthiness assessment, with the loan designed to be as fit as possible for avoiding over-indebtedness, but on the other hand efforts made in the ongoing relationship too. This includes a certain good-faith collaboration in solving problems that later arise, and in principle also default rules designed so as not to accelerate risks of over-indebtedness. The contribution also stresses the link beyond mere contract law (both at formation and going forward) – namely the link with the public good – to more general policies of consumer financial literacy, but, very importantly, also to organisational rules, such as avoidance of remuneration schemes that might give incentives to engage in irresponsible lending techniques. Finally, the contribution also discusses over-regulation with respect to information requirements. It rightly points out that the regime takes sound steps, but nevertheless cannot solve all problems of over-indebtedness once and for all, or extinguish risk as such – as the roots of risk also lie in external causes (divorce, illness and unemployment).

4. PARTICIPATION REGIME FOR PRIVATE PARTIES

4.1. PARTICIPATION AS THE CORE THRUST IN EU COMPANY LAW – SUMMARY

As is the case with public good orientation (discussed above in section 3), European Company Law is also a protagonist with respect to strongly increased participation rights, and contrary to what was the conclusion for public good, with respect to private parties' participation, European Company Law was even the forerunner in time as well. Indeed, in *European Company Law*, strongly increased participation rights – for a multitude of affected parties and situations – could be seen as a core thrust of the development since as far back as the turn of the century. This constitutes a development which can be viewed as a '*red-box* approach' – with a host of tools for incentivising *intense participation and heated discussion* – and which completely diverges from the US experience where no such federal policy can be sensed at all.[62]

[62] For all this, see more extensively, including the underlying change in EU politics and development of theoretical approaches, the contribution by S. Grundmann (above n. 2) section II. This section forms the basis of the summary given here.

In European Company Law, this refers to an increase in 'having a say' on company issues (including work conditions) and company strategies (for the parallel question of what this refers to in the context of banking and contract law, see below section 4.2.). This development in company law can be analysed against the background of a Union that became a political Union (not only an internal market) and of a broad theory trend towards diversification in decision-making, which can best be summarised by pointing to the concept of 'wisdom of the crowds'.[63] The main body of EU legislative acts now focuses on actors with particular economic weight, large listed companies or groups, who are the sole addressees of the duties spelt out.[64] This core of EU legislative acts consists of three main groups – acts on intensification of the exit rights of shareholders, on intensification of the voice rights of shareholders, and on inclusion of labour and stakeholders in the decision processes.

Intensification of the *exit rights of shareholders* was related, as a forerunner, to the enactment of a general EC Prospectus Directive at the time when the political Union was first conceived. The legal measure opened the core primary information tool – the prospectus – to all capital markets, i.e., it introduced a

[63] In detail on this, see S. GRUNDMANN (above n. 2) section II., where reference is made (i) to the Maastricht Treaty (1992), with its landmark introduction of a common currency 1999/2002, increased common foreign policy [including defence policy] and increased common security policy [justice and home affairs] – and later, of course, the Lisbon Treaty, the concept of citizenship and the EU Charter of Fundamental Rights, but also (ii) to (theoretical) concepts developed or put in practice at these times. They include competition of legislatures also in Europe (as featured in Case C-212/97 *Centros Ltd. v. Erhvervs- og Selskabsstyrelsen*, ECLI:EU:C:1999:126), diversity as a quality condition in decision-making, heterogeneity in decision-making (with bounded rationality) and shareholders' democracy (new economic sociology focusing again more on the study of 'relations' and 'embeddedness', and more generally 'wisdom of the crowds'). On the wisdom of the crowds and diversity of decision-making bodies in relation to the quality of decision-making, see H. OINAS-KUKKONEN, 'Network analysis and crowds of people as sources of new organisational knowledge' in A. KOOHANG, J. BRITZ and K. HARMAN (eds.), *Knowledge Management: Theoretical Foundation*, Informing Science Press, Santa Rosa CA 2008, p. 173; C. SUNSTEIN, *Infotopia: How Many Minds Produce Knowledge*, Oxford University Press, Oxford 2006; J. SUROWIECKI, *The Wisdom of Crowds: Why the Many Are Smarter than the Few and How Collective Wisdom Shapes business, Economies, Societies and Nations*, Random House, New York 2004. The parallelism to J. Habermas' discourse theory, on the political scene, is noteworthy; see survey in M. RENNER, 'Private Law and Theories of Communication' in S. GRUNDMANN, M. RENNER and H.-W. MICKLITZ (above n. 43), chapter 4.

[64] Interestingly enough, all key legal acts of company law listed below, are indeed targeted now solely at this segment of large and *listed* companies, from the Takeover Directive (2004) to the two Shareholder Rights Directives (2007, 2017), and in principle and de facto also the main developments in accounting law (the IFRS Regulation 2002 and the CSR Directive 2014). Conversely, from an internal market perspective, all limited liability companies and their reliability were important and were indeed included in the (earlier) harmonisation programme tailored for the internal market's needs.

duty to issue a prospectus for all public offerings (issues of securities).[65] This, however, brought Europe only to what was the standard in the US already (with the Securities and Securities Exchange Acts of the early 1930s), individual standardised information (disclosure) at issues of securities. The core act, which also demonstrates a proactive policy of *including all shareholders* (and treating them equally) at supranational level, was to be seen only in the EC Takeover Directive of 2004, more than a decade later.[66] With these acts began a policy of a participation at many levels, not only through voting by shareholders in general meetings as the traditional form of shareholder voice. Rather, this legal measure not only gave each shareholder the right to have his equal share (mandating that bids be made to all shareholders according to Article 3) – quite different already from the law in most US States, and certainly with no parallel at US federal level. Moreover, this act empowered shareholders as well at the moment of takeovers to take a collective vote, and to do so with all shareholders, and even with a view to adapting the charter (see Articles 9 and 11, in part optional) – unthinkable in the US.

Intensification of the *voice option of shareholders*, through the legal measures taken in this respect, continued on the same path. Participation of shareholders no longer remained mostly formal but was rendered more material as a de facto possibility. This is empowerment for all shareholders, even where long intermediation chain would traditionally frustrate their voting rights in practice; for all shareholders, even when information and access costs would traditionally make them abstain from voting; and for all shareholders, where traditionally they would abstain because of problems of collective action, i.e., cooperating and organising themselves. The Shareholders Rights Directive I of

---

65 See Council Directive of 17 April 1989 coordinating the requirements for the drawing-up, scrutiny and distribution of the prospectus to be published when transferable securities are offered to the public, [1989] OJ L 124/8; today Regulation (EU) 2017/1129 of the European Parliament and of the Council of 14 June 2017 on the prospectus to be published when securities are offered to the public or admitted to trading on a regulated market, and repealing Directive 2003/71/EC, [2017] OJ L 168/12. On a second, concurrent line of legislation that introduces a philosophy of broad trust into capital markets in the EU (insider dealing, market abuse), see S. Grundmann (above n. 2) section II.; today Regulation (EU) No. 596/2014 of the European Parliament and of the Council of 16 April 2014 on market abuse (market abuse regulation) and repealing Directive 2003/6/EC of the European Parliament and of the Council and Commission Directives 2003/124/EC, 2003/125/EC and 2004/72/EC, [2014] OJ L 173/1.

66 See Directive 2004/25/EC of the European Parliament and of the Council of 21 April 2004 on takeover bids, [2004] OJ L 142/12; on the directive's disclosure and voting regime and on the mandatory inclusion of *all* shareholders, see S. Bartman, 'Analysis and Consequences of the EC Directive on takeover bids' (2004) 1 *European Company Law* 5-8; G. Ferrarini and G. Miller, 'A Simple Theory of Takeover Regulation in the United States and Europe' (2009) 42 *Cornell Int'l. L.J.*, 301, 313 et seq.; summary in S. Grundmann, *European Company Law – Organization, Finance and Capital Markets*, 2nd ed., Intersentia, Antwerp/Oxford 2012 – forthcoming in its 3rd. ed. 2024), § 30 paras. 39-54.

2007 prescribed the infrastructure to be guaranteed for all these issues in all Member States' company laws.[67] Therefore, notice periods long enough even for long intermediation chains were imposed. Therefore, the possibility to appoint a proxy and to instruct such representative electronically – while following the streaming of the general meeting from a distance – was foreseen as a minimum protection in harmonisation (Article 5(1), Recital 6, with Articles 8 and 10, also 12). Finally and most importantly, organised representation – by professionals acting for and in the interest of individual shareholders – has to be guaranteed as a possibility by national law (such as shareholders' associations or depositary voting by depositary banks for their clients, see Articles 10(3) and 11, Recitals 10 and 11). All these framework conditions form a federal policy of participation rights; these rights are still underpinned by disclosure duties on important issues such as shareholder structure (which allows for a better assessment of potential trends and coalitions) and on strategies envisaged by large block-holders and their advisors ('no surprise moves').[68] All this is without any parallel in US State law and even less so at the federal level. This holds true both for active participation of shareholders of the target company and then in the new shareholder structure following takeovers and for the empowerment of (small) shareholders in the regular voting processes (general meetings).[69] What remains to be said on labour participation is even less of a

---

67 See Directive 2007/36/EC of the European Parliament and of the Council of 11 July 2007 on the exercise of certain rights of shareholders in listed companies, [2007] OJ L 184/17 (Shareholders' Rights Directive I); then followed, complemented and not replaced by Directive (EU) 2017/828 of the European Parliament and of the Council of 17 May 2017 amending Directive 2007/36/EC as regards the encouragement of long-term shareholder engagement, [2017] OJ L 132/1 (Shareholders' Rights Directive II; see below). On the Shareholders' Rights Directive I, see A. Hainsworth, 'The Shareholder Rights Directive and the challenge of re-enfranchising beneficial shareholders' (2007) 1 *Law and Financial Markets Review* 11; F. Xiangxing Hong, 'Protection of Shareholders' Rights at EU Level' (2009) 6 *ECL* 124; see summary in S. Grundmann, *European Company Law* (above n. 66), § 13.

68 The former is regulated in (Arts. 9-18 of) Directive 2004/109/EC of the European Parliament and of the Council of 15 December 2004 on the harmonisation of transparency requirements in relation to information about issuers whose securities are admitted to trading on a regulated market and amending Directive 2001/34/EC, [2004] OJ L 390/38; later amended several times; the core substance, however, is unchanged. On the disclosure duties with respect to structure of shareholdings, see H. Fleischer and K.U. Schmolke, 'The Reform of the Transparency Directive: Minimum or Full Harmonisation of Ownership Disclosure' (2011) 12 *EBOR* 121; summary in S. Grundmann, *European Company Law* (above n. 66), § 21, paras. 22-32. The latter in: Shareholders Rights Directive II of 2017 (above n. 67).

69 On the lack of a mandatory bid and of a regime empowering shareholders to have a collective vote in US corporate law, see J. Armour and D. Skeel, 'Who Writes the Rules for Hostile Takeovers, and Why? The Peculiar Divergence of US and UK Takeover Regulation' (2007) 95 *Georgetown Law Journal* 1727; G. Ferrarini and G. Miller, 'A Simple Theory of Takeover Regulation in the United States and Europe' (2009) 42 *Cornell International Law Journal* 301; also, C. Ryngaert, 'Cross-Border Takeover Regulation: a Transatlantic Perspective' (2007) 4 *ECFR* 434. This is all the more astonishing, if one considers how

standard in the US. Overall, Hirschman's seminal distinction between exit and voice of 1970 seems to take impressively form in the 2000s and later in the EC/EU law of the large and listed enterprise.[70]

However, the EU policy of strengthening participation rights goes beyond shareholders. It includes also labour – certainly for work environment-related issues, with the so-called Works Council Directive of 2009, with mandatory participation, at least in terms of information and consultation,[71] but also in some inchoate way even for issues not directly labour related, such as entrepreneurial issues and strategies. For the latter, there is at least an EC/EU guarantee of – national! – co-determination regimes to 'survive' structural changes cross-border and remain intact unless otherwise consented also by labour. This (EC) solution (of mutual recognition of national regimes in place) applies both in the case of European Companies (always created by structural changes)[72] *and* in the case of national companies involved in cross-border structural changes,[73] i.e., in the important structural changes cross-border in

---

important take-overs are in U.S. practice, how much they form a core part of the image of corporate law and if one considers the dominance of a shareholder value paradigm as the prime benchmark in US corporate law in the 2000s. See K. Hopt, 'Comparative Corporate Governance, the State of the Art and International Regulation' in A. Fleckner and K. Hopt (eds.), *Comparative Corporate Governance*, CUP, Cambridge 2013, p. 3, p. 10; J. Gordon, 'The Rise of Independent Directors in the United States, 1950-2005: Of Shareholder Value and Stock Market Prices' (2007) 59 *Stanford Law Review* 1465, 1526 et seqq.

70 A. Hirschman, *Exit, Voice and Loyalty – Responses to Decline in Firms, Organizations, and States*, Harvard University Press, Cambridge MA and London 1970; see the contextualisation in S. Grundmann, in S. Grundmann, M. Renner and H.-W. Micklitz (above n. 43), chapter 21.

71 See Directive 2009/38/EC of the European Parliament and of the Council of 6 May 2009 on the establishment of a European Works Council or a procedure in Community-scale undertakings and Community-scale groups of undertakings for the purposes of informing and consulting employees, [2009] OJ L 122/28. On this participation regime, see A. Alaimo, 'The New Directive on European Works Councils: Innovations and Omissions' (2010) 26 *International Journal of Comparative Labour Law & Industrial Relations* 217; S. Laulom, 'Flawed Revision of the European Works Council Directive' (2010) 39 *Industrial Law Journal* 202; summary in K. Riesenhuber, *European Employment Law*, 2nd ed., Intersentia, Cambridge 2022), § 31.

72 See Council Regulation (EC) No. 2157/2001 of 8 October 2001 on the Statute for a European company (SE), [2001] OJ L 294/1 (European Company – SE – Regulation); Council Directive 2001/86/EC of 8 October 2001 supplementing the Statute for a European company with regard to the involvement of employees, [2001] OJ L 294/22. On the labour codetermination regime, see C. Leca, 'The Participation of Employees' Representatives in the Governance Structure of the Societas Europaea' (2007) 18 *EBLR* 403; E. Roelofs, 'Shelf SEs and Employee Participation' (2010) 7 *ECL* 120; C. Schubert, 'The National Implementation of Employee Participation in the Administrative Board of the SE in the One-tier Model – A Legal Comparison on the Basis of Germany, Austria, Sweden, and France' (2008) 5 *ECFR* 422. Summary in S. Grundmann, *European Company Law* (above n. 66), § 33, paras. 50-58.

73 See Art. 16 of the Directive 2005/56/EC of the European Parliament and of the Council of 26 October 2005 on cross-border mergers of limited liability companies, [2005] OJ L 310/1 (Cross-Border Merger Directive); then integrated into Art. 118 et seqq., namely 133 of the Directive 2017/1132/EU of the European Parliament and of the Council of 14 June

Europe. The most co-determination-friendly solution imposes itself absent consent by all parties.

Finally, as of 2014, still reaching further, the CSR policy – for the protection of ecological and human rights interests – adopts a strategy to inform the public at large, governments, NGOs and activists[74] – and increasingly does so also with signalling tools and with liability attached to failure.

Altogether, the '*red-box* approach' would seem to imply two things. Firstly, the legal regime tries to empower as large a 'crowd' of affected persons as possible – shareholders, stakeholders, the public at large – to take part in the decision-making process of the large enterprise. Secondly, it tries to render the (informational and organisational) basis for such broader decision-making as suitable as possible for empowering the persons affected to really take decisions in their best interest. The overall thrust is that this will also enhance the quality of decision-making, and certainly the legitimacy. Finally, all this is perceived as a federal policy, at EC/EU level, that materialises in a number of EC/EU legislative acts.

4.2. PARTICIPATION IN EU BANKING, CONTRACT AND MARKET LAW

Private participation rights or instruments in private party relationships proper – as distinguished from private claims within the supervisory architecture (see above section 2.3.) – take on multiple forms. While in company law, the development was about giving more extensively and also *de facto* 'a say' to a number of affected parties and circles (including deeper information), in banking and contract law, broader and enhanced participation is different. It is mostly about deriving claims and rights from the banking supervision regulatory scheme and its violation, or about enhancing their enforcement, especially in case of highly dispersed and fragmented loss. More intense participation in EU Banking law points, however, not only in the direction of more rights, voting rights or claims, but of potentially more responsibility

2017 relating to certain aspects of company law, [2017] OJ L 169/46 (so-called Codification Directive); finally modified in the so-called Mobility Directive, Directive (EU) 2019/2121 of the European Parliament and of the Council of 27 November 2019 amending Directive (EU) 2017/1132 as regards cross-border conversions, mergers and divisions, [2019] OJ L 321/1 (also integrated into the Codification Directive). On the labour codetermination regime in cross-border mergers, see M. Pannier, 'The EU Cross Border Merger Directive – A New Dimension for Employee Participation and Company Restructuring' (2005) 16 *European Business Law Review* 1424; M. Siems, 'The European Directive on Cross-Border Mergers: An International Model?' (2005) 11 *Columbia Journal of European Law* 167, 176-179. Summary in S. Grundmann, *European Company Law* (above n. 66), § 29, para. 15.

[74] See more in detail above section 3.1.

too. The European Banking Union, as has been explained, in its completely novel aspect of a recovery and resolution regime, is indeed primarily aimed at encouraging a more responsible attitude by investors and shareholders towards the common good of stability (see above sections 2.2. and 3.2.). This constitutes as well, even without additional claims for private parties, a move via which these groups are more intensely involved ('participate') in the safeguard of that common good. This other side of 'participation' would seem well in line with the old ethical stronghold that more autonomy should entail as well stronger responsibility.[75] It can be put differently as well: investors have more actively to choose between bail-in-able instruments and general financial instruments.

Chapter 7 starts out with an analysis of an area of regulation on which claims can be based – before the other chapters then discuss substantive issues, namely claims and enforcement. This chapter's analysis is therefore about yet another form of increased participation, this time with respect to standard-setting itself.[76] Codes of conduct and codes of ethics are self-regulatory tools in which the banking community itself lays down best practices and which, after the intensification of regulation via the EU Banking Union, did not decrease, but rather increased. The contribution illustrates this increase in sheer numbers, but with concrete single examples too. Thus, the codes of conduct related to the EU Banking Union form yet another (but also rather special) case of private ordering and its ever-growing importance in business law, namely transnational law[77] – special because of its particular relationship and reciprocity with increased EU regulation. On this basis, the contribution mainly analyses the question of how far the promises made in such codes of practices – despite the lack of direct contractual relationships – may serve as a basis also for liability claims by investors in cases of breach. Yet, the hurdles seem high and the enforceability of unilateral promises form an exception that requires careful consideration. The added efficiency of enforcement of supervisory standards, but also the network character of the banking industry

---

[75] See only K. Riesenhuber (ed.), *Das Prinzip der Selbstverantwortung – Grundlagen und Bedeutung im heutigen Privatrecht*, Mohr-Siebeck, Tübingen 2011.

[76] M. Renner, 'Bank Codes of Conduct and European Contract Law', below chapter 7.

[77] Path-breaking: R. Ellickson, *Order without Law: How Neighbours Settle Disputes*, Harvard University Press, Cambridge MA 1991; L. Bernstein, 'Opting Out of the Legal System: Extralegal Contractual Relations in the Diamond Industry' (1992) 21 *Journal of Legal Studies* 115; primarily for the transnational scene L. Backer, 'Economic Globalization and the Rise of Efficient Systems of Global Private Lawmaking: Wal-Mart as Global Legislature' (2007) 39 *Connecticut Law Review* 1739; G. Teubner, 'Global Bukowina' – Legal Pluralism in the World Society' in G. Teubner (ed.), *Global Law without a State*, Aldershot, Dartmouth 1997, p. 3; T. Dietz, *Global Order Beyond Law*, Hart Publishing, Oxford 2014; D. Wielsch, 'Global Law's Toolbox: Private Regulation by Standards' (2012) 60 *American Journal of Comparative Law* 1075. See as well monograph by G. Bachmann, *Private Ordnung: Grundlagen ziviler Rechtsetzung*, Mohr-Siebeck, Tübingen 2006; contextualization and later developments in M. Renner, in S. Grundmann, M. Renner and H.-W. Micklitz (above n. 43), chapter 26.

as a highly regulated 'cooperative' endeavour, would appear to serve as powerful arguments in this vein.

Chapter 8 then addresses directly the core issue of private law claims based on the violation of EU Banking Union regulatory standards – if damage ensues from such violation.[78] The key question is whether violations of the EU Banking Union regime should follow the same path, which the most relevant parallel regulatory regimes have taken. Claims for violation of regulatory standards have been imposed – after decades of dispute about the question – via CJEU judgments and EU legislation in the area of competition law, which at the same time forms the very model of market regulation and the starting point in the European Union.[79] At least in practical outcome, the same holds true in virtually all cases in EU Capital Market Law. For the EU Banking Union, Chapter 8 strongly insists on the fact that customers' rights and claims have been largely increased as a reaction to the crisis, for instance under the deposit guarantee scheme; hence core private law claims explicitly grew via a legislative decision – in other words, the regime envisages the private parties' individual rights. Moreover, CRD IV and forthcoming CRD V (with CRR/ CRR II) have as their core aim depositor (and as well investor) protection, i.e., the clientele of banks and their management, the typical or at least potential respondents if claims based on violations of the supervisory regime are admitted. The contribution additionally refers to banking contract law, with the duty of responsible lending (see above section 3.2.), which is considerably increasing clients' protection. The conclusion is simple. The area would seem ripe – as was competition law at the time of the *Courage* case – for conceiving all standards as protecting individual parties of private law too. Such view could then constitute the basis for annulling contracts in violation of such standards or for interpreting contracts in conformity with such standards. The contribution appeals, however, also for liability beyond contracts, if the aggrieved party falls within the protective scope of the legal measures of the EU Banking Union regime in a precise enough way.

---

78 N. Badenhoop, 'Individual Protection Goals in EU Banking Regulation – A Process Towards Private Law Enforcement', chapter 8 below in this volume.

79 See CJEU case C-453/99 *Courage v. Crehan*, ECLI:EU:C:2001:465, esp. paras. 19-28 ('The full effectiveness of Article 85 of the Treaty and, in particular, the practical effect of the prohibition laid down in Article 85(1) would be put at risk if it were not open to any individual to claim damages for loss caused to him by a contract or by conduct liable to restrict or distort competition'). On this basis then also harmonisation of the regime of claims via Directive 2014/104/EU of the European Parliament and of the Council of 26 November 2014 on certain rules governing actions for damages under national law for infringements of the competition law provisions of the Member States and of the European Union, [2014] OJ L 349/1. See important monograph by J.-U. Franck, *Marktordnung durch Haftung: Legitimation, Reichweite und Steuerung der Haftung auf Schadensersatz zur Durchsetzung marktordnenden Rechts*, Mohr-Siebeck, Tübingen 2016. For that role of competition law as a forerunner in the Union, see references above n. 22.

In the area of enforcement, *Chapter 9* then addresses the problem of difficulties in enforcement, namely one increasingly prominent alternative.[80] It analyses the broad trend towards Alternative Dispute Resolution (ADR), i.e., out-of-court proceedings – cheaper (for clients, often even free), faster, less formal – both in the Member States and then harmonised and fine-tuned by Directive 2013/11/EU and – for consumers in particular – Regulation (EU) No. 524/2013. It analyses the close involvement specifically of the banking supervisory system itself, setting up ADR panels or Ombudsman services, the typically binding character – at least *de facto* binding character – of the final decision for the side of the credit institutions, and gives a comparative survey of some of the most important national systems (Italy, France, England). The chapter finds a change in approach – from a rather traditional 'access to justice' approach, in the tradition of the late Mauro Cappelletti's,[81] to a more mass consumer-oriented summary proceeding of reduced precision. The chapter therefore insists that, for reasons of quality of the law, the path of recourse to the courts needs to remain active and vigorous. It also addresses the strongly consumer-oriented character of ADR and deduces from this important differences to arbitration, namely with respect to publication and open discussion, but with respect to incentives and punitive elements as well – all these being of much higher importance than in the area of arbitration.

Finally, *Chapter 10* takes up a line of CJEU case law that concerns another loan segment (mainly in Central European Countries) that could provoke a systemic crisis (albeit only regional). This is the segment of foreign currency loans, the Polish bank sector being most severely affected.[82] Chapter 10 starts from contextualising this type of loan – in most cases truly existential for consumers, but truly existential as well for Central European Countries (in terms of numbers) – and the contractual terms often used in Central European Countries – foreign currency terms that, rather by mistake than on purpose, were drafted in a way that is unlawful under the Unfair Contract Terms Directive. The contribution extensively discusses the CJEU's case law in *Dziubak*, framing the legal scenario by totally annulling the loan contracts. It

---

80 P. Sirena, 'ADR Systems in the Banking and Financial Markets', chapter 9 below in this volume.

81 Mauro Cappelletti. 20th century comparative law scholar and general editor of the 4 volumes *Access to Justice*, Sijthoff and Noordhoff/Giuffre, Alphen aan den Rijn/Milan 1978 and 1979.

82 P. Tereszkiewicz, 'Making Foreign Currency Indexed Mortgage Loans Sustainable? The CJUE on Adjusting the Mortgage Loan Contracts', below Chapter 10 in this volume. Good recent comparative law survey on this topic in P. Tereszkiewicz and M. Golecki (eds.), *Protecting Financial Consumers in Europe – Comparative Perspectives and Policy Choices*, Brill Nijhoff, Leiden 2023. See as well lately S. Grundmann and N. Badenhoop, 'Foreign Currency Loans and the Foundations of European Contract Law – A Case for Financial and Contractual Crisis?' (2023) 19 *ERCL* 1; P. Sirena (ed.), *Unfair Contract Terms and Restitution in European Private Law – the National and ECJ Litigation on House Loans Indexed in a Foreign Currency*, Cambridge University Press, Cambridge 2024, forthcoming.

continues with the aspect of legal consequences. It shows how little, however, the Unfair Contract Terms Directive specifies them, namely the extent of restitution claims, how strongly recourse is to be had to general principles, and how it is open to discussion at what level they are to be found and located in a two-level system such as the EU. Thereby, interestingly enough, the seemingly very specific case pattern – foreign currency loans with a particular conversion mechanism that has been nullified – served as the basis for an unheard-of discussion on such a broad field as the European private law of restitution (including restitution damages). Altogether, the contribution sees parts of the case law as 'outcome-specific', others as mere 'guidance' and some as complete 'deference' to national law.

5. CONCLUSIONS

Strongly enhanced and diversified participation (rights) and pronounced common-good orientation would appear to be the two main thrusts of EU Company and Capital Market Law as a 'federal' (i.e. EU) policy. This diverges significantly from the US development, where such federal policy is largely missing, but as well parallel State law initiatives are rather weak. Not only the main actor in economies and markets, the large, listed firm, is subject to these developments in Europe. Banking law and Contract law are as well. At least for the latter two, it would seem as if certain general trends in this direction would have substantially grown and strengthened in reaction to the global financial crisis and the Euro sovereign debt crisis. Indeed, with respect to the public good, the European Banking Union – and the parallel enactment of the Mortgage Credit Directive 2014 with a strong focus on the duty of responsible lending – should probably be seen as trend-setters. It is all the more consistent with this development that private participation instruments too should increase and flourish within this context. This is the core topic of this volume. The European Banking Union is seen as an important triggering element with respect to private party participation rights in the financial arena and in regulation.

PART II

Stability Regime of the EU Banking Union

CHAPTER 2

PRE-INSOLVENCY IN THE BANK RECOVERY AND RESOLUTION DIRECTIVE

How to Enhance Recovery Measures

Alessandra DE ALDISIO and Carlo LANFRANCHI*

* The views expressed in this contribution are those of the authors and do not involve the responsibility of the Bank of Italy.

1. INTRODUCTION

The Directive 2014/59/EU[1] has considerably widened the crisis prevention measures used to intervene when a bank is experiencing difficulties, to prevent them from worsening. Indeed, due to the limitation on shareholders and creditors' rights that is entailed as a consequence of a decision adopted by a public authority, 'resolution' should be only adopted as a last resort measure when there are no reasonable prospects that any alternative supervisory action or private sector measure can prevent the bank's failure.

Yet, the new recovery and resolution framework provides for neither special negotiated solutions of the crisis, nor harmonised rules on financing arranged by the bank during the recovery or early intervention phase ('funding for recovery'). In addition, the more volatile market environment linked to the new 'bail-inable' regime and the lack of a credible public backstop[2] may make it more difficult to arrange early intervention measures and private sector solutions.

Crisis prevention measures[3] and the resolution framework[4] provided for in the Bank Recovery and Resolution Directive (BRRD) can affect the contractual relationships between banks and investors and the incentives to the latter to provide funding for recovery.

We will first recall the current provisions in the Bank Recovery and Resolution Directive on preventive, preparatory and early intervention measures that are especially relevant for the effects that they may have on contracts. After some general thoughts on the effects of insolvency and resolution proceedings on contracts, we will examine the possibility to introduce additional regulatory measures that could increase the effectiveness of preventive measures.

To this end, one option that is worth exploring is the possibility to harmonise rules on clawback actions and funding for recovery, both in the form of debt and equity, to facilitate restructuring processes and avoid a failure. The possibility to introduce a special financial instrument (a mandatory convertible

---

1 Directive 2014/59/EU of the European Parliament and of the Council of 15 May 2014 Establishing a framework for the recovery and resolution of credit institutions and investment firms and amending Council Directive 82/891/EEC, and Directives 2001/24/EC, 2002/47/EC, 2004/25/EC, 2005/56/EC, 2007/36/EC, 2011/35/EU, 2012/30/EU and 2013/36/EU, and Regulations (EU) No. 1093/2010 and (EU) No. 648/2012, of the European Parliament and of the Council [2014] OJ L 173/90, also called the 'Bank Recovery and Resolution Directive': hereinafter, the BRRD.

2 The implementation of the European Stability Mechanism backstop for the Single Resolution Fund and the possibility for Deposit Guarantee Schemes (DGS) to access public funds for financing could improve the situation but not solve the problem.

3 The BRRD provides for a definition of 'crisis prevention measures': see Art. 2(1), point 101.

4 See, in particular, 'resolution actions' as defined by Art. 2(1), point 40 of the BRRD.

bond) to incentivise capital injections into banks in financial distress – with the aim to overcome the problems of possible collective action – will also be investigated.

2. THE PRE-INSOLVENCY POWERS IN THE BRRD

The Bank Recovery and Resolution Directive framework has two main objectives: (i) to prevent insolvency through 'recovery', (ii) to minimise the adverse effects of insolvency through 'resolution', should a bank, notwithstanding the preventive actions undertaken, fail.

Accordingly, the Bank Recovery and Resolution Directive has introduced a comprehensive approach to banking crisis prevention and crisis management, covering both the going-concern and the gone-concern perspectives. Not only does it introduce a harmonised resolution regime, alternative to ordinary insolvency proceedings, to manage banking crises; it also provides for ex-ante regulatory instruments to prevent banks' failure and prepare them for a potential orderly resolution.

On the one hand, the financial crisis of 2007–2008 showed that many ordinary insolvency proceedings were not suited to address the failure of firms that, as banks, have a very special nature; on the other hand, it revealed the need to strengthen the toolkit at the disposal of the authorities to remedy the deterioration of a bank's financial and economic situation.[5]

As underlined by the De Larosière Report, there were substantial differences in the crisis prevention powers granted to supervisors in different Member States; therefore the report recommended action to bring all supervisors up to a high-level minimum standard.[6] The response was the introduction of a broad set of harmonised tools in the Bank Recovery and Resolution Directive, aimed at increasing the chances that developing problems will be identified and addressed at an early stage and at enhancing the preparedness of firms and authorities to deal effectively with serious difficulties.[7]

Some of these arrangements and measures – such as those aimed at ensuring that the bank has adequate access to contingency funding sources

---

5 See BRRD, Recital 40.

6 See Report of the High-Level Group on Financial Supervision in the EU (De Larosière Group), February 2009, available at: https://www.esrb.europa.eu/shared/pdf/de_larosiere_report_en.pdf?351e1b35ec1ca5e855d2e465383a311f, para. 160.

7 Communication from the Commission to the European Parliament, the Council, the European Economic and Social Committee, the Committee of the Regions and the European Central Bank, 'An EU Framework for Crisis Management in the Financial Sector', Brussels, 20.10.2010, COM(2010) 579 final.

or those aimed at restructuring liabilities – may have a specific impact on the contractual relationships between banks and investors.

The De Larosière Report also noted that

> company law provisions in some countries prevent in times of crisis the transfer of assets from one legal entity to another within the same group. This makes it impossible to transfer assets where they are needed, even though this may be crucial to safeguard the viability of the group as a whole.[8]

A special framework for intra-group financial support was therefore introduced by the Bank Recovery and Resolution Directive.

3. CRISIS PREVENTION MEASURES

We can identify three types of measures: (i) preventive measures, including recovery planning and intra-group financial support; (ii) preparatory measures, i.e., resolution plans and resolvability assessments; and (iii) early intervention measures, i.e., pre-resolution measures.

The set of supervisory powers enshrined in the prudential directives has been widened with early intervention measures. Furthermore, firms and authorities are required to plan in advance the actions aimed at overcoming difficulties (recovery plans and intra-group financial support agreements) and to ensure orderly resolution (resolution plans).

Planning the activities to be taken in case of resolution is a truly innovative aspect of the new resolution framework that requires both the firms and the authorities to contemplate a crisis well before it materialises: banks must imagine scenarios of difficulty, assess their potential impacts, and identify effective response actions. In turn, the authorities must identify in advance the potential obstacles to the application of the resolution tools and specify all actions to be put in place to manage the crisis in an orderly manner.

3.1. RECOVERABILITY: RECOVERY PLANS

As a first step, banks should prepare and regularly update recovery plans that set out the measures that the management could take to restore the financial position of the bank, following a significant deterioration in the capital or liquidity situation. Early action based on recovery plans can prevent the escalation of problems and reduce the risk of a bank's failure.[9]

8 See Report of the De Larosière Group, February 2009, n. 6 above, para. 130.
9 BRRD, Arts. 6 and 7 and Annex, Section A.

The plan should identify a range of capital and liquidity actions required to maintain or restore the viability and the financial position of the bank. Accordingly, it should identify arrangements and measures to conserve or restore the bank's own funds. In addition, it should take into account the nature of the bank's sources of funding and the degree to which group support would be credibly available. More specifically, it should include (i) arrangements and measures to ensure that the bank has adequate access to contingency funding sources, including potential liquidity sources and liquidity facilities provided by central banks, (ii) an assessment of available collateral, and (iii) an assessment of the possibility to transfer liquidity across group entities and business lines.[10]

Banks are required to submit their plans to competent authorities for an assessment. Such assessment includes consideration of whether the plans are comprehensive and could feasibly restore a bank's viability, in a timely manner, even in periods of financial stress.

Where a bank does not present an adequate recovery plan, competent authorities may require the banks to take measures necessary to redress the shortcomings of the plan. More specifically, the competent authority has the power to direct the bank to (i) reduce its risk profile, including liquidity risk, (ii) enable timely recapitalisation, (iii) review the bank's strategy and structure; (iv) make changes to the funding strategy, and (v) make changes to the governance structure.

3.2. INTRA-GROUP FINANCIAL SUPPORT

The Bank Recovery and Resolution Directive has introduced a framework for intra-group financial support aimed at increasing the legal certainty of transfers of assets within groups: group entities may enter into an agreement to provide financial support to any other party that meets the conditions for early intervention.

The possibility to transfer liquidity, collateral and other assets within a banking group, in particular when this is a cross-border transfer, may enhance the group's ability to cope with severe stresses, preventing difficulties from worsening in parts of the group.

The experience of the 2007–2008 crisis showed how quickly a liquidity crisis may turn out into a solvency crisis and how the parent company's support may be crucial to ensure the viability of subsidiaries. An additional tool at the disposal of groups and authorities to prevent this situation was thought to be very useful, especially for integrated groups.

---

[10] BRRD, Annex, Section A, point 11.

However, the provision of financial support from one entity of a transnational group to another entity of the same group is restricted by a number of provisions, laid down in national law in some Member States, that make ring-fencing possible. These provisions are designed to protect the creditors and shareholders of each entity, but they do not take into account the interdependency of the entities of the same group. It is therefore appropriate to set out under what conditions financial support may be provided among entities of a transnational group with a view to ensuring the financial stability of the group as a whole without jeopardising the liquidity or solvency of the group entity providing the support.[11]

The Bank Recovery and Resolution Directive therefore has introduced a special framework aimed at enabling mutual financial support, on a voluntary basis, through the transfer of assets to the group entities experiencing temporary difficulties.[12] The *ex ante* approval of the agreement by the shareholders of the entities concerned and by the authorities provides more certainty to transfers that are made on that basis, thus reducing the risks that they are challenged by minority shareholders and creditors of the transferring entity.

Financial support may be provided only if: (i) there is a reasonable prospect of recovery, (ii) the support will not jeopardise the liquidity or solvency of the provider, (iii) there is a reasonable prospect that the consideration for the support will be paid and the loan reimbursed. In addition, the interest in the stability of the group as a whole is recognised as a condition of the validity of the transfer.[13]

The transferring authority may, however, prevent the transfer even though an agreement has been signed if it considers it to be in conflict with the terms of the agreement and if the transfer threatens the liquidity or solvency of the transferor or financial stability, in particular, in the Member State of the group entity providing support.[14]

During the negotiations of the Bank Recovery and Resolution Directive at the Council, some delegations proposed to make the Directive the prevailing law with respect to national corporate and bankruptcy laws, in order to avoid

---

11 BRRD, Recital 38.

12 BRRD, Arts. 19–25.

13 Legal theories on groups of companies are several and still under debate. See, for example, the 'Rozenblum' doctrine, the theory of compensatory group advantages (*teoria dei vantaggi compensativi*) and the 'source of strength' doctrine.

14 A different solution has been advanced by the ECB, more agile and effective than the group financial support agreements currently envisaged in the BRRD, as the safeguards envisaged would be triggered at an earlier stage and would require less stringent conditions, due to an enforcement power that could be attributed to the supervisor. See A. Enria and E. Fernandez-Bollo, 'Fostering the cross-border integration of banking groups in the banking union', ECB Supervision Blog, Frankfurt am Main, 09.10.2020, available at: https://www.bankingsupervision.europa.eu/press/blog/2020/html/ssm.blog201009~bc7ef4e6f8.en.html.

the risk of clawback actions and to ensure legal certainty for transfers made on the basis of agreements between the companies concerned and approved by the authorities.[15] The final text of the Bank Recovery and Resolution Directive states that Member States should remove any legal impediments in national law to intra-group financial support transactions, with the exception of limitations on intra-group transactions envisaged by the prudential directives.[16]

Unfortunately, such agreements have not been widely adopted so far. This shows that the framework is not fully equipped to tackle ring-fencing problems and should be further improved. One possible way to support a deeper integration of cross-border banking groups while ensuring an effective and fair crisis management mechanism applicable to group entities could be the introduction of a cross-border capital waiver. However, in order to address host countries' concerns, a cross-border capital waiver should be combined with a credible statutory claim by the subsidiary against the parent entity to provide adequate capital. In this regard, for the Euro area, an option to explore would be to require that the collateral is deposited at a centralised level (e.g., at the European Central Bank as custodian), while continuing to be managed by the parent company at the group level. In this scenario, the European Central Bank may be vested with supervisory powers to limit the use of these funds and securities to avoid their diversion or misuse and ensure that they are available to be down-streamed to the subsidiaries' level in case of need. Moreover, the involvement of the European Central Bank would trigger the common jurisdiction of the European Court of Justice in the event of a dispute.

3.3. RESOLVABILITY: RESOLUTION PLANS

Resolution planning is an essential component of effective resolution. It is aimed at ensuring that the group's structure and the liabilities' structure facilitate the application of resolution tools by the resolution authority, so as to ensure the continuity of critical functions and preserve financial stability.

The resolution plan identifies ex-ante the actions and the tools that the authorities can apply in case of a crisis. The plan is prepared by the resolution authorities, after consulting the supervisory authorities, on the basis of the

15 The initial legislative proposal of the Commission did not contain such provision. See 'Proposal for a Directive of the European Parliament and of the Council establishing a framework for the recovery and resolution of credit institutions and investment firms, and amending Council Directives 77/91/EEC and 82/891/EC, Directives 2001/24/EC, 2002/47/EC, 2004/25/EC, 2005/56/EC, 2007/36/EC and 2011/35/EC and Regulation (EU) No. 1093/2010', Brussels, 06.06.2012, COM(2012) 280 final, Art. 16.

16 BRRD, Art. 19(4).

information provided by the intermediaries, and has to consider several scenarios, including a generalised difficult situation.[17]

When drafting the plan, the authorities must identify in advance the potential obstacles to the application of the resolution strategy and the resolution tools (for example, the transfer of critical functions to a bridge bank) and define all actions to be put in place to effectively manage the crisis.

On the basis of the assessment of resolvability, resolution authorities have the power to require banks to take measures which are necessary to reduce or remove material impediments to the application of resolution tools, including the option to request changes to the legal and operational structure of the groups in order to reduce their complexity and to isolate and separate the critical functions of the intermediary, and the issuance of liabilities that are eligible to meet the Minimum Requirement for Own Funds and Eligible Liabilities (MREL). In addition, resolution authorities may require the bank (i) to renegotiate eligible liabilities, additional Tier 1 instruments or Tier 2 instruments it has issued, with a view to ensuring that any decision of the resolution authority to write down or convert those liabilities or instruments would be effected under the law of the jurisdiction governing those liabilities or instruments and (ii) to change the maturity profile of the liabilities to ensure compliance with the MREL.[18]

The group resolution plans are prepared for the group as a whole and identify measures in relation to the parent company and its subsidiaries.

The Financial Stability Board (FSB) has identified two resolution strategies for groups, in particular transnational groups: the Single Point of Entry (SPE) strategy envisages that the resolution tools are applied by one authority only at the level of the parent company, which should have a loss-absorbing capacity adequate to recapitalise the individual subsidiaries. The subsidiaries will not be subject to resolution, but they will continue to operate by transferring the losses exceeding their capital to the parent company. The parent company will have to issue bail-inable instruments in adequate amounts to absorb losses and to recapitalise its subsidiaries.[19]

The mechanism for transferring the losses from the subsidiary to the parent company is the write-down or conversion of subordinated debt issued by the subsidiary and subscribed by the parent company. The first step involves transferring losses exceeding a subsidiary's equity to its parent.

> In essence, the solution is for key subsidiaries to issue super-subordinated debt (or extra equity) to their parent group/subgroup (the so called Internal TLAC). The subsidiary's

---

[17] BRRD, Arts. 12–17.

[18] BRRD, Art. 17.

[19] Financial Stability Board, 'Guidance on Developing Effective Resolution Strategies', July 2013; and Financial Stability Board, 'Guiding Principles on the Internal Total Loss-absorbing Capacity of G-SIBs ('Internal TLAC')', July 2017.

> 'excess' losses are covered and its solvency is restored by writing-down and converting into equity as much as is needed of the intra-group debt. Thus, the subsidiary is recapitalised without going into default itself and the group as a whole is preserved.

As has been noted, that 'will at last make a reality of the long-standing doctrine – underpinning all consolidated supervision but without binding substance up to now – that groups should be a source of strength for their component parts'.[20]

The Multiple Point of Entry (MPE) strategy instead implies that resolution tools are applied by multiple authorities to different parts of the group, identified as part of the same jurisdiction or business line, with a self-sufficient capacity to absorb losses and easily separable from other components of the group. In this case, the group would be fragmented into the different components subject to separate resolutions. It is possible to combine the two strategies.

The SPE strategy fits best with integrated groups characterised by interconnections between the individual entities of the group, resulting from the centralisation of functions such as liquidity management (cash-pooling), risk management, and essential services such as IT. The MPE strategy requires instead that interconnections are reduced and the group is organised for substantively self-sufficient individual entities or subgroups.

The Bank Recovery and Resolution Directive review of 2019, aiming to implement the TLAC standard for the European global systemically important banks (G-SIBs) and to adapt the provisions on MREL, has – among other things – introduced the concepts of resolution group, resolution entity and internal TLAC in the Union law.[21]

3.4. EARLY INTERVENTION MEASURES

In order to preserve financial stability, it is important that competent authorities are able to remedy the deterioration of a bank's financial and economic situation before that bank reaches a point at which authorities have no other alternative than to resolve it.

To this end, competent authorities have been granted early intervention powers to remedy the problems before they compromise the viability of the bank. These are aimed at restoring the bank's financial soundness, and range from the power to require the management to adopt remedial measures, to the power to remove the management and appoint a temporary administrator,

---

20 P. Tucker, 'The Resolution of Financial Banks without Taxpayer Solvency Support: Seven Retrospective Clarifications and Elaborations', European Summer Symposium in Economic Theory, Gerzensee (Switzerland), 03.07.2014.

21 See n. 16 above.

either to replace or to temporarily collaborate with the management body and senior management of the bank, applicable when certain trigger conditions are met.[22]

Among these measures, we specifically recall (i) the power of the authorities to request a bank that has breached or is likely to breach the prudential requirements to implement the arrangements or measures that are set out in the recovery plan, including activating the intra-group financial support where such an agreement has been concluded, and (ii) the power to require the management body to draw up a plan for negotiating the restructuring of the bank's debt with some or all of its creditors according to the recovery plan.[23] [24]

The write-down or conversion powers in relation to capital instruments, when exercised independently of resolution, can be included among the measures that can prevent resolution.[25] Just as intra-group financial support can address a liquidity problem within a group, the write-down or conversion of capital instruments when a bank has reached the point of non-viability may help in restoring the solvency and viability of the bank and thereby avoid resolution.

4. CONTRACTS IN PRE-INSOLVENCY AND PRE-RESOLUTION

As a general principle, outside of formal insolvency proceedings, contracts could not be affected without the consent of the parties.[26] However, this general principle does not mean that the applicable legal framework on insolvency has no impact (indirect or *de facto*) on parties' *ex ante* incentives and therefore on how contracts are concretely settled upon.

The Italian legal framework provides, as many others do, also for out-of-court composition agreements[27] and hybrid pre-bankruptcy proceedings;[28] both

---

22 BRRD, Arts. 27–29.

23 BRRD, Art. 27(1)(a) and (e).

24 For a stronger link between the recovery plan and a group financial support agreement, coupled with the power of the supervisor to enforce the agreement included in the group's recovery plan and adequate incentives to enter into group financial support agreements, see 'The yin and yang of banking market integration – the case of cross-border banks', speech by A. Enria at the 7th Annual Digital Conference on the Banking Union, Frankfurt am Main, 18.11.2020.

25 BRRD, Art. 59(1)(a).

26 See Art. 1372, Italian Civil Code (*Codice civile*: Royal Decree 16.03.1942, No. 262) that sets forth the principle of consensuality of contracts.

27 See Attested plan for restructuring (*Piani di risanamento*: Art. 67(3)(d), Italian Insolvency Act (*Legge fallimentare*: Royal Decree 16.03.1942, No. 267) and Agreements for the restructuring of debts (*Accordi di ristrutturazione*: Arts. 182-bis and 67(3)(e) of the Italian Insolvency Act).

28 See Scheme of arrangement with creditors (*Concordato preventivo*: Art. 160 of the Italian Insolvency Act).

of them were conceived as a preventive alternative to fully public insolvency proceeding.[29] The former are strictly based on a consensus of all parties involved (unanimity rule); the latter instead are based on a voting procedure whose outcome is binding for all the relevant creditors (majority rule).[30] At the current stage, both of them are often unlikely to be applicable to banks because of legal[31] and feasibility constraints. However, some room could be found and expanded for the former: namely, crisis solutions agreed upon by creditors.

On the matter of these tools, the new recovery and resolution framework does not provide useful guidance. Indeed, in the Bank Recovery and Resolution Directive, the role played by the above-mentioned pre-crisis management tools is only partially played by crisis prevention measures which – notwithstanding a specific provision on a possible plan for restructuring of debt with creditors as an early intervention measure – provide neither for special negotiated solutions to the crisis, nor for harmonised rules on financing arranged by the bank during the recovery or early intervention phases ('funding for recovery'). Indeed, the preventive restructuring framework for banks still remains almost completely unharmonised among Member States, while some steps forwards in this direction have been taken with the Directive (EU) 2019/1023 on preventive restructuring frameworks (see section 7.1 below).

4.1. CONTRACTS AND CRISIS PREVENTION MEASURES

As extensively described in the previous paragraphs, the Bank Recovery and Resolution Directive provides for a comprehensive crisis prevention framework that is deemed to be a notable innovation for addressing a banking crisis. As said, according to this framework, the competent authority may exercise a number of powers by which it may deeply intervene in the financial and governance structure of the bank. To some extent, this intervention could indirectly affect contracts entered into by the bank. The exercise of such powers cannot result in a direct modification of contractual terms regarding third parties (except for subsidiaries, due to the exercise of management and coordination activity by

29 See Bankruptcy (*Fallimento*: Art. 1 of the Italian Insolvency Act), Compulsory Administrative Liquidation (*Liquidazione coatta amministrativa*: Art. 80, Consolidated Law on Banking (*Testo unico bancario*: Legislative Decree 01.09.1993, No. 385), Extraordinary Administration for 'large' undertakings (*Amministrazione straordinaria delle grandi imprese in crisi*).

30 It is useful to note that the Italian legal framework provides also for a third option: a decision taken by a majority without a formal meeting that is binding for an entire class of creditors. It is a special agreement between the borrower and his financial lenders (see Art. 182-*septies* of the Italian Insolvency Act); *accordo di ristrutturazione con intermediari finanziari*).

31 According to Art. 80(6) of the Consolidated Law on Banking, 'banks shall not be subject to insolvency proceedings other than compulsory administrative liquidation'.

the parent bank) but the possibility of *ex post* intervention by the resolution authority is sufficient to affect contracts models *ex ante*.

For example, new contracts models arranged by banks might start providing for specific clauses aimed at taking into account the possibility that a competent authority may request the bank to renegotiate liabilities as an early intervention measure.[32]

Likewise, a resolution authority assessing resolvability could require the insertion of specific contractual clauses to ensure that internal MREL/TLAC can be triggered at the point of non-viability to absorb losses and recapitalise subsidiaries in an SPE strategy.[33]

Again, it is required that banks assess their available collateral to ensure adequate and continuous access to contingency funding sources.[34] This requirement, together with MREL/TLAC, might diminish asset encumbrance and then improve use of covenants by adjusting creditors.[35]

The need to ensure that bail-inable bonds could be effectively bailed-in in resolution is having, as well, some implications for contracts models when the law governing the bond is the law of a non-EU country. Indeed, in this case, the contract must include a term by which the parties recognise that the liability may be subject to bail-in.[36]

Even where a statutory power is envisaged and is enforceable to achieve specific outcomes, the insertion of a contractual clause that recognises the authority's power is encouraged by the Bank Recovery and Resolution Directive, presumably to increase the awareness of investors.[37]

4.2. CONTRACTS AND RESOLUTION

As is well known, even more than crisis prevention measures, the broader resolution framework could indirectly affect contracts in pre-insolvency.

---

32 See BRRD, Art. 17(5)(j), and Annex, Section A, point. 13.

33 See Financial Stability Board, 'Guiding Principles on the Internal Total Loss-absorbing Capacity of G-SIBs ('Internal TLAC')', July 2017, Annex III.

34 See BRRD, Annex, Section A, point. 11, which requires the bank to create a sort of buffer of contingency-eligible collateral.

35 I.e., creditors that are capable of protecting themselves. See L.A. Bebchuk and J.M. Fried, 'The Uneasy Case for the Priority of Secured Claims in Bankruptcy' (1996) 105 *Yale Law Journal* 857, 934; also (1996) *Harvard Law and Economics Discussion Paper No. 166*, available at:
https://ssrn.com/abstract=417960 or http://dx.doi.org/10.2139/ssrn.417960.

36 See BRRD, Art. 55.

37 See for example BRRD, Recital 81, requiring that the statutory power to write-down or convert capital instruments is recognised in the term governing the instruments and in any prospectus or offering document.

Indeed, legal risks arising from applicable insolvency law are essential elements of the risk assessment conducted by prospective investors. Unlike crisis prevention measures, normal insolvency proceedings, when formally initiated, could directly and substantially interact with contracts, both already executed and pending. Insolvency necessarily impacts on contracts' enforceability and execution, whatever the crisis management procedure adopted is. As the insolvency law defines the contract's outcome when the debtor goes bankrupt, the agents will take it into account when negotiating contract terms like, at least, price and duration. More specifically, the agents could be influenced when taking investment decisions by the treatment that contracts they are going to enter into would have under the applicable insolvency law. For example, and in particular, the applicable treatment of loan agreements according to insolvency law could encourage or discourage agents from providing new finance to a debtor in financial distress, while it is well known how much fresh finance can be a key factor for the successful solution of a crisis, particularly in case of a temporary lack of liquidity.

The same clearly holds true for resolution; as it is a special procedure to address a bank failure, it deeply interacts with contracts.

For example, the decision of the resolution authority on the strategy to be adopted in resolution (SPE or MPE) determines the risk profile of the group's liabilities among the group's entities: according to an SPE strategy, the liabilities issued by the parent company (structurally subordinated) are riskier than liabilities issued by the subsidiaries and, more significantly, the liabilities issued by the subsidiaries are riskier in an MPE strategy than in an SPE strategy.

5. CONTRACTS IN NORMAL INSOLVENCY PROCEEDINGS

Traditionally, insolvency law could affect executed contracts through clawback actions and pending contracts through decisions upon their continuation or termination.

A clawback action is brought by a creditor to demand that acts by which the debtor disposes of his assets to the prejudice of his rights be declared ineffective as regards him. The successful outcome of a clawback action could severely harm the creditors against which the action is brought. Also, for that reason, prospective creditors are discouraged from entering into a lending relationship with a debtor that is in a 'twilight zone' and at risk of going bankrupt.

As for ongoing contractual relationships, they are continued or terminated *ex lege* or upon the decision of a special manager and their treatment could harm contractual parties involved, as well.

6. CONTRACTS IN RESOLUTION

As said, resolution too deeply interacts with contracts when it is formally commenced. More precisely, the Bank Recovery and Resolution Directive does not provide properly for a complete formal procedure but rather for a toolkit and a set of powers that resolution authorities will have at their disposal where necessary in the public interest.

Accordingly, the Bank Recovery and Resolution Directive provides for a number of general powers that allow resolution authorities to modify contractual terms in different ways.[38] For example, (i) the power to amend or alter the maturity of debt instruments issued by the bank under resolution, or alter the amount of interest payable, or the date on which the interest becomes payable; (ii) the power to close-out and terminate financial or derivatives contracts; (iii) the power to remove third parties' rights from transferred instruments or assets; (iv) the power to cancel or modify the terms of a contract to which the institution under resolution is a party, or to substitute a recipient as a party.

In addition, or as generalisations of these powers, we identify two main types of resolution authority intervention: continuation or termination of contracts, and exercise of clawback actions.

6.1. CONTINUATION OF CONTRACTS

Since resolution is deemed to be a reorganisation and restructuring procedure, it requires, as a general rule, the continuation of contracts. Only a few exceptions are provided: close-out netting of derivative contracts[39] (aimed at determining possible liabilities to bail-in), and the provision of powers[40] to suspend for a very short period of time certain obligations and rights arising from contracts.[41]

In addition, in order to ensure the continuity of critical functions and minimise the destruction of value, resolution shall not be deemed to be an enforcement event or an insolvency proceeding for the purposes of contracts entered into by the bank. It is assumed that resolution is not a reason for counterparties not to fulfil their obligations.[42]

---

38 See Arts. 63 and 64, BRRD.

39 See Art. 49, BRRD.

40 See Arts. 69 and 70, BRRD.

41 An extension of the moratorium period is discussed in the context of the review of the BRRD. See Proposal for a Directive of the European Parliament and of the Council amending Directive 2014/59/EU on loss-absorbing and recapitalisation capacity of credit institutions and investment firms, COM(2016) 852 final – 2016/0362(COD).

42 See BRRD, Art. 68.

6.2. CLAWBACK ACTIONS

The Bank Recovery and Resolution Directive does not provide for any legal remedies against fraudulent and preferential transfers. In particular, it does not provide for a framework for clawback actions.

In contrast, the Italian transposition of the Bank Recovery and Resolution Directive has extended the application of clawback actions to resolution too, to avoid a difference in treatment in respect of the normal Italian insolvency proceeding for banks (i.e., the Compulsory Administrative Liquidation).[43]

Clawback actions aim at granting equal treatment among creditors and a (limited) source of funding for the resolution. Most importantly, they aim at (i) avoiding delay in unveiling the crisis, (ii) preventing its worsening because of over-investment decisions taken by the debtor willing to gamble with the firm's assets, and (iii) making lenders accountable for their lending decisions.

As mentioned above, the application of clawback actions has also some downsides, since it could harm the legal certainty of valid acts.

The threat of clawback action could discourage prospective investors from establishing contractual relationships with the bank when it is in the 'twilight zone'.

In order to neutralise these unintended consequences that may compromise the success of a restructuring, some exceptions to the general avoidance provision seem necessary.

In the Italian transposition of the Bank Recovery and Resolution Directive, a waiver has been provided: clawback actions do not apply to contracts executed in application of an intra-group financial support agreement approved by the competent authority. This provision seems to be in line with Article 19(4) of the Bank Recovery and Resolution Directive, according to which 'Member States shall remove any legal impediment ... to intra-group financial support transactions'.

Further steps in this direction seem, however, to be necessary given that any action *ex post facto* that aims at restoring the *par condicio creditorum* (*pari passu* principle) could have *ex ante* worsening effects on the crisis due to reduction in the bank's borrowing capacity: the more aggressive the clawback actions are, the less willing to provide new funding the investors would be.

On the other hand, the risk that these exceptions and similar measures aimed at encouraging fresh finance injections would threaten other creditors should be considered. Therefore, a trade off has to be addressed with the purpose of striking the right balance between the protection of the existing creditors and the encouragement of prospective new finance providers.

[43] See n. 29 above.

A proposal could be that clawback actions do not apply at least to those acts that are undertaken by the bank in execution of the recovery plan and in good faith, following a request by the competent authority to implement the plan as an early intervention measure.[44] Essentially, this proposal would be a transposition into the bank recovery legal framework of the tool provided for by Article 67(3)(d) of the Italian Insolvency Act: attested plan for restructuring, which still is applicable to banks. According to this provision, acts concluded in compliance with a plan for restructuring attested by an independent expert are protected from clawback actions if bankruptcy proceedings are commenced.

7. A PROPOSAL: FUNDING FOR RECOVERY

Introducing new exceptions to the general rule on clawback actions could certainly be useful but probably not enough to encourage injections of new finance and give the bank a chance to preserve or restore its viability.

Differentials in recovery rates between bankruptcy and alternative measures make it possible to imagine a larger role for private prevention measures. Indeed, it is well known that recovery rates are higher through restructuring than through liquidation and this could be even more relevant for banks due to the role of confidence in preserving customer relationships and the franchise value.

Accordingly, in order to improve a bank's chances of recovery from a significant deterioration of its financial situation, and particularly to enable timely recapitalisation or other funding measures, liquidity injections from current and, most importantly, new investors should be encouraged as a measure envisaged by the recovery plan.[45]

However, under the current framework prospective investors are discouraged from providing new finance, and even more so, from participating in capital increases, when the bank is in the 'twilight zone'. Indeed, their investments could be wiped out by a subsequent bail-in if the new finance injection ultimately proves to be insufficient to preserve or restore the viability of the bank. This conclusion holds true both for equity and debt financing. In particular, in case of equity financing, collective action issues may arise and need to be tackled. If an ailing bank needs a capital increase, but, due to the impossibility of setting up an underwriting syndicate or finding a single 'white

[44] On this issue see L. Stanghellini and A. Zorzi, 'Il piano di risanamento attestato' in A. Jorio and B.N. Sassani (eds.), *Trattato delle procedure concorsuali*, Giuffrè, Milan 2017, pp. 527 et seq.

[45] Indeed, according to the BRRD, 'the recovery plan shall include the following information: ... a range of capital and liquidity actions required to maintain or restore the viability and financial position of the bank' (BRRD, Annex, Section A, point 4)).

knight' investor, it is forced to tap a highly fragmented market, the outcome of a last-ditch attempt at a pre-resolution capital increase may be uncertain, since prospective investors may be discouraged from providing financial resources if they are not shielded from bail-in.

7.1. 'DIP' FINANCING

A proposal could be to introduce in the Bank Recovery and Resolution Directive an exclusion from bail-in (or a super-priority) for finance received by the bank during recovery or early intervention phases (in line with 'debtor-in-possession (DIP) financing' under US bankruptcy law).[46]

DIP financing is often an essential component of a US corporate reorganisation. US law gives the bankruptcy judge authority to allow the restructured firm to borrow in a way that subordinates the claims of prior creditors. A DIP loan can increase the eventual recovery value for prior creditors by allowing the firm to keep operating and earn profits, in particular in cases of debt overhang.

Under the proposed rule, new financing provided to a bank in financial distress upon approval by the competent authority would be excluded from bail-in. According to this proposal, if a bank that has entered into a recovery or an early intervention phase cannot roll over its debt on ordinary market terms, the competent authority may authorise the bank to receive loans that have priority over pre-recovery creditors or are excluded from bail-in, provided that the receipt of such new finance is necessary to preserve the bank as a going concern.

Such preferential treatment[47] would be justified as aimed at restoring the financial situation of a bank. However, as already noted above, it has to be carefully considered because it implies some risks, too. In the event that the liquidity injection is not enough to restore the bank's ability to comply with minimum capital requirements and the bank is put under resolution, non-preferred creditors could incur greater losses than they would have incurred without DIP financing.

So, it is crucial to identify the moment from which a bank would be eligible to receive loans that have priority: on the one hand, this moment should be set sufficiently early to increase the prospect of a successful restructuring; on

---

[46] See for an example, the US Bankruptcy Code, 11 US Code § 364(d). Also, the Italian Insolvency Law provides for similar financing schemes.

[47] This special treatment should be extended also to shareholders' financing and intra-group financial support. In order to avoid breaches of the 'no creditor worse off' (NCWO) principle (see BRRD Art. 34(1)(g)), the same preferential treatment should be applied to new finance also in normal insolvency proceedings (as already provided for under insolvency law of many jurisdictions).

the other hand, it should not be set too early, that is before difficulties arise, as this could have distorting effects on the funding conditions and level playing-field. The request to implement the recovery plan by the competent authority as an early intervention measure could be considered an appropriate trigger condition.

Since the competent authority would be empowered to authorise the bank to receive such financing and this authorisation could expose the former to legal and operational risks, special safeguards should be envisaged.

In addition, since these new liabilities would not be bail-inable, they could not count towards the MREL/TLAC requirement: nevertheless, the possibility to issue these liabilities may still be valuable for the bank, since it would facilitate its capacity to roll-over its existing debt.

It is worth noting that Directive (EU) 2019/1023 on preventive restructuring frameworks sets up a DIP procedure and protects both new financing (i.e., financing which is necessary to implement the restructuring plan) and interim financing (allowing the business to continue to operate during the negotiation of the restructuring plan) under specific conditions, in order to support the restructuring process of the company while negotiations are ongoing.

According to the European Commission, 'this incentivises new lenders to financially support a restructuring plan and should ensure that a restructuring plan can successfully be implemented'.[48]

In addition, transactions undertaken in good faith and closely connected with the adoption or implementation of a restructuring plan are also protected from avoidance actions in subsequent insolvency proceedings.

7.2. EQUITY FINANCING

One of the conditions of starting resolution is the lack of a reasonable prospect for any alternative private solution, including an increase of capital by existing or new shareholders. A proposal[49] could be to introduce a new set of special provisions derogating from or clarifying the possible derogation from ordinary

[48] See European Commission fact sheet, available at: http://europa.eu/rapid/press-release_MEMO-16-3803_en.htm.

[49] The proposal may require a partial revision of Directive 2012/30/EU of the European parliament and of the council of 25 October 2012 on coordination of safeguards which, for the protection of the interests of members and others, are required by Member States of companies within the meaning of the second paragraph of Article 54 of the Treaty on the Functioning of the European Union, in respect of the formation of public limited liability companies and the maintenance and alteration of their capital, with a view to making such safeguards equivalent [2012] OJ L 315/74.

EU rules on capital increases[50] and a mandatory bid to facilitate the raising of new equity. In particular, when the interest of the company so requires and/or in a specific period of time,[51] banks should be able – also upon request by the competent authority and with a smaller majority than that currently required – to launch capital increases with exclusion, alternatively or in combination, of pre-emption rights, mandatory previous capital reduction and the mandatory bid rule[52] and, if necessary to offset losses incurred or expected, at a price below par value. This proposal is aimed at eliminating some of the existing impediments[53] to the timely[54] approval of a capital increase by the relevant corporate body and, in some cases, at facilitating a change in corporate control.

This approach seems to be legally and economically justified, considering that shareholders start 'losing' their property rights when the company becomes likely to fail and they 'lose' them completely when corporate assets become less than corporate liabilities.[55] At the former stage, it seems correct, ideally, to transfer shareholders' decision rights (at least on the rescue[56] of the company) to creditors, as new de facto owners, and, in particular, to recognise that the directors of the near-insolvent company owe duties of loyalty and care also to them as creditors.[57] As a consequence, company directors should be required to balance a dual duty to both creditors and shareholders. This approach seems to be in line with the proposal[58] to assign a role in the corporate governance

50 In this regard, it has to be noted that Directive 2007/36/EC of the European Parliament and of the Council of 11 July 2007 on the exercise of certain rights of shareholders in listed companies [2007] OJ L 184/17, does not apply in the case of the use of resolution tools.

51 See the DIP financing proposal (section 7.1 above).

52 See for example Art. 106(5)(a), Consolidated Law on Finance (*Testo unico delle disposizioni in materia di intermediazione finanziaria*. Legislative Decree 24.02.1998, No. 58).

53 See EBA, 'Recovery planning comparative report on recovery options', 01.03.2017 available at: http://www.eba.europa.eu/documents/10180/1720738/EBA+Comparative+report+on+recovery+options+-+March+2017.pdf.
EBA recognises as an impediment to prompt execution of recovery options the limitations on capital increases coming from the bank's Articles of Association or lack of market appetite for the bank's capital instruments (on the latter issue, see the proposal for a special convertible bond below in the text).

54 See Consolidated Law on Banking, Art. 77-bis, and BRRD, Art. 121, which provide for derogations from some rules of procedure for shareholders' meetings.

55 See *ex multis* M.C. Jensen and W.H. Meckling, 'Theory of the Firm: Managerial Behavior, Agency Costs and Ownership Structure' (1976) 3 *Journal Financial Economics* 308.

56 See for example Italian Insolvency Act, Art. 163(5), on capital increases proposed by creditors.

57 Contra *Nacepf, Inc. v. Gheewalla*, 930 A.2d 92, 101 (Del. 2007). However, it seems that this principle of law should not be applicable at least to systemically important financial institutions.

58 See S.L. Schwarcz, 'Rethinking Corporate Governance for a Bondholder Financed, Systemically Risky World' (2017) 58 *William & Mary Law Review* 1345; also *Duke Law School Public Law & Legal Theory Series No. 2016-22*, available at: https://ssrn.com/abstract=2741794.

framework to holders of contingent convertible bonds and subordinated bondholders with the purpose of reducing systemic risk.

Accordingly, it should be legally feasible to exclude pre-emption rights, dilute existing shareholdingsand, through capital increase, promote even a change in corporate control (that still should be compensated by granting a proper share premium), even by a board decision.[59]

If 'hidden' value is present that is owed to shareholders, corrective measures, like assignment of warrants or bonus shares (*azioni di godimento*) that should be deemed to be ex-post adjustment measures, should be legally feasible, as well.

In light of this approach, a special financial instrument could also be proposed to incentivise capital injections into banks in financial distress for which collective action problems make the outcome of a capital increase *ex ante* uncertain (see above section 7). The proposed instrument would be a mandatory convertible bond (to be underwritten by current or prospective shareholders) that is converted into equity in the following two alternative scenarios:

(i) if the value of instruments subscribed is enough to restore the bank's ability to comply with minimum capital requirements, the bonds are converted upon conclusion of their offering period. In this scenario, since minimum requirements are complied with, resolution is avoided;[60]

(ii) if the value of instruments subscribed is not enough to restore the bank's ability to comply with minimum capital requirements, the bank will have to undergo resolution. In this case, the mandatory convertible bonds will be converted into equity (either of the bank or of a bridge bank, as appropriate) only after losses have been absorbed and the bank (or the bridge bank) has been recapitalised through bail-in. As a consequence, since these bonds would be excluded from bail-in, their holders will gain an ownership stake in a fully recapitalised bank.

This instrument would provide the bank with new finance and, through conversion, would help, in the best-case scenario, to avoid the entry into resolution and, in the second-best-case scenario, to lower the value of liabilities to be converted to restore the minimum amount of own funds.

---

59 The European Court of Justice has stated that Directive 2012/30/EU must be interpreted as not precluding measures 'adopted in a situation where there is a serious disturbance of the economy and the financial system of a Member State threatening the financial stability of the European Union, the effect of that measure being to increase the share capital of a public limited liability company, without the agreement of the general meeting of that company, new shares being issued at a price lower than their nominal value and the existing shareholders being denied a pre-emptive right to subscribe' (Case C-41/15, *Dowling and others v. Minister for Finance*, ECLI:EU:C:2016:836, para. 55).

60 A similar goal, but not the other ones, is pursuable by a divisible capital increase.

8. CONCLUSIONS

To conclude, given the clear interlinks between funding for recovery and subsequent potential resolution, a harmonised approach is necessary to strengthen the role of private prevention measures. To this end, a wider exemption from clawback actions and some form of privilege for funding for recovery, both in the form of debt and equity, could be explored. This would be in line with the proportionality principle that requires exploration of any alternative private sector measures that can prevent the failure, and adoption of resolution only as a last resort measure.

In a sense, the need to protect taxpayers and to limit the use of public funds to resolve banking crises leads us to consider the adoption for banks of tools that are already in place in corporate insolvency law to avoid the disruptive effects that the failure of any kind of firm usually has, such as the attested plans for restructuring under the Italian Insolvency Act.

In this regard, we note that after a period of time where the rules for the banking sector have inspired some reforms in company law – for example, the provisions in the Italian Civil Code on groups of companies mirrored those in the Consolidated Law on Banking for banking groups – an opposite tendency is now in place and tools of corporate law could be exported to the banking framework with appropriate safeguards.

However, given the special role of banks in the economy and their involvement in systemic risk, it is worth noting that such developments could never be considered as a substitute for a public backstop or for the involvement of the Deposit Guarantee Scheme or the central bank.

As underlined by many authors, DIP loans are generally small and

> the mismatch between the availability of private DIP funding and the potential losses of a [Systematically Important Financial Institution] seriously understates the case for temporary government funding to make resolution credible. In a financial crisis, several systemic intermediaries may require speedy resolution at the same time. Precisely at such a juncture, private DIP funding is likely to shrivel,

and a public backstop may thus be necessary.[61]

---

[61] S. Cecchetti and K. Schoenholtz, 'Bank resolution: The importance of a public backstop', 29.05.2017, available at: http://voxeu.org/article/bank-resolution-importance-public-backstop. See also Financial Stability Board, 'Guiding principles on the temporary funding needed to support the orderly resolution of a global systemically important bank ('G-SIB')', August 2016, p. 10, available at: http://www.fsb.org/wp-content/uploads/Guiding-principles-on-the-temporary-funding-needed-to-support-the-orderly-resolution-of-a-global-systemically-important-bank-"G-SIB".pdf.

CHAPTER 3
THE TRANSFORMATION OF PROPERTY RIGHTS IN CORPORATE INSOLVENCY AND BANK RESOLUTION

Michael Anderson Schillig

1. INTRODUCTION

Relying on a 'tragedy of the commons/anti-commons' analysis, this contribution seeks to develop a conceptual framework that explains and justifies both the procedural and substantive transformation of property rights in corporate insolvency and bank resolution. On that basis, the chapter further seeks to predict one of the unintended consequences of the new bank resolution framework: a likely increase of the costs of capital for medium-sized and less complex institutions, that may result in a further consolidation of the banking sector over the long term. This goes against the underlying rationale of the bank resolution framework to effectively tackle 'too-big-to-fail'.

The commencement of proceedings with a view to resolving financial distress,[1] and to a lesser extent the financial state of insolvency, can have a transformative effect on the property rights held by counterparties of the debtor. The term 'property right' is here used in a broad – economic – sense, encompassing personal (contractual) rights as well as proprietary interests (*ius in re*). Depending on the legal system, contractual obligations and security interests may no longer be enforceable;[2] after-acquired property clauses in security agreements may be ineffective;[3] rights acquired pre-commencement may be subject to a challenge under voidable transfer laws;[4] mutual obligations may be reduced to a net balance;[5] and debt may be deferred, written down or converted to equity.[6] As a general principle, in a market economy parties are free to agree on any amendment of their rights and obligations. In the insolvency context, they may do so *ex post* through a contractual workout,

---

1 According to the Commission's Proposal for a Directive on preventive restructuring frameworks, '[i]nsolvency rules cover a wide range of measures from early intervention before a company gets into serious difficulties, timely restructuring to ensure that viable business parts are preserved, liquidation of assets were companies cannot otherwise be saved and finally giving a second chance to honest entrepreneurs via discharge of debt'. Proposal for a Directive of the European Parliament and of the Council on preventive restructuring frameworks, second chance and measures to increase the efficiency of restructuring, insolvency and discharge procedures and amending Directive 2012/30/EU, COM(2016) 723 final (Commission Proposal). For our purposes, there would be little merit in formally distinguishing among 'preventive' or pre-insolvency proceedings, insolvency proceedings, restructuring proceedings, and liquidation. Across jurisdictions, the boundaries between these concepts are fluid and the terminology is far from settled. See also H. Eidenmüller, 'Contracting for a European Insolvency Regime' (2017) 18 *European Business Organisation Law Review (EBOR)* 273 289–290: '[W]hat the Commission has in mind is, in essence a workout or out-of-court restructuring with minimalistic rules to discipline holdouts ... However, ... [i]f an American reader studies the draft [Commission Proposal], he or she probably will think that it looks quite similar to a full-blown Chapter 11 proceeding'.

2 11 USC § 362(a) (automatic stay); Insolvency Act 1986, Schedule B1 paras. 42–44 (moratorium, interim moratorium in administration); InsO, §§ 88, 89 (*Rückschlagssperre, Vollstreckungsverbot*); see also Arts. 6, 7 Directive (EU) 2019/1023 of the European Parliament and of the Council of 20 June 2019 on preventive restructuring frameworks, on discharge of debt and disqualifications, and on measures to increase the efficiency of procedures concerning restructuring, insolvency and discharge of debt, and amending Directive (EU) 2017/1132 (Directive on restructuring and insolvency), [2019] OJ L 172/18.

3 Uniform Commercial Code, § 9-204; 11 USC § 552(a).

4 Uniform Voidable Transactions Act 2015, §§ 4, 5; 11 USC §§ 547, 548; Insolvency Act 1986, ss. 238, 239, 423; InsO, §§ 129–134.

5 Insolvency Rules 2016, rr. 14.24, 14.25 (insolvency set-off in administration and liquidation); 2002 International Swaps and Derivatives Association (ISDA) Master Agreement, para. 6.(f).

6 On the basis of a plan of reorganisation (11 USC §§ 1121–1129), a company voluntary arrangement (Insolvency Act 1986, ss. 1–7B) or scheme of arrangement (Companies Act 2006, ss. 895–901), or an insolvency plan (InsO, §§ 217–269); see also Arts. 8–15 Directive (EU) 2017/1132. Write down and/or conversion may occur automatically upon a certain trigger event for so called 'contingent convertible' instruments or 'CoCo bonds'; M. Schillig, *Resolution and Insolvency of Banks and Financial Institutions*, OUP, Oxford, 2016, paras. 11.04–11.09.

deferring and/or reducing payment obligations and agreeing on a stand still.[7] *Ex ante* agreed *ipso facto* clauses linked to insolvency may bring a contractual relationship or property right of the debtor to an end, either automatically or subject to the discretion of the counterparty.[8] However, the transformations that are of interest here are those that occur without a party's (*ex ante* or *ex post*) consent and which, therefore, require a legal or statutory basis. These statutory transformations may be categorised in accordance with their trigger mechanism. On that basis, transformation may occur automatically, as with an automatic stay or moratorium.[9] Further, transformation may be in the power and subject to the discretion of the debtor, represented by the office-holder, as where the office-holder may assume or reject an executory contract[10] or seek to avoid a pre-commencement transaction.[11] Finally, the parties' rights and obligations may be transformed on the basis of a negotiated solution that is imposed on dissenting parties, for example, through a plan of reorganisation, restructuring plan or scheme of arrangement.[12] Given that bank resolution is generally understood as an administrative process that relies to a large extent on the resolution authority exercising its discretion, a more useful categorisation for present purposes may be derived from the effect that a transformation may have on property rights. This effect may be either procedural or substantive. In the former case, the transformation concerns predominantly the remedies emanating from the respective property right, without affecting the right's substantive content. In the latter case, the transformation goes to the heart of the entitlement, modifying its immanent cash flow and/or control rights.

Under the Bank Recovery and Resolution Directive (BRRD) and Single Resolution Mechanism (SRM), the application of resolution tools and powers is conceptualised as an *ultima ratio* alternative to normal insolvency proceedings where resolution is justified in the public interest on systemic risk grounds. Where the public interest requirement as a condition for resolution is not satisfied, normal insolvency proceedings apply as the default option for resolving failing banks. The purpose of the present contribution is twofold. It first seeks to develop a conceptual framework that explains and justifies both the procedural and substantive transformation of property rights in corporate

---

7 K. van Zwieten, *Goode on Principles of Corporate Insolvency Law*, 5th student ed., Sweet & Maxwell, London 2019, paras. 12-01–12-11.

8 E.g. 2002 ISDA Master Agreement, para. 6; *Butters and others v. BBC Worldwide Ltd and others* [2009] EWHC 1954 (Ch.) (concerning the termination of a media licensing agreement upon insolvency of the licensee); see also BGH, 15.11.2012, IX ZR 169/11 (*ipso facto* clause invalid and unenforceable if the counterparty is subject to German insolvency law).

9 Above n. 2.

10 11 USC § 365; Insolvency Act 1986, s. 178 (power to disclaim onerous property); InsO, §§ 103.

11 Above n. 4.

12 Above n. 6.

insolvency and bank resolution. In this respect, the contribution relies on a 'tragedy of the commons/anti-commons' analysis.[13] Initially developed as a descriptive and normative theory of corporate insolvency law, this analytical framework may be used in order to explain and justify the characteristic features of a bank resolution regime and its deviations from general corporate insolvency law.[14]

Secondly, based on this analysis the contribution seeks to highlight one of the potential unintended consequences of the new bank resolution framework. From a social welfare point of view,[15] any transformation of property rights can be justified only where the right's underlying risk profile is being maintained as a benchmark. Otherwise, the enhanced volatility would drive up the costs of capital with the consequence that fewer welfare-enhancing positive net present value projects would be realised. Whereas corporate insolvency law utilises a range of *ex ante* mechanisms for preserving a property right's underlying risk profile, bank resolution law relies predominantly on the 'no-creditor-worse-off' principle as an *ex post* safeguard. In combination with bank-specific complexities, the *ex post* nature of the 'no-creditor-worse-off' principle renders it less effective than traditional corporate insolvency law mechanisms in this respect. Although theoretically sound, this adds to the practical difficulties of the application of the resolution framework. Conceived as an *ultima ratio* alternative to standard insolvency law, the framework may end up being applied only in simple cases that could be resolved on the basis of domestic insolvency law, whereas the large and complex cases with systemic implications are likely to be bailed out. As a consequence, the funding costs of smaller, less complex banks may increase over time, resulting over the long term in a consolidation of the banking sector.

In what follows, we will analyse, in turn, the procedural transformation of property rights and their substantive transformation. For each category, we will start with the theoretical framework as it applies to standard corporate insolvency law and will then introduce the modifications that a bank-specific resolution framework necessitates. The analysis of corporate insolvency law will rely on comparative law, taking into account mainly English, German and US

13 M. Schillig, 'Corporate Insolvency Law in the 21st Century – State-Imposed or Market-Based?' (2014) 14 *Journal of Corporate Law Studies* 1. See n. 63 below.

14 M. Schillig, above n. 6, paras. 3.37–3.42.

15 As opposed to the standard human rights analysis; see K.-P. Wojcik, 'Bail-In in the Banking Union' (2016) 53 *Common Market Law Review* 91, 116–126.

law. For the bank resolution framework, the SRM[16] (and the BRRD)[17] will be the main focus. The conclusion contains a tentative prediction for the future.

2. PROCEDURAL TRANSFORMATION

Procedural transformation (mainly) concerns the remedies attached to a property right. In insolvency these will be severely curtailed. Individual enforcement rights are transformed into participation rights in a collective procedure. A right's substantive entitlements – notably cash-flow rights – remain intact and form the basis for the right-holder's participatory entitlements.

2.1. NON-FINANCIAL FIRMS

Their individual enforcement rights give creditors access to the debtor's assets. In the debtor's insolvency, the creditors' incentives are misaligned. The exercise of any one creditor's individual enforcement right (in priority to others) may result in a fully internalised benefit for this creditor – full satisfaction of their claim – whereas the costs emanating from the destruction of a potential going concern value are externalised and borne by all the other creditors as a group. Even if there is no going concern surplus, individual enforcement action may still result in negative externalities imposed on the other creditors who may only receive a lower dividend compared to what they would have received on the basis of a *pari passu* sharing rule.[18] The misalignment of incentives is a result of the combination of individual enforcement rights with a common pool of assets. These individual rights can be used to impose costs on the common pool whilst at the same time the pool of assets can be accessed in order to

---

16 Regulation (EU) 806/2014 of the European Parliament and of the Council of 15 July 2014 establishing uniform rules and a uniform procedure for the resolution of credit institutions and certain investment firms in the framework of a Single Resolution Mechanism and a Single Resolution Fund and amending Regulation (EU) No. 1093/2010, [2014] OJ L 225/1; as amended by Regulation (EU) 2019/877 of the European Parliament and of the Council of 20 May 2019 amending Regulation (EU) No. 806/2014 as regards the loss-absorbing and recapitalisation capacity of credit institutions and investment firms, [2019] OJ L 150/226.

17 Directive 2014/59/EU of the European Parliament and of the Council of 15 May 2014 establishing a framework for the recovery and resolution of credit institutions and investment firms, [2014] OJ L 173/190; as amended by Directive (EU) 2017/1132 of the European Parliament and of the Council of 14 June 2017, [2017] OJ L 169/46; Directive (EU) 2017/2399 of the European Parliament and of the Council of 12 December 2017, [2017] OJ L 345/96; Directive (EU) 2019/879 of the European Parliament and of the Council of 20 May 2019, [2019] OJ L 150/296.

18 M. Schillig, above n. 13, 5.

obtain private benefits.[19] Consider a debtor whose assets have a break-up value of 8 and a going concern value of 12. Each of two creditors has a claim against the debtor of nominal 7.[20]

The payoff bimatrix looks as follows:

		Creditor 2	
		Enforce (don't cooperate)	Don't enforce (cooperate)
Creditor 1	Enforce (don't cooperate)	4; 4	7; 1
	Don't enforce (cooperate)	1; 7	6; 6

The socially optimal outcome would be the realisation of the going concern value through cooperation (non-enforcement of individual rights). The creditors as a whole would be better off and the amount of 12 could be split equally (bottom-right). In the absence of corporate insolvency law it may not be possible for either creditor to credibly commit to cooperation. In that case, each creditor will always be better off by enforcing (not cooperating) regardless of what the other creditor does.[21] We end up with a 'Nash equilibrium' in the top-left scenario. This means greater volatility of returns for creditors[22] and thus a higher cost of capital[23] with the consequence that fewer positive net present value projects will be pursued.

---

19 L.A. Fennell, 'Commons, anticommons, semicommons' in K. Ayotte and H. Smith (eds.) *Research Handbook on the Economics of Property Law*, Edward Elgar, Cheltenham 2011, pp. 35, 36–37.

20 M. Schillig, above n. 13, 8.

21 Under the assumption that each creditor has an equal chance of coming first in the race for the debtor's assets, the payoff for each creditor would have an expected value of 4 (50% × 7 + 50% × 1). By contrast, each creditor will have a payoff of only 1 when he cooperates and the other enforces, realising a payoff of 7. Thus, the dominant strategy of each creditor is to enforce (not cooperate).

22 Assume that our debtor company has an equal chance of being either solvent or insolvent (with the stated asset values above) at the end of year 1. In scenario A, there is no mandatory insolvency law that imposes an automatic stay. As a consequence, a creditor has a 50% chance of receiving 4 if the company goes bust and a 50% chance of receiving 7 if the company is solvent. The expected value of the claim is 5.5 (50% × 4 + 50% × 7). In scenario B, mandatory insolvency law ensures that the going concern value is preserved so that a creditor has a 50% chance of receiving 6 in insolvency and a 50% chance of 7 if the company remains solvent. The expected value of the claim is 6.5 (50% × 6 + 50% × 7). In scenario A, the difference between the expected value and the possible outcomes is 1.5; whereas in scenario B the difference is only 0.5. The range of dispersion is greater in scenario A; W. Klein, J. Coffee and F. Partnoy, *Business organization and Finance*, 11th ed., Foundation Press, New York 2010, p. 243.

23 Leaving time value of money aside, in scenario A the rational investor would pay no more than 5.5 in order to receive a promised return of 7 at the end of the one-year period. Thus, in order to obtain the loan the debtor must promise a rate of return of (at least) 27% (r =

This 'tragedy of the commons' can be addressed by delinking individual rights from the right of access to the common pool. Most legal systems effectuate this delinking through a consolidation of individual enforcement rights in the hands of a collectivity that can act as one ('collectivisation').[24] This usually entails the appointment of an office-holder with far-reaching powers over the debtor's assets[25] and a duty to act in the best interest of all creditors.[26] Individual enforcement rights are transformed into participation rights in a collective procedure into which creditors are forced whilst retaining their substantive entitlements – that is, the nominal value of cash-flow rights and the underlying risk profile as determined, in particular, by their position within the hierarchy of claims.[27] Participation takes place primarily through voting on the office-holder's proposals as to how to deal with the debtor's assets in order to maximise their value and the allocation and distribution of future cash flows and proceeds.[28]

The transformation of individual enforcement rights into participation rights entails, as an essential first step, the removal of the remedies attached to these rights outside of corporate insolvency proceedings. Consequently, the commencement of insolvency proceedings normally triggers a more or less comprehensive moratorium or automatic stay.[29] This seeks to prevent a run on the debtor's assets with a view to preserving a potential going concern surplus, and also addresses potential negative externalities from distributions other than on a *pro rata* basis.[30] The scope of the automatic stay or moratorium may vary significantly between jurisdictions and procedures. Generally, a stay will prevent the enforcement of non-proprietary remedies against the debtor and its property; judicial proceedings to that end can no longer be initiated; pending

7/5.5-1). In scenario B, the promised rate of return is only 7.7% (r = 7/6.5-1).

24 L.A. Fennell, above n. 20, pp. 38–39.

25 Insolvency Act 1986, Schedule B1, paras. 59–64 and 70–72, and Schedule 1; InsO, §§ 56, 80. Under the US Bankruptcy Code, the incumbent management remains in control as the Debtor in Possession in a Chapter 11 reorganisation, with all the rights and powers of a Trustee in Bankruptcy; 11 USC § 1107. Subject to the court ordering otherwise, the Debtor in Possession continues to operate the debtor's business; 11 USC § 1108. A party in interest may request the court to appoint a Trustee in Bankruptcy for cause, subject to strict preconditions; 11 USC § 1104.

26 Insolvency Act 1986, Schedule B1, para. 3(2); InsO, § 60; as a representative of the estate, the Debtor in Possession owes fiduciary duties to all parties in interest; 11 USC §§ 321, 1107.

27 T. Jackson, *The Logic and Limits of Bankruptcy Law*, Beard Books, Washington DC 2001 reprint, p. 29: 'The bankruptcy process should duplicate the relative standing among claimants that would exist outside of bankruptcy's collective framework. This is the concept of relative value.' – 'we are in a world where one needs to think not in terms of abstract rights but of measuring *relative values.*

28 11 USC § 1126; Insolvency Act 1986, Schedule B1 paras. 50–53; Companies Act 2006, s.899(1); InsO, §§ 235–244.

29 Above n. 2.

30 T. Jackson, above n. 27, p. 150.

proceedings may be placed on (temporary) hold. The effect on the holders of security interests is more varied and may range from a comprehensive stay on all types of security interests[31] to exempting (certain) secured creditors from collectivisation altogether.[32] The treatment of *ipso facto* clauses – under which a contract may be terminated automatically or at the discretion of the counterparty – is equally varied. *Ipso facto* clauses may be enforceable,[33] non-enforceable[34] or enforceability may be subject to subtle distinctions.[35]

From a theoretical perspective, secured creditors and *ipso facto* clauses should be included in an automatic stay or moratorium, provided the risk profile of the underlying claim is not adversely affected. For present purposes, security interests and *ipso facto* clauses are similar in that they allow the beneficiary to withdraw a resource from the common pool of assets – say, an essential piece of equipment or a service contract – and to realise its value, to the detriment of the common pool – by, for example, selling the equipment or offering the service contract to a third party at current market price. We can modify our example as follows: our debtor's assets still have a break-up value of 8 and a going concern value of 12. Amongst other items, the assets consist of equipment with a (break-up) value of 6. Each of two creditors has a claim against the debtor of nominal 7, however C2's claim is secured on a recourse basis by way of a security interest on the equipment.[36]

31 11 USC § 362(a)(3)–(7); Insolvency Act 1986, Schedule B1 para. 43(2)–(4).

32 Under German law, creditors who hold a right that entitles them to retrieve an asset from the estate based on the holder's ownership or on a personal right ('right to separation'), are not constrained by the collective procedure, and retain their individual enforcement rights; InsO § 47.

33 This used to be the case under English law: the moratoria in administration did not prevent the exercise of a right to terminate a contract, either on the basis of a contractually stipulated right or by accepting the administrator's repudiation of the contract; K. van Zwieten, above n. 7, para. 11-72. The Corporate Insolvency and Governance Act 2020 introduced a new sec. 233B pursuant to which *ipso facto* clauses in contracts for the supply of good and services to the debtor company, in principle, cease to have effect upon commencement of a relevant insolvency procedure.

34 11 USC §§ 365(e)(1), 541(c)(1)(B); see further *Lehman Brothers Special Financing Inc v. BNY Corporate Trustee Services Ltd.*, 422 BR 407 (US Bankruptcy Court, SDNY, 2010); InsO § 119 and BGH, 15.11.2012, IX ZR 169/11.

35 On the English law anti-deprivation principle, concerning *ipso facto* clauses affecting property of the estate (as opposed to mere contracts) see M. Schillig, above n. 13, 32–37 and *Belmont Park Investments PTY Ltd. v. BNY Corporate Trustee Services Ltd. and Lehman Brothers Special Financing Inc.* [2011] UKSC 38.

36 We can modify the example by assuming that, on the basis of an *ipso facto* clause, C2 can terminate its relationship with the debtor and instead contract with a third party for 6. The analysis would be the same.

The payoff bimatrix looks as follows:

		Creditor 2	
		Enforce (don't cooperate)	Don't enforce (cooperate)
Creditor 1	Enforce (don't cooperate)	1.5; 6.5	2; 6
	Don't enforce (cooperate)	1; 7	5.5; 6.5

The socially optimal outcome would be the realisation of the going concern value through cooperation (bottom-right). However, in the absence of a credible commitment to cooperate, each creditor will prefer enforcement (non-cooperation), resulting in the destruction of the going concern surplus. The Nash equilibrium is represented by the top-left corner. Again, this can be remedied through the procedural transformation of individual enforcement rights and an automatic stay that extends to secured creditors.[37] The preferential treatment of secured creditors results in lower volatility of returns, a lower required rate of return and reduced costs of capital.[38] In order to retain this beneficial effect the inclusion of secured creditors in the automatic stay must guarantee that they will not be made worse off by joining the collective procedure.[39] At this stage of the process, this means (at least) that the value of the collateral must be adequately protected for the duration of the process.[40] For *ipso facto* clauses, similar considerations apply: their inclusion in the automatic stay may

37 Under Thomas Jackson's famous 'creditors' bargain model', secured creditors are unlikely to profit directly from the cost savings resulting from preventing a race on the debtor's assets. However, Jackson argues, because the collective regime minimises the debtor's total credit costs to the advantage of debtor and unsecured creditors, one would expect the unsecured creditors to pay the secured creditors to agree to join in the collective proceeding. In order to maintain the (assumed) efficiency gains of secured credit, secured creditors are still required to be paid first out of the secured creditors' collateral. Consequently, secured creditors would not be worse off by joining a collective proceeding and the unsecured creditors could be better off; T. Jackson, 'Bankruptcy, Non-Bankruptcy Entitlements, and the Creditors' Bargain' (1982) 91 *Yale Law Journal* 857, 869–870.

38 We may revisit and modify our earlier example (above nn. 21–23). In scenario A, our secured creditor has a 50% chance of receiving 6.5 and a 50% chance of receiving 7. The expected value of the claim is 6.75, the difference between expected value and possible outcomes is 0.25, and the required rate of return is 3.7%.

39 If we did not ensure that, in scenario B, our secured creditor obtains at least the value of the collateral we would end up with the same values as above (see nn. 21–23): expected value of the claim of 6.5; difference between expected value and possible outcomes of 0.5; and required rate of return of 7.7%. As a consequence, at least part of the cost savings associated with secured credit would be lost.

40 11 USC § 361; InsO § 169.

be subject to past defaults being cured and security being given for the future performance under the contract.[41]

2.2. FINANCIAL INSTITUTIONS

Financial institutions face a much more severe common pool problem.[42] This is due to the presence of large numbers of 'financial creditors' holding 'financial claims' on the firm. These are claims for which the credit nature (right to a future cash flow) is merely incidental to additional functions they serve, notably a liquidity function (deposits, repos) or a risk-shifting function (derivatives). As a corollary of these functions, the counterparty must be able to immediately (or almost immediately) withdraw their funds from the firm, terminate their exposure and hedge their risk elsewhere.[43] Liquidity and risk-shifting add value to a financial claim beyond the net present value of the future cash flow; value that will be impaired if 'immediacy' is lost and the 'financial creditor' is prevented from immediately accessing what is owed to them.[44] Generally, in non-financial firms, the common pool problem becomes acute only where the firm is in general default. However, 'financial creditors' can withdraw their money and liquidate their claims (almost) immediately, and they have an incentive to withdraw their funds while it is still possible to get full recovery. This may trigger a (bank) run, causing illiquidity and insolvency, and exacerbates the common pool problem by accelerating it and deepening its severity.[45]

Consider a bank with two depositors and deposits of nominal 7 each. The bank's assets (loans and securities) are volatile. If sold at current market conditions (and at fire sale prices) they may realise a value of only 8; whereas under normal market conditions their value would probably be 12. To each nominal deposit claim we may add a 'liquidity premium' of 4.

The payoff bimatrix looks as follows:		**Depositor 2**	
		Withdraw	Don't withdraw
Depositor 1	Withdraw	4+1; 4+1	7+4; 1+0
	Don't withdraw	1+0; 7+4	6+0; 6+0

41 11 USC § 365 (an executory contract may only be assumed if any defaults are cured and adequate assurance of future performance is provided).

42 M. Schillig, above n. 6, para. 3.37. The problem is related, but not identical, to the maturity mismatch issue which renders banks vulnerable to runs.

43 J. Sommer, 'Why Bail-In? And How?' (2014) 20(2) *Economic Policy Review, Special Issue: Large and Complex Banks* 1, 6.

44 Ibid.

45 P. Swire, 'Bank Insolvency Law Now That It Matters Again' (1992) 42 *Duke Law Journal* 469, 495.

This liquidity premium can be salvaged only to the extent that the depositor can withdraw their money immediately. Thus, by leaving their money in the bank, the depositors would forgo their liquidity premium. Taking into account the liquidity premium, both depositors have an incentive to withdraw immediately as their dominant strategy. This incentive is stronger – i.e. the common pool problem is more severe – because the difference in payoffs between withdrawal and non-withdrawal is greater (4+1 / 1+0 and 7+4 / 6+0, respectively). At the same time, it is no longer so obvious what the socially optimal outcome is: the aggregate payoff values for the bottom row and top-right are the same.[46] This may be explained on the basis that immediate access to liquidity is vital for paying bills and keeping the economy going.

As a consequence, whereas in insolvencies of non-financial companies an automatic stay or moratorium is essential for remedying the commons problem, in bank resolution it is problematic. Under a comprehensive moratorium or automatic stay, 'financial creditors' would lose the key benefit of 'immediacy': immediate access to the amounts due to them.[47] This prevents an analogy being drawn with the treatment of secured creditors under the commons analysis as it applies to non-financial companies: for depositors, temporarily losing access to their accounts is extremely costly; in order to ensure that they are not worse off, continued immediate access would have to be provided in some other way, possibly through a deposit guarantee scheme. However, in order to reduce moral hazard, deposit insurance cannot be complete, and significant amounts will have to remain outside its coverage.[48] For other 'financial creditors' – repo and derivatives counterparties – the situation becomes more complex where systemic risk implications are taken into account.

Assume our bank[49] has two creditors, a repo counterparty and a derivatives counterparty, with each currently having a net exposure of 7. To the derivative exposure we may add a 'hedging premium' of 4, and to the repo a 'liquidity premium' of 4. On that basis, the payoff bimatrix would look as before. However, we must now take into account potential negative externalities imposed on the financial system as a whole. By forcing a fire sale of the bank's assets through closing out and immediately liquidating net exposures, asset prices may deteriorate and other banks may fail with negative consequences for other financial market participants and the wider economy.[50] Our counterparties

46 The liquidity premium adds value to a claim in addition to and above the net present value of the cash flow. This explains why the aggregate payoff in, say, the top-left scenario is higher than the firm's asset value.

47 P. Swire, above n. 45, 490–491; G. Kaufman, 'Depositor Liquidity and Loss-Sharing in Bank Failure Resolutions' *Federal Reserve Bank of Chicago WP 2003-02*, 3–4.

48 M. Schillig, above n. 6, paras. 12.07–12.09.

49 Loans and securities with a fire sale value of 8 and a market value of 12.

50 On direct and indirect transmission of systemic risk and contagion see M. Schillig, above n. 5 paras. 3.19–3.21.

may feel this effect indirectly and in the long term through losses across their trading book.[51] In order to take account of these externalities we may add a 'systemic risk discount' of (-4) to our payoff bimatrix in those scenarios where assets will be liquidated:

		Derivative	
		Close out	Don't close out
Repo	Close out	4+1; 4+1 (-4)	7+4; 1+0 (-4)
	Don't close out	1+0; 7+4 (-4)	6+0; 6+0

Under these assumptions we can again identify the socially optimum outcome (bottom-right corner). Preventing counterparties from liquidating their positions immediately may at least slow down the demise of a financial firm and may have a mitigating effect on systemic implications. Through the loss of immediacy, negative externalities imposed on the financial system as a whole are internalised and borne by the financial creditors themselves. On the other hand, the loss of immediacy and access to liquidity may itself have adverse systemic risk implications. Allowing counterparties to immediately liquidate their positions and thereby minimise their exposure to a failing firm may prevent the spreading of systemic risk to other market players and enhance the financial system's resilience. Whether in any concrete scenario the former or the latter should prevail depends on a multitude of circumstances, including the nature of the respective financial claims, the systemic relevance of the financial creditors involved, and the overall structure of the financial system as a whole.[52] In addition, financial assets are notoriously volatile and, depending on market movements, may quickly turn into financial liabilities and *vice versa*. This requires a finely balanced system under which a moratorium cannot be automatic and comprehensive; it may be discretionary, temporary, and limited, as the individual situation requires.[53]

---

51 see also J. Armour and J. Gordon, 'Systemic Harms and Shareholder Value' (2014) 6 *Journal of Legal Analysis* 35, 39: Although diversified shareholders are insensitive to idiosyncratic (firm-specific) risk and therefore prefer management to invest in high-risk/high-return projects, where these investment strategies generate systemic risk that is non-diversifiable shareholders may see their overall portfolio returns reduced.

52 This is at the core of the discussion concerning the 'safe harbours' for qualified financial contracts in bankruptcy; M Schillig, above n. 6, paras. 13.50–13.56.

53 Pursuant to the International Swaps and Derivatives Association (ISDA) 2015 Universal Resolution Stay Protocol, derivatives counterparties can contractually opt into provisions within certain resolution regimes that limit the exercise of termination and close-out rights so as to make the respective resolution provisions effective on a cross-border basis; ISDA 2015 Universal Protocol. Where parties adopt the ISDA 2015 Universal Protocol, this can perhaps be interpreted as an actual creditors' bargain for a limited stay on 'financial claims'.

In accordance with these considerations, the BRRD and SRM do not provide for an automatic stay or moratorium. Rather, resolution authorities have the power to suspend any payment or delivery obligation under any of the institution's contracts from the time of the publication of the suspension until midnight at the end of the following business day. At the same time, the obligations of the institution's counterparties will be suspended. The claims of eligible depositors, of eligible investors and of payment and settlement systems are exempt.[54] Contracts are subject to a prohibition of *ipso facto* clauses linked to the exercise of resolution tools and powers. The resolution action itself may not constitute a credit event and may not trigger a right to terminate or accelerate a contract to which the institution is a party.[55] This does not, in principle, affect any rights that arise by virtue of an event of default that is not the resolution action itself. However, these latter termination rights may be suspended by the resolution authority from the time of notice until midnight at the end of the following business day.[56] This allows the resolution authority to effectuate a transfer of assets and liabilities, and prevents the value inherent in a bank's trading book from immediately evaporating because of counterparties closing out their contracts. Consequently, where the respective contract is being transferred to a private-sector buyer or a bridge bank, the exercise of termination rights is suspended until a subsequent trigger event occurs.[57]

Where it is necessary for the effective application of resolution tools and powers, resolution authorities can request the court to impose a stay on any judicial action or proceedings in which the institution is or becomes a party. The stay may only be for a period that is appropriate for the resolution objective pursued.[58] Resolution authorities also have the power to restrict the enforcement of security interests against any of the institution's property. This

---

54 BRRD, Art. 69.

55 Similarly, it may not result in obtaining possession of, or exercising control over, any property of the institution and may not affect any of its contractual rights; BRRD, Art. 68(3).

56 BRRD, Art. 71.

57 BRRD, Art. 71(5). The contracts remaining with the residual entity may be terminated immediately when the suspension period comes to an end, or even before that, upon notice by the resolution authority that the contract will not be transferred or will not be subject to bail-in; BRRD, Art. 71(4).

58 BRRD, Art. 86(3). Resolution prevents the commencement of normal insolvency proceedings under national law, except on the initiative of or with the consent of the resolution authority. For that purpose, competent and resolution authorities must be informed without delay of any application for the initiation of normal insolvency proceedings in respect of an institution. The court deciding on a petition to commence insolvency proceedings in respect of an institution under resolution, or for which the conditions for resolution have been determined to be met, can do so only where the resolution authority has notified the court that it will not take any resolution action, or a 7-day period has expired since the resolution authority was informed of the petition to begin proceedings; BRRD, Art. 86(1) and (2).

restriction can only be for a limited period, until midnight at the end of the business day following publication of the notice of the restriction.[59]

The BRRD does not contain any provisions that would protect a secured creditor against the depreciation in value of the collateral, by granting him either adequate protection or leave to enforce his security, even in the event that the collateral would not be required for the realisation of resolution objectives. This omission is probably less problematic than it would appear against the background of general insolvency law. The restriction on the enforcement of security interests can only be for a limited period of time. Moreover, under the 'no-creditor-worse-off' principle, a creditor must be put in the position he would have been in in the event of liquidation under normal proceedings. This seems to entail an assessment of to what extent the creditor could have obtained adequate protection under normal proceedings and/or leave of the court to enforce the security.

3. SUBSTANTIVE TRANSFORMATION

A financially distressed firm expects to be unable to meet its fixed obligations out of its future earnings. These firms are unlikely to survive as going concerns without a new capital structure. Consequently, corporate insolvency and restructuring law must aim to enable firms to acquire a new capital structure.[60] This can be achieved in two principal ways. First, the business remains with the debtor company and the latter's capital structure is amended through substantive transformation of property rights, by reducing the company's debt load through a write-down or deferral of payment obligations and/or converting some debt into equity or new reduced or deferred debt. Alternatively, the business (assets and certain liabilities) may be transferred to a new corporate entity with a more sustainable capital structure, leaving some of the existing creditors behind with a more or less empty shell. This also entails a substantive transformation of the property rights of those (senior) creditors with an economic interest in the business:[61] their previous debtor will be replaced by a new one, and their initial claims will be substituted for new debt or equity issued by the new corporate holding structure. In practice, both approaches may be combined to a greater or lesser extent.[62]

59 Assets pledged as margin or collateral to a central counterparty are exempt; BRRD, Art. 70.

60 B. Adler, D. Baird and T. Jackson, *Bankruptcy: Cases, Problems, and Materials*, 4th ed., Foundation Press, New York 2007, p. 26.

61 Usually, the property rights of the left-behind junior creditors will not be substantively transformed. These rights retain their nominal value and may participate in any distribution of the liquidation value of the residual entity on a *pro-rata* basis.

62 K. Asimacopoulos and J. Bickle (eds.), *European Debt Restructuring Handbook: Leading Case Studies from the Post-Lehman Cycle*, Global Law and Business, London 2013.

3.1. NON-FINANCIAL FIRMS

The collective corporate insolvency or restructuring process provides a forum for ascertaining whether there is any going concern surplus; and if there is, for negotiating a solution that is most suitable for preserving that surplus and allocating it amongst the various constituencies. However, where the creditors are locked into a collective procedure, the 'tragedy of the commons' may be transformed into a 'tragedy of the anti-commons'.[63] At a very basic level, whereas the commons problem may be said to derive from too many private access rights or 'use privileges' resulting in 'over-use' of a common resource, the anti-commons is characterised by private exclusion or veto rights resulting in 'under-use' of a common resource.[64] However, the key for a proper understanding of the distinction seems to lie in the different strategic behavior patterns of commons and anti-commons.[65] A general moratorium solves the commons problem by removing individual enforcement rights, thus preserving the potential going concern value inherent in the common pool. Parties must then decide how to realise and distribute a potential surplus.

If they don't reach agreement the going concern surplus will be lost and they will share the break-up value on a *pro rata* basis.[66]		**Creditor 2**	
		Don't cooperate	Cooperate
Creditor 1	Don't cooperate	4; 4	7; 5
	Cooperate	5; 7	6; 6

[63] R. de Weijs, 'Harmonisation of European Insolvency Law and the Need to Tackle Two Common Problems: Common Pool & Anticommons' (2012) 21 *International Insolvency Review* 67, 68–72; D.G. Baird and R.K. Rasmussen, 'Anti-Bankruptcy' (2010) 120 *Yale Law Journal* 648, 652–653.

[64] M. Heller, 'The Tragedy of the Anticommons: Property in the Transition from Marx to Markets' (1998) 111 *Harvard Law Review* 621, 677.

[65] The commons problem resembles the strategic pattern of a Prisoner's Dilemma, with one dominant strategy and one Nash equilibrium: in the absence of a credible commitment by the other creditors to cooperate, every creditor is always better off by enforcing his individual rights. By contrast, the anti-commons problem is more akin to the 'game of chicken' with multiple equilibria and no dominant strategy, where the best strategy for each individual player depends on what the other does; Fennell (n. 19) 43–45; D.G. Baird, R.H. Gertner and R.C. Picker, *Game Theory and the Law*, Harvard University Press, Cambridge MA 1994, pp. 44–45. See also R. de Weijs, 'Too Big To Fail as a Game of Chicken with the State: What Insolvency Law Theory has to say about TBTF and vice versa', *Centre for the Study of European Contract Law Working Paper Series No. 2012-13.*

[66] M. Schillig, above n. 13, 7–8.

The socially optimal outcome is the realisation of the going concern surplus; from a social welfare point of view, its allocation is immaterial (bottom row, and top-right). However, each creditor has an incentive to extract as much of the surplus for itself as possible.[67] By misreading the other party's intentions or by being in error of the amount of surplus, a party may push too far, a deal may collapse and the surplus may be lost (top-left corner).[68] Corporate insolvency law addresses these issues through information rights, possibly channelled through a creditors' committee, majority voting instead of unanimity and possibly a cram-down in order to overcome holdouts within a class and across various classes.

From a cost of capital perspective, it is again essential that a claim's risk profile will not change without the claim-holders' consent. If a claim's risk profile were subject to an adverse change through a non-consensual restructuring solution, the increased volatility would result in higher costs of capital.[69] Legal systems rely on a number of safeguards in this respect. For example, under Chapter 11 of the US Bankruptcy Code, a plan of reorganisation may be confirmed by the court and imposed on dissenting creditors within a class only if each member of the class receives at least the liquidation value of the claim (the 'best interest' test).[70] A cram-down across classes may only be confirmed subject to the absolute priority rule that seeks to ensure that the plan respects the order of priority outside of bankruptcy, in particular, a class of secured creditors must receive at least the discounted net present value of their secured claims, and in order to cram-down a class of dissenting unsecured creditors, any class junior to the dissenting class must not receive any value under the plan.[71] A scheme of arrangement will be sanctioned by

---

67 Thus, where creditor 2 holds out and creditor 1 is willing to forgo some of the surplus in order to reach agreement the payoffs may look like in the bottom-left corner with creditor 2 receiving a payoff of 7 and creditor 1 of 5 (or *vice versa*: top-right). Creditor 1 may be willing to cooperate because his payoff in that case still exceeds his payoff were the agreement to fail and both creditors would share equally in the break-up value (top-left corner).

68 L.A. Fennell, above n. 19, pp. 44–45. In this game there are multiple Nash equilibria and each creditor's optimal strategy depends on what the other does; D.G. Baird, R.H. Gertner and R.C. Picker, above n. 65, p. 44.

69 Assume we have an insolvency law system that allows for liquidation on a break-up basis only. Thus, if the firm is solvent our creditors will be paid in full (7 each); in case of insolvency they will share *pro rata* in the break-up value of 8 and receive 4 each. If we assume that the firm has a 50% chance of being solvent at the end of the year, each claim has an expected value of 5.5 (as above n. 23). The required rate of return would be 27%. If we now add a restructuring option in case of insolvency under which a creditor's entitlement maybe reduced without consent to 3 with a probability of 50%, this creditor's claim has an expected value of 5.25 (50% x 7 + 25% x 4 + 25% x 3), and the required rate of return will be 33.3%.

70 11 USC § 1129(a)(7)(A)(ii) ('best interest of the creditor test': non-consenting creditor receives at least liquidation value); similarly InsO § 245(1)No.1.

71 11 USC § 1129(b)(2); similarly InsO §§ 245(1)No.2, (2), 223.

the court only where the scheme is fair to creditors in general; that is, the scheme is 'one as to which persons acting honestly, and viewing the scheme laid before them in the interests of those whom they represent, take a view which can reasonably be taken by business men.'[72] This would seem to entail an assessment as to whether the dissenting minority would be (significantly) worse off under the scheme than without it. Confirmation of a restructuring plan is subject to a 'best interest of the creditor' test[73] with the court making sure that, under the plan, dissenting creditors are no worse off than in the next best alternative, which may be piecemeal liquidation or a going concern sale. A cross-class cram-down additionally requires adherence to 'relative priority': the dissenting senior class must not be treated less favourably under the plan than any other equally ranking class and must be treated more favourably than any junior class.[74] These mechanisms realise their effect *ex ante* – if in breach, a plan of reorganisation cannot be confirmed, a scheme will not be sanctioned, and the envisaged restructuring will not take effect.

Financial and technological innovation increasingly allows investors to rearrange their property rights by de-coupling and reassembling economic interests and control rights, resulting in significantly more complex and fragmented proprietary interests.[75] With hedge funds and private equity groups replacing traditional commercial banks as sources of capital in some areas,[76] new and opaque financial market actors have emerged with their own agendas, which do not necessarily include a successful corporate rescue of the debtor's business.[77] The heightened complexity and fragmentation and the resulting realignment of incentive structures, as well as the appearance of new and opaque players, amplify the significance of the 'tragedy of the anti-commons'. It has become more difficult for participants to correctly identify and assess the incentives of the other players and calculate their behaviour in a scenario where there is no dominant strategy.[78] This increases the likelihood that any one party will overreach and push too far so that a surplus-enhancing deal may collapse. The resulting deadlock may perpetuate the tragedy. This situation may be overcome by switching from a collective procedure to a

---

72 *Re APCOA Parkings Holding GmbH* [2014] EWHC 3849 (Ch) paras. 126–134 with extensive references to the case law.

73 UK Companies Act 2006, s. 901G(3); Directive (EU) 2019/1023, Arts. 10(2)(d), 2(1)(6); 11 USC § 1129(7).

74 Directive (EU) 2019/1023, Art. 11(1)(c).

75 H.T.C. Hu and B. Black, 'The New Vote Buying: Empty Voting and Hidden Ownership' (2006) 79 *Southern California Law Review* 811; 'Equity and Debt Decoupling and Empty Voting II: Importance and Extensions' (2008) 156 *University of Pennsylvania Law Review* 635; 'Debt, Equity, and Hybrid Decoupling: Governance and Systemic Risk Implications' (2008a) 14 *European Financial Management* 663.

76 D.G. Baird and R.K. Rasmussen, above n. 63, 659.

77 H.T.C. Hu and B. Black (2008a), above n. 75, 693–694.

78 L.A. Fennell, above n. 19, 45.

process under which the procedural participation rights are bundled in the hands of a single lead creditor (or group of creditors) in control of the process and its destination ('individualisation').[79] This can be observed in today's international restructuring practice. Most reorganisations of non-financial companies are effectuated through a sale of the business, or parts thereof; frequently to previous management and/or previous owners and investors.[80] Prior to Brexit taking effect, the 'pre-pack administration', combined with schemes of arrangement, had emerged as an internationally extremely popular restructuring technique. In a deal between the debtor and the senior lenders, the debtor's business (or the viable parts thereof) would be transferred to a new corporate entity, which would be equipped with a more sustainable capital structure. Without the need to consult junior creditors, shareholders or the court,[81] the pre-pack administration allowed for a quick and easy sale by the administrator of the debtor company's assets to a new entity as soon as the adminstrator's appointment became effective. Under a scheme of arrangement between the debtor company and the senior lenders, the latter would exchange their claims in the debtor company for equity or new debt in the new corporate structure. Junior creditors would not be part of the scheme and would retain their entitlement against the debtor company, which, following the transfer of its assets to the new entity, would be an empty shell.[82] This constituted a form of (partial) 'individualisation' because the business's future was decided by a group of lead creditors – the senior lenders – that essentially controlled the process through the administrator without any procedural input from the remaining (junior) creditors. The collectivity of creditors had been replaced with the procedural dominance of a group of lead creditors that determined the process and its outcome.[83] The risk profile of the affected claims remained protected: a pre-pack sale required the consent of secured creditors;[84] and non-voting creditors with an economic interest in the company's business could object to a scheme of arrangement at the sanctioning stage, and would be successful if they could demonstrate that they should have been included in the scheme because firm value exceeded the nominal value of any class senior to theirs (i.e.

---

79 M. Schillig, above n. 13, 6, 13.

80 K. Asimacopoulos and J. Bickle, above n. 62.

81 *Re T&D Industries plc* [2000] 1 WLR 646; *Transbus International Ltd. (in liquidation)* [2004] 2 BCLC 550; *DKLL Solicitors v. Revenue and Customs Commissioners* [2007] BCC 908.

82 e.g. *Re McCarthy & Stone Plc* [2009] EWHC 1116 (Ch); *Re Bluebrook Ltd.* [2009] EWHC 2114 (Ch); *Re Countrywide Plc* [2009] EWHC 1347 (Ch); *Re APCOA Holdings GmbH* [2014] EWHC 3849 (Ch).

83 M. Schillig, above n. 13, 24–27.

84 Under English law, assets subject to fixed charges and other asset-based lending techniques may be sold by the administrator only with either the consent of the creditor or by order of the court; Insolvency Act 1986, Schedule B1, paras. 70–73. The holder of a qualifying floating charge will participate by either appointing the administrator or by not interfering with the company's appointment.

firm value broke within their class).[85] The introduction of the restructuring plan process allowing for a cross-class cram-down has reduced the need for pre-pack sales under English law. Also, because of a tightening of their regulatory prerequisites, pre-pack administrations have lost some of their appeal.[86]

3.2. FINANCIAL INSTITUTIONS

The tragedy of the anti-commons is more acute in the context of banks and financial institutions. Financial institutions' balance sheets are notoriously complex, with a multitude of different debt instruments issued to finance a multitude of difficult-to-value and volatile assets. Exposures may be hedged for risk-mitigation or speculative purposes, resulting in immense complexity and opacity. These interactive complexities create a huge collective action problem that makes negotiations among stakeholders very difficult. Moreover, time will normally be of the essence in order to prevent a further deterioration of asset values and the possible spread of 'contagion'. As a consequence, a collectivised negotiation mechanism under traditional corporate insolvency law – majority voting, cram-down, and information rights – is largely inadequate.[87] The anti-commons problem can be overcome effectively through the consolidation of individual rights in the hands of a single rights-holder with decision-making powers to drive forward and administer the process – an administrative receivership with significant discretionary authority.[88] The single rights-holder can quickly take control of an ailing institution and, equipped with extensive powers, can substantively transform the parties' rights and obligations. In a bank restructuring, the overall form of a substantive transformation of rights is not so very different from the restructuring of any other business. After having determined to what extent the business is viable, the viable parts must be equipped with a new capital structure, either within the same legal entity or through a new one. The main difference is the availability of extensive discretionary tools and powers to effectuate the restructuring. Moreover, bank restructurings are essentially pre-packs:[89] the preferred resolution strategy will have been agreed between the failing institution and the resolution authority as the 'lead creditor'; after all, the resolution authority represents the resolution fund as the likely main provider of resolution financing, backed by an implicit state guarantee.

---

85 *Re Bluebrook Ltd.* [2009] EWHC 2114 (Ch).

86 The Administration (Restrictions on Disposal etc. to Connected Persons) Regulations 2021.

87 M. Schillig, above n. 6, para. 3.40.

88 J. Gordon and W.-G. Ringe, 'Bank Resolution in Europe: The Unfinished Agenda of Structural Reform' (January 2015) *ECGI Law Working Paper No. 282/2015*, p. 4, referring to the Financial Stability Board (FSB)'s Key Attributes.

89 L. Janssen, 'Bail-in from an insolvency law perspective' (2017) 26 *Norton Journal of Bankruptcy Law and Practice* 457, 470.

3.2.1. *Going Concern Transfers*

Via the sale of business tool, resolution authorities have the power to transfer the shares of an institution under resolution, or all or some of its assets, rights or liabilities to a private-sector purchaser or purchasers.[90] The transfer requires neither the consent of the shareholders of the institution nor of any third party other than the purchaser. The procedural requirements under company or securities laws are suspended.[91] The bridge institution tool provides a temporary solution where no private-sector buyer is readily available.[92] Normal insolvency law does not allow for debtor substitution without the creditors' consent (at least on the basis of a majority decision). Where the debtor is to be replaced with a new entity, this can only be achieved through a form of novation: debtor, creditor and third party agree and enter into a new arrangement, perhaps on the basis of a plan of reorganisation or scheme of arrangement – the new corporate structure issues new debt and/or equity in exchange for the senior lenders' claims against the debtor company. By contrast, the resolution powers include the power to transfer all or some of an institution's liabilities to a new corporate structure,[93] subject to the discretion of the resolution authority and with the consent of the transferee entity. Pursuant to the 'no-creditor-worse-off' principle, no creditor or shareholder shall incur greater losses in resolution than they would have incurred if the institution had been wound up under normal insolvency proceedings. As a consequence, in deciding on which liabilities are to be transferred, the resolution authority must take the order of priority of claims under applicable national insolvency law as a baseline.[94] However, the resolution authority may deviate from this national

---

[90] BRRD, Art. 38(1).

[91] BRRD, Art. 38(1).

[92] Following the transfer to a bridge institution, the total value of liabilities transferred must not exceed the total value of the rights and assets transferred or provided from other sources (BRRD, Art. 40(3); Single Resolution Mechanism(SRM) Regulation, Art. 25(3)), thus providing the viable parts of the business with a new capital structure. When market conditions improve, the bridge's business is to be sold to a private-sector purchaser; BRRD, Art. 41(2).

[93] BRRD, Art. 63(1)(d).

[94] See the resolution principles in BRRD, Art. 34(1)(b), (f) and (g). The BRRD has harmonised the ranking of depositors and deposit guarantee schemes to some extent. Pursuant to BRRD, Art. 108(1), eligible deposits of natural persons and SMEs have a higher priority under national law than ordinary creditors; covered deposits rank even higher, with the Deposit Guarantee Scheme subrogating to the ranking of covered depositors. The new Art. 108(2) has introduced the asset class of non-preferred senior debt, ranking below ordinary unsecured claims and above capital instruments. This new asset class aims to facilitate the meeting of the subordination requirement as a prerequisite for TLAC/MREL (see text to nn. 108, 110) eligibility with a view to enhancing the effectiveness of the bail-in tool. Moreover, the newly introduced BRRD, Art. 48(7) ensures that own funds items (Common Equity Tier 1, Additional Tier 1 and Tier 2 instruments) have a lower priority in national insolvency law than any other claim that does not qualify as an own funds item.

order of priority, subject only to the principle that creditors of the same class are to be treated equitably, not equally. Discrimination between various groups of creditors equally ranked under national insolvency law is likely to be the rule, rather than the exception. The application of resolution tools and powers with a view to ensuring the continuity of critical functions and to preserving financial stability by necessity entails the selection and transfer of certain systemically important contractual relationships that are essential for achieving the resolution objectives, and the leaving behind and eventual liquidation of the remaining non-systemic arrangements.[95]

Under the transfer powers, the property rights of the creditors whose entitlements are transferred to the new entity experience a substantive transformation in two respects: (i) the previous debtor is replaced by another entity; and (ii) transferred liabilities have obtained preferred status to the extent that equally ranking liabilities have been left behind. The left-behind creditors are subject to a substantive transformation of rights only in this second respect: their claims have been subordinated in relation to equally ranking creditors whose claims have been transferred. In addition to specific safeguards for certain security arrangements that protect both transferred and left-behind creditors,[96] the risk profile of the left-behind creditors' claims is further protected by the 'no-creditor-worse-off' principle. Shareholders and creditors whose interests have not been transferred and who have received less than they would have received if the institution had been wound up under normal insolvency proceedings immediately before the transfer,[97] are entitled to be paid the difference between the two sums, from the resolution financing arrangements.[98]

95 J.-H. Binder, 'The Position of Creditors Under the BRRD', in *Commemorative Volume in memory of Professor Dr. Leonidas Georgakopoulos*, Bank of Greece's Centre for Culture, Research and Documentation, Athens 2016, 37, 49 (available at: SSRN: https://ssrn.com/abstract=2698086).

96 Rights and liabilities that are protected under a title transfer financial collateral arrangement or a set-off or netting arrangement may only be transferred in their entirety. Also, these rights and liabilities may not be terminated or modified. Member States are required to provide 'appropriate protection' in this respect. In respect of liabilities secured under a security arrangement, Member States are required to ensure that the secured liability and the benefit of the security can only be transferred together. Moreover, the modification or termination of a security arrangement may not result in a secured liability ceasing to be secured. In each case, an exception may apply for covered deposits in order to ensure their availability; BRRD, Arts. 76–78. In a similar vein, Member States must ensure that the property, rights and liabilities subject to a structured finance arrangement to which the institution is a party may only be transferred in their entirety; and cannot be terminated or modified; BRRD, Art. 79.

97 BRRD, Art. 73; SRM Regulation, Arts. 15(1)(g), 29.

98 BRRD, Arts. 75, 74; SRM, Art. 20(16) and (17).

3.2.2. *Bail-in*

Whereas the transfer powers may effectuate a transformation in the person of the obligor, the special restructuring tools in the form of a power to write-down capital instruments[99] and to 'bail-in' eligible liabilities[100] may have a direct transforming effect on the actual content of property rights. Under the bail-in tool, a negotiated debt for equity and/or new debt swap is replaced by the application of the resolution powers specified in BRRD, Article 63(1)(e)–(k):[101] to reduce, if necessary to zero, the principal or outstanding amount due in respect of eligible liabilities; to convert eligible liabilities into ordinary shares; to cancel shares and debt securities; and to require an institution under resolution to issue new shares or other capital instruments. These powers may be used to either (i) recapitalise an institution in order to restore its viability (open bank scenario);[102] or (ii) reduce the debt to be transferred to a bridge institution or a private-sector buyer (closed bank scenario).[103] The bail-in trigger is the determination by the resolution authority[104] that the general conditions for resolution have been met.[105] The vagueness of the bail-in trigger

---

99 BRRD, Arts. 59–62; SRM Regulation, Art. 21. A write-down of capital instruments may occur independently of a resolution action or as part of a resolution; BRRD, Art. 59(1) (a) and (b). Capital instruments must be written down, irrespective of whether or not subsequently resolution tools and powers are exercised, as soon as the appropriate authority (which may be the competent authority or the resolution authority, BRRD, Art. 61(1)) determines that in the absence of a write-down the institution will no longer be viable; which are essentially the conditions for resolution minus the public interest requirement; BRRD, Art. 59(3) and (4). In applying the write-down power, depending on the amount of losses, common shares may be cancelled in their entirety. Thereafter, the principal amount of the relevant capital instruments is reduced to zero, permanently, and, in principle, without compensation. Following the write-down no liability to the holder shall remain, except for any liability already accrued; BRRD, Art. 60(1)(a), (b) and (c), and (2).

100 BRRD, Arts. 43–55; SRM Regulation, Art. 27.

101 BRRD, Art. 43(1).

102 BRRD, Art. 43(2)(a); SRM Regulation, Art. 27(1)(a).

103 BRRD, Art. 43(2)(b); SRM Regulation, Art. 27(1)(b). In both scenarios the conditions for resolution must be met. In the latter scenario, application of the bail-in tool seems to be straightforward: transferred debt is reduced or converted to the extent necessary to adequately capitalise the bridge institution or to facilitate a sale of business. In the open bank scenario, the bail-in tool may be exercised only if there is a realistic prospect that the application of bail-in in conjunction with other measures implemented in accordance with a business reorganisation plan by the management or an administrator appointed for that purpose will achieve, not only the relevant resolution objectives, but will restore the institution to financial soundness and long-term viability. Where these conditions are not fulfilled, resolution authorities may use any of the other resolution tools and the bail-in tool in order to capitalise a bridge institution or facilitate a transfer; BRRD, Art. 43(3); SRM Regulation, Art. 27(2).

104 BRRD, Art. 82.

105 Pursuant to BRRD/SRM, in respect of a credit institution or investment firm, resolution action may be taken if (i) the competent authority, after consulting the resolution authority, determines that the institution is failing or is likely to fail; (ii) there is no reasonable prospect

gives resolution authorities a rather wide, essentially political discretion. The bail-in tool applies to all liabilities that are not excluded.[106] In exceptional circumstances, resolution authorities may exclude certain eligible liabilities where this is strictly necessary and proportionate to ensure continuity of critical functions or to prevent widespread contagion.[107] This 'escape clause' appears to be very flexible. For the largest systemically important banks it will be very easy to invoke the 'risk of contagion' exception. The delineation of the scope of the bail-in tool means that basically all unsecured debt with an original maturity of seven days or more will be bail-inable, leaving as the main loophole for circumvention secured liabilities and short-term inter-institutional debt. In order to prevent circumvention, banks and financial institutions are required to maintain at all times a certain minimum requirement for eligible liabilities (MREL) in form of a sufficient aggregate amount of own funds and eligible liabilities, expressed as a percentage of total liabilities[108] and own funds, in accordance with Regulation (EU) 575/2013.[109] For global systemically

that, in the absence of a resolution action, the failure of the institution could be prevented within a reasonable timeframe; and (iii) resolution action is necessary in the public interest. An institution is deemed failing or likely to fail if it is in breach or will be in breach, in the near future, of the capital requirements for continuing authorisation in a way that would justify the withdrawal of the authorisation by the competent authority, including, but not limited to, the institution having incurred or being likely to incur losses that will deplete all or substantially all of its own funds. An institution will also be deemed to be failing, or likely to fail, if its assets are, or will in the near future be, less than its liabilities; or if it is, or will in the near future be, unable to pay its obligations as they fall due. Moreover, the institution is deemed to be failing when it requires extraordinary public financial support. A resolution action will be in the public interest if it achieves, and is proportionate to, one or more of the resolution objectives, and the winding up of the institution pursuant to normal insolvency proceedings would not meet those objectives to the same extent; BRRD, Art. 32(1); SRM Regulation, Art. 18(1).

106 BRRD, Art. 44(1). Excluded liabilities are limited to covered deposits; secured liabilities up to the amount of the value of the collateral; liabilities arising from the holding of client assets or client money; fiduciary liabilities; short term liabilities with an original maturity of less than seven days (where owed to a clearing or settlement system with a remaining maturity of less than seven days); and certain liabilities owed to employees, commercial and trade creditors, and tax and social security claims provided they are treated as preferential under national insolvency law; as well as contributions owed to a Deposit Guarantee Scheme; BRRD, Art. 44(2); SRM Regulation, Art. 27(3).

107 BRRD, Art. 44(3); SRM Regulation, Art. 27(5). When doing so, resolution authorities must have regard to the order of preference under national law.

108 Derivative liabilities are to be included in total liabilities, taking into account the netting rights of counterparties.

109 Resolution authorities, after consulting the competent authorities, may determine the required minimum on a case-by-case basis depending on the risks associated with a specific institution and its resolvability. BRRD, Art. 45(1); SRM Regulation, Art. 12(1) and (2). Commission Delegated Regulation (EU) 2016/1450 of 23 May 2016 supplementing Directive 2014/59/EU of the European Parliament and of the Council with regard to regulatory technical standards specifying the criteria relating to the methodology for setting the minimum requirement for own funds and eligible liabilities, [2016] OJ L 237/1.

important banks (G-SIBs), the Financial Stability Board (FSB) has issued a new minimum total loss-absorbing capacity (TLAC) requirement.[110] MREL and TLAC constitute complementary elements of a common framework that seeks to ensure that institutions have sufficient loss-absorbing and recapitalisation capacity. [111]

In order to apply the bail-in tool, resolution authorities must first establish, on the basis of a fair and reasonable valuation, the aggregate amount by which eligible liabilities should be reduced or converted.[112] By application of the bail-in tool, existing shares in an institution are either cancelled or 'severely diluted' by converting eligible liabilities into shares at an appropriate rate of conversion.[113] Thereafter, the BRRD and SRM Regulation establish a waterfall for exercising the bail-in tool that, in principle, follows the reverse order of priority under general corporate insolvency law.[114] Within each class, losses are to be allocated on a *pro rata* basis.[115]

To the extent that bail-in respects the order of priority under national corporate insolvency law, a claim's risk profile is not subject to alteration. However, the exclusion of certain liabilities, automatically or at the discretion of the resolution authority, from the scope of the bail-in tool may constitute a deviation from the ranking of creditors under national insolvency laws. The exclusion of certain liabilities from bail-in transforms them into preferred liabilities, whereas equally ranking bail-inable instruments will be subordinated.

---

110 FSB, Principles on Loss-absorbing and Recapitalization Capacity of G-SIBs in Resolution (09.11.2015).

111 Directive (EU) 2019/879 of the European Parliament and of the Council of 20 May 2019 amending Directive 2014/59/EU as regards loss-absorbing and recapitalisation capacity of credit institutions and investment firms and Directive 98/26/EC, [2019] OJ L 150/296, Recital (2); Regulation (EU) 2019/877 of the European Parliament and of the Council of 20 May 2019 amending Regulation (EU) No. 806/2014 as regards the loss-absorbing and recapitalisation capacity of credit institutions and investment firms, [2019] OJ L 150/226, Recital (2).

112 BRRD, Art. 46(1). Where the bail-in tool is applied in order to recapitalise an institution or to capitalise a bridge bank, the aggregate amount thus established must be sufficient to restore the CET1 capital ratio of the institution, to sustain sufficient market confidence in it and to allow it to continue to comply with the conditions for authorisation and to carry on the activities for which it was authorised for at least one year; BRRD, Art. 46(2).

113 BRRD, Art. 47(1).

114 BRRD, Art. 48; SRM Regulation, Arts. 27(15), 17. Consequently, CET1 instruments are written down first in proportion to the losses and up to their capacity with the relevant shares being cancelled. If, and only if, this is insufficient to arrive at the aggregate amount, resolution authorities reduce the principal amount of Additional Tier 1 instruments followed by Tier 2 instruments. If, and only if, this is still insufficient, resolution authorities reduce the principal amount of subordinated debt (other than Additional Tier 1 or Tier 2 capital) to the extent necessary in accordance with the reverse ranking under national law. Only if this is still insufficient, may the outstanding senior eligible debt be reduced in accordance with its reverse ranking under national law to the extent necessary to arrive at the aggregate amount; BRRD, Art. 48(1)(a)–(e).

115 BRRD, Art. 48(2).

If the institution were to be wound up under normal insolvency law all unsecured general creditors would share in the proceeds of the pool of assets available for distribution on a *pro rata* basis. Consequently, bailing-in certain unsecured creditors but not equally ranked others may potentially result in the former being worse off in resolution than they would have been under otherwise applicable corporate insolvency law. This possible subordination adversely affects a claim's risk profile and the ensuing increase in volatility seems likely to push up the costs of capital for claims subject to bail-in and subordination;[116] whereas the cost of capital for excluded liabilities with preferential status is likely to be lower.[117] Similar considerations apply in the going concern transfer scenario in respect of left-behind and transferred creditors, respectively. The 'no-creditor-worse-off' principle seeks to restore the initial risk profile of subordinated claims. Those creditors whose claims were bailed in (or left behind) in order to absorb losses may be compensated *ex post* – through a payout from the resolution financing arrangement – to the extent that they are worse off than they would have been in a standard insolvency process.[118] If the 'no-creditor-worse-off' principle were effective as a risk profile preservation device, an institution subject to resolution and bail-in would be unlikely to suffer adverse cost of capital consequences, as compared to an institution resolved under standard insolvency law. Those creditors holding liabilities that are exempt from bail-in (or to be transferred) would be better off, and bail-in (or left-behind) creditors would not be worse off. Thus, all else being equal, subjecting an institution to resolution instead of standard insolvency law should at least be neutral in terms of the institution's weighted average cost of capital. However, this hinges on the effectiveness of the 'no-creditor-worse-off' principle.

3.2.3. *Risk Profile Preservation through 'No-Creditor-Worse-Off'*

Under both the going concern sale scenario and bail-in, deviations from the applicable order of priority under national law are likely to be the rule, rather than the exception. As a consequence, risk profile preservation is more likely to take the form of *ex post* compensation, rather than adhering to the 'no-creditor-worse-off' principle *ex ante*. The special treatment of systemically important liabilities is inherent in the resolution process, even its *raison d'être*.[119] Thus, *ex post* compensation will be essential as a risk profile preservation device.

---

116 Above n. 69.

117 J. Chan-Lau and H. Oura, 'Bail-in Power, Depositor Preference, and Asset Encumbrance: The End of Cheap Senior Unsecured Debt? A Structural Pricing Perspective' (March 2016), (available at http://ssrn.com/abstract=2785992).

118 BRRD, Art. 75.

119 J.-H. Binder, above n. 95, pp. 46–47.

In order to determine whether any shareholder or creditor is worse off following resolution as compared to their likely status in normal insolvency proceedings, an independent *ex post* valuation is to be carried out as soon as possible after the resolution action has taken effect.[120] This valuation seeks to determine: (i) the (hypothetical) treatment that the shareholder or creditor would have received if the institution had entered normal insolvency proceedings instead of resolution; (ii) their actual treatment under resolution; and (iii) whether there is any difference between (i) and (ii).[121] Where, on that basis, a shareholder or creditor has suffered greater losses under (ii) than they would have suffered under (i), they are entitled to compensation from the resolution financing arrangement.[122] Under the 'no-creditor-worse-off' principle the likely loss given default under bail-in will at least not be worse than the loss given default in a hypothetical liquidation. Thus, the cost of capital of eligible liabilities could be based on this 'worst-case scenario' as a benchmark.[123] Theoretically, this would prevent an increase in volatility as compared to standard insolvency law (discounting a public bailout). However, there are a number of reasons for assuming that the 'no-creditor-worse-off' principle is less effective than traditional corporate insolvency law mechanisms in preserving a claim's risk profile.

Whereas in standard insolvency procedures, a plan or scheme cannot be imposed on dissenting creditors that would be worse off, in resolution bail-in (or a transfer of liabilities) can be enforced, but is subject to compensation only *ex post*.[124] This deviation can be justified on the basis of the systemic risk implications in the context of resolution and the fact that time will normally be of the essence.[125] However, whether compensation is due will by necessity be assessed with hindsight. The eventual economic outcome of a resolution is likely to materialise only after months or even years from the time the relevant resolution action was taken and implemented. Assessing the counterfactual outcome of standard insolvency proceedings will be difficult under these circumstances, also because the taking of resolution action may itself have an impact on market conditions, with implications for the factual basis of the valuation to be carried out.[126] The valuation of a financial

---

120 BRRD, Art. 74(1); SRM Regulation, Art. 20(16). This valuation is separate and distinct from the valuations prior to commencement, and, presumably is to be carried out by a different person; S Schelo, *Bank Recover and Resolution*, Kluwers Law International, Alphen aan den Rijn 2015, p. 108.

121 BRRD, Art. 74(2); SRM Regulation, Art. 20(17).

122 BRRD, Art. 75.

123 S. Gleeson, 'Legal Aspects of Bank Bail-Ins' *LSE Financial Markets Group Paper Series, Special Paper No. 205* (January 2012), 8–10.

124 L. Janssen, above n. 89, 477.

125 J.-H. Binder, above n. 95, p. 61.

126 Ibid., p. 47.

institution is a notoriously difficult process and highly contingent on financial market conditions, particularly in a crisis scenario when liquidity dries up and assets are no longer readily marketable. The Lehman Bros collapse is a case in point. Moreover, the hypothetical liquidation assessment is fraught with uncertainties, in respect of the applicable corporate insolvency law and the order of priority, in particular where institutions operate across borders. Valuation is likely to be a lengthy and expensive process, carried out under the auspices of the resolution authority. There seems to be an unlimited potential for litigation concerning the factual correctness and appropriateness of the valuation outcome, which could drag on for years and further postpone the compensation process. The longer it takes to arrive at a valuation that is acceptable for the stakeholders concerned, the less likely that they will recover full compensation for the difference between the hypothetical liquidation value and the resolution value of their claim.[127] On that basis, the 'no-creditor-worse-off' principle may be nothing more than a 'weak promise'.[128] In any case, the principle offers no protection for any liquidity shortfalls that may occur during the implementation of the resolution action and the eventual valuation and compensation.[129] This would suggest that the 'no-creditor-worse-off' principle cannot fully restore a claim's risk profile. As a consequence, bail-inable (and left-behind) debt is likely to be more expensive than it would be in the absence of the resolution framework. At the same time, exempt (and to be transferred) liabilities may become cheaper than they would be outside of resolution. However, it is not plausible to assume that the cost savings on exempt liabilities can completely compensate for the cost increase on bail-inable debt. This is because of an adverse selection problem that exists at two levels. An investor in (automatically) excluded liabilities cannot be sure whether the institution will be subject to resolution at all; and if resolved under standard insolvency law the exclusion will count for nothing. This uncertainty emanating from the political discretion afforded the resolution authority will be factored into the pricing decision and increase the cost of capital relative to a situation where resolution would be the only applicable regime. In addition, *ex ante* no investor can be sure whether their liability will obtain preferential status – by being transferred to a private-sector buyer or bridge bank, or exempted from bail-in on the basis of the 'escape clause' – even if resolution has been triggered. Again, this uncertainty[130] has to be factored in, with adverse effects on the cost of capital as compared to a situation where exemption would be a certainty. On that basis, it is fair to assume that the weighted average cost of capital of an institution subject to resolution will be higher, all else being equal,

127 Ibid., p. 48.
128 Ibid., p. 48.
129 Ibid., p. 50.
130 J. Chan-Lau and H. Oura, above n. 117, 23.

than for an institution for which the resolution framework would never apply. A bank resolved through normal insolvency proceedings would benefit from the more robust risk profile preservation mechanisms available under standard corporate insolvency law.[131]

At the other end of the spectrum, there is reason to believe that the largest and most complex institutions will not be subject to resolution and bail-in either. The bank resolution framework contains many loopholes that allow authorities to circumvent its strict loss-sharing principles.[132] The resolution trigger, and in particular the public interest requirement, is notoriously vague; the exercise of discretion is subject to regulatory and political capture, a tendency that will be amplified by the bail-in tool's redistributive effects. Bail-inable instruments are likely to be held predominantly by other non-bank financial institutions: pension funds, insurance companies and other institutional investors.[133] The application of the bail-in tool would impose losses on these institutional investor classes, and indirectly, on their customers: pensioners, savers and policyholders.[134] The issue becomes politically even more charged where bail-inable instruments are held directly by retail investors. As a consequence, resolution and bail-in are likely to be applied only in cases that are 'easy', i.e. where the application of resolution tools and powers is straightforward, the potential spillover effects limited, and/or the political implications minimal, as in the case of the Spanish bank Banco Popular, the first application of the SRM.[135] By contrast, the 'hard' cases are likely to be bailed out, using any of the escape routes available, as was the case with the Italian lender Monte dei Paschi di Sienna, Italy's fourth-largest lender, that was bailed-out by the Italian state

[131] J.-H. Binder, above n. 95, p. 60: 'In the "brave new world" of innovative resolution tools prescribed by the BRRD and the SRM Regulation, creditors are bound to find themselves in a considerably less comfortable position than they would enjoy in traditional insolvency proceedings.'

[132] E.g. 'precautionary recapitalisation' (below n. 136). Where the resolution authority decides that resolution is not in the public interest due to a lack of systemic relevance, the institution will then be resolved under national corporate insolvency law. This opens the door for a public bailout, as has been the case with Banca Popolare di Vicenza and Veneto Banca, two regional Italian banks. Such a bailout is subject to the EU state aid framework, which is less stringent in respect of the sharing of losses.

[133] Under the FSB's TLAC principles, G-SIBs will be required to deduct from their own TLAC their exposures to eligible external TLAC liabilities issued by other G-SIBs. This penalisation of cross-holdings is aimed at reducing the risk of contagion; M. Schillig, above n. 6, para. 11.17.

[134] E. Avgouleas and C. Goodhart, 'A Critical Evaluation of Bail-In as a Bank Recapitalisation Mechanism' (2014) *Centre for Economic Policy Research, Discussion Paper Series No. 100065*, 16.

[135] Decision of the Single Resolution Board in its Executive Session of 07.06.2017 concerning the adoption of a resolution scheme in respect of Banco Popular Español, SA, (the institution) with a Legal Entity Identifier: 80H66LPTVDLMOP28XF25, addressed to FROB (SRB/EES/2017/08).

on the basis of a so-called 'precautionary recapitalisation', one of the loopholes in the BRRD/SRM framework.[136]

This leaves us with three different categories of institutions in terms of their resolvability: (i) insignificant institutions that may be resolved through national corporate insolvency law; (ii) 'easy' cases which will be resolved under the BRRD and SRM; and (iii) 'hard' cases which will be resolved through a public bailout. Category (iii) benefits from an implicit state guarantee, and category (i) may benefit from the more robust risk profile preservation mechanisms in corporate insolvency in addition to generous state aid. As a consequence, the adverse cost of capital implications will be most significant for category (ii). In order to keep their costs of capital competitive, institutions that fall within category (ii) could seek to transition into either one of the other categories. As a consequence, the universe of category (ii) institutions subject to resolution and bail-in will likely be populated more and more sparsely. For political reasons, resolution authorities will not be inclined to extend the application of the resolution framework to 'hard' cases; neither are they likely to extend the ambit of the resolution framework at the other end of the spectrum, by encroaching upon the domain of national corporate insolvency law and state aid. When there are two or more parallel systems for resolving banks in financial distress, different substantive entitlements in these systems invite potentially wrong deployment decisions because of the varying incentives regarding distributional outcomes.[137] The new resolution framework will have the unintended consequence of increasing the costs of capital for medium-sized and less complex institutions. In the long term, this middle class of banking institutions may disappear, to be replaced with possibly a few large banks and many similarly situated smaller banks, a trajectory running contrary to the objective of effectively tackling 'too-big-to-fail' and 'too-many-to-fail'.

136 Whereas, in principle, an institution will be deemed to be failing or likely to fail where extraordinary public financial support is required, exceptionally this won't be the case where: (i) public financial support is given in order to remedy a serious disturbance in the economy of a Member State and to preserve financial stability; (ii) it takes the form of an injection of own funds or the purchase of capital requirements on terms that do not confer an advantage on the institution; (iii) the institution is not deemed to be failing or likely to fail on other grounds (cash-flow insolvency, balance-sheet insolvency, infringement of own funds requirements) and is solvent; (iv) the measure is of a precautionary and temporary nature and cannot be used to offset losses; (v) it is subject to the EU state aid framework and necessary to address a capital shortfall established in a stress test; BRRD, Art. 32(4)(d); SRM Regulation, Art. 18(4)(d).

137 T. Jackson, above n. 27, p. 61: 'When there are two parallel systems of debt collection, different substantive entitlements in the two systems invite wrong deployment decisions for the group as a whole because of individual incentives regarding distributional outcomes'.

4. CONCLUSION

The transformation of rights in insolvency and resolution is theoretically sound and can be explained seamlessly based on a commons/anti-commons analysis. However, the application of the bail-in tool, and the resolution framework more generally, is beset with practical problems: the vagueness of the resolution trigger, the reliance on authority discretion, flexible 'escape clauses', the 'no-creditor-worse-off' principle as an inadequate risk profile preservation mechanism, to name but a few. Consequently, large systemically important financial institutions are likely to be bailed out; smaller banks are likely to be resolved under national corporate insolvency law with generous state aid support. This may have adverse consequences for the costs of capital of medium-sized institutions, and, over time, may exacerbate the 'too-big-to-fail' and 'too-many-to-fail' problems.

CHAPTER 4

DEPOSIT GUARANTEE SCHEMES: TOWARDS HARMONISATION THROUGH THE EU?

François BARRIÈRE

The economic and financial difficulties encountered by European States since the global 2007–2009 financial crisis have led to a loss of trust in the banking and financial system, and have made the previous theoretical assumption of the bankruptcy of credit institutions perceptible. The financial crisis showed the importance of maintaining depositor confidence in the financial system, and using such tools as increases in deposit insurance coverage and strengthening of funding arrangements, to support financial stability.[1] In a changing world, challenges with respect to deposit schemes are numerous. In June 2017 (i) an agreement was reached at the EU and Italian levels to recapitalise the Italian Banca Monte dei Paschi di Siena, and (ii) the Spanish Banco Popular Espanol S.A. was put into resolution and its equity instruments were transferred to Banco Santander S.A. The failure of those two credit institutions illustrates the fact that bankruptcies of banks are not hypothetical, 10 years after the Lehmann Brothers collapse. March 2023 proved that risks on deposits still exist. Indeed, US regulators rushed to seize the assets of Silicon Valley Bank (SVB) after a run on that bank, the largest failure of a financial institution since the height of the financial crisis more than a decade ago. Pursuant to a 12 March 2023 Joint Statement by the US Department of the Treasury, US

[1] S.M. Seyad, 'The Impact of the Proposed Banking Union on the Unity and Integrity of the European Union's Single Market' (2013) 28(3) *Journal of International Banking Law and Regulation (J.I.B.L.R.)* 99.

Federal Reserve, and US FDIC, the resolution of Silicon Valley Bank was announced to be executed in a manner that fully protects all depositors. The US Federal Reserve stated, also in March 2023, that it would offer funding to banks through a new facility to help ensure that banks can meet all depositor withdrawals, essentially backstopping all deposits – both insured and uninsured – across the US financial system. While US regulators hoped to shore up confidence by guaranteeing deposits at SVB and also the crypto-focused Signature Bank – which faced severe difficulties only a few days apart from SVB – the collapse of Swiss historic bank Credit Suisse in March 2023 reignited fears of contagion across the financial sector. In March 2023, UBS took over its troubled Swiss rival Credit Suisse for $3.25 billion following crunch talks, aimed at stopping the stricken bank from triggering a wider international banking crisis. Soon after the announcement, the US Federal Reserve, European Central Bank and other major central banks came out with statements to reassure markets that had been walloped by a banking crisis that started with the collapse of two regional US banks earlier the same month.

Deposit insurance is deemed to help mitigate moral hazard on the behaviour of shareholders and bank management, as banks may fail without being saved by the State while depositors will benefit from deposit insurance. Moral hazard may indeed be reduced by stating that banks may fail, that there is no 'too-big-to-fail', due to the fact that depositors will in any event benefit from a guarantee with a timely intervention by the deposit insurer.

Typically, depositors are often unable to differentiate between safe and unsafe banks. A deposit insurance scheme provides for a guarantee of repayment in case the insured credit institution fails to reimburse depositors, which is to the benefit of depositors due to the fact that deposits are usually not held on a segregated basis by banks. Depositors of a credit institution in the EU, and of any branch of a credit institution in the EU, should benefit from a protection, irrespective of the domicile of the depositor. Pursuant to EU legislation, every credit institution should join a statutory deposit guarantee scheme, and EEA Member States may no longer exempt credit institutions from joining such a scheme, e.g., European cooperative banks may no longer belong solely to their own deposit protection scheme, and must belong to a statutory deposit guarantee scheme. A sufficiently efficient protection of eligible deposits is a tenet of a resilient financial system, in particular because it should facilitate prevention of capital flight and deposit outflows if a bank goes bankrupt.

A deposit should mean any credit balance which results from funds left in an account, and which a financial institution is legally obliged to repay. A deposit insurance scheme should provide for (i) what is an eligible deposit (and what is not), (ii) what is the protected amount, (iii) what is the payout delay, and

(iv) the funding of the deposit insurance scheme (as adequate funding will be key for determining to what extent said scheme will have sufficient resources to reimburse the depositors). However, functions of deposit insurers may vary, as the institutional framework is not uniform throughout jurisdictions. Indeed, the mandate of deposit insurers varies across the globe, being more or less narrow. At a minimum, a deposit insurer should be responsible for the reimbursement of insured deposits. Sometimes, a deposit insurer also has a limited role in resolution, which usually will take the form of a financial support, or even a more active role in connection with the selection of resolution strategies. At most, the deposit insurer may have a full suite of resolution powers and prudential oversight. A large majority of deposit insurers are subject to *ex ante* funding throughout the world, including pursuant to the EU framework. In any event, the deposit guarantee scheme should kick-in when deposits become unavailable, e.g., when a credit institution fails, therefore improving financial consumer protection.

Deposit insurers' regulatory landscape has been moving, and is expected to continue to evolve. Recent EU directives have strengthened the protection of deposits throughout the EEA, mainly via deposit guarantee schemes, i.e., entities responsible for reimbursing depositors for the loss of their deposit if a credit institution is unable to meet its obligations to the depositors. The latter contributes to overall financial stability, and offers protection to depositors, in particular those that are unable to easily assess the solvency situation of a bank. Recently, the Deposit Guarantee Directive No. 2014/49/EU of 16 April 2014 amended the current European framework, to provide, among other things, (i) a broader scope of the guarantee to all type of deposits, irrespective of their currency, (ii) the shortening of the indemnification period, (iii) the creation of a higher threshold than the standard one to guarantee so-called 'exceptional temporary' deposits, and (iv) new information obligations to the benefit of depositors. The latter Directive does not permit exclusion of medium-to-large entities from the benefit of the deposit guarantee.

The next currently contemplated step at the Eurozone level is the implementation of the European Deposit Insurance Scheme (EDIS), which is aimed at disentangling the link between credit establishments and their Member State. Indeed, if deposit insurers are usually regarded as last resort payers, to date, National Treasuries are usually regarded as ultimate guarantors and Central Banks as last resort lenders. In short, EDIS, as currently contemplated, would be implemented in three successive stages over a seven-year period, and will aim to be initially a Eurozone-wide reinsurance fund, then a co-insurance fund, and finally a Eurozone-wide deposit scheme, to the benefit of Member States' depositors. A Eurozone, or even a pan-European, common deposit guarantee scheme may prove to have some beneficial effects, but does raise a number of questions.

An effective deposit scheme is a concern that is not limited to European jurisdictions. The International Association of Deposit Insurers (IADI)[2] has issued its 'Core Principles for Effective Deposit Insurance Systems', dated November 2014, which are intended as a framework-supporting effective deposit insurance practices. Core Principles are a way to ensure international harmonisation, in a similar way to how the Basel Principles impact bank regulation throughout a great number of countries. The number of jurisdictions that have become members of the IADI has been growing significantly over the years, e.g., 94 are members in 2023, as compared to 78 in 2016 and 41 in 2005.

Depositors are in a similar legal position to that of unsecured creditors, i.e., as if they had lent money to the credit establishment. If the credit establishment goes bankrupt and the depositor is deemed to be an unsecured creditor of the bank, in the absence of sufficient liquidity, the depositor will not be paid back. That is why depositor insurance aims to protect retail depositors from bank failures. It also aims to avoid a run on a bank: depositors are less likely to rush to a bank to withdraw money if they benefit from an insurance to receive their deposit back. Deposit insurance schemes therefore promote public confidence.

This leads to the question as to what justifies a special protection to the benefit of bank depositors, as opposed to other investors. Bank deposits and investments, e.g., bonds, are similar in a number of respects.[3] From the point of view of the owner, both are assets, whereas both are liabilities from the point of view of their debtor. Bank deposits are one of the investment options on the table, irrespective of whether the return is low. Bank deposits are not risk-free placements, as the bankruptcy of the UK bank 'Northern Rock' has showed. However, bank deposits yields returns, similarly to debt investments, but unlike capital investments. The main difference seems to be that bank deposits do not imply the transformation of capital into an asset, as opposed to an investment. The differences between deposits and investments do not seem conclusive enough to justify a different legal treatment. What does, however, matter is the public perception of deposits. Depositors do not intend to take any investment risk when they deposit their cash in a bank account – risk is a hallmark of an investment. Nor do they believe that they are speculating when depositing cash in a bank. Depositors perceive deposits as risk-free, though banks use deposits to conduct proprietary trading. The mere fact that bail-in may transform depositors into shareholders is not sufficient to consider that the investment perception of a depositor is that of a risk-investment. However, from a public policy perspective, if resolution and other bail-in measures are justified by a financial stability need, unsecured depositors should not be

---

2 The International Association of Deposit Insurers and the Basel Committee on Banking Supervision had issued Core Principles in a similar vein in June 2009.

3 P. Athanassiou, 'On the Legal and Economic Treatment of Bank Deposits as Investments: Some Reflections' (2014) 29 *J.I.B.L.R.* 715.

exempted from bail-in measures. As an exception to the latter, guarantees should be provided for the benefit of depositors within a certain limit – that is the purpose of deposit guarantee schemes.

Therefore, in order to reassure depositors, thus avoiding bank runs, e.g., preventing another Northern Rock (the lack of liquidity of the latter resulted in depositors queuing to withdraw their funds), and support the stability of the banking system, current deposit-guarantee mechanisms (section 2 below) have been established and strengthened in favour of depositors under the auspices of the European Union (section 1 below).

1. DEVELOPMENTS IN LEGAL INSTRUMENTS: FROM NATIONAL LEGISLATION TO AN EU-WIDE DEPOSIT GUARANTEE SCHEME

1.1. THE PREMISES OF A DEPOSIT GUARANTEE SYSTEM IN FRANCE

In 1980, in France, a regulation of the French Banking Association (*Association Française des Banques*) first outlined an *ad hoc* depositor compensation scheme based on the solidarity of its members: the reimbursement of the deposits of defaulting members was therefore provided for up to a limit of 200 million French francs per year.

French Law No. 84-46 of 24 January 1984 (Article 52(2)), known as the Banking Law, mimicked this mechanism by introducing an optional and non-binding depositor compensation procedure by other credit institutions, at the initiative of the Governor of the Bank of France.

1.2. IMPLEMENTATION OF A FRENCH ORGANISED DEPOSIT GUARANTEE SYSTEM UNDER EU INFLUENCE

An organised deposit guarantee system only truly emerged in France with the implementation of Directive No. 94/19/EC of the European Parliament and of the Council of 30 May 1994, which required that Member States adopt such a system, whilst granting them considerable discretion for its implementation. The 1994 Directive was transposed into French law by Law No. 94-679 of 8 August 1994: credit institutions were required to adhere to a deposit guarantee fund intended to compensate depositors in the event that deposits were unavailable.

It was within this framework that French legislation continued to strengthen the guarantee system, by establishing the Deposit Guarantee Fund (*Fonds de Garantie des Dépôts*) pursuant to Law No. 99-532 on savings and financial security of 25 June 1999, which then became the Deposit Guarantee and Resolution Fund (*Fonds de Garantie des Dépôts et de Résolution,* FGDR) pursuant to Law No. 2013-672 of 6 July 2013. The provisions of the French law of 25 June 1999, implemented by various regulations of the Banking and Financial Regulatory Committee (*Comité de la Règlementation Bancaire et Financière,* CRBF), contributed to the implementation of a harmonised deposit guarantee system in France, in order to better protect depositors.

1.3. EU-DRIVEN STRENGTHENING OF DEPOSIT GUARANTEE SCHEMES IN THE CONTEXT OF THE FINANCIAL CRISIS

1.3.1. Directive 2009/14/EC of 11 March 2009

The onset of the 2007–2008 major financial crisis compelled the European Union to urgently adopt a Directive to reassure depositors. Directive No. 2009/14/EC of the European Parliament and of the Council of 11 March 2009 introduced substantial changes to the provisions of Directive No. 94/19/EC of the European Parliament and of the Council of 30 May 1994, in order to create a deposit guarantee scheme that was more protective of depositors, and complete the harmonisation of the mechanisms of the different Member States.

1.3.2. Directive 2014/49/EU of 16 April 2014

Directive 2009/14/EC, which was adopted urgently, remained incomplete. For the purposes of completing it, Directive No. 2014/49/EU on deposit guarantee schemes was adopted on 16 April 2014. The latter, with the same purpose of simplifying and harmonising existing mechanisms, considerably strengthens the means of deposit-guarantee systems. It has been transposed into French law by Law No. 2014-1662 of 30 December 2014, Ordinance No. 2015-1024 of 20 August 2015, and five decrees of 27 October 2015.

The Deposit Guarantee Scheme Directive (DGSD) No. 2014/49/EU required EU Member States to, among other things, introduce a deposit guarantee scheme in their jurisdiction, to (i) provide for depositors' protection, and (ii) reduce the risk of bank runs.

1.4. TOWARDS A BANKING UNION AND A EUROPEAN DEPOSIT GUARANTEE FUND

1.4.1. The 2015 EDIS Proposal

The EU regulatory landscape still faces challenges, which include the lack of sufficient harmonisation throughout the EU, EU market fragmentation, deposit guarantee scheme resources, identical risk calculations, and equivalent governance of deposit insurance schemes issues.

To continue the harmonisation process, and in order to implement the third pillar of the Banking Union,[4] a proposal for a regulation was presented on 24 November 2015 by the European Commission, for the purposes of implementing the proposed EDIS. EDIS aims to provide for a common system for the protection of depositors in the Eurozone, in connection with the Single Supervisory Mechanism (SSM), and, at the end of the process, an integrated/single deposit guarantee scheme. SSM and the Single Resolution Mechanism (SRM) – provided for by the Banking Recovery and Resolution Directive (BRRD) No. 2014/59/EU and the Single Resolution Mechanism Regulation (SRM Regulation) No. 806/2014 of 15 July 2014 – are the two other pillars of the Banking Union.

Questions arise as to whether depositors will be better off with EDIS, and whether they can hold EDIS accountable. National deposit guarantee schemes are potentially vulnerable to the insolvency of a systemic bank, e.g., national deposit guarantees are unlikely to have sufficient funding to reimburse depositors of a bank with a significantly high level of deposits.

In short, EDIS would provide extra-finance compared to a sole Member State's deposit guarantee scheme, which should result in additional confidence in a bank's stability for a depositor. Wherever the bank operates within the SSM territorial scope, depositors should benefit from the same aggregate of money available to guarantee their deposits. The risk that a banking crisis would become a national treasury crisis should therefore be reduced. EDIS aims to increase the resilience in the banking union, by reducing the link between a bank and its home Member State.[5]

This proposal provides for the creation of a European Deposit Guarantee Fund (EDGF), and an implementation in three stages:

- between 2017 and 2020, the EDGF would implement a re-insurance mechanism for defaulting national deposit guarantee regimes within the Eurozone, i.e., EDIS could provide limited funding and cover a limited share in a deposit guarantee scheme if the latter has a liquidity shortfall when requested to make a payment, acting therefore as a back-stop for national insurance schemes; more precisely, the EGDF would ensure (i) liquidity up to 20 per cent of shortage (measured against DGSD2 theoretical resources,

[4] M. Huertas, 'EDIS – The Third-Pillar of the EU's Banking Union: Big, Bold, but Can it Be Beautiful?' (2016) 31(11) *J.I.B.L.R.* 587.

[5] A. Minto, 'The Introduction of an EU-Wide Deposit Insurance Scheme: Advantages and Disadvantages from a Depositor Perspective – Survey, Challenges, and a Way Forward by Means of a Comparative Analysis' (2017) 32(2) *J.I.B.L.R.* 49.

after depletion), and (ii) cost sharing up to 20 per cent of shortage measured against DGSD2 theoretical resources and recoveries, after depletion;

- between 2020 and 2024, a co-insurance mechanism would provide for the co-financing of the EDGF and the national deposit guarantee systems; EDIS would provide funding of a percentage of the participating deposit guarantee scheme's liquidity need, arising from a payout event (the main difference in this phase is that a national scheme would not have to exhaust its own resources prior to accessing the European fund), i.e., the EGDF would ensure (i) liquidity in a 20 to 80% range (increasing year upon year) of the anticipated costs of the payout, and (ii) cost sharing in a 20 to 80% range (increasing year upon year) of the costs, less recoveries;
- from 2024 onwards, the EDGF would replace national Eurozone deposit guarantee systems, therefore implementing a shared comprehensive insurance mechanism, e.g., the EGDF would have liquidity for the whole anticipated costs of the payout, and would ensure cost financing for the whole costs (less recoveries).

EDIS would apply to deposit guarantee schemes in Eurozone Member States participating in the SSM. Payouts from EDIS would be made from a deposit insurance fund, to be funded by risk-based contributions paid by banks. In any event, the system should provide that funding should be on an *ex ante* basis. EDIS will mainly affect the funding of the deposit insurance scheme and the administration of a common deposit insurance fund, which probably should imply a greater harmonisation of national guarantee schemes, including definitions of guaranteed deposits and coverage rules. Local deposit insurance funds will end up wound-up into a single deposit insurance fund, centrally administered by a single board. This shift of authority from a national deposit insurance fund to a Eurozone deposit insurance fund will have, *prima facie*, little effect on the depositors themselves, as the definition of their rights will remain unchanged, and the administrative procedure put in place at the level of the EU deposit fund should not directly concern them, e.g., EDIS centralises existing deposit guarantee schemes in place in each Eurozone Member State. Whether the scheme is funded at a national level or at an EU-wide level does not directly impact the rights of the depositors. It does impact the effectiveness of their rights, in so far as they will have access to a deeper pocket. For banks, the perspective will be different, as banks will have to contribute at the end to a Eurozone-wide deposit guarantee fund, and therefore banks may need to pay additional contributions at the EU level, even if no bank from their Member State fails, in order to fund payouts to the benefit of depositors from banks that fail in another Member State. In addition, from a depositor point of view, perception is important, and its trust would probably be greater if the funds which will serve as a guarantee are held locally, at a national level, as opposed to at an EU level. In any event this would ensure easy and rapid access to the funds which indemnify the depositors, as well as ensuring an absence of conflict of laws that could undermine or render more complex the rights of the depositor from one specific EU country if the funds were held at EU level.[6]

1.4.2. The Rapporteur de Lange's 2016 Proposal

Rapporteur de Lange's draft report on the EDIS Proposal, dated 4 November 2016, is sceptical on the so-called EDIS proposal, and makes a different proposal, which would provide for a two-step plan at the Eurozone level:

- a reinsurance phase until 2024,
- followed by an insurance phase.

More specifically, de Lange's draft report supports a more cautious and conditional approach and changes the substance, with only two stages of implementation, and the timeline of the Commission proposal (2024 earliest). While a reinsurance period would be introduced only in 2019, the second and final stage (EDIS) would only be introduced after the fulfilment of four conditions, hence after:

- the date of application, or, where relevant, the expiry of the transposition period for the international standard for Total Loss Absorbing Capacity (TLAC), for Global Systemically Important Banks (G-SIBs), and for revised rules in relation to a minimum requirement for own funds and eligible liabilities (MREL), for all credit institutions affiliated to the participating DGSs;
- the date of application, or, where relevant, the expiry of the transposition period for an insolvency ranking for credit institutions, harmonised at Union level, in relation to subordinated debt;
- the date of application, or, where relevant, the expiry of the transposition period for a framework for business insolvency, harmonised at EU level, in relation to the early restructuring of companies in order to prevent and better handle the pressing issue of non-performing loans;

---

6 The European Forum of Deposit Insurers (EFDI) has published a report on technical considerations for the design of the European Deposit Insurance Scheme (EDIS), dated 19.11.2018, which provides, among other things, that a 'golden rule' should be introduced that EDIS at no stage should lead to a decrease in (expected) available financial means to cover individual DGS events compared to the situation before EDIS.

- the date of application, or, where relevant, the expiry of the transposition period for an act amending Regulation (EU) No. 575/2013 and Directive No. 2013/36/EU, resulting in a binding leverage ratio requirement.

There are therefore discussions at EU level as to the scheme that should be put in place. The current status of discussions at EU level raises the question as to which of those two ways, or which alternative way, should be considered.

1.4.3. Assessment of the Current Situation in Terms of an EU Deposit Guarantee Scheme and Proposals

1.4.3.1. Should the BRRD be Implemented Prior to an EU Deposit Guarantee Scheme?

Mutualising risks across the Eurozone implies that banking risks will be properly assessed and minimised. The reinsurance period should be long enough to enable banks to make progress in the area of risk reduction, and for additional EU regulation to be put in place in this regard. A legitimate question is to what extent there should not be full implementation of the BRRD prior to an EU deposit guarantee scheme, including the Minimum Requirement for own funds and Eligible Liabilities (MREL).

The counterpart of a Euro-zone mutualisation of bank risks through a European deposit reinsurance scheme could be that a Member State's deposit guarantee scheme may only benefit from EDIS if such Member State complies with EU rules. However, once the final phase of EDIS enters into force, it seems that the absence of compliance with EU rules and/or the absence of appropriate implementation of EU rules by a Member State will not impact the access of depositors of a bank in such a Member State to the EU-wide deposit guarantee fund. Some States and credit institutions may be at risk that the EDIS scheme results in having to prop-up lenders in more fiscally lax States. To mitigate this risk, the EU deposit guarantee scheme should be available only if the EU rules on deposit guarantees have been fully implemented, though that seems to have potential effect mainly during the reinsurance phase, as opposed to when EDIS will replace national deposit schemes. In other words, it may therefore seem preferable to give the benefit of the Eurozone deposit scheme prior to the final phase only if the banking package is fully implemented by Member States, e.g., CRD IV (Capital Requirement Directive), BRRD, as opposed to merely the Deposit Guarantee Directive. It seems legitimate that Member States fully comply with the EU legislative banking package, in order to benefit from the contemplated EU fund to be created via EDIS. As a consequence, it seems preferable that harmonisation be made at a maximum level, i.e., without leaving options at Member States' level, and that due implementation at National level be verified, prior to implementing a mutualised deposit guarantee scheme.

1.4.3.2. Should Banks be Subject to Supervision at EU Level if a Mutualisation of Deposit Guarantees is Put in Place?

If the deposit guarantee scheme is managed solely at EU level, i.e., in the event of full mutualisation, the supervision of the banks that are involved may also need be made at EU level, as opposed to merely being locally supervised. There would be some paradox to have an EU-managed deposit scheme fund, without direct supervision of financial institutions at the same level.

1.4.3.3. Should Resources Remain at Local Levels, as Opposed to EU Level, in Order to Strengthen Depositors' Confidence?

To ensure depositors confidence, the bulk of resources may need to remain local (it is uncertain that depositors' confidence will be strong if the resources are at EU level), and, at a strict minimum, a local entity should remain to facilitate communication with depositors, including in the language of depositors, and to better understand local products and regulations.

1.4.3.4. Is there a Need for Deeper Economic Analysis to Determine How to Best Reduce EU Market Fragmentation?

Funding of the Eurozone-wide deposit guarantee scheme and/or deposit guarantee scheme throughout the EU (not only the Eurozone) may need to be harmonised to reduce EU market fragmentation. Further economic analysis would be recommended in this regard. An EU-wide mechanism may seem more appropriate than a Eurozone one only in connection with a Banking Union perspective.

1.4.3.5. Should Reinsurance be Considered Instead of Mutualisation?

It is true that a euro might be worth less than another euro, depending on whether or not the depositor's guarantee is equivalent from one Member State to another. However, an option to be considered – as an alternative scheme to the current EDIS or de Lange's proposals – could be to offer resources at EU level, and to maintain current resources at local level; a reinsurance mechanism would permit cost sharing, as EDIS or its equivalent would then provide additional resources to national deposit schemes in the event of a short-fall. It is unclear to what extent any step further than a reinsurance phase, i.e., the first phase of the currently contemplated EDIS, should be considered at this stage of the Banking Union. A European deposit scheme could intervene in the event that a local deposit scheme falls short of resources, and that local banks have contributed *ex post* to the local guarantee scheme, as applicable, to offer an effective guarantee to depositors.

1.4.3.6. Should the European Deposit Guarantee Scheme be to the Benefit of EEA Depositors?

It is unclear why a European deposit guarantee mechanism should benefit solely depositors within the Eurozone, as opposed to throughout the EEA. Creating a full mutualisation scheme does not seem realistic within the EEA, due to the discrepancies between local jurisdictions' implementation of the EU Banking Union package as well as different types of local supervision. However, a mere reinsurance mechanism should be easier to set-up with a full EEA coverage. That seems to be one more advantage of a reinsurance mechanism.

1.4.3.7. Would an EU Deposit Guarantee Scheme be Beneficial to Individual Depositors?

From a depositor perspective, the EDIS regime does not seem, *prima facie*, to have direct impact on them, as they will continue to be able to access a deposit guarantee scheme for equivalent amounts to the ones currently available, and the geographical scope of coverage as the definition of covered deposits is not subject to significant changes. Even better, the EU-wide fund would be expected to have more cash available to guarantee depositors, and the funding of the EU-wide fund would benefit from a broader base of funding.

In addition, the board of such of an EU-wide fund could be held accountable to the benefit of depositors,[7] e.g., in the event of an administrative error or a wrongful error of the board of the EU-wide fund. EDIS will mainly have effect on the resourcing of the fund and the administration of the EU-wide fund, in light of the fact that the national deposit insurance funds will end up being replaced by a single EU-wide fund administered by a single board (though some administrative procedures may be handled at the national level).

1.4.4. The April 2024 Proposal

Rapporteur Karas presented a draft report at EU level on 4 March 2024, which was adopted in ECON on 18 April 2024, but this proposal for a regulation amending Regulation (EU) 806/2014 in order to establish a European Deposit Insurance Scheme is yet to be definitively voted.

---

7 A. Minto, above n. 5.

As stated in said amending regulation, financial support to reimburse depositors enhances the financial stability not only in the participating Member State concerned but also in other Member States, by preventing any spill-over of bank crises into non-participating Member States.

This amending regulation proposes to establish the first stage of a European Deposit Insurance Scheme ("EDIS I"), operating as a liquidity scheme that provides loans to participating deposit guarantee schemes. EDIS I would therefore establish a liquidity scheme that provides loans to the local deposit guarantee schemes in need of liquidity. It would be supported by a deposit insurance fund funded by other deposit guarantee schemes and, if needs be, by additional loans from the latter. The Single Resolution and Deposit Insurance Board would have decision-making, monitoring and enforcement powers. There will therefore be a central authority.

In order to limit the liability for the European Deposit Insurance Fund and to reduce moral hazard risk at the national level, assistance from the yet to be implemented Deposit Insurance Fund should only be requested if the participating deposit guarantee scheme has raised *ex ante* contributions and if such funds proved not to be sufficient.

If a Member State has received liquidity support, that liquidity support should be repaid within six years.

The first phase that the amending regulation aims to implement would thus ensure liquidity provisions to local deposit guarantee schemes in need, not risk sharing.

The next step would be to provide for regulations that would move from the provision of liquidity support to the establishment of a full insurance scheme with loss coverage. The aim is indeed to move towards the establishment of a full insurance scheme with loss coverage at a later stage.

2. DEPOSIT GUARANTEE MECHANISMS

2.1. SCOPE OF APPLICATION

2.1.1. Ratione Personae: Institutions Concerned

2.1.1.1. Credit Institutions

As a general principle, under applicable EU directives, every credit institution should join a deposit guarantee scheme. As a consequence, cooperative banks, for example, may not adhere solely to their own deposit protection scheme.

Pursuant to the EU Deposit Guarantee Directive No. 2014/49/EU (Article 4), all depositors should benefit from the deposit guarantee scheme, irrespective of their legal status or size. EU legislation does not permit exceptions for medium and large entities, as there was for example under the previous German law regime.

2.1.1.2. Branches

Foreign branches also fall within the scope of the obligation to become a member of a deposit guarantee scheme when they are located in a state which is a party to the European Economic Area Agreement, or if a similar agreement exists in the country where they are established.[8] Conversely, the branches of non-EEA institutions located in France or in other EEA states are only required to adhere to the Deposit Guarantee and Resolution Fund if they are not covered by a similar mechanism in their country of origin.[9]

2.1.2. Ratione Materiae

2.1.2.1. Type of Reimbursed Deposits

The 1994 EU Directive mentioned in section 1.2 above adopts a broad definition of deposit by defining it as

> any credit balance which results from funds left in an account or from temporary situations deriving from normal banking transactions, and which a credit institution must repay under the legal and contractual conditions applicable, and any debt evidenced by a certificate issued by a credit institution.[10]

It excludes from any repayment by guarantee schemes: (i) the deposits made by other credit institutions on their own behalf and for their own account, (ii) all instruments which would fall within the definition of 'own funds', and (iii) deposits arising out of transactions in connection with which there has been a criminal conviction for money laundering.[11] It also adds a list of optional exclusions[12] to such mandatory exclusions, left to the discretion of each State.

---

8 Arts. 14 and 15 of Directive 2014/49/EU of the European Parliament and of the Council of 16 April 2014 on deposit guarantee schemes [2014] OJ L 173/149; CRBF Regulation No. 99-05 of 09.07.1999, Art. 2.

9 Arts. 14 and 15 of Directive 2014/49/EU of the European Parliament and of the Council of 16 April 2014 on deposit guarantee schemes [2014] OJ L 173/149; CRBF Regulation No. 99-05 of 09.07.1999, Art. 3.

10 Art. 1(1) of Directive 94/19/EC of the European Parliament and of the Council of 30 May 1994 on deposit-guarantee schemes [1994] OJ L 135/5.

11 Art. 2 of Directive 94/19/EC of the European Parliament and of the Council of 30 May 1994 on deposit-guarantee schemes [1994] OJ L 135/5.

12 Art. 7(2) and Annex 1 of Directive 94/19/EC of the European Parliament and of the Council of 30 May 1994 on deposit-guarantee schemes [1994] OJ L 135/5.

The current definition of reimbursed deposits[13] has been harmonised at European level by the 2014 EU Directive (Article 2(1)(3)), and includes:

- Funds left in an account with a credit institution, which must be reimbursed to their holder under the legal, regulatory or contractual conditions applicable, and which do not constitute the pledge or collateral for an existing undertaking entered into by their holder towards the credit institution.
- Sums corresponding to ongoing payment transactions or resulting from temporary situations, carried out for the benefit of an identified individual, and deriving from normal banking transactions.

The exclusions, now also harmonised (Article 5(1) of the 2014 DGSD), include own funds, deposits arising out of transactions in connection with which there has been a criminal conviction for money laundering, anonymous deposits or any debt instrument issued by a credit institution.[14]

2.1.2.2. Covered Depositors

The benefit of the deposit guarantee is offered to depositors regardless of where the depositor is domiciled.[15] Depositors should be regarded as having a direct relationship with the deposit guarantee scheme, allowing the depositor to act as claimant via courts. The current exclusions include credit institutions and investment funds for deposits made on their own behalf and for their own account, finance companies and their parent companies, financial holding companies, electronic money institutions and payment institutions, insurance and reinsurance companies, collective investment undertakings, pension schemes, Member States and local authorities, and certain other institutions.

Credit institutions are required, pursuant to the EU framework, to inform depositors of the deposit guarantee scheme's guarantees, including the value and scope of protection offered. Confirmation that deposits qualify for the protection should even be provided to depositors on their statements of account. The level of information is provided for by EU legislation and the local implementation measures; it appeared that under certain local jurisdictions, e.g., Germany, it might prove difficult for depositors to determine precisely the scope of their right and of their protection. It may, however, be good practice

[13] Art. L. 312-4-1 I of the French Monetary and Financial Code.

[14] Art. 5(1) of Directive 2014/49/EU of the European Parliament and of the Council of 16 April 2014 on deposit guarantee schemes [2014] OJ L 173/149, and Art. L. 312-4-1 III of the French Monetary and Financial Code.

[15] Art. 2(1)(6) of Directive 2014/49/EU of the European Parliament and of the Council of 16 April 2014 on deposit guarantee schemes [2014] OJ L 173/149.

for banks to go beyond those EU information requirements, in order to ensure full understanding of the legal regime by depositors. Courts will have to decide to what extent banks could be bound by higher standards, in order to ensure full understanding by depositors of the legal regime applicable. It seems that a number of individual depositors are not aware that the non-covered deposits, i.e., deposits above EUR 100,000.00, may be used for bail-in purposes. More generally, if the legal regime is not the same for deposits above EUR 100,000.00 as for those below EUR 100,000.00, the characterisation would be better using two different terms, which could be covered deposits, and non-covered deposits. Characterisation implies a specific regime, if the amounts of cash deposited are all characterised as mere deposits, that may lead to confusion as to the two different regimes that may apply, depending whether the EUR 100,000.00 threshold is met or not.

2.2. FUNCTIONING OF THE DEPOSIT GUARANTEE SCHEME

2.2.1. Framework of the Compensation Mechanism

The 2014 EU Directive improved the governance of Member States' deposit guarantee systems by requiring sound governance practices,[16] as well as the implementation of stress tests.[17] It also reinforced their financial resources by providing that they must, following a 10-year transitional period, hold 0.8 per cent of the eligible deposits, and that they are able to demand extraordinary contributions up to the limit of 0.5 per cent of eligible deposits per year. The possibility for deposit-guarantee schemes to borrow funds within the European Union is also provided for.[18] All of these EU provisions have been transposed into French law.

2.2.2. Procedures for the Compensation of Depositors

In terms of deposit guarantees, the French Deposit Guarantee and Resolution Fund's involvement may be preventive (section 2.2.2.1) or remedial (section 2.2.2.2).

Depositors will benefit from a direct claim against the statutory deposit guarantee scheme,[19] as opposed to a merely indirect protection of the system

16 Art. 4(12) of Directive 2014/49/EU of the European Parliament and of the Council of 16 April 2014 on deposit guarantee schemes [2014] OJ L 173/149.
17 Ibid., Art. 4(10)–(11).
18 Ibid., Art. 12 - L. 312-8-2 V of the French Monetary and Financial Code.
19 Art. 9(1) of Directive 2014/49/EU of the European Parliament and of the Council of 16 April 2014 on deposit guarantee schemes [2014] OJ L 173/149.

that protects the credit institution itself, as was for example the case for German cooperative banks.

2.2.2.1. Preventive Procedure[20]

In the event that the situation of the credit institution should raise fears as to the unavailability of funds, a preventive procedure in order to improve the situation of the credit institution may be triggered on the proposal of the French Prudential Supervisory Authority (*Autorité de contrôle prudentiel et de resolution*, ACPR) leaving full discretionary power to the French Deposit Guarantee and Resolution Fund.

The French Deposit Guarantee and Resolution Fund sets out the conditions of its intervention after obtaining the opinion of the ACPR. It has several means of intervention[21] and may make its intervention subject to the total or partial transfer of the credit institution or to the extinction of its business activity, or may even acquire the institution's shares.

2.2.2.2. Remedial Procedure[22]

When it is established that the credit institution is no longer able to return the funds covered by the deposit guarantee either immediately or in the near future, the French Prudential Supervisory Authority may refer to the Deposit Guarantee and Resolution Fund in order to initiate the compensation mechanism.

Since the introduction of the first depositors' guarantee scheme pursuant to the 1994 EU Directive, the successive amendments to the scheme, both at European and at national level, have enhanced the protection of depositors in a number of ways.

(a) Shortening of Procedural Timelines

Pursuant to Directive No. 2014/49/EU, the deposit guarantee scheme needs to compensate the depositors after having established the unavailability of funds. From mid-2015 depositors are to be reimbursed within a maximum of 20 working days. This time limit will be gradually reduced to seven working days by 2024.

Depositors do not have to formally make a request to the deposit guarantee scheme, in light of the fact that the credit institution has to transmit the relevant information on deposits and depositors in due course. However, if not repaid in time, the depositor should make a formal request. Member States

20 Art. L. 312-5 II of the French Monetary and Financial Code.
21 Art. L. 312-4 IV of the French Monetary and Financial Code.
22 Art. L. 312-5 I of the French Monetary and Financial Code.

are authorised to provide for a statute of limitation, pursuant to which claims will not be accepted after a specified deadline.

(b) Harmonisation of the Level of Guarantee

The 1994 Directive required Member States to adopt a deposit-guarantee system providing for minimum compensation of ECU 20,000.00.[23] In France, such Directive had been transposed by providing for a minimum threshold of EUR 70,000.00 per depositor and per credit institution.[24]

The discretion left to each Member State to fix the minimum amount led to significant disparities between the Member States that the 2009 Directive intended to reduce by harmonising the threshold. It therefore raised the minimum threshold to EUR 50,000.00 from 30 June 2009, and provided for a fixed and harmonised level of guarantee at EUR 100,000.00, needing to be implemented prior to 31 December 2010.[25] The coverage level applies to aggregate deposits placed in the same credit institution, irrespective of the number and currency of the deposits.

(c) Ranking

Deposits rank higher in priority, during an insolvency period applicable to a credit institution, than claims of unsecured, non-preferred creditors (Article 108 of the 2014 EU Directive). The treatment of depositors in the creditor hierarchy has an impact on the costs incurred by the deposit insurer, as it can reduce the costs of liquidation (and of depositor reimbursement where subrogation is present). However, such preference does not preclude non-deposit creditors from taking action to better protect themselves too, e.g., shortening terms of maturity, taking collaterals, which would off-set the benefit of the statutory ranking of depositors.

(d) Subrogation of Rights

The deposit guarantee scheme, both in the remedial and the preventive procedure, is subrogated to the rights of the beneficiaries of its intervention in direct proportion to the sums it has paid, and may bring any action for damages against the executives, shareholders and holders of securities.[26] Thus, the deposit guarantee scheme will be entitled to receive the benefit of any

---

23 Art. 7(1) Directive 94/19/EC of the European Parliament and of the Council of 30 May 1994 on deposit-guarantee schemes [1994] OJ L 135/5.

24 CRBF Regulation No. 99-05 of 09.07.1999, Art. 5.

25 Art. 6(1) of Directive 2014/49/EU of the European Parliament and of the Council of 16 April 2014 on deposit guarantee schemes [2014] OJ L 173/149.

26 Art. 9(2) of Directive 2014/49/EU of the European Parliament and of the Council of 16 April 2014 on deposit guarantee schemes [2014] OJ L 173/149. For the French implementation, see: Art. L. 312-6 of the French Monetary and Financial Code.

repayments that the depositor would have been entitled to under the insolvency of the credit institution.

(e) Islamic Banking

The Islamic financial services industry has been growing rapidly over the past few years in certain EU jurisdictions. Islamic deposits should comply with Islamic principles. Deposit insurance coverage for the Islamic banking sector should not necessarily be automatic, as Sharia principles may imply that a risk be taken, and therefore that there should not be a full safety-net.

(f) Excluded Deposits

The EU legislation excluded certain unsecured liability from the scope of application of the bail-in tool: in order to protect holders of covered deposits, the bail-in tool does not apply to those deposits that are protected under the Deposit Guarantee Directive No. 2014/49/EU.[27] Other eligible deposits are potentially available for loss absorbency purposes, including deposits over EUR 100,000.00.[28] The fact that two legal regimes will apply depending on the amount of cash deposited in a bank account should imply that the characterisation be different, in order for depositors to distinguish the two applicable legal regimes more easily.

This means that individuals having deposits of more than EUR 100,000.00, as well as companies above the same threshold, at a bank should consider alternative means in order to protect their deposits. One measure could be to open accounts at different banks in order to avoid crossing the EUR 100,000.00

27 Arts. 31 and 32 of Directive 2014/59/EU of the European Parliament and of the Council of 15 May 2014 establishing a framework for the recovery and resolution of credit institutions and investment firms and amending Council Directive 82/891/EEC, and Directives 2001/24/EC, 2002/47/EC, 2004/25/EC, 2007/36/EC, 2011/35/EU, 2012/30/EU and 2013/36/EU, and Regulations (EU) No. 1093/2010 and (EU) No. 648/2012, of the European Parliament and of the Council [2014] OJ L 173/190, and Art. 18 of Regulation (EU) No. 806/2014 of the European Parliament and of the Council of 15 July 2014 establishing uniform rules and a uniform procedure for the resolution of credit institutions and certain investment firms in the framework of a Single Resolution Mechanism and a Single Resolution Fund and amending Regulation (EU) No. 1093/2010 [2014] OJ L 225/1.

28 See also: Art. 44(3) of Directive 2014/59/EU of the European Parliament and of the Council of 15 May 2014 establishing a framework for the recovery and resolution of credit institutions and investment firms and amending Council Directive 82/891/EEC, and Directives 2001/24/EC, 2002/47/EC, 2004/25/EC, 2007/36/EC, 2011/35/EU, 2012/30/EU and 2013/36/EU, and Regulations (EU) No. 1093/2010 and (EU) No. 648/2012, of the European Parliament and of the Council [2014] OJ L 173/190, and Art. 27(3) of Regulation (EU) No. 806/2014 of the European Parliament and of the Council of 15 July 2014 establishing uniform rules and a uniform procedure for the resolution of credit institutions and certain investment firms in the framework of a Single Resolution Mechanism and a Single Resolution Fund and amending Regulation (EU) No. 1093/2010 [2014] OJ L 225/1. The latter articles provide that resolution authorities may choose, under certain circumstances, to exclude certain liabilities from the bail-in procedure. The various conditions that need to be met in order to proceed should limit any arbitrary decision by a resolution authority.

threshold. They may also prefer to invest their deposit in state-bonds, which are deemed to be at low risk.

(g) Critical Analysis of the Legal Regime Applicable to Deposits

Article 44(2) of the so-called BRRD provides for the scope of bail-in tools. It provides, among other things, that resolution authorities shall not exercise the write-down or conversion powers in relation to covered deposits whether they are governed by the law of a Member State or of a third country.

Investors are at risk when they invest as shareholders. Shareholders are at risk that they get no return on their investment, and ultimately that their investment is not worth any money. Asking shareholders of a bank to be diluted in connection with a bail-out does not seem outrageous, however, in light of the fact that the value of their shares is worth little if anything when the bank is subject to resolution procedures.

Depositors, which are a type of lender to the benefit of the bank, need to be adequately protected. The EU frameworks provides that non-covered depositors are at risk of being subject to bail-in measures, prior to any State Aid. In light of the asymmetry of information, of the lack of understanding by depositors – who are, once again, a type of lender –, of the complexity of financial institutions' balance sheets, and in light of the fact that most depositors are unable to distinguish between safe and unsafe banks, depositors may never adequately assess the risk that their deposit will be used in connection with a bail-in procedure, being unable to assess the risk of a resolution procedure to be applied to a financial institution.

Depositors of the failing financial institutions are at risk of having bail-in measures applied, whereas financial contributions are a burden for all depositors/tax payers in connection with a bail-out, and, to some extent, it may – *prima facie* – seem fairer to have all tax payers contribute in proportion to their tax level, as all tax payers will then bear such a burden as opposed to only some of them in connection with a bail-in. The main and major drawback of such proposal is, however, keeping a link with the State and National Treasuries, which proved during the 2007–2009 financial crisis to have far more drawbacks than advantages.

3. CONCLUSION

The effectiveness of a deposit insurance system is influenced by the environment in which it operates, e.g., prudential regulation, supervision, and resolution, and not only by its design features. The SSM seems inconceivable without an SRM and a harmonised deposit scheme framework. The EU banking reform package aims to complete the reforms that the EU implemented in the wake of the financial crisis, which made the financial system more stable and resilient. The

23 November 2016 'EDIS' proposal of the EU Commission follows that route. However, in light of the difficulty of having a mutualised deposit guarantee scheme such as the one proposed by the contemplated EDIS scheme, it seems preferable to implement a reinsurance deposit guarantee scheme in the near future, in order to offer a deeper pocket for the benefit of depositors without having some banks consider that they would be treated unfairly as compared to banks located in more fiscally lax states. Such reinsurance scheme would not necessarily be limited to the benefit of Eurozone depositors but rather operate throughout the EU. The April 2024 EDIS I proposal to amend the relevant regulation is a first step, out of three, to obtain a full reinsurance scheme; at this stage, it only proposes a liquidity support to the benefit of local deposit guarantee schemes; it may though be a limited but needed first step in order for the banking harmonisation to move forward. Once a full harmonisation of the EU banking package has been tested, once the banking rules have been fully implemented throughout Member States, and once supervision of banks at the EU level has been proven effective, then a step further than reinsurance should be considered. At this stage, the Banking Union will be incomplete. It seems necessary to go one step further with respect to deposit guarantee schemes, and a reinsurance mechanism at the EU level, which would provide extra-funding to national deposit guarantee schemes, seems to be one easy way forward, which should prove useful to help break the link between the failure of a systemic bank and a National Treasury crisis.

CHAPTER 5

CIVIL LIABILITY OF NATIONAL FINANCIAL SUPERVISORY AUTHORITIES

Ewa Bagińska

1. INTRODUCTION[1]

The problem of liability of national financial supervisory authorities (FSAs) transcends the classical division between public and private law. The duties of the authorities are regulated by public law, but liability claims by aggrieved persons are rooted in private law. Entitlement to private law remedies is not limited to individuals such as depositors and embraces other actors in the financial markets (banks, insurers, stock exchange, etc.) which can suffer damage to reputation or to their financial position in the market, and possibly their shareholders.[2]

---

[1] An earlier and abridged version of this chapter was published as E. Bagińska, 'Liability in Tort of Financial Supervisory Authorities – a comparative analysis' (2018) 23 *Studia Iuridica Toruniensia* 11–30. This unabridged version has also been updated.

[2] R.J. Dijkstra, 'Is limiting financial supervisory liability a way to prevent defensive conduct? The outcome of a European survey' (2017) 43 *European Journal of Law and Economics* 59, 60 et seq.

In recent years European courts have increasingly admitted the possibility of seeking civil remedies, specifically based on tort law, against FSAs and/or the state.[3] The nature of the liability of FSAs is tortuous, as a contractual relationship between a public authority and an injured individual cannot be established. This contribution reviews the case law and provides a theoretical framework for such claims. Latest comparative research by R.J. Dijkstra has shown that no common approach to financial supervisory liability exists in the EU Member States.[4] Nevertheless, we should try to identify some convergences or at least common trends in the present developments.

2. PUBLIC AUTHORITY LIABILITY MATRIX

We should begin with a sketch of the current state of the liability of public authorities in Europe.[5] Depending on the national system, the rules on liability of public authorities belong to either the private or public law domain, or to both. Thus, the problem discussed here may be approached from different angles: civil law, constitutional law, administrative law and EU law. In the vast majority of European systems, public authority liability is presently governed by special rules that are stricter than the ordinary rules of tort liability. Only the common law countries have, in principle, retained uniform rules of liability for public and private persons. The classification (whether private or public law), however, does not have a great influence on the substance of the liability question, its prerequisites and limitations.[6]

Moreover, because a claim for compensation always remains a civil law claim,[7] its core elements are common for most of the legal systems: an event giving rise to liability, damage and causation. Additional requirements can flow

---

[3] R.J. Dijkstra, 'Liability of Financial Supervisory Authorities in the European Union' (2012) 3 *Journal of European Tort Law* 346.

[4] R.J. Dijkstra, above n. 3, 368–369.

[5] J. Bell and A. Bradley, 'Governmental liability: a comparative study' in D. Fairgrieve, M. Andenas and J. Bell (eds.), *Tort liability of public authorities in comparative perspective*, BIICL, London 2002, and D. Fairgrieve, 'State liability in tort. A comparative law study' in K. Oliphant (ed.), *The Liability of Public Authorities in Comparative Perspective*, Intersentia, Cambridge 2016.

[6] E. Bagińska, *Odpowiedzialność odszkodowawcza za wykonywanie władzy publicznej*, C.H. Beck, Warszawa 2006, p. 125, K. Oliphant, 'The liability of public authorities in comparative perspective' in K. Oliphant (ed.), *The Liability of Public Authorities in Comparative Perspective*, Intersentia, Cambridge 2016, p. 849, p. 881.

[7] C. Harlow, 'State liability: problem without solution' (1995) 6 *National Journal of Constitutional Law* 67, 70.

from the particularisation of special rules, for example in cases of the liability of the judiciary or for the legislative functions, if admitted.[8]

Despite *prima facie* differences in the scope of public authority liability in the main legal systems, general objectivisation and extension of public authority liability should be noted. On the one hand, liability can be triggered by illegal conduct; hence anyone's negligence is not subject to scrutiny. On the other hand, albeit quite exceptionally, subjective fault still plays a role in cases of specific governmental activities, where usually the proof of gross negligence is required. As will be shown below, the latter limitation of liability is clearly accepted in the sphere of regulatory banking and financial activities. Accordingly, a breach of public rules or failure to fulfil public tasks must be intentional or grossly unreasonable in order to trigger liability, assuming that the other elements of a tort claim have been met.

The nature of damage suffered by the injured persons in the discussed context is typically characterised as pure economic loss. This is another argument used by European courts to limit public authority liability, as public resources are usually deficient (section 4.2 below). We should note, however, that an important exclusion of the liability of FSAs concerns losses that have been or could have been covered by a deposit guarantee fund or scheme.

Finally, there may arise a question of legal standing. Should a claimant sue the institution itself or the state which stands behind the institution? The organisation of domestic supervisory systems for financial markets is not uniform in Europe; the legal nature of the supervisors and their connection to the state budget varies.[9] In many continental legal systems, a public supervisory authority that has its own legal capacity and budget should be sued. To illustrate, in Poland, as a result of the evolution of the supervisory system, a consolidated supervision model was adopted for all financial market sectors. The supervision authority used to be the Financial Supervision Commission (KNF), which had a *statio fisci* status. The status of KNF changed as of 1 January 2019.[10] Pursuant to Article 3(1) of the Financial Market Supervision Act, the state's legal person is the Office of the Financial Supervision Authority (*Urząd Komisji Nadzoru Finansowego, UKNF*), and the Financial Supervision

---

8 Liability in respect of primary and secondary legislation has been admitted in Belgium, Greece, Portugal, Poland.

9 There can be state administrative bodies with varying degrees of dependence on the government, state self-regulatory bodies that include representatives of brokers and investors, or self-regulatory bodies of financial market participants. Budgetary separation is recommended by the Financial Sector Assessment Programme by the IMF and the World Bank: https://www.imf.org/external/np/fsap/fssa.aspx.

10 Act of 09.11.2018 amending certain acts in connection with the strengthening of supervision over the financial market and the protection of investors in that market, *Official Journal* [*Dziennik Ustaw*] 2018, item 2243.

Commission itself was granted the status of an organ (named the KNF Board) of this state legal person.

Further problems arise in the systems which have shifted from the exclusive liability of the individual servant to the joint liability of the public institution by which the servant was engaged, and frequently to the exclusive liability of that institution.[11] However, even in those systems, where, as a matter of policy, liability is channelled onto a public institution, the latter is granted a limited right of recourse against the servant, in particular where they acted with gross negligence or intent. As might be expected, the institution's deep pockets attract claims even where the servant bears notional joint liability.[12]

It is clear from the above that a civil servant of a financial supervisory authority will most likely not be sued personally, although, it cannot be excluded that the institution will in turn seek recourse by way of indemnity for damages already paid.

Interestingly, what can make the question of who to sue more complicated, also in the context of causation (see section 4.3 below), is the use of professional auditors by a supervising body. The problem is illustrated by an Austrian case of 2003.[13] Under the facts of the case, the plaintiffs, who had deposits or saving accounts with a bank that went bankrupt, brought an action for a declaratory judgment establishing the liability of the Republic of Austria for the loss suffered as a consequence of the bankruptcy. The plaintiffs argued that the bankruptcy and the ensuing anticipated loss was caused by insufficient banking supervision by the state (the Federal Ministry of Finance). According to the findings, the criminal conduct of two executives and a secretary led to the bankruptcy. Their malversation was not detectable for the bank auditor or the organs of the banking supervision authority. However, a properly organised and functioning internal control would, most probably, have uncovered the malversation. Had the bank auditor informed the supervisory organs appropriately about the inadequately organised internal control, the bank's bankruptcy could very probably have been avoided. In this case the bank auditor had been mandated contractually by the bank and not by the Ministry of Finance. The Austrian Supreme Court held that banking auditors should be treated as state organs, because when they are appointed[14] they support the supervisory authority, get

---

[11] K. Oliphant, The liability of public authorities in comparative perspective', above n. 6, p. 868.

[12] Ibid.

[13] Oberster Gerichtshof (Supreme Court) (OGH), 25.03.2003, 1 Ob 188/02g, [2003] ecolex, 416, B.C. Steininger, 'Austria' in H. Koziol and B.C. Steininger (eds.), *European Tort Law 2003*, Springer, Vienna/New York 2004, p. 34 nos. 27–40, 40–41.

[14] In Austria there are two situations where the banking supervision authority calls upon the bank auditor to fulfil its duties. The first one imposes a duty on a bank auditor to notify the supervision authority of certain facts, especially violations of regulations relevant for banking supervision. Secondly, the bank auditor is obliged to prepare a banking supervisory audit report and to present this report to the competent organs.

involved in the fulfilment of the banking supervision authority's duties and, therefore, have to be qualified as a state organ.[15]

3. AN EVENT GIVING RISE TO NATIONAL FINANCIAL SUPERVISORY AUTHORITIES' LIABILITY

3.1. EXERCISING REGULATORY AND SUPERVISORY POWERS

Both the regulation of a financial market (setting rules) and the supervision over it (by which we mean monitoring and enforcement of rules) are conduct which can result in someone's unwanted losses and thus lead to liability. Most often individuals suffer from omissions by supervising authorities, which in themselves enjoy a wide margin of discretion in taking actions and implementing measures. Other (institutional) market actors are exposed if the authorities interfere with their business activities or overreact to certain facts. It is underlined in the doctrine that sometimes FSAs seem to have fallen short of fulfilling their statutory obligation of preventing reckless market conduct in order to diminish improper financial risks.[16]

In general, as noted earlier, the contemporary model of public authority liability in Europe, and specifically in newly democratic states, is liability based on unlawfulness (public illegality, wrongfulness). The objective standard is rooted in constitutional values and principles. However, the sphere of application of the objective standard of liability of public authorities sometimes excludes licensing and supervisory activities, especially those performed by financial regulators. First and foremost, it is argued that regulatory and supervisory powers are regarded as non-justiciable.[17] Administrative decision-makers are allowed a degree of discretion in the exercise of their powers and the courts cannot second-guess their decision;[18] deciding on liability would

15 B. Steininger, ibid., above n. 13, p. 41.

16 E. Karner, 'Tort Law and the Financial Crisis: Basic Questions' (2013) 4 *Journal of European Tort Law* 125.

17 Except for countries, such as France, where a finding of public law illegality is sufficient to establish faute, consideration of discretion and justiciability is obviated. However, for financial regulators faute lourde is the standard. See D. Fairgrieve and F. Lichere, 'The liability of public authorities in France' in K. Oliphant (ed.), *The Liability of Public Authorities in Comparative Perspective*, Intersentia, Cambridge 2016, pp. 155, 165 et seq.

18 The English courts debate in each case over the likely economic effects of establishing the cause of action through expanding the duty of care of public bodies. See *Dorset Yacht Co. v. Home Office* [1970] AC 1004, *Anns v. Merton London Borough Council* [1978] AC 728, *Stovin v. Wise* [1996] AC 923 (Lord Hoffman), *Three Rivers District Council v. Bank of England III* [2000] 2 WLR 1220.

mean infringing on the administrative organ's sphere of discretion.[19] As will be elaborated on below, in some countries this argument leads to statutory immunity of FSAs.

In practice, the problem of using discretionary powers in the financial market can be illustrated by a Spanish case concerning the National Securities Market Commission's (CNMV) alleged failure to discharge statutory duties on the occasion of the bankruptcy of investment agencies.[20] Spanish case law assumes that the current legislation does not confer upon the CNMV absolute powers of immediate inspection and intervention, or even power to suspend activities, when there is news or indication that irregularities in an investment agency are occurring. The Spanish Supreme Court held that the CNMV had the discretion required to assess the circumstances of the case according to its experience and expertise. A prudent exercise of power has to take account of the possible effect of a planned action on the stock market, on which the company operates. 'It is not considered reasonable for the CNMV to take drastic measures without having made the necessary checks or without having given the managers the opportunity to explain themselves and, if necessary, to rectify procedures'.[21] Hence, technical discretion and attention to the likely impact of the actions of public authorities on the economic or social area in question influence the assessment of liability.

3.2. NO UNIFORM STANDARD OF LIABILITY – THE EVOLUTION OF CASE LAW

Comparative research reveals that the standard of liability of national FSAs, as shaped by legislation and case law, seems to vary significantly. The liability can be based on simple negligence in supervision (Denmark, Sweden, Hungary), unlawfulness (Czech Republic, Poland,[22] Greece, Spain), gross negligence (France, Belgium, Italy, Croatia) and solely intent (UK, Ireland, the Netherlands, Bulgaria, Malta, Estonia). In some countries liability has *de facto* been abolished (Germany, Austria).[23] Despite this variety in the approaches

19 K. Oliphant, 'The liability of public authorities in comparative perspective', above n. 6, p. 866.

20 STS judgment of 16.05.2008, RJ 2008/2756, M. Martin-Casals and J. Ribot, 'The liability of public authorities in Spain' in K. Oliphant (ed.), *The Liability of Public Authorities in Comparative Perspective*, Intersentia, Cambridge 2016, pp. 463, 488 et seq. See also STS 20.12.2011 (RJ 2012\758).

21 M. Martin-Casals and J. Ribot, ibid., 489 no 83.

22 See in more detail E. Bagińska, 'Podstawy odpowiedzialności cywilnej krajowych organów nadzoru finansowego w świetle doświadczeń zagranicznych' (2019) *Wiadomości Ubezpieczeniowe* 1-22, doi.org/10.33995/wu2019.1.1 [in Polish].

23 R.J. Dijkstra, 'Liability of Financial Supervisory Authorities in the European Union', above n. 3, 370 et seq.

to the preliminary condition of liability (unlawfulness/fault), negligent supervision (simple negligence/fault) or maladministration[24] will likely not be sufficient to hold the state or the FSA itself liable in damages in most European jurisdictions. A plaintiff will have to prove gross negligence (*culpa lata*) or bad faith, which means that discretionary activities remaining within the parameters of reasonableness will not trigger liability.[25]

Gross negligence depicts a situation where the given FSA should have uncovered fraud or other irregularities at the institution,[26] or should have recognised signs of financial difficulties, or should have acted more decisively (e.g. revoke a licence, impose other sanctions) applying the ordinary standard of care. Bad faith, on the other hand, is a notion unorthodox to continental civil law systems, which prevails in common law. By 'bad faith' continental lawyers would most likely understand a situation that is quite close to intentional infliction of damage.[27]

An interesting evolution of the liability standard is to be observed in those countries where public authority liability is based on general liability rules.[28] Two illustrations – from the Netherlands and Italy – are worthy of closer analysis.

In the Netherlands, before 2012, the general tort liability clause contained in Article 6:162 of the Dutch civil code was held applicable to the liability of financial authorities. The Dutch Supreme Court (*Hoge Raad*) took this position first in 2006 in its *Vie d'Or* judgment,[29] which concerned the liability of the insurers' supervising authority, and later in the judgment *X v. Autoriteit Financiële Markten* (2014).[30]

In *Vie d'Or* case, the lawsuit involved claims of several persons who incurred loss when their life insurance company had gone bankrupt. The claims were subrogated to a foundation who sued the Insurance Chamber – an independent

24 The word 'maladministration' is used to embrace various forms of unreasonable (wrongful) conduct, negligent supervision – simple negligence/fault.

25 M Martin-Casals and J. Ribot, 'The Liability of Public Authorities in Spain', above n. 20, 483.

26 See e.g. *Three Rivers District Council v. Bank of England III* [2000] 2 WLR 1220.

27 D. Nolan, 'The Liability of Financial Supervisory Authorities' (2013) 4 *Journal of European Tort Law* 190, 191.

28 Equivalent in the English common law is the tort of misfeasance in public office. B.S. Markesinis, J.P. Auby, D. Coester-Waltjen and S. Deakin, *Tortious liability of Statutory Bodies: A Comparative and Economic Analysis of Five English Cases*, Hart Publishing, Oxford-Portland OR 1999, pp. 45–54, 87, J. Murphy, *Misfeasance in a Public Office: A Tort Law Misfit?* (2012) 32 *Oxford Journal of Legal Studies (OJLS)* 51.

29 Judgment of 13.10.2006, NJ 2008, 527, commented by M.G. Faure and T. Hartlief, 'The Netherlands' in H. Koziol and B.C. Steininger (eds.), *European Tort Law 2007*, Springer, Vienna/New York 2008, 416, nos. 11-13.

30 Judgment of 21.11.2014, *X v. Autoriteit Financiële Markten*, RvdW 2014, 1310, J.M. Emaus and A.L.M. Keirse, 'The Netherlands' in E. Karner and B.C. Steininger (eds.), *European Tort Law 2014*, Springer, Vienna/New York 2015, 429 et seq.

supervisory authority –, the accountants, and the actuary involved. The basis of the claim against the Insurance Chamber was its failure to exercise the duty of supervision with reasonable care and to take early measures to protect the claimant's interests. The *Hoge Raad* held that the crucial question was whether the supervisory authority under the circumstances at the time of the decision and with the information available to it at that moment could reasonably have come to its decision. The Court thus rejected the hindsight test. The defendant authority was under a duty to take effective measures, and if they failed, other measures should have been implemented. However, because the authority had been granted a large margin of discretion when taking decisions and intervening in insurance companies, the courts' power to investigate and test those decisions should be curbed.[31]

Several years later, in 2014, the *Hoge Raad* applied a similar approach to test the reasonableness of the conduct of banking authorities. In the *Autoriteit Financiële Markten* case the plaintiff concluded a deposit agreement with DSB Bank in 2008. The plaintiff had made sure that the bank had a licence and had also read the annual accounts before she deposited EUR 500,000. Furthermore, she had read the bank's brochure on 'subordinated deposits', with an explanation of 'subordinated' (i.e. not covered by the deposit insurance). DSB Bank went bankrupt in October 2009. The Minister of Finance held an inquiry into the situation at the DSB Bank, the actions taken by the Central Bank (*De Nederlandsche Bank*) and the regulator in this regard, as well as into the cooperation between the two financial institutions. The plaintiff alleged that the regulator failed to fulfil the duties under the relevant laws and that it had acted unlawfully against her and was thus liable for the damage inflicted. The court of appeal held that the rules of the Financial Supervision Act on disclosure of information had not been violated by DSB Bank. Secondly, the regulator, had it conducted research on subordinated deposits in 2008, would not have acted unlawfully if it had decided not to oblige DSB Bank to provide potential clients with certain information. The Hoge Raad agreed with both arguments – lack of unlawfulness and lack of *causa sine qua non* – and upheld the court of appeal's judgment. The Court stated that that it is not sufficient to argue that the regulator did not prevent the damage. The Court also underlined the so-called 'regulators' dilemma'. One of the aims of the FSA is to protect the clients' interests in the best way it can. But taking measures to enforce compliance with legal rules may at the same time hurt the financial institution's business. In this regard, the Court's inquiry should be whether the regulator actually contributed to the development of the dilemma.[32]

---

31 Ibid.

32 Ibid., nos. 62–66.

The depicted evolution of case law has led to the reduction of the liability of financial supervisory authorities by the legislator. Since 1 July 2012 *Autoriteit Financiële Markten* and the Dutch Central Bank are liable for intentional acts only.[33]

Let us now turn to the example of Italy, and the judgment of the Italian Supreme Court (*Corte di Cassazione*) of 3 March 2001 (no. 3132[34]). Before handing down this high-profile precedent the *Corte di Cassazione* had denied civil liability of the Italian FSA – the Securities and Investments Board (*Commissione Nazionale per la Società e la Borsa*, hereafter CONSOB), arguing that the investors did not have any claims based on a legally protected interest. The 2001 case involved claims of consumers who had underwritten a public offer concerning the purchase of shares of a limited liability company. The press published information concerning irregularities committed by the issuing company (false information in the prospectus). Despite the initial success of the public offer the company went bankrupt a couple of years later. The investors then demanded damages from CONSOB for failure to control the truthfulness of the information contained in the prospectus. The claimants argued that they had been wrongly induced to subscribe to the proposal. A diligent analysis of the document filed with CONSOB would have been sufficient to discover the irregularities. The *Corte di Cassazione* held that the investors had a subjective right to sue CONSOB in tort in the event that it had failed to use its statutory powers in order to prevent the publication of false information in a prospectus. CONSOB had a duty to undertake both preventive and subsequent verification of the prospectus, a duty to eventually stop the transaction and, if necessary, to make inspections of the supervised market. Therefore, the claimants could invoke the general clause of tort liability (Article 2043 of the Italian Civil Code). Interestingly, the prospectus contained terms purporting to exonerate CONSOB from liability for non-discovered breaches of law, which was declared null and void by the Court.[35]

Similarly to the Dutch response, the Italian legislator reacted to the above precedent by reducing the liability of FSAs to cases of gross negligence or intention.[36]

---

33 Based on the *Wet aansprakelijkheidsbeperking DNB en AFM*, see J. Emaus and A. Keirse, 'The Netherlands' in E. Karner and B.C. Steininger (eds.), *European Tort Law 2012*, Springer, Vienna/New York 2013, pp. 469, 470, nos. 5–9.

34 E. Navarretta and E. Bargelli, 'Italy' in H. Koziol and B.C. Steininger (eds.), *European Tort Law 2001*, Springer, Wien/New York 2002, p. 347 nos. 47–48.

35 A. Scarso, 'Tortious liability of regulatory authorities' in E. Karner and B.C. Steininger (eds.), *European Tort Law 2005*, Springer, Wien/New York 2006, pp. 94, 102–105.

36 Art. 24(6) of the Law 28 of December 2005.

In a subsequent case of 23 March 2011 (no. 6681[37]), the *Corte di Cassazione* confirmed that CONSOB is not only a supervisory authority, but the objective of its work is also protecting private and national investments. In consequence, CONSOB carries fault-based liability for the grossly negligent omission to comply with the duty to protect private and national savings, which is covered by the Italian Constitution (Article 47). In the given case 130 investors lost the investments they made in the period 1990–1992 with two financial intermediary companies (*Società Servici Finanziari Amministrativi*) which afterwards were compulsorily wound up. In 1997 the investors brought a tort action for damages against CONSOB, alleging that it had allowed the above-mentioned companies to provide financial services notwithstanding several irregularities in their accounts, and, after subsequent inspections, it had omitted to take the necessary measures to protect investors. The court of appeal awarded compensation, but CONSOB appealed to the Cassation Court. The latter ruled that even if the investment contracts were concluded between 1990 and 1992, when the original statute no. 216/1974 granted CONSOB only limited power to supervise companies, the tort committed by CONSOB had continuing and permanent harmful effects. As a consequence, the investments were subject to the statute, which imposed upon CONSOB the duty to supervise companies in the interests of investors. Interestingly, the Court held that CONSOB was not only obliged to comply with standards of conduct stated in legislation on financial markets, but was also subject to Article 2043 of the Italian Civil Code. As a consequence, the appeal of CONSOB was dismissed.

3.3. SELECTED LEGISLATIVE CHOICES LIMITING OR EXCLUDING LIABILITY

In other countries the legislature also stood by the central supervisory organs and introduced the criteria of gross negligence and /or intent (or bad faith) to limit their potential liability in damages. At least with regard to the banking services sector, this policy is in line with Principle 2 of Basel Committee on Banking Supervision's Core Principles for Effective Banking Supervision (2012),[38] which recommends (quite self-explanatory) legal protection of supervisors and their staff through immunity regarding actions/omissions taken in good faith. This standard of liability is specific to the common law

---

37 Judgment of 23.03.2011, no. 6681, E. Bargelli, 'Italy' in K. Oliphant and B.C. Steininger (eds.), *European Tort Law 2011*, Springer, Vienna/New York 2012, pp. 339, 346, nos. 30–38.

38 Available at: www.bis.org/publ/bcbs230.pdf. Principle 2, at point 9 of 'essential criteria' provides: 'Laws provide protection to the supervisor and its staff against lawsuits for actions taken and/or omissions made while discharging their duties in good faith. The supervisor and its staff are adequately protected against the costs of defending their actions and/or omissions made while discharging their duties in good faith.'

jurisdictions. The enactment of an immunity or essential restriction on liability in a few civil law countries led to the domino effect in other countries where many internationally operating large financial institutions were located and remained subject to general tort liability rules with no cap or limitations.[39]

This notwithstanding, the discussed regulatory trend has also been marked in countries that are not centres of international financial business, such as Poland, Lithuania and Croatia, among others.[40]

In accordance with Article 133(4) of the Act of 29 August 1997 on Banking Law, the Polish Financial Supervision Authority and persons performing banking supervision shall not be liable for damage resulting from actions or the omission thereof that are in compliance with the provisions of the law and which are exercised by the Financial Supervision Authority when supervising the activities of banks, branches, and representatives of foreign banks and branches of credit institutions.[41]

In Lithuania, the Law on financial sustainability provides that the court, having investigated a claim concerning the acts of the Lithuanian government, an institution authorised by it, the Bank of Lithuania or other institutions has the right to award compensation for damage. The court cannot affect the validity of the act, nor can it order specific performance resulting in cancellation or suspension of the act of supervision.[42] In 2015 a new Article 45 of the Law on the Bank of Lithuania made a shift in the standard of liability from any kind of fault to intent or gross negligence.[43]

The Croatian Credit Institutions Act no. 159/2013 provides for the exclusion of liability of the Croatian National Bank, its employees and members of its Council for damage caused in the course of exercising their duties according to this Act, unless it can be proven that damage was caused with intent or gross

---

39 M. Faure and T. Hartlief, 'The Netherlands' in H. Koziol and BC Steininger (eds.), *European Tort Law 2007*, Springer, Wien/New York 2008, p. 419, no. 7.

40 The bad faith standard (or intent), has also been introduced in Bulgaria, Malta and Estonia. See R.J. Dijkstra, 'Liability of Financial Supervisory Authorities in the European Union', above n. 3, 370.

41 Consolidated text: Journal of Laws of 2022, item 2324.

42 S. Selelionyte-Drukteiniene and L. Saltinyte, 'Lithuania' in K. Olphant and B.C. Steininger (eds.), *European Tort Law 2011*, Springer, Vienna/New York 2012, p. 386, nos. 6–10.

43 S. Selelionyte-Drukteiniene and L. Saltinyte, 'Lithuania' in E. Karner and B.C. Steininger (eds.), *European Tort Law 2015*, Springer, Vienna/New York 2016, p. 349, no. 1 et seq.

negligence.[44] The Capital Market Act no. 65/2018,[45] which comprehensively regulated liability for damage arising from conduct of various actors in capital markets, similarly limited the liability of the Croatian Financial Services Supervisory Agency, and of the Ministry of Finance as well as of their employees. The immunity of the Croatian supervisory agency and its employees concerns the accuracy or comprehensiveness of prospectus information.

Exceptionally the approach of German and Austrian legislators is to confer on FSAs complete immunity from liability toward third parties. The absence of liability is partially due to the theoretical restraints which flow from the design of the law of civil liability in those countries (see below at section 4.1), and partially due to the intervention of the legislator. The respective legislators introduced stipulations that supervisors owe their duties to the public at large rather than to individual depositors. In consequence, in the absence of a specific duty to protect individual interests, financial supervisors (or the state) cannot be held liable for any pecuniary losses that depositors (or shareholders) may suffer as a result of the supervisors' deficient performance of their public law tasks.

In Germany, the revision of the law was a reaction to the judgment of the *Bundesgerichtshof* (BGH) of 15 February 1979,[46] in which the Court held that the rules of conduct for banking supervisors also had the purpose of protecting individual investors. In 1984 Article 4(4) the *Finanzdienstleistungsaufsichtsgesetz* (Financial Services Supervision Act) was introduced. It specified that the German financial regulator, the *Bundesanstalt für Finanzdienstleistungsaufsicht* (BaFin), is an independent public law body that performs its financial supervision only in the general public interest.

In Austria, the state is liable pursuant to the provisions of the *Amtshaftungsgesetz* (Public Liability Act)[47] for damage caused by the *Finanzmarktaufsicht* (FMA) organs and employees in the enforcement of federal Acts. The rule dictates that reparable damage is such that was directly caused to the legal entity that is subject to supervision pursuant to this federal Act. The FMA as well as its employees and bodies shall not be liable towards the injured

[44] See Art. 325 of the Act, in M. Baretić, 'Croatia' in K Oliphant and B.C. Steininger (eds), *European Tort Law 2013* Springer, Vienna/New York 2014, pp. 110–111. Similarly, Art. 15 of the Council for Financial Stability Act no. 159/2013 as concerns the members of the Council for Financial Stability; see S. Baretić, 'Croatia' in E. Karner and B.C. Steininger (eds.), *European Tort Law 2015,* Springer, Vienna/New York 2016, p. 76, no. 2.

[45] Law no. 65/2018, Arts. 216, 601, 617, as amended in 2020 by the Act no. 17/2020. The same model of regulation is found in Art. 11 of the Credit Institutions and Investment companies Recovery Act (No. 146/2020). M. Baretić and I. Kanceljak, 'Croatia' in E. Karner and B.C. Steininger (eds.), *European Tort Law 2018*, Springer, Vienna/New York 2019, pp. 70, 75; M. Baretić, 'Croatia' in E. Karner and B.C. Steininger (eds.), *European Tort Law 2020*, Springer, Vienna/New York 2021, pp. 66, 69, 71.

[46] BGHZ 74,144 (*Wetterstein-Wertbrief-Fonds*).

[47] Federal Law Gazette no. 20/1949.

party. The immunity thus covers third-party claims, but not the directly injured entities that are subject to the supervision[48]. The legislative change (following the 2007 crisis) has met with doctrinal criticism in Austria for incompatibility with constitutional law and EU law.[49] However, a constitutional argument failed before the German BGH in an earlier case of 20 January 2005,[50] in which BGH held that the then actual statutory immunity of a supervisory authority organ from liability for negligent supervision towards individual depositors did not infringe either Article 34 (concerning state liability[51]) or Article 14 § 1 (concerning protection of property) of the German Constitution. The holding puts emphasis on the wide margin of appreciation in the realisation of *Schutzpflichten* by public regulatory and supervisory agencies. A positive duty to protect through a specific legislative measure is owed solely by the parliament.[52]

The Austrian Supreme Court held that the statutory exemption from liability for pecuniary loss suffered by bank customers also applies to banking supervision carried out by the Austrian National Bank. Hence, according to the Austrian judicial practice on banking supervision, the liability towards bank customers due to deficient banking supervision by FMA attaches neither to the Republic of Austria (as the legal representative of FMA) nor to the Austrian National Bank.[53]

The special legal protection granted to financial supervisory authorities in the jurisdictions referred to above is typically motivated by the concern that the threat of liability is likely to be detrimental to the effective exercise of their functions.[54] Other policy arguments include the need to preserve limited financial resources. It has also been argued that the rules providing for full immunity save claimants the trial costs, while the result is close to the same as it would have been were the standard of gross negligence or bad faith applicable.[55] Thus, the efficiency argument would favour full immunity over the prerequisite of gross negligence or/and intent.

---

48 See § 3 Finanzmarktaufsichtsbehördengesetz (FMABG).

49 B.C. Steininger, 'Austria' in H. Koziol and B.C. Steininger (eds.), *European Tort Law 2008*, Springer, Vienna/New York 2009, pp. 108, 114–115, 18.

50 NJW 2005, 742.

51 The German Constitution (Basic Law) stipulates that everyone whose rights are violated by acts or omissions of the German public authority has the right to a judicial remedy (Art. 19 § 4) and sets out the principle of liability of the state for tortious acts of its agents (Art. 34). However, in light of the German courts' case law, the right to an effective remedy can be claimed only in connection with a subjective right conferred on the individual in the Basic Law, statutory law or international human rights law.

52 A. Scarso, 'Tortious liability of regulatory authorities', above n. 35, 110.

53 OGH 14 July 2022, 1 Ob 91/22x= ÖBA 2023, 2883. See S. Nitch, 'Austria' in E. Karner and B.C. Steininger (eds.), *European Tort Law 2022*, Springer, Vienna/New York 2023, pp. 21-24.

54 D. Nolan, 'The liability of Financial Supervisory Authorities', above n. 27, p. 221.

55 D. Nolan, 'The liability Financial Supervisory Authorities', above n. 27, pp. 221–222.

4. OTHER CONDITIONS FOR A COMPENSATORY CLAIM AS OBSTACLES TO LIABILITY

4.1. THE PROTECTIVE PURPOSE OF RULES (NORMS)

In the so-called Germanic legal family, as well as in Denmark, the Netherlands,[56] or Italy, the liability of FSAs is additionally curbed through the doctrine of the protective purpose of legal rules. This doctrine means that a tort law claim requires the violation of a strongly protected and precisely described right (sometimes referred to as absolute rights, such as a property right). The damage suffered by the victim must fall within the scope of protection of the particular norm that has been violated. This scope may be construed differently in various legal systems.

As has been indicated, the purpose of the rules on financial supervision was interpreted positively for investors in Italy (see the cases reported in section 3.2). Also in the Austrian case of 25 March 2003 (cited in section 2 above) the Austrian Supreme Court held expressly that 'savers are included in the protective purpose of the provisions on banking supervision'.[57] In that case it was, however, unclear whether the state should be liable also towards the bank's shareholders, and whether the auditors bear any additional liability besides the state.[58]

An interesting illustration of how the 'protective purpose of the norm' concept may limit the liability of supervising authorities in a system where unlawfulness is generally sufficient to hold a public authority liable, comes from Switzerland. In a decision of 11 April 2012 the *Schweizerisches Bundesgericht* (SB) accepted that the Swiss Confederation could not be held liable towards bank shareholders for faulty bank supervision.[59] Under the facts of the case, in 2000, the Canton of Geneva had to subject its own bank, the Cantonal Bank of Geneva, to a capital reconstruction for CHF 3.4 billion in order to prevent bankruptcy. As a consequence, the Canton of Geneva filed a liability lawsuit for that amount against the Swiss Confederation, alleging that the supervisory authority for banks (then the Federal Banking Commission[60]) had failed to exercise due care in supervision of the bank. The Federal Administrative

[56] The relativity argument was raised in the *Vie d'or* case cited earlier. M. Faure and T. Hartlief, *European Tort Law*, p. 419, no 14.

[57] Oberster Gerichtshof (Supreme Court) (OGH), 25.03.2003, 1 Ob 188/02g, [2003] ecolex, 416, B.C. Steininger, 'Austria' in H. Koziol and B.C. Steininger (eds.), *European Tort Law 2003*, Springer, Vienna/New York 2004, pp. 34, 27–40.

[58] B.C. Steininger, ibid., p. 43.

[59] Judgment of 11.04.2012, A7111/2010, at: http://www.bvger.ch. P. Loser, 'Switzerland' in E. Karner and B.C. Steininger (eds.), *European Tort Law 2013*, Springer, Vienna/New York 2014, pp. 673, 686.

[60] Since 2007 the Swiss Financial Market Supervisory Authority (FINMA).

Court rejected the lawsuit, reasoning that the federal provisions on banking supervision serve to protect depositors from the risk of losing their deposited funds in the case of the bank's insolvency. However, the purpose of such a regulation is not to protect shareholders or cantons which guarantee the liabilities of their cantonal bank from the risk of having to restructure the bank's capital. The canton guaranteeing the deposits is only technically and indirectly protected. Hence, the supervisory duties are not supposed to protect the bank's shareholders in Switzerland.

In the context of the protective purpose of the rule, it should also be recalled[61] that in instances where individuals' deposits were unavailable because of negligent bank supervision, the so-called 'Codified Banking Directive'[62] did not confer upon depositors the right to have banking supervisory authorities take appropriate supervisory measures or to hold that supervisory body or a given country liable in situations in which the payment of damages is provided for by the Directive on deposit guarantee schemes.[63] It should be added, however, that the incorrect implementation and application of the Directive's provisions, e.g. those concerning the conditions for determining the unavailability of deposits, and the consequent malfunctioning of the compensation mechanism, may, in specific circumstances, constitute a sufficiently serious breach of Union law capable of rendering the Member State concerned liable.[64] Furthermore, in light of the European Court's judgment of 4 October 2018 (*Kantarev v. Balgarska Narodna Banka*),[65] national legislation may not make the right of individuals to be compensated for a breach of EU law subject to an additional

---

[61] Case C-222/02 *Peter Paul, Cornelia Sonnen-Lütte and Christel Mörkens v. Bundesrepublik Deutschland*, ECLI:EU:C:2004:606. That case concerned the interpretation of Articles 3 and 7 of Directive 94/19/EC on deposit guarantee schemes. Customers of the German bank BVH sought compensation from the state for lost deposits caused by the delay in the transposition of the directive and negligence committed by the federal supervisory authority in the supervision of the bank where they had deposits. The interpretation of Directive 94/19/EC was justified by recital 24, which states that a Member State or its competent authorities cannot be made liable with respect to depositors.

[62] Directive 2000/12/EC of 20 March 2000 on the taking up and pursuit of the business of credit institutions, which was repealed by Directive 2006/48/EC of the European Parliament and of the Council of 14 June 2006 relating to the taking up and pursuit of the business of credit institutions (recast) [2006] OJ L 177/1–200.

[63] Currently Directive 2014/49/EU of the European Parliament and of the Council of 16 April 2014 on deposit guarantee schemes (recast), at: http://data.europa.eu/eli/dir/2014/49/2014-07-02.

[64] Opinion of Advocate General Kokott, Case C-571/16, *Nikolay Kantarev v. Balgarska Narodna Banka*, ECLI:EU:C:2018:412 – Concerning Art. 1(3)(i) of Directive 94/19/EC, currently Art. 2(1)(8) Directive 2014/49/EU.

[65] Case C-571/16 *Nikolay Kantarev v. Balgarska Narodna Banka*, ECLI:EU:C:2018:807. The CJEU held that Article 1(3)(i) of Directive 94/19, as amended by Directive 2009/14, has direct effect and constitutes a rule of law intended to confer rights on individuals, allowing depositors to bring an action for damages for the harm sustained by late repayment of deposits.

condition relating to the intentional nature of the damage caused by the national authority. Nor may the condition of culpable action by the central bank be interpreted in a way that goes beyond the condition of a sufficiently serious breach of the EU law.

4.2. COMPENSABLE DAMAGE

In all surveyed jurisdictions the principle of full compensation applies to tort claims and predominantly also to public authorities' liability.[66] Compensation caps are designed for some cases of insolvency of supervised entities, namely when actual losses fall under the coverage of a mandatory deposit guarantee scheme – mentioned in the preceding section. The existence of a deposit scheme, on the one hand, means stricter liability towards the depositors, but on the other hand, constitutes a departure from the principle of full compensation in cases of negligent supervision of banking authorities. Moreover, other injured parties (e.g. the supervised entities themselves) remain outside special protection regimes.

For other cases, a possible argument against limiting the state liability for pure economic loss through compensation caps is rooted in constitutional values and fundamental rights, which include protection of property and may include the principle of public authorities' liability for damage to individuals.[67]

This notwithstanding, the purely economic nature of damage inflicted upon individuals and supervised institutions through the negligent conduct of FSAs may serve as a tool to circumscribe the liability.[68] In Romanistic legal systems – based on the general principle of liability for faulty conduct – which do not apply the concept of pure economic loss because *prima facie* all interests, including pure economic loss, deserve legal protection in tort, this task is left to the courts.[69] The courts hence use the traditional toolbox in order to prevent

---

66 K. Oliphant, 'The liability of public authorities in comparative perspective', above n. 6, p. 859. See also an exception in Latvia which was successfully challenged before the CJEU in the judgment of 10 December 2020 (Case C-735/19, *Euromin Holdings (Cyprus) Limited*, ECLI:EU:C:2020:1014 – according to Latvian state liability law, compensation for pecuniary loss can be limited to 50% of the actual damage if the amount of damage exceeds EUR 1,420,000). In consequence, this limitation cannot be applied to state liability for breach of EU law.

67 See for example Art. 34 of the German Constitution 1949, Art. 23 of the Austrian Constitution of 1920 as amended in 1929 and 1948, Art. 48 of the Italian Constitution 1948, Art. 106(2) of the Spanish Constitution 1978, Art. 77 of the Polish Constitution 1997.

68 See E. Karner, 'Tort Law and the Financial Crisis: Basic Questions', above n. 16, p. 126.

69 In France, for example, the liability for pure economic loss is established more often than in England, but the awards are very low, while in England the rare awards are much higher See D. Fairgrieve, 'State liability in tort. A comparative law study', above n. 5, pp. 203, 237.

an unpredictable and limitless expansion of liability, such as the concepts of 'damage' and 'adequate causation'.[70]

In the systems based on the concept of protected interests (i.e. the Germanic systems, Denmark,[71] and other Scandinavian legal systems) pure economic loss of third parties must be included (by courts) in the list of protected interests to be compensable in tort. A telling, but rather isolated, example of holding the supervisory authorities liable for pure economic loss comes from an Austrian judgment of 2012.[72] The Austrian Republic was held liable to investors for omissions by the public supervisory agency in charge at that time of supervising the securities market (the *Bundeswertpapieraufsichtsbehörde*). The authority was held to have failed to adequately control a private financial services provider that acted fraudulently. By contrast, the doctrine of protective purpose of the rule is the main justification for dismissal of claims brought by individual investors in the numerous Austrian cases on banking supervision.[73]

4.3. CAUSATION

In order to determine the liability of FSAs, a causal link between the alleged violation of the latter's duty and the claimant's loss should be established.

Causation proves to be a tricky element of a compensatory claim against FSAs, among other reasons because national authorities are obliged to cooperate with EU supervisory authorities (including the European Commission and the three European Supervisory Authorities – the European Banking Authority (EBA), the European Securities and Markets Authority (ESMA) and the European Insurance and Occupational Pensions Authority (EIOPA), as well as the European Central Bank). Circumstances of a systemic nature may thus have a direct impact on causation and the legal standing to be sued in a damages action.

In principle, when damage is the result of a failed business activity of a financial institution, this institution should in the first instance bear the burden of compensation. Financial supervision for the most part consists of examining whether legal rules have been complied with. Therefore, the causal link between economic losses and negligent omission in supervision is almost always indirect. However, indirect causation is not an obstacle to liability in

---

70 See D. Nolan, 'The Liability of Financial Supervisory Authorities', above n. 27, 202 et seq.

71 See V. Ulfbeck, 'The liability of public authorities in Denmark' in K. Oliphant (ed.), *The Liability of Public Authorities in Comparative Perspective*, Intersentia, Cambridge 2016, pp. 105, 118.

72 OGH 22 June 2012, 1 Ob 186/11a = ÖBA 2013, 52.

73 OGH 14 July 2022, 1 Ob 91/22x = ÖBA 2023, 2883.

most countries, where the test of adequate causation is used, unlike the systems where the test of direct causation prevails (such as France, for instance).

Illustrative of how causation can create an obstacle to holding the FSA liable is French case law. In the famous *El Shikh* case, the French appellate administrative court dismissed the claims of depositors due to the lack of causal link between the alleged failures of the *Banque de France* and the loss of the deposits by the claimants (clients of the bankrupt bank).[74] As established by the court, the bankruptcy of the bank was largely attributable to the fraudulent conduct of its London office, so – according to the court – there was not a direct causal connection between omissions on the part of the French supervisory authorities and the losses sustained by the depositors.[75] Also the failure to revoke the bank's licence did not give rise to liability because it had not been established that the bank's collapse was attributable to its failure to comply with the requirements of its licence. The key question for the establishment of the causation (Would the revocation of the licence have prevented the loss?) was thus answered in the negative. This case shows that although the French philosophy of holding the state liable for damage is based on a particular assumption that all losses suffered by individuals due to governmental activities must be borne by society, there are two important limitations to the liability in the regulatory financial sector: the requirement of *faute lourde* and the requirement of causation.

This general conclusion notwithstanding, attention should be drawn to the solution applied in the judgment of 25 January 2000 by the Court of Appeal in Paris. The Court held that while inadequate supervision had been causally significant in the failure of another bank, it had only deprived depositors of the chance of avoiding their losses. Hence, damages should be limited to 1/5 of the funds each had lost.[76] The 'loss of chance' doctrine served to overcome the problem of uncertain causation (i.e. the condition *sine qua non*). As a result, the burden of losses was allocated proportionally between the injured parties and the liable institution.[77]

The all-or-nothing approach to the causation condition can be illustrated by the judgment of the *Corte di Cassazione* of 2001 (the CONSOB case no. 3132 – cited in section 3.2). The Court disagreed with the rejection of the compensatory claims by the Court of Appeal of Milan, reasoning that the existence of the causal relationship between CONSOB's conduct and

---

74 CAA Paris, 30.03.1999, *El Shikh*. See D. Fairgrieve, *State liability in tort. A comparative law study*, Oxford University Press, Oxford 2003, pp. 109–110.

75 See D. Nolan, 'The Liability of Financial Supervisory Authorities', above n. 27, 216 et seq.

76 CAA Paris, 25.01.2000; see D. Nolan, 'The Liability of Financial Supervisory Authorities', above n. 27, p. 217.

77 I. Gilead, M.D. Green and B.A. Koch (eds.), *Proportional liability: Analytical and Comparative Perspectives*, De Gruyter, Berlin-Boston 2013.

the damage suffered by investors should not be confused with the aspects related to the assessment of compensable damage. The causal inquiry should examine what should have been the result of a timely and correct fulfilment of CONSOB's duties on the subscriber's investment. On remand, the Court of Appeal of Milan held that even risk-friendly investors would have turned their attention to different forms of investment if CONSOB had properly fulfilled its duties. In consequence, the claimants received full compensation.[78]

More recently, the Croatian Supreme Court[79] tackled the problem of causation in a rather simplistic manner. Croatia is a civil law system, which follows the adequate causation theory. In this case the plaintiff invested money with a financial agency, an independent private undertaking, which undertook an obligation to repay him money with interest after a certain period. Although presented as a regular financial activity, in reality this was a fraudulent pyramid scheme designed to function as long as newcomers were joining. Subsequently, the plaintiff lost his investment and brought an action against both the financial agency and the state. He argued that the state's liability should be based on failure to supervise the financial market, in particular the failure to conduct appropriate surveillance of the financial agency, which consequently brought about the damage. The lower courts dismissed the claim against the state, holding that even if there were certain omissions in the conduct of state bodies responsible for the supervision of the financial market, no relevant causal link existed between these omissions and the damage sustained by the plaintiff. The Supreme Court upheld this argumentation and held that the liability of the state could not be based on the Croatian rules on public authorities' liability, which govern the liability for damage inflicted to the party in administrative proceedings. According to the Supreme Court, the idea that the state could be liable for all damage that may occur to anyone because some public bodies were perhaps not as active as they should have been, would be too far-fetched. The Court also denied the liability of the state under the general rules of tort liability, finding that no relevant causal link existed between the alleged omissions of the defendant authorities and the damage sustained by the plaintiff. In the case of multiple causes, which all may have influenced the emergence of certain damage, only that cause which typically results in certain damage shall be considered legally relevant. The motives, but not the result, were rightly criticised by Baretić.

---

78 A. Scarso, 'Tortious liability of regulatory authorities', above n. 35, p. 105.

79 Judgment of 21.05.2013, Vrhovni sud Republike Hrvatske (VsRH), Rev-x 262/13-2, M Baretić, 'Croatia' in E. Karner and B.C. Steininger (eds.), *European Tort Law 2013*, Springer, Vienna/New York 2014, p. 119, nos. 104, 114.

5. CONCLUSIONS

As the foregoing analysis reflects, the liability of national financial supervisory authorities is part of a wider debate on public authorities' liability, which increasingly separates itself from the public/private terminology.[80]

The field of financial markets' supervision displays the persistent need for balance in weighing the countervailing policy arguments and social values.[81] Several of those arguments have been raised and used against the expansion of financial authorities' liability, including the need to preserve limited financial resources, the risk of detrimentally defensive action by the authorities, the alleged conflict between the duty to the public (in particular a duty to protect the stability of the banking system)[82] and the private duty,[83] discretionary powers granted to FSAs – especially in the area of disciplinary (quasi-judicial) powers –,[84] and unjust redistribution of wealth. It is also argued that public authorities should not be deterred from using their powers to achieve public benefit. As a matter of fact, it is difficult to evaluate the deterrent effects of liability in this context, because there are no empirical data which support the thesis that tort law liability has a deterrent effect on the conduct of financial regulatory authorities.[85]

To recapitulate the arguments pro-liability, they include the need for consumer protection (due to information asymmetry),[86] promotion of 'awareness of liability', and the transparency and efficiency of financial markets.[87] It should be stressed that these arguments are raised alongside the traditional motives supporting public authority liability. The constitutional provenance of the principle of liability of public authorities should be

---

80 G. Eörsi, 'Private and governmental liability for the torts of employees and organs' in A. Tunc (ed.), *International Encyclopaedia of Comparative Law*, Vol. XI (Torts) (J. Mohr, Tübingen/ Mouton, Paris 1975) at 149; C. Harlow, 'State liability: problem without solution', above n. 7, 71.

81 K. Oliphant, 'The liability of public authorities in comparative perspective', above n. 6, p. 862, no 28; Martin-Casals and J. Ribot, 'The liability of public authorities in Spain', above n. 22, pp. 463, 479.

82 Financial regulators are under an obligation to protect a plurality of interests, including, more specifically, the stability of the banking system.

83 K. Oliphant, 'The liability of public authorities in comparative perspective', above n. 6, pp. 860–861 no 21, case *Three Rivers District Council v. Bank of England III*, [2000] 2 WLR 1220.

84 D. Nolan, 'The liability of Financial Supervisory Authorities', above n. 27, 211.

85 R.J. Dijkstra, 'Is limiting financial supervisory liability a way to prevent defensive conduct?', above n. 2, 61.

86 See on this aspect C. Amato and Ch. Perfumi, 'Financial investors as consumers and their protection: Recent Italian legislation from a European perspective' (2010) 3 *Opinio Juris*, Paper no. 3, pp. 1–23. https://papers.ssrn.com/sol3/papers.cfm?abstract_id=1684460# online publication September 2010.

87 A. Scarso, 'Tortious liability of regulatory authorities', above n. 35, 114.

considered an essential argument for controlling the use of the powers of public authorities and extending the protection of interests of citizens. Indeed, it should be underlined that the fact that FSAs are granted powers with which to achieve public goals provides a valid reason for holding them accountable for their proper exercise.[88] The discretionary powers of those authorities require a reaction of the law to arbitrariness (disproportionality) in their actions and failure to relinquish functions and powers.

Moreover, it is clear from the above review of European jurisdictions that a claim for compensation is of a civil nature and hence traditional tort law instruments are used to handle the claims for compensation of economic losses arising from a tort of a national FSA. Civil law has developed different paths to avoid a proliferation of the liability: among others, the concepts of the scope of the duty and protective purpose of the rule, the concept of adequate causation, and the concept of pure economic loss. The courts, acting as guardians of individual rights, have used the tort law toolbox with attentiveness to those rights and regard to the individual circumstances of the case. The condition of gross negligence or bad faith seems to curtail the liability, but its content is also shaped by courts and remains objectivised. To conclude, a closer examination of the practical results of applying the different private law doctrines and theories to the cases of the liability of FSAs, as well as the methodology that the courts use to solve actual conflicts, have revealed a certain level of convergence of the systems under survey.[89] The convergence leads to the acceptance of FSAs' liability, although the standard of liability is not uniform. Hence, the opinion according to which 'full immunity' (i.e. no liability) of the national supervisory authorities from liability toward third parties indicates a broader trend in Europe, is unsupported by actual case law.[90]

This general conclusion remains valid even though some particular problems, such as for example the scope of compensation for pure financial losses, might be given different answers. The scope of the liability discussed here varies because the legal solutions are closely dependent on constitutional values, social and legal policy, and are applied in their particular economic, moral and cultural contexts.[91]

---

88 K. Oliphant, 'The liability of public authorities in comparative perspective', above n. 6, pp. 860–861, no. 21.

89 A. Scarso, 'Tortious liability of regulatory authorities', above n. 35, 94, 110, no. 38.

90 E. Karner, 'Tort law and the Financial Crisis: Basic Questions', above n. 16, 126.

91 B. Markesinis, 'Unity or division: the search for similarities in contemporary European law' in D. Fairgrieve, M. Andenas and J. Bell (eds.), *Tort Liability of Public Authorities in Comparative Perspective*, BIICL, London 2002, pp. 458 et seq., K. Zweigert and H. Kötz, *An Introduction to Comparative Law* (Trans. T. Weir), Oxford University Press, Oxford 1998, p. 34.

PART III

Common Good and Participation Regime for Private Parties

CHAPTER 6
RESPONSIBLE LENDING

Esther Arroyo Amayuelas*

* The research leading to these results falls within the scope of the I+D+I Project PID2021-127197NB-I00, funded by MCIN/AEI/10.13039/501100011033/ and FEDER 'A Way of Doing Europe'; and Project 2021 SGR 00347, funded by the Generalitat de Catalunya. It is also part of the EU Private Law Jean Monnet Chair research funded by the EU Commission.

1. INTRODUCTION

The European Union incorporated the responsible lending programme into legislation in an attempt to tackle the high levels of indebtedness resulting from the expansion in access to credit and new credit products and lending practices. It did so first, and rather timidly, into Directive 2008/48/EC of 23 April 2008 on Consumer Credit,[1] and then more forcefully into Directive 2014/17/EC of 28 February 2014 on Credit Agreements for Consumers Relating to Residential Immovable Property.[2] The aim was to ensure that professional lenders took consumer needs and interests into account throughout the entire duration of the credit agreement, which entailed both the need to enable consumers to make maximum savings (e.g. via early repayment without penalty) and to prevent borrowers from succumbing to the temptation to commit themselves to risky loan agreements. The expression 'responsible lending' is generally associated with good practices in the granting of credit (unfair practices in credit card approval and subprime mortgages would be clear examples of irresponsible practices to be tackled) and with the measures proposed to prevent over-indebtedness: e.g. transparency in the marketing of loans, creditworthiness assessment and the granting of a right of withdrawal. However, it also covers creditors' obligation to show reasonable forbearance when claiming repayment, for example, by limiting default interest, preventing the abuse of acceleration clauses and seeking to avoid foreclosure actions being carried out before attempts have been made to negotiate with debtors. It also entails implementing policies to improve consumers' financial education and, last but by no means least, involves addressing institutions' internal structural problems such as incentive policies promoting the misleading marketing of credit products; this would also affect intermediaries to a large extent and would apply to the remuneration linked to transactions concluded, and the sale of credit cards and insurance policies associated with loans, for example.[3]

---

1 Directive 2008/48/EC of the European Parliament and of the Council of 28 April 2008 on credit agreements for consumers and repealing Council Directive 1987/102/EEC, [2008] OJ L 133/66, of 22.05.2008.

2 Directive 2014/17/EU of the European Parliament and of the Council of 4 February 2014 on credit agreements for consumers relating to residential immovable property, [2014] OJ L 60/34, of 28.02.2014.

3 See U. Reifner, 'European Coalition for Responsible Credit – Principles of Responsible Credit' in C. Twigg-Flessner *et al.* (eds.), *The Yearbook of Consumer Law 2008*, Ashgate Publishing, Aldershot 2007, p. 419; Y.M. Atamer, 'Duty of Responsible Lending: Should

The pages that follow aim to provide a brief overview of the European Union's efforts to implement the responsible lending policy in Member States, paying special attention to lenders' duty to assess the risk of borrower default and the consequences that failure to fulfil this duty should entail. While this paper was in the process of being published, Directive (EU) 2023/2225 of the European Parliament and of the Council of 18 October 2023 on credit agreements for consumers and repealing Directive 2008/48/EC has been published.[4] It has therefore only been possible to make a brief mention of this legislation at the very end of this study.[5]

2. THE WEAK REPONSIBLE LENDING PROGRAMME IN DIRECTIVE 2008/48 ON CONSUMER CREDIT

The revision of Directive 1987/102 on Consumer Credit first materialised in a 2002 Proposal,[6] the aims of which included the need to incorporate the idea of responsible lending; that is, the need for lenders to observe prudential supervision or management rules. Examples of this were the provisions concerning measures to prevent excessive indebtedness and others obliging lenders to consult central databases in order to improve the quality of lending and reduce the risk of consumers falling victim to unbalanced agreements, which they were incapable of fulfilling, and which resulted in financial exclusion and costly social interventions on the part of Member States. The principle of responsible lending also required consumers seeking credit to exercise the same prudence and to respect their contractual obligations.[7]

the European Union Take Action' in S. Grundmann and Y.M. Atamer (eds.), *Financial Services, Financial Crisis and General European Contract Law*, Kluwer, Alphen aan den Rijn 2011, p. 179; I. Ramsay, 'Regulation of consumer credit' in G. Howells *et al.* (eds.), *Handbook of Research on International Consumer Law*, 1st ed., Edward Elgar, Cheltenham 2010, p. 366, pp. 394 et seq.

4 Directive (EU) 2023/2225 of the European Parliament and of the Council of 18 October 2023 on credit agreements for consumers and repealing Directive 2008/48/EC, OJ L 2023/2225, of 30.10.2023.

5 For further information, E. Arroyo Amayuelas, "A Third Directive on Consumer Credit", (2024) 20(1) *European Review of Contract Law* 1.

6 Proposal for a Directive of the European Parliament and of the Council on the harmonisation of the laws, regulations and administrative provisions of the Member States concerning credit for consumers, Brussels, 11.09.2002 (COM(2002) 443 final.

7 Proposal for a Directive on consumer credit 2002, above n. 6, p. 16 (commentary on Art. 9).

2.1. MEASURES TO REDUCE THE RISK OF UNBALANCED AGREEMENTS

The principle of responsible lending materialised in Article 9 of the Proposal, which made lenders responsible for ascertaining consumers' ability to repay before granting loans. This could require cooperation on the part of consumers, and the provision therefore had to be complemented by Article 6, which established reciprocal duties of information (consumers, as to their financial situation; lenders, as to the description of the product they offer and its advantages and drawbacks) and a duty to provide advice which entailed choosing the most suitable loan for applicants' circumstances. Article 9 also had to be viewed in relation to Article 8, which established mandatory consultation of a central database that included a record of repayment defaults, although it could also include a record of credit and surety agreements.

A consumer protection instrument that went beyond lenders' pre-contractual duties of information was thus adopted to encourage responsible practices in granting credit.[8] However, the duties of information did not disappear; on the contrary, they increased, perhaps to the detriment of other essential measures such as determining EU-level criteria for defining maximum interest rates and what constitutes usury.[9]

2.2. CREDITWORTHINESS ASSESSMENT: A DUTY OF CARE

Assessing the ability to repay was an obligation of means and, consequently, consumers' failure to discharge their obligations should not automatically entail lender liability; rather, the facts of every particular case had to be examined by the legal authorities.[10] What is important here is that the Commission expressly stressed the relationship between concluding credit agreements and the prior assessment of debtors' ability to repay, as this would suggest that when the prognosis was not favourable for granting a loan (the loan requested or any other), the lender should not conclude the credit agreement, and to do so would imply a lack of care that should have civil consequences. In the model provided

---

8 I. Ramsay, 'From Truth in Lending to Responsible Lending' in G. Howells *et al.* (eds.), *Information Rights and Obligations*, Ashgate, Aldershot 2005, p. 47.

9 One of the measures called for by the European Economic and Social Committee (EESC) in Opinion (OJ C 234/1-10 of 30.09.2003), points 2.2.4 et seq. The EESC also criticised the Proposal's general philosophy, according to which 'consumer protection' is the same as 'consumer information' (e.g., points 2.4.3, 2.4.5).

10 Proposal for a Directive on consumer credit 2002, above n. 6, pp. 15–16 (commentary on Art. 9).

by Belgian legislation[11] – and undoubtedly also the Swiss one,[12] although the latter was not specifically mentioned – this was illustrated by the possibility of lenders forfeiting the interest and costs and consumers maintaining repayment of the total amount of the loan in instalments (Article 31(2)). All this was the measure of what the Commission considered a penalty that was effective, proportionate and constituted a deterrent (Article 31(1)), although administrative penalties were not ruled out.[13] In a subsequent and detailed Opinion, the European Economic and Social Committee (EESC) examined the question of whether the Proposal should clearly set out the consequences of failing to consult or take into account database information about borrowers, coming down decisively in favour of the view that the penalties for lenders that failed to respect the provisions concerning responsible lending would entail the loss of the right to the interest and costs.[14]

2.3. A DIFFERENT WAY OF LOOKING AT THE ISSUE

These levels of stringency were lowered at the first reading of the Commission's Proposal in the European Parliament, however.[15] The Proposal was interpreted as making access to credit tougher, with the risk of social exclusion that this could entail for innumerable members of the public. It was warned that the Commission was not approaching the question in the right way, because over-indebtedness is normally the consequence of either a series of unexpected life events (unemployment, divorce and illness) or of debtors' own illicit practices.[16] For this reason, although the Parliament did not delete the obligation to assess creditworthiness, it did delete Article 9 as drafted by the Commission, aiming to clarify that responsibility extended to the duty to supply information and also to highlight the idea that both lending and borrowing should be responsible. The duty to provide advice on the most suitable loan for consumers' financial

---

11 For details, see P. Rott, E. Terryn and C. Twigg-Flesner, 'Kreditwürdigkeitsprüfung: Verbraucherschultzverhinderung durch Zuweisung zum Öffentlichen Recht' (2011) 5 *Verbraucher und Recht* 163, 164.

12 For details, see Y.M. Atamer, above n. 3, pp. 192–193.

13 Proposal for a Directive on consumer credit 2002, above n. 6, p. 28 (commentary on Art. 31): 'Possibilities include a loss of interest and/or penalties as well as the withdrawal of their licence'.

14 [2003] OJ C 234/1, sections 3.4.1, 3.12.2 on pp. 7 and 8.

15 Committee on Legal Affairs and the Internal Market (Rapporteur: Joachim Wuermeling), Final A5-0224/2004: Second Report on the proposal for a European Parliament and Council directive on the harmonisation of the laws, regulations and administrative provisions of the Member States concerning credit for consumers (02.04.2004), available at: https://www.europarl.europa.eu/doceo/document/A-5-2004-0224_EN.pdf.

16 Second Report (Explanatory Statement), above n. 15, p. 83, p. 84.

situations was also deleted.[17] The Committee on Economic and Monetary Affairs had maintained that the obligation to provide advice could only be met by carrying out detailed investigations into consumers' personal affairs, and complained that this would not only mean an intolerable intrusion into their private lives but would also be unviable in many cases (e.g. offers of distance loans).[18] In its opinion, it was also pointless to introduce the principle that lenders could not conclude credit agreements unless they were convinced that consumers or guarantors could meet their obligations; lenders by definition have an interest in carefully assessing debtors' ability to repay by virtue of the criteria of sound and prudent management, and the technical arrangements for this assessment form part of the free exercise of business activity.[19] The Committee also considered that evaluating lender behaviour when a guarantor was required raised problems because it was unclear whether this indicated that the lender was convinced that the borrower would not repay the loan and should therefore also be understood to be acting irresponsibly. It was also felt that any negative effects of adopting this regulation would be projected onto lenders that were unable to recover their loans for reasons beyond their control. Lastly, it was argued that the supply of credit would contract, which would clearly be to the detriment of consumers because no lender would run the risk of offering loans to consumers with a history of default.[20]

The European Parliament consequently understood that the principle of 'responsible lending' should be totally deleted, since it only contained a repetition of obvious contractual obligations and was therefore redundant and should not appear in a legal text.[21] It was also said that in practice lenders already acted to reduce risk by checking whether consumers or guarantors were in a position to meet their obligations.[22] On the other hand, the need for both consumers and lenders to behave prudently and respect their contractual obligations should be expressly stated.[23] In other words, while lenders' prudence could be taken for granted (because it is in their interests to be sure of borrowers' ability to repay), the same could not be said of borrowers, whose behaviour was not above suspicions of recklessness. What should therefore be encouraged was responsible consumer borrowing, an aspect that the 2002 Proposal reflected only timidly.[24]

17 Second Report, above n. 15, amendment 17, deleting Recital 15, pp. 14–15; amendment 65, which affected Arts. 6 and 9, pp. 34–37.

18 Second Report, above n. 15, amendment 17, deleting Recital 15, p. 93.

19 Second Report, above n. 15, amendment 55, deleting Art. 9, p. 109.

20 Second Report, above n. 15, amendment 55, deleting Art. 9, p. 109.

21 Second Report, above n. 15, amendment 17, deleting Recital 15, p. 15.

22 Second Report, above n. 15, amendment 17, deleting Recital 15, p. 15.

23 Second Report, above n. 15, amendment 18, introducing new paragraph 15*a* in the Explanatory Statement (p. 15).

24 Proposal for a Directive on consumer credit 2002, above n. 6, p. 16 (commentary on Art. 9).

2.4. A NEW SOLUTION IN SUPPORT OF BANKS

These objections obliged the Commission to present a new text in 2005,[25] in which the principle of responsible lending was reduced to the duty to provide pre-contractual information and assess consumer creditworthiness on the basis of detailed data obtained from consumers themselves and, where appropriate (this was no longer mandatory), from consulting the relevant databases (Article 5(1)). In addition, the duty to propose the most suitable loan according to borrowers' needs in view of their financial positions, the risks, the advantages and disadvantages and the purpose of the loan, was deleted (Article 6(3) 2002 Proposal).[26] The new text instead introduced a lender duty to provide adequate explanations so that consumers could assess whether the proposed agreement suited their needs and financial position, in addition to the duty to clarify the meaning of the pre-contractual information and give details of the advantages and disadvantages associated with the proposed products if necessary (Article 5(5)). *Mutatis mutandis*, these provisions would subsequently correspond to Article 5(6) (adequate explanations; Recital 27), Article 8 (creditworthiness assessment; Recital 26) and Article 9 (database access).

2.5. THE FINAL OUTCOME

Directive 2008/48 accepted that consumers were ultimately responsible for their decisions and did not include the prohibition on granting credit if they turned out not to be creditworthy. On this basis, the adequate, tailored explanations that lenders were obliged to give could not supplant consumers' wishes, as the latter were ultimately responsible for their own decisions to enter into contracts and to obtain the loans that they wanted. The Directive neither required the creation of a central default database nor even obliged lenders to consult any database at all;[27] it did not stipulate what information consumers

---

25 Amended proposal for a Directive of the European Parliament and of the Council on credit agreements for consumers amending Council Directive 93/13/EC [Brussels, 23.11.2005, COM(2005) 483 final/2], available at: https://eur-lex.europa.eu/LexUriServ/LexUriServ.do?uri=COM:2005:0483:FIN:EN:PDF.

26 Favouring this approach, S. Grundmann and C. Hofmann, 'EC Financial Services and Contract Law - Developments 2007–2010' (2010) 4 *European Review of Contract Law* 467, 480.

27 For more detail, F. Ferretti, 'The Legal Framework of Consumer Credit Bureaus and Credit Scoring in the European Union: Pitfalls and Challenges - Over-indebtedness, Responsible Lending, Market Integration, and Fundamental Rights' (2013) 46 *Suffolk University Law Review* 791, 802–807.

had to provide,[28] and did not rank the criteria that lenders should use to decide on creditworthy applicants. In practice, positive credit assessments were frequently achieved thanks to the provision of extremely long repayment terms, and the risk of default served merely to increase the interest rate for borrowers who appeared less likely to repay their debts. The bursting of the housing bubble highlighted these and other practices, some of them dishonest, and showed that the duty to take due account of borrowers' needs had been systematically ignored in the field of mortgage credit.

3. GREATER PROTECTION FOR MORTGAGE CREDIT CONSUMERS IN DIRECTIVE 2014/17

Member States had until the end of May 2010 to transpose the Consumer Credit Directive (Article 27), but it was useful to examine responsibility in the granting of mortgage credit in more detail, bearing in mind the serious consequences of over-indebtedness in this market, both for consumers and the financial system as a whole.[29] So, while the first directive cited above had the clear function of expanding credit in the domestic market, the second, which was enacted after the housing crash, needed stricter requirements to tackle irresponsible banking practices.[30]

3.1. THE SYSTEM'S VULNERABILITY

The financial crisis – and with it the avalanche of foreclosures in many European Union countries, in which financing possibilities had been extended to enable people to purchase their own homes – revealed the system's vulnerability.[31] In the years leading up to the crisis, banks encouraged fictitious valuations, granted very long mortgage repayment terms, were very flexible with interest rates and, above all, did not correctly assess borrowers' ability to repay, among other reasons because they were excessively confident that property prices

---

28 In contrast, amendment 65 on the reform of Arts. 6 and 9, of the Committee on Legal Affairs and the Internal Market did provide for this, although the consumer was responsible for paying for the assessment supplying this information (Second Report, n. 16 above, p. 38).

29 G. Comparato, 'The Design of Consumer and Mortgage Credit Law in the European System' in H.W. Micklitz and I. Domurath (eds.), *Consumer Debt and Social Exclusion in Europe*, Ashgate, Farnham 2015, p. 9, pp. 18–19.

30 G. Comparato, above n. 29, p. 15.

31 See the reports in H.W. Micklitz and I. Domurath, above n. 29, pp. 29 et seq. See also, M. Anderson and E. Arroyo Amayuelas (eds.), *The Impact of the Mortgage Credit Directive in Europe. Contrasting Views from Member States*, Europa Law Publishing, Groningen 2017.

would continue to rise. In addition, new mortgage and financial products and ancillary services to loans were invented, whose risks were not made clear to consumers. Moreover, credit institution staff were ignorant of the risks and supervision was inadequate. In Spain[32] credit intermediaries were not subject to control until 2009,[33] and the need to carry out borrower creditworthiness checks was unregulated until levels of indebtedness reached vertiginous heights (2011).[34] There was no regulation of insolvency proceedings by natural persons until very recently (2015),[35] clearly long after it was introduced in Italy, which was wrongly said to be the last country in Europe whose national legislature addressed the problem (in 2012).[36]

3.2. THE LESSONS TO BE DRAWN FROM THE FINANCIAL CRISIS

Directive 2014/17 aimed to draw lessons from the financial crisis and eradicate irresponsible lending practices (Recitals 4 and 5) on the basis of incorporating stricter provisions than the previous Directive (Recital 22). Following the White Paper on the integration of EU mortgage credit markets,[37] the Commission launched a consultation on responsible lending and borrowing, which helped to define its profile more clearly.[38] The Proposal for a Directive was submitted in 2011,[39] the European Parliament issued its amendments report in 2012[40] and

---

32 With regard to realities in Spain, underlining the impact of irresponsible lending and the lack of adequate control, see M. Anderson and H. Simón Moreno, 'The Impact of the Mortgage Credit Directive in Spain' in M. Anderson and E. Arroyo Amayuelas (eds.), above n. 31, pp. 50 et seq; S. Nasarre Aznar, 'Malas prácticas bancarias en la actividad hipotecaria' (2014) 727 *Revista Crítica de Derecho Inmobiliario* 2665; F. Zunzunegui, 'Sobreendeudamiento y prácticas hipotecarias de las entidades bancarias' (2013) 129 *Revista de Derecho Bancario y Bursátil* 35.

33 Act 2/2009 of 31 March regulating consumer loans and mortgage credit agreements and intermediary services for concluding loan or credit agreements (BOE no. 79 of 1 April 2009).

34 Essentially, Order EHA/2899/2011 of 28 October on transparency and customer protection in banking services (BOE no. 261 of 29.11.2011).

35 Act 25/2015 of 8 July on the fresh start mechanism, reducing financial burdens and other social order measures (BOE no. 180 of 29 July 2015).

36 R. Montinaro, 'The consumers' over-indebtedness under an Italian contract law perspective: The current status and the way ahead' (2016) 4 *Europa e Diritto privato* 1215, 1217.

37 Brussels, 18.12.2007 (COM(2007) 807 final, pp. 7–9 on responsible lending and borrowing.

38 See Public Consultation on Responsible Lending and Borrowing in the EU (Brussels, 15.06.2009).

39 Proposal for a Directive of the European Parliament and of the Council on credit agreements relating to residential property [Brussels 31.02.2011, COM(2011) 142 final].

40 Report on the proposal for a Directive of the European Parliament and of the Council on credit agreements relating to residential property (Rapporteurs: Antolín Sánchez Presedo/Kurt Lehner). Document PE469.842v04-00 of 11.10.2012, available at: https://www.europarl.europa.eu/doceo/document/A-7-2012-0202_EN.pdf.

the Proposal was approved shortly after, extensively re-touched but without major problems.[41] The EESC, which strongly advocated responsible lending, had called for some significant adjustments such as the regulation of usury or the incorporation of an adequate loan-to-value ratio,[42] but these aspects ultimately failed to materialise.

3.3. HOW COULD CONSUMERS BE PROTECTED?

The 2014 Directive incorporates *ex novo* rules disciplining lender conduct based on the requirement for adequate levels of knowledge and competence, imposing transparency on intermediary remuneration and regulating the requirements for the performance and establishment of credit intermediaries. With the aim of encouraging responsible borrowing, there is a new suggestion for improving consumers' financial education (Articles 6, 22(7)); while this may turn out to be of dubious practical efficiency when the information is highly complex, it could at least help in making decisions related to managing household finances.[43] The legislation also enhances consumer protection by requiring new warnings to be included in advertising and more complete and tailored information for borrowers (Articles 11, 13–14) together with adequate explanations (Article 16).

3.3.1. *Information, Explanations and the Provision of Advice*

As consumers often decide to take out loans on the basis of advertisements, it is essential for advertising to contain basic information such as the duration of the loan, the number of instalments and the price (at least the APR). If, on the other hand, advertising or pre-contractual information confronts consumers with an avalanche of mandatory statements that they are not always

41 For the vicissitudes in its gestation, F.L. Schäfer, 'Wohnimmobilienkreditrichtlinie. Geschichte und Umsetzung im Verbraucherdarlehensrecht' (2014) 6 *Verbraucher und Recht* 207, 207-212; E. Arroyo Amayuelas, 'Directiva 2014/17, sobre los contratos de crédito con consumidores para bienes inmuebles de uso residencial' (2017) 3 *InDret* 1, esp. 1–12.

42 Opinion of the EESC on the Proposal for a Directive of the European Parliament and of the Council on credit agreements relating to residential property, 29.10.2011 ([2011] OJ C 318/133), points 1.10 and 3.3.8 and 3.3.9.

43 Regarding the measure's somewhat limited effects, in part as a consequence of the EU's lack of competence to put it into practice, see I. Domurath, 'A Map of Responsible Lending and Responsible Borrowing in the EU and Suggestions for a Stronger Legal Framework to Prevent Over-Indebtedness of European Consumers' in H.W. Micklitz and I. Domurath, above n. 29, p 155, pp. 163–164. Equally sceptical is V. Mak, 'The Myth of the "Empowered Consumer": Lessons from Financial Literacy Studies' (2012) 1(4) *Journal of European Consumer and Market Law* 254, 258–259. On the subject of consumers' financial education, COM(2007) 808 final, 18.12.2007 and Opinion of the EESC, 29.10.2011 ([2011] OJ C 318/24).

capable of understanding, rational decision-making becomes more difficult.[44] This problem was only partly solved by the precautions adopted to make the language used in the European Standardised Information Sheet (ESIS) less technical than the legal terms in the Directive (Recital 41).

As in the previous Directive 2008/48 (Article 5(6)), Directive 2014/17 (Article 16) maintains the need to provide explanations that enable consumers to choose the most suitable credit products for their needs and financial situation, and, if necessary, the requirement to explain the pre-contractual information, the features of the proposed product, the services associated with it, the obligations to be undertaken and the risks in the event of default. There is, of course, no guarantee that consumers will abandon their decision to take out credit in spite of explanations of the adverse consequences of their decision; there appears to be an almost natural tendency to ignore what is complex, to assume exaggerated optimism over future income, and a disregard for the possible setbacks that may arise during the long life of a loan (e.g. divorce, illness or job loss).[45] However, it would be said that such warnings could be redirected to the 'advisory services' regulated in Article 22 (cf. Article 22(3)(a) Directive 2014/17). The 2007 White Paper had considered it highly desirable for consumers to be given 'objective advice, which is based on their individual profile and commensurate with the complexity of the products and risks involved', so as to acquire the most suitable product for them, but it also recommended that credit institutions should not be under a legal obligation to offer this advice for fear that this would have negative repercussions on mortgage prices and limit the range of products available to consumers.[46] This is undoubtedly why Directive 2014/17 does not make this mandatory, either for credit institutions or for independent third parties. It is clear that if advice were provided by lenders (or tied intermediaries) these would only have to

---

44 For a general critique of this model of consumer protection in the financial context, see Y.M. Atamer, above n. 3, pp. 188–189; J. Köndgen, 'Policy Responses to Credit Crises: Does the Law of Contract Provide an Answer?' in S. Grundmann and Y.M. Atamer, above n. 3, pp. 47–49. Concerning Directive 2014/17, B. Zapf, 'Die Wohnimmobilienkreditrichtlinie 2014/17/EU - Am Ziel einer langen Reise?' (2016) 3 *Zeitschrift für europäisches Privatrecht* 656, 657–658, 664–675.

45 Y.M. Atamer, above n. 3, pp. 184–185; I. Domurath, above n. 13, p. 160. With detail, I. Ramsay, above n. 8, pp. 52 et seq. Regarding borrowers' imperfect reasoning in the context of subprime mortgages, see O. Bar-Gill, 'The Law, Economics and Psychology of Subprime Mortgage Contracts' (2009) 94 *Cornell Law Review* 1073, esp. 1119 et seq.

46 White Paper, above n. 37, p. 7. Agreeing, B. Zapf, above n. 44, 680. Regarding the possible conflict of interests, see Public Consultation, above n. 38, p. 8, pp. 13–14. Against converting lenders into consumer affairs managers, A. Piekenbrock, 'Die geplante Umsetzung der Wohnimmobilienkreditvertragsrichtlinie' (2015) 1 *Zeitschrift für das Privatrecht der Europäischen Union* 26, 35.

take into account their own range of products (Article 22(3)(b)).[47] In reality, this would always be the case, as in order to assess borrowers' ability to repay, lenders would first have to establish which loan is in their best interests.

3.3.2. *Cooling-off Period/ Right of Withdrawal*

The cooling-off period (period of reflection, according to the Directive) and the right of withdrawal (Article 14(6)) are signs of responsible borrowing, and the latter also appeared in Directive 2008/48 (Article 14). The benefits of the right of withdrawal are more apparent than real, because consumers only seem to remember their right of withdrawal when they start to have repayment problems and the right has expired.[48] Moreover, it will not be exercised if the loan has already been invested in the purchase of property and/or the mortgage has been registered. In such scenarios, it falls to Member States to decide whether the right has lapsed (Recital 23). Neither does the cooling-off period seem to be very useful for preventing over-indebtedness if consumers can accept offers at any time during this period (Article 14(6)(b).[49] Ensuring speedy access to the money is incompatible with the purpose of the measure, which is that consumers can seek advice before concluding credit agreements.[50]

3.3.3. *An Understanding Approach to Borrowers*

Directive 2014/17 introduces for the first time provisions on the reasonable forbearance that creditors must show to reduce the number of repossessions and/or alleviate the effects of falling into arrears and foreclosure (Article 28).[51] The philosophy is that it is better to adjust the conditions of a loan than to

[47] This issue has been the object of detailed analysis in the UK. See Financial Services Authority, 'Mortgage Market Review: Distribution & Disclosure', Consultation Paper 10/28, Chapter 2; Financial Services Authority, Mortgage Market Review: Proposed Package of Reforms, Consultation Paper 11/31, December 2011, sections 5.46–5.53, where it is explained that the general rule is that 'an intermediary must always assess whether a mortgage is appropriate for the consumer based on the consumer's particular needs and circumstances' (section 5.52). Later, see Mortgage Conduct of Business Rules, 4.7A [advised sales] and 4.8A [execution-only sales].

[48] Describing the experience in Germany, P. Rott, 'A plea for special treatment of financial services in unfair commercial practices law' (2013) 2(2) *Journal of European Consumer and Market Law* 61, 66.

[49] It is so in Belgium (Art. VII.127(3) Code de Droit économique), the United Kingdom (Mortgage Conduct of Business Rules, 6A.3.4 R(2)(b)), or Italy (Art. 120-*novies* (3) *Testo Unico Bancario*). For a more general overview, see E. Arroyo Amayuelas, 'Crisis, what Crisis' in M. Anderson and E. Arroyo Amayuelas, above n. 31, p. 13.

[50] In contrast, see B. Zapf, above n. 44, p. 681.

[51] See Commission Staff Working Paper 'National measures and practices to avoid foreclosure procedures for residential mortgage loans', document accompanying the Proposal for a Directive on credit agreements relating to residential property, Brussels, 31.03.2011

terminate the credit agreement, and it is consequently necessary to make every effort to avoid early termination of loans if this could lead to the premature enforcement of the collateral. Furthermore, charges must be restricted to what is needed to cover the real cost of the default: administration expenses and interest for default. It would be fair if interest payable were equivalent to the cost to the lender of refinancing, but Directive 2014/17 allows higher default interest rates to be imposed in accordance with the limit provided by national legislatures.[52] It seems to have been precisely the experience in Spain that encouraged the European Parliament to introduce these and other measures into Directive 2014/17, especially the possibility for Member States to recognise the voluntary *datio in solutum* in order to discharge debts.[53] Shortly afterwards, the European Parliament itself drew attention to the shocking consequences of over-indebtedness and foreclosures in Spain and warned that adopting a purely voluntary code of conduct to alleviate the effects of the crisis would merit mistrust.[54]

Among the measures adopted in Spain from 2011 to 2015 were increasing the minimum level of income that could be seized, debt relief/ reduction, extending the repayment period, enabling fresh starts in the event of insolvency proceedings, and accepting transfer of property in lieu of payment (*datio in solutum*), sometimes together with allowing debtors to rent back the property they had transferred. Legislation was accompanied by a good number of ECJ rulings on the unfairness of some mortgage loan terms, a matter on which Directive 2014/17 is silent.[55] However, it should be noted that the effect of these measures has been suboptimal in Spain, since the new laws adopted have been highly restrictive and have failed to benefit a significant number of people.

Where default interest rates are concerned, Article 28(2) and (3) Directive 2014/17 provide the opportunity for the legal setting of lower default interest rates than those established in national law for mortgage credits, as well as extending the rule to other types of loan. However, Article 25 of the Spanish

---

(SEC(2011) 357 final). Art. 28(1) has recently been revised by Art. 28(2) of Directive 2021/2167 of 24 November 2021 on credit servicers and credit purchasers, which exemplifies some potential forbearance measures that could be implemented by Member States.

52 See U. Reifner, above n. 3, p. 424. On Art. 28(2) and (3) Directive 2014/17, see E. Arroyo Amayuelas, 'Límites a los intereses moratorios' in M. Anderson, E. Arroyo Amayuelas and A. Aparicio (eds.), *Cuestiones hipotecarias e instrumentos de prevision. El impacto de la jurisprudencia de la Unión Europea*, Marcial Pons, Barcelona 2021, p. 77, pp. 93–94.

53 I. Ramsay, 'Two Cheers for Europe: Austerity, Mortgage Foreclosures and Personal Insolvency' in H.W. Micklitz and I. Domurath, above n. 29, p. 189, p. 217.

54 European Parliament Resolution 'Mortgage legislation and risky financial instruments in the EU: the case of Spain' of 08.102015 (P8_TA-PROV(2015)0347). Previously, Human Rights Watch, 'Shattered Dreams: Impact of Spain's Housing Crisis on Vulnerable Groups', May 2014 (available at: https://www.hrw.org/report/2014/05/27/shattered-dreams/impact-spains-housing-crisis vulnerable-groups).

55 M. Anderson and H. Simón Moreno, above n. 32, pp. 95 et seq.

Act 5/2019 and Article 114.3 of the *Ley Hipotecaria* (LH) transposing the Directive,[56] establish that these should be three points above the agreed ordinary interest rate. The Spanish legislature tries to prevent unfair terms and to ensure the necessary economic and financial balance between the parties, but it is against EU legislation for the regulation to be mandatory and this does not admit exceptions, even when these would be to the benefit of consumers.[57]

4. THE PARTICULAR DUTY TO ASSESS CONSUMER CREDITWORTHINESS

Long before any EU directives were enacted, some national legal systems already prohibited lending to prospective borrowers without positive credit assessments (e.g. Belgium,[58] the Netherlands[59]); while others only imposed a duty on lenders to warn of the risk of over-indebtedness, undoubtedly with the aim of ensuring that they refused to approve loans that exceeded borrowers' ability to repay, but without making this an obligation. In France this rule was developed through case law and as a rule only applied to poorly informed consumers.[60] In Germany, there was no such restriction and borrowers were held responsible for their own actions.[61] The duty to assess creditworthiness was recognised for the first time in Directive 2008/48 (Article 8, Recital 26), although it is Article 4(17) Directive 2014/17 that explains what this consists of: 'the evaluation of the prospect for the debt obligation resulting from the credit agreement to be met'.

---

56 Act 5/2019, of 15.03.2019 *reguladora de los contratos de crédito inmobiliario* (BOE no. 65 of 16.03.2019). On the unfairness of interest rates by default in Spain, see E. Arroyo Amayuelas, 'The Dialogue Between Courts Concerning Directive 93/13 with Special Regard to the Default Interest Terms' in H. Schulte-Nölke and A. Janssen (eds.), *Festschrift Researches in European Private Law and Beyond – Contributions in Honour of Reiner Schulze's Seventieth Birthday*, Nomos, Baden-Baden 2020, p. 141.

57 On the incorrectness of that transposition, see E. Arroyo Amayuelas, above n. 52, pp. 87 et seq.

58 P. Rott, E. Terryn and C. Twigg-Flesner, above n. 11, p. 164.

59 Art. 4:34 Act of 28 September 2006, on rules regarding the financial markets and their supervision (Act on Financial Supervision). On this subject, see V. Mak, 'What is Responsible Lending? The EU Consumer Mortgage Credit Directive in the UK and the Netherlands' (2015) 38 *Journal of Consumer Policy* 411, 422–423; J. Braspenning, 'Mortgage credit in the Netherlands' (2017) 6(4) *Journal of European Consumer and Market Law* 180, 181–182.

60 P. Rott, E. Terryn and C. Twigg-Flesner, above n. 11, p. 164; J. Köndgen, above n. 44, p. 52. In detail, J. Benedict, 'Responsible Lending – Das europäische Vertragsrecht zwischen caveat emptor und caveat creditor!' (2008) 2 *Zeitschrift für europäisches Privatrecht* 394, 408 et seq.

61 See C. Hofmann, 'Die Pflicht zur Bewertung der kreditwürdigkeit' (2010) 25 *Neue Juristische Wochenschrift* 1782, 1783–1784.

However, Directive 2008/48 did not oblige lenders to refuse credit if borrowers were not sufficiently creditworthy. To some authors the opposite is true and can clearly be deduced from Recital 26,[62] but the Directive has generally been interpreted to mean that lenders only have a duty to warn of the risk and should ultimately leave borrowers to decide whether to take out the loan.[63] The fact that some Member States have also made provision for this outcome[64] undoubtedly accounts for the fact that shortly after Directive 2008/48 was enacted the European Parliament felt obliged to recommend that neither consumer credit nor mortgage credit should be granted to consumers whose creditworthiness had not been established or who had not provided suitable collateral.[65] In fact, this would later be mentioned in ECJ judgments *CA Consumer Finance*[66] and *OPR-Finance s.r.o*,[67] which stated that this obligation (assessing creditworthiness) aimed to make lenders responsible and avoid loans being granted to uncreditworthy consumers. On the other hand, according to the ECJ judgment *Michel Schyns*,[68] a national rule establishing the lender's obligation to refrain from concluding a credit agreement in the event of a consumer's lack of creditworthiness is clearly possible.

Europe did not previously oblige lenders to carry out credit checks before granting mortgages because Directive 2008/48 did not refer to loans of this type, but it should be assumed that individual assessments were regarded as part of standard banking practice in Member States before they became mandatory.

---

62 Thus, in Italy, G. De Cristofaro, 'La nuova disciplina comunitaria del crédito al consumo: La direttiva 2008/48/CE e l'armonizzacione "completa" delle disposizioni nazionali concernenti "taluni aspetti" dei "contratti di credito ai consumatori"' (2008) 3 *Rivista di Diritto Civile* 255, 274. Qualifying this idea, M. Francisetti Brolin, 'L'art. 124-*bis* del TUB e gli incerti riflessi civilistici del c.d. "merito crediticio" nel credito al consumo: dalla *culpa in contrahendo* al vizi del volere' (2014) (2) *Contratto e Impresa/Europa* 541, 559–560.

63 S. Grundmann and C. Hofmann, above n. 26, p. 481; P. Rott, 'Consumer Credit' in H.W. Micklitz *et al.*, *Understanding EU Consumer Law*, Intersentia, Antwerp 2009, pp. 177–213, p. 199; V. Mak and J. Braspenning, '*Errare humanum est:* Financial Literacy in European Consumer Credit Law' (2012) 3 *Journal of Consumer Policy* 307, 327.

64 In Germany, C. Hofmann, above n. 61, 1785–1786. In Austria, § 7(2) DaKRÄG (*Darlehens- und Kreditrechts-Änderungsgesetz*): '[W]enn diese Prüfung erhebliche Zweifel an der Fähigkeit des Verbrauchers ergibt, seine Pflichten aus dem Kreditvertrag vollständig zu erfüllen, hat der Kreditgeber den Verbraucher auf diese Bedenken gegen dessen Kreditwürdigkeit hinzuweisen'. B. Zöchling-Jud, § 7 VKrG in C. Wendehorst and B. Zöchling-Jud, *Verbraucherkreditrecht*, Manz, Wien 2010, Rn. 28–29. In general, J. Köndgen, above n. 44, pp. 51–52, with references to other legal systems. In Spain it has been argued that consumers can only annul agreements in exceptional cases, when the credit institution has wilfully concealed essential information about the debtor's ability to repay. See L. De la Peña and J. López-Frías, 'Crédito responsable: un nuevo concepto en nuestro ordenamiento' (2013) 130 *Revista de Derecho Bancario y Bursátil* 47, 68–69, 77.

65 Opinion of the Committee on Economic and Monetary Affairs (08.06.2012).

66 Case C-449/13, *CA Consumer Finance v. Ingrid Bakkaus*, ECLI:EU:C:2014:2464, (paras. 35, 43).

67 Case C-679/18, *OPR-Finance s.r.o v. GK*, ECLI:EU:C:2020:167, (para. 20).

68 Case C-58/18, *Michel Schyns v. Belfius Banque SA*, ECLI:EU:C:2019:467, (paras. 45–49).

However, it has become clear that there were a number of incentives for not actually carrying these out: first, loans could be approved more quickly, thus saving costs and attracting new clients; secondly, salaries were linked to the number of loans approved. Furthermore, risk was transferred to third parties (through securitisation, sale of the loan portfolio, collateral or mortgage to third parties) and there was the certainty that the property could be sold.[69] This laxity led to an increase in the costs linked to claims and enormous harm, not only to borrowers themselves but also to third party guarantors and the ultimate purchasers of the loan, and finally, through the need to bail out the banks.

This is certainly why Directive 2014/17 imposes the obligation to carry out 'thorough' creditworthiness assessments (Article 18(1)), regulating this issue in some detail in Articles 18–20. The assessment must be carried out before the credit agreement is concluded (Recital 55); in fact, this must be done before lenders provide tailored information, given that they need to consider which loan best meets borrowers' needs (Article 14(1)(a))[70] and, as a general rule, must be repeated whenever there is to be any significant increase in the loan (Article 18(6)).

4.1. HOW CAN THE LIKELIHOOD OF CONSUMERS MEETING THEIR OBLIGATIONS BE ASSESSED?

Directive 2014/17 consigns to Member States the question of what factors should be used to assess the likelihood that consumers will repay the capital and the interest (Article 18 (1)), and indicates that the main consideration here should *not* be the hypothetical increase in value of the property used as collateral (except when the purpose of the loan is to build or renovate the property, Article 18(3)). That is why guarantors' ability to repay cannot be taken into account when assessing that of borrowers,[71] without prejudice to the opportunity to assess this if the guarantor is the person liable for repayment of the debt; naturally, this is not referred to in any of the directives, as contracts

69 Public Consultation, above n. 38, pp. 7–8. See Recital 57, Directive 2014/17.

70 Of this view is P. Rott, 'Die neue Immobiliarkredit-Richtlinie 2014/17 und ihre Auswirkungen auf das Deutsche Recht' (2015) 8 *Zeitschrift für Bank- und Kapitalmarktrecht* 9, 10. This time sequence could not be deduced from the articles of Directive 2008/48, as ECJ judgment C-449/13, *CA Consumer Finance* had the opportunity to point out, without prejudice to the fact that a subsequent creditworthiness assessment might require adapting the explanations already given previously (paras. 45, 49).

71 Recital 57 is clear in this sense. See in Spain, Annex IX para. 12, of the Circular 4/2016, of 27.04.2016, from the Banco de España (BOE no. 110, of 06.05.2016). With regard to consumer credit, see A. Simionato, 'Prime note in tema di valutazione del merito creditizio del consumatore nella Direttiva 2008/48' in G. De Cristofaro (ed.), *La nuova disciplina europea del credito al consumo*, Giappichelli, Turin 2009, pp. 183–193, p. 186.

of guarantee are not credit agreements.[72] However, guarantors are debtors (subsidiary or joint) and are exposed to lender actions in the same way as the main debtor.[73] Some legal systems expressly refer to assessing guarantor creditworthiness (e.g. Spain,[74] Belgium[75] and the United Kingdom[76]), as do the new European Banking Authority (EBA) Guidelines on loan origination and monitoring.[77]

The 2014 legislation imposes no limits on either loan-to-value or loan-to-income ratios and, therefore, does not preclude Member States from setting limits on the amount that can be lent on the basis of 'x' times salary, as is standard practice in the United Kingdom. This would be an additional guideline and should not preclude the prior assessment of consumers' income and expenditure and other financial and economic circumstances (Recital 55, Article 20(1)).[78] The information required is not specified, only that it must take account of 'appropriate account of factors' (Article 18.1), 'shall not be based predominantly on the value of the property' (Article 18.3), and has to be 'necessary, sufficient and proportionate' (Article 20.1). All these expressions are too vague.[79]

Lenders certainly need details of both the nature and duration of consumers' employment, the amount and type of their assets and of their sources of income; that is, whether or not these are independent of paid work, whether this is permanent or temporary, and whether they have rental income (expressly mentioned in Recital 56, but only in the context of buy-to-let agreements),

---

72 Case C-45/96, *Bayerische Hypotheke- und Wechselbank AG v. Edgar Dietzinger*. ECLI:EU:C:1998:111.

73 For the purpose of applying Directive 93/13, Order ECJ Case C-74/15, *Dumitru Tarcău v. Banca Comercială Intesa Sanpaolo România SA*, ECLI:EU:C:2015:772, opens the door to non-professional guarantors being just as protected as consumers.

74 Art. 11.1 Act 5/2019 of 15.03.2019 *reguladora de los contratos de crédito inmobiliario* (BOE no. 65 of 16.03.2019). For details, see B. Saenz de Jubera, *Los contratos de Crédito inmobliario tras la Ley 5/2019, de 15 de marzo*, Tirant lo Blanch, Valencia 2019, p. 184. Earlier, see A. Gálvez Criado, 'Los terceros garantes en los préstamos hipotecarios con consumidores: deberes de información y de evaluación de la solvencia' (2016) 14 *Revista de Derecho Bancario y Bursátil* 15, 31.

75 *Code de Droit économique*, Arts. VII.69(1), VII.77(1) (consumer credit), VII.126(1) and VII.133(1) (mortgage credit).

76 In relation to mortgage credit, Mortgage Conduct of Business Rules, 11.6.2(1)R.

77 See EBA, *Guidelines on Loan Origination and Monitoring. Final Report*. 29.05.2020, Section 5.2, para. 100, p. 35.

78 See, in the United Kingdom, the Mortgage Conduct of Business Rules, 11.6.5R and 11.6.7G.

79 See § 505e BGB and § 18a(10a) KWG and the *Immobiliar-Kreditwürdigkeitsprüfungsleitl inien-Verordnung* of 24.04.2018. For a general assessment of the rules in Germany, The Netherlands and Ireland, see recently A. Van't Hof, 'The First Years of the Creditworthiness Assessment under the Mortgage Credit Directive: is it enough?' (2021) 10(1) *Journal of European Consumer and Market Law* 4, 9–12. In Spain, see the rather generic Art. 11.1 Act 5/2019 of 15.03.2019 *reguladora de los contratos de crédito inmobiliario* (BOE no. 65 of 16.03.2019). Art. 18.2 of Orden EHA/2899/2011 (fn. 32) and Annex IX paras. 12, 15 of the Circular 4/2016, of 27.04.2016, from the Banco de España (BOE no. 110 of 6.05.2016).

investments or family benefits or assistance. Other information needed would include the number of adults and/or children that are dependent on applicants' income, as well as the amount and type of regular expenditure (vehicle maintenance, insurance policies, food, lease payments or other expenditure linked with building maintenance, social security benefits, savings accounts, taxes, etc.).[80] Recital 55 suggests that calculations should take into account necessary adjustments, not only in relation to a possible future reduction in income but also on the basis of a simulation of the effects of a likely variation in interest rates during a specific time period.[81]

Customer information already held by the lender may be sufficient to assess whether borrowers are likely to meet their debt obligations, but as a general rule financial institutions have replaced human intervention with sophisticated risk assessment systems (scoring) – the automated assessment alluded to in Article 18(5)(c) – carried out by agencies specialising in customer assessment (rating), that handle the data on customers' payment behaviour; however, banking institutions can also consult public records (Article 9 Directive 2008/48; Article 18(5)(b), Article 21 Directive 2014/17). Even so, none of the directives makes it mandatory to check solvency records or databases; nor do they even set out any criteria for credit registers (e.g. registration thresholds or terms that should be used).[82]

The personal circumstances of borrowers that may affect their ability to repay the mortgage can rightfully be considered when assessing borrowers' creditworthiness (e.g. planned age for retirement, which will result in a reduction in income), but according to Directive 2014/17 (Article 20(1) and (3)) lenders are not allowed to ask for other personal data not directly related to financial circumstances (e.g. medical history, detail of social media accounts).[83] However, it must not be overlooked that FinTech companies' algorithms are using non-classical sources or unstructured data (i.e. information that cannot be stored in traditional databases, e.g. images, video or audio, collected via

---

80 Focusing on those points in order to encourage responsible borrowing, see the 'Stellungnahme des Gesamtsverbands der Deutschen Versicherungswirtschaft e.V. zum Konsultationspapier der EU-Komission "Verantwortliche Kreditvergabe und Kreditaufnnahme in der EU"', Berlin, 27.09.2008, pp. 7–8. See also, EBA (above n. 75) Sections 5.1 and 5.2, pp. 33, 35–38 and Annex 2, pp. 71–72.

81 See, in the United Kingdom the Mortgage Conduct of Business Rules, 11.6.5R (3) and (4).

82 In contrast, see Art. 16(2) of the 2011 Proposal for a Directive, deleted by the European Parliament (amendment 82).

83 For the right to be forgotten for cancer patients in France, Belgium and Luxembourg, see information provided by Risk & Policy Analysts, 'Evaluation of the Mortgage Credit Directive (Directive 2014/17/EU)'. Final Report, November 2020, p. 116. At: https://op.europa.eu/s/xnl9. See now the new Directive (EU) 2023/2225 of the European Parliament and of the Council of 18 October 2023 on credit agreements for consumers and repealing Directive 2008/48 ([2023] OJ L, of 30.10.2023), Recital 57 and Art. 19(5), according to which personal data found on social media platforms or health data, including cancer data, should not be used when conducting a creditworthiness assessment.

Twitter, YouTube, LinkedIn, or Instagram) to build consumer profiles that can also be used to assess the creditworthiness of individuals.[84] This may be useful for assessing consumers who do not have a credit history (e.g. young people or immigrants), but raises the risk of certain vulnerable persons or groups not being granted the mortgage credit they are applying for. Furthermore, the question arises as to whether consumers' consent to the processing of such data is entirely freely given, not only because of the cognitive biases that prevent credit applicants from seeing the risks, but also because of the difficulty of understanding the complexity of the system of data collection, profiling, and the functioning of algorithms.[85] Consumer associations have already expressed their concern at the lack of transparency behind these types of algorithms.[86]

Online mortgage lending is not yet common, but future regulatory requirements on the assessment of creditworthiness should take account of different distribution channels of mortgage credit services. For the time being, the new Directive 2023/2225 on consumer credit provides that when the creditworthiness assessment is based on automated processing, including profiling, consumers have the right: to request and obtain human intervention on the part of the creditor, to be given a clear explanation of the assessment of creditworthiness, to express his or her point of view, and to request a review of the assessment of the creditworthiness and the decision on the granting of the credit by the creditor.[87] Therefore, it is possible to know which personal data are taken into account, although it is less clear to what extent this knowledge should include the specific weight that the score gives to each specific data. Be it as it may, the possibility to request a review of the initial assessment and of the decision should not necessarily lead to the granting of credit to the consumer, which means that freedom of contract prevails over the result of the creditworthiness assessment.[88]

4.2. BETWEEN FREEDOM OF CONTRACT AND PROHIBITION

A fundamental difference between Directive 2008/48 and Directive 2014/17 is that the latter prohibits the granting of credit to consumers with negative creditworthiness ratings, although this is expressed less decisively in Article

---

84 See on that, Risk & Policy Analysts, above n. 83, pp. 81–83.

85 F. Ferretti, 'Consumer access to capital in the age of FinTech and big data: The limits of EU law' (2018) 25(4) *Maastricht Journal of European and Comparative Law* 476, 484 et seq.

86 EBA Consumer Trends Report 2018/2019, of 20.02.2019, para. 184, p. 54.

87 See Art. 18(8) and Recital 56, n. 83 above.

88 See General Approach on the Proposal. Document 10382/21 + REV1 * ADD1-4 (Brussels, 07.06.2022). Council amendment to Recital 48 and the new Recitals 54, 56 of Directive 2023/2225.

18(5)(a) than in Article 14(2)(a) of the 2011 Proposal.[89] Transposing the legislation has required Member States to include this prohibition in their national laws (e.g. France[90] and the United Kingdom[91]). The prohibition is less explicit in other states (Italy[92]) and there are still countries such as Spain that establishes prudential norms that 'creditworthiness assessments shall be undertaken without prejudice to the freedom of contract … and in no case … shall the liability for customers' failure to fulfil their obligations be passed on to institutions'.[93] Nevertheless, Article 11(5) of the Spanish Act 5/2019 should take precedence; it is therefore clear that national law interpretation in accordance with European law requires this freedom to be understood in the sense that even if creditworthiness assessments produce positive ratings, this must not result in lenders being under any obligation to grant credit (Recital 57). For the rest, it would not make sense for regulatory changes to be reflected only in the governance of mortgage credit. This was unfortunately the approach adopted by the Catalan legislature;[94] the Belgian legislature has used better criteria and

---

89 Warning of the change and suggesting that the prohibition on granting credit is not obvious, see F.L. Schäfer, above n. 39, p. 210; R. Simon, 'Transposition of the Mortgage Credit Directive into Hungarian and Czech Law – The Problem of Credit Intermediaries' (2017) 6(3) *Journal of European Consumer and Market Law* 106, 107. In Spain, hesitating, see S. Nasarre Aznar and H. Simón Moreno, 'Un paso más en la protección de los deudores hipotecarios de vivienda: La Directiva 2014/17/UE y la reforma del Código de Consumo de Cataluña por Ley 20/2014' (2015) 139 *Revista de Derecho Bancario y Bursátil* 11, 13, 16, 19. Other authors state that the prohibition does not exist, but on the other hand they hold lenders responsible for the consequences of granting credit irresponsibly. Thus, see M. Cuena Casas, 'El sobreendeudamiento privado como causa de la crisis financiera y su necesario enfoque multidisciplinar' in L. Prats Albentosa and M. Cuena Casas (eds.), *Préstamo responsable y ficheros de solvencia*, Aranzadi-Thomson Reuters, Cizur Menor 2014, pp. 27–89, p. 77; S. Pagliantini, 'Statuto dell'informazione e prestito responsabile nella direttiva 17/2014/UE (sui contratti di credito ai consumatori relativi a beni immobili residenziali)' (2014) (2) *Contratto e impresa/Europa* 523, 537. However, the general sense expressed by academia in Europe is that reflected above in the text. See, among many others, G. Comparato, above n. 29, p. 19; M. Anderson and H. Simón Moreno, above n. 32, p. 84; I. Domurath, above n. 43, p. 168; P. Kalamees, K. Lilleholt and K. Sein, 'Responsible Lending in Estonian and Norwegian Law' (2014) 3(1) *Journal of European Consumer and Market Law* 29, 35; V. Mak, above n. 59, p. 426.

90 *Code de la Consommation*, Art. L 313-16(1). But see H. Aubry, 'Mortgage credit in France' (2017) 6(4) *Journal of European Consumer and Market Law* 173, 174, 175.

91 Mortgage and Home Finance Conduct of Business Handbook. 11.6.2R(1)(b).

92 Art. 120-*undecies* Testo Unico Bancario.

93 See Art. 18(6) Order EHA/2899/2011 of 28 October on transparency and customer protection in banking services (BOE no. 261 of 29.11.2011). Agreeing with the system and thus critical of the Directive 2014/17 is E. Muñiz Espada, *El deterioro del mercado hipotecario y la necesidad de su reconstrucción. Aportaciones desde el Derecho europeo*, Thomson Reuters, Cizur Menor 2016, pp. 124–125.

94 See the original Art. 263-2(4) *Codi de Consum*, before the provision was annulled by the Spanish Constitutional Court (STC 54/2018 of 24.05.2018). Art. 252-9(2)(b) *Codi de Consum* extends the prohibition to the contracting of financial investment services when

extended the prohibition to consumer credit.[95] Mortgage credit can only be granted in Germany if 'repayment is likely' and consumer credit only if 'there are no substantial doubts'. This distinction shows that the checks used to assess creditworthiness are also stricter for mortgage credit, which could perhaps be justified by the fact that the sums to be repaid are relatively large as a rule.[96]

The prohibition certainly encroaches on private autonomy: it conditions lender criteria for choosing prospective customers and for putting their business strategies into practice, and it also conditions consumers' choice of credit. Greater respect for free will would have required lenders to be obliged to inform borrowers of negative credit ratings but would not keep them from concluding contracts if consumers were aware of the risks and thus acted on the basis of an informed decision. The negative effects of the prohibition could also be considered: on one hand there is a risk of not holding debtors liable, who could use strategic and opportunistic litigation to complain about lender behaviour; on the other, the costs of borrowing are increased for creditworthy individuals. However, both arguments disregard the fact that lenders are not only better informed but are also better placed to know the risks, and that the prohibition not only protects consumers from their own short-sightedness, but also from banks' tendency towards excessive lending and taking advantage of cognitive biases among borrowers.[97] If over-indebtedness poses a threat to society as a whole, and consumers also usually turn out to be vulnerable, preventative and more general solutions are needed, undoubtedly together with a certain dose of paternalism.[98] On the other hand, excluding members of the public in a high-risk category from credit provision – another of the arguments usually raised against the prohibition[99] – should not lead to greater social exclusion than decisions to grant it, as shown by the subprime mortgage

creditworthiness assessments are negative. In Andalusia, Art. 13(3) L. 3/2016, only prevents lenders from granting credit when applicants or guarantors refuse to provide the necessary information.

95 *Code de Droit économique*, Art. VII.77(2) (consumer credit) and Art. VII.133(2) (mortgage credit). See also Case C-58/18, *Michel Schyns v. Belfius Banque SA*, ECLI:EU:C:2019:467, paras. 45–49.

96 Cf. § 505a(1). See J. Schürnbrand, § 505a BGB, *Münchener Kommentar zum BGB*, III, 7. Auflage, C.H. Beck, München 2017, Rn. 6–7; M. Artz, '§ 505a BGB' in P. Bülow and M. Artz, *Verbraucherkreditrecht*, 9th ed., C.H. Beck, München 2016, Rn. 9.

97 In this respect, see I. Ramsay, above n. 3, pp. 394–395. On the effectiveness of credit bureaus for creating a subprime market in the United Kingdom, see F. Ferretti, above n. 27, p. 796.

98 Admitting that it is not easy to say which protection model is best because not all consumers are the same, and acknowledging that the question depends greatly on local markets, see V. Mak, above n. 43, pp. 259 et seq. V. Mak and J. Braspenning, above n. 63, p. 327, believe that a general prohibition for all types of consumers is an extreme solution. Also, raising objections, see F. Ferretti, above n. 27, pp. 815–816.

99 E. Gallego Sánchez, 'La obligación de evaluar la solvencia del deudor. Consecuencias derivadas de su incumplimiento' in L. Prats Albentosa and M. Cuena Casas, above n. 89, pp. 207–242, p. 222, pp. 238–239.

crisis, which has forced thousands of borrowers out of their homes as a result of foreclosure by unsatisfied creditors.[100] What would not be acceptable would be to refuse credit on the basis of arbitrary or unjustified decisions. In any case, setting reasonable limits is always possible because being unable to repay a specific loan does not necessarily mean being unable to repay another. Furthermore, it should be noted that Directive 2014/17 permits loans granted to a specific sector of the public on special terms by social banks, cooperatives and local authorities to be excluded from its scope (Article 3(3)(c)), which includes being able to dispense with creditworthiness assessments for such cases; hence, there is no total prohibition on granting credit should the debtor be at risk of over-indebtedness.

4.3. THE CONSEQUENCES OF CREDITWORTHINESS ASSESSMENT

Member States are responsible for determining the consequences of granting credit contrary to the prohibition (Article 38 Directive 2014/17). Directive 2014/17 only provides for the remedies available to lenders when it is consumers who are imprudent and do not meet their pre-contractual obligations (Articles 18(4), 20(3) third sub-paragraph and (4)). This is one more sign that the responsible lending policy cannot work effectively according to the European Union if borrowers do not behave appropriately,[101] especially if they are capable of lying to obtain credit.[102] However, if in accordance with Article 20(1) final sentence and 20(3) Directive 2014/17, consumers are required to provide documentary evidence of information (salary slips, tax returns, average current account balance statements)[103] and credit cannot be granted if the information is withheld or cannot be verified (Article 20(4)), deception will certainly not be easy. It would consequently constitute a lack of diligence on the part of the lender not to detect it (e.g. it is easy to spot whether salary slips are for months in which bonuses were paid). This is especially true since institutions have to be able to request clarification and independently verify what consumers tell them (Article 20(1) and (3)), although they are not always obliged to do so

---

100 G. Comparato, above n. 29, pp. 12–14; I. Domurath, above n. 43, p. 168; U. Reifner, above n. 3, p. 426.

101 Public Consultation (above n. 38), p. 3, p. 10.

102 Public Consultation (above n. 38), p. 10. The problem seems to refer specifically to self-certification mortgages, which require no proof of income and have been common practice in the USA, UK and Ireland. See Financial Services Authority, Mortgage Market Review: Responsible Lending, July 2010, paras. 2.19–2.20.

103 On the basis of Art. 8 Directive 2008/48, see Case C-449/13, *CA Consumer Finance*, ECLI:EU:C:2014:2464, para. 37.

(Article 20(1), 'when necessary').[104] Nonetheless, there will always be scenarios that are difficult to check: consumers may hide the fact that they know they are going to lose their jobs and their incomes will therefore fall; they may not give details of all their financial obligations, or they may fail to give details of outstanding repayments on loans granted by other institutions. It is impossible to check the latter without consulting customer credit histories, and these records may differ from one country to another (there are both public records [credit registries] and private records [credit bureaus], which hold positive and/or negative information), or may not function efficiently in all countries, perhaps because loans for a particular amount are not recorded, or because there is no historical record of data, or because not all lenders have access to them, or, finally, because borrower consent is needed for the data to be processed.[105]

The Directive says nothing about what happens if lenders give credit without previously assessing creditworthiness (a scenario that would have to be considered unlikely nowadays) or if they do so when risk assessments are negative or are manipulated to produce positive results. All that Articles 18(4) and 20(3) second sub-paragraph provide for is the inability of lenders to modify, cancel or terminate agreements when they realise, after the signature of the credit agreement, that the assessment of creditworthiness was incorrectly conducted due to incomplete information at the time of the assessment (Recital 58). Therefore, leaving aside cases when debtors are to blame for manipulating the information,[106] lender error, misconduct or negligence would not prevent consumers from continuing to enjoy the capital. However, what if they could not pay it back?

4.3.1. Between Public and Private Law

Since the duty to assess creditworthiness is frequently incorporated into prudential standards whose aim is to control and supervise the banking system as a whole there is some debate over whether any infringement could entail private law penalties in addition to administrative sanctions

---

104 Once more, Case C-449/13, *CA Consumer Finance*, paras. 38–39.

105 See, for instance, A. Fejős, 'Mortgage Credit in Hungary' (2017) 6(3) *Journal of European Consumer and Market Law* 139, 141–142. Arguing in favour of positive creditworthiness records to prevent over-indebtedness, M. Cuena Casas, 'Intercambio de información positiva de solvencia y funcionamiento del mercado de crédito' (2017) 3 *InDret* 1. In contrast, questioning the role of credit bureaus, F. Ferretti, above n. 27, pp. 815–817.

106 In seems that in these cases termination would indeed be possible (Art. 20(3) third sub-para., Recital 58). In many legal systems there is speculation in such cases about challenging void contracts that are vitiated by error. Italian academic writing is an example of this rationale. See M. Francisetti Brolin, above n. 62, p. 569. If these were contracts regarding immovable property, it is not clear what advantages this solution would have over the more forceful remedy of declaring the loan due and initiating the enforcement procedure.

(expressly provided for in Article 38(2) Directive 2014/17), among them, lenders' civil liability.[107]

Directive 2014/17 suggests that private law remedies should only be applied when it is borrowers that do not act responsibly (Recital 83), and thus appears to avert the risk that Article 18(5)(a) will be understood to have been transposed incorrectly if the prohibition is only incorporated into prudential standards. It would then be said that, as the legal policy objective of regulations of this kind is to defend the public interest, avoiding over-indebtedness is in the general interest of the financial system and the particular interest of banks, in whose business risk is implicit.[108] Consequently, the administrative sanctions provided for in each case, according to the severity of the infringement, would be sufficient. However, the Directive pursues not only the stability of the financial system, but also a high degree of consumer protection (Recitals 5–7, 49, 81–82). No doubt should be cast on the fact that this includes borrowers' individual rights to a creditworthiness assessment, and any violation of this duty on the part of lenders should naturally have civil consequences. Administrative sanctions serve to drive unfair competitors out of the market, but they have no individual or direct benefits for consumers. Two ECJ judgments have confirmed that civil sanctions are both possible and necessary.[109] In any case, the prohibition on extending credit to those who do not have the appropriate profile should not lead to contract annulment.[110]

---

107 For more detail, A. Simionato, above n. 71, pp. 188–192. Case C-222/02, *Peter Paul, Cornelia Sonnen-Lütte and Christel Mörkens v. Bundesrepublik Deutschland* ECLI:EU:C:2004:606, understands that no right to individual protection derives from the prudential standards for supervising the banking sector (paras. 44, 46–47).

108 Concerning Directive 2008/48, S. Grundmann, 'EC Financial Services – Developments 2002–2005' (2005) 1(4) *European Review of Contract Law* 482, 488: 'a behaviour which so far rather aimed at self-protection would now be imposed on banks'. For the arguments, with references to German writing, see C. Hofmann, above n. 61, p. 1783. In Spain, see E. Gallego Sánchez, above n. 99, pp. 239–240.

109 Case C-565/12, *LCL Le Crédit Lyonnais v. Fesih Kalhan*; Case C-449/13, *CA Consumer Finance*. See M. Artz, above n. 96, Rn. 5; A. Rank and M. Schmidt-Kessel, 'Mortgage Credit in Germany' (2017) 6(4) *Journal of European Consumer and Market Law Review* 176, 177.

110 Expressly, in Germany, see *Referentenentwurf*: 'Die Verbote des Absatzes 1 verdeutlichen den Zweck der Kreditwürdigkeitsprüfung, stellen aber kein Verbot gemäß § 134 BGB dar, das zur Nichtigkeit des Darlehensvertrags führt (vgl. § 505d BGB)', p. 95. In Italy, E. Bargelli and G. Donadio, 'The Impact of Directive 2014/17 in Italy' in M. Anderson and E. Arroyo Amayuelas, above n. 31, pp. 304–331, p. 318 and n. 45, who refer to the doctrinal debate. In Portugal, J. Morais Carvalho, *Manual de Direito do Consumo*, 4th ed., Coimbra, Almedina 2017, p. 373. In favour of partial nullity, in Spain, M. Anderson and H. Simón Moreno, above n. 32, p. 85; B. Sáenz de Jubera, above n. 74, pp. 182–183.

4.3.2. *Between Interest Loss and Reduction*

It has already been noted that the 2002 Consumer Credit Directive Proposal included the possibility of loss of interest (Article 31(2)). As its incorporation into the final draft of the Directive was rejected, if adopted in Member States the measure could have run the risk of being considered disproportionate were it possible to understand that protecting consumers did not always entail disregarding lenders' interest in remuneration.[111] To some extent this is the philosophy behind § 505d(1) BGB, which only provides for reducing interest that would have been earned had the lender used the capital for a secure investment instead of providing the loan.[112] Accordingly, a fixed interest rate will be replaced by the customary interest rate for German mortgage-backed bonds and German public-sector bonds, and a flexible interest rate will be replaced by a customary interbank rate, provided these are not higher than those agreed upon in the contract.[113] As well as France,[114] countries such as Belgium[115] and Switzerland[116] have provided for the forfeiture of interest; in Switzerland lenders may even lose the right to the repayment of capital in case of serious violation, something which Germany expressly rejects,[117] and the consumer can also ask for the repayment of the amounts he has already paid, though this does not apply to credit secured on real estate.[118]

111 Thus, C. Brenner, *Die Verbraucherschützenden EG-Richtlinien im Bereich des Schuldrechts und Ihre Umsetzung in Deutschland und Frankreich. Auf dem Weg zu einem europäischen Privatrecht?*, Akademischer Verlag, Munchen 2000, p. 180. Also, J. Köndgen, above n. 44, p. 51, believes that there is a risk of unfair consumer enrichment. Stressing the effectiveness of this sanction, on the other hand, see S. Díez Alabart, 'Evaluación de la solvencia del consumidor, tasación de inmuebles y consultas en ficheros de solvencia' in S. Díaz Alabart and P. Represa Polo (eds.), *La protección del consumidor en los créditos hipotecarios (Directiva 2014/17)*, Reus, Madrid 2015, pp. 223–276, p. 237.

112 M. Artz, above n. 96, '§ 505a BGB',§ 505d', Rn. 6. The reduction is excluded if a proper assesment of the creditworthiness would have had a positive result. See also, A. Rank and M. Schmidt-Kessel, above n. 109, p. 178.

113 A. Rank and M. Schmidt-Kessel, above n. 109, p. 178.

114 *Code de la Consommation*, Arts. L. 341-27, L. 341-28. See also L. 341-31, L. 341-33. For a general view, see Aubry, above n. 90, pp. 175–176. In Case C-565/12, *LCL Le Crédit Lyonnais v. Fesih Kalhan*, the ECJ understood that the penalty involving the forfeiture of contractual interest was a poor deterrent if not also accompanied by the loss of statutory interest (para. 55).

115 *Code de Droit économique*, Arts. VII.201, VII.209 (1er).

116 *Loi fédérale sur le crédit à la consommation*, Art. 28(1), Art. 32.

117 M. Artz, '§ 505d BGB', above n. 96, Rn. 4 et seq.

118 Art. 7.1(a) *Loi fédérale sur le crédit à la consummation*. See A.-C. Fornage, 'Vers un droit de crédit à la consommation plus responsable' (2017) II *Journal des Tribunaux* 4, 28 et seq., esp. 34–35.

4.3.3. *Claim for Damages*

Should the national laws not provide for a specific private law penalty, it should be possible to hold lenders liable by applying the general rules,[119] perhaps even additional to administrative sanctions (which may not always be required; if the lender's behaviour is not repeated, for example). This would not contradict Recital 56 Directive 2014/17, which, given its systematic positioning, only refers to scenarios in which creditworthiness has been assessed correctly. In Spain, the nature of this liability is debated,[120] and part of the academic community considers this option to be very impractical.[121]

The civil liability claim requires proving the causal link, i.e. that if the solvency check had been carried out and its negative results communicated to the consumer, the consumer would never have concluded the contract. It is not necessary for the courts to start from the presumption that this is exactly what would have happened, in a similar way to how they reason when it comes to holding the bank liable for negligent marketing of complex investment products, because, as has already been repeatedly stated, the lender has a legal duty to refrain from concluding the contract when the borrower is not creditworthy and, consequently, the mere fact of creating a risk for the consumer must be sufficient for liability to arise. The causal link is therefore always present.[122]

If the possibility of claiming damages is accepted, the problem lies in determining exactly what borrowers can claim.[123] The answer would be that the

---

119 In favour of an individual right to redress, regarding Art. 8 Directive 2008/48, P. Rott, E. Terryn and C. Twigg-Flesner, above n. 11, pp. 166–168. In Germany, see C. Hofmann, above n. 61, p. 1785; in Estonia, P. Kalamees, K. Lilleholt and K. Sein, above n. 89, p. 32, pp. 36–37; in Spain, see M.C. Mayorga Toledano, 'Obligaciones de la entidad de crédito en la concesión de crédito adecuado a la solvencia y capacidad de endeudamiento del cliente', in M. Flores Doña and J.T. Raga Gil (eds.), *El préstamo hipotecario y el mercado del crédito en la Unión Europea*, Tirant lo Blanch, Valencia 2016, pp. 353–377, p. 373. Concerning Directive 2014/17, stating this in Italy, see P. Sirena, 'Introduzione. Autonomia privata e vigilanza bancaria nel diritto europeo dei contratti di finanziamento' in P. Sirena (ed.) *I mutui ipotecari nel diritto comparato ed europeo. Comentario alla direttiva 2014/17/UE*, Grupo24ore, Milano 2016, pp. 3–8, p. 8.

120 See P. Álvarez Olalla, 'La obligación de evaluar la solvencia', in: Asociación de Profesores de Derecho Civil (ed.), *Vivienda e Hipoteca*, Tecnos, Madrid 2018, pp. 135–184, p. 171; S. Díaz Alabart, above n. 111, p. 235.

121 Among others, M. J. Marín López, 'La obligación del prestamista de evaluar la solvencia del prestatario', in Carrasco (ed.), *Comentario a la Ley de Contratos de Crédito Inmobiliario*, Aranzadi, Cizur Menor 2019, pp. 211–256, pp. 254–255.

122 Similar, P. Buck-Heeb, 'Rechtsfolgen fehlender oder fehlerhafter Kreditwürdigkeitsprüfung' (2016) 29 *Neue Juristische Wochenschrift* 2065, 2070.

123 J. Köndgen, above n. 44, p. 51. Part of German academia rejects the possibility that the sanction provided for in § 505a BGB can be cumulated with claims for compensation, ex § 280 BGB. Thus, M. Artz, '§ 505a BGB', above n. 96, Rn. 15. But see A. Rank and M. Schmidt-Kessel, above n. 109, p. 178.

damage is the agreement itself, so judges will have to consider the difference that should ideally exist between the agreement actually concluded and the agreement that the consumer could really have afforded. If not even this is possible – that is, if the consumer really had no ability at all to repay – then it would probably be necessary to consider the possibility that the loan was unenforceable and the consumer will be released from repaying both the capital and the interest.[124] In short, the borrower ought to be in the same position as if the contract had never been concluded.[125]

5. CREDITWORTHINESS ASSESSMENT IN THE RECENT DIRECTIVE (EU) 2023/2225 ON CREDIT AGREEMENTS FOR CONSUMERS

Directive (EU) 2023/2225 adopts an approach to assessing creditworthiness, which is no longer based on trust in the decisions of informed consumers, but on lenders' duty to act in their interests (Article 18(1)).[126] This means that credit can only be granted when the results of the creditworthiness analysis are positive (Article 18(6)). However, firstly, it is still up to Member States to decide on the procedures by which lenders conclude that consumers are likely to repay the credit (Article 18(4)); and secondly, it is also up to national law to stipulate the consequences of disregarding negative creditworthiness (Article 44). Credit that was formerly granted in less than 24 hours and without paperwork is not exempt from this creditworthiness assessment, but some may perhaps benefit from the circumstances provided for in Recital 55, when it concerns, *inter alia*, the financing of studies or one-off health care expenses.

The increasing use of alternative data sources and the transparency of assessments made using machine learning techniques are real preoccupations in the new Consumer Credit Directive. This Directive (and other recent legislation) emphasises that it is no longer possible to look at responsible lending without accounting for consumer data protection.

124 In relation to consumer credit in Austrian law, see B. Zöchling-Jud, above n. 64, Rn. 45–46, pp. 193–194. In Germany, C. Hofmann, above n. 61, p. 1786; M. Artz, '§ 505a BGB', above n. 96, Rn. 15.

125 P. Buck-Heeb, above n. 122, p. 2070.

126 Cfr. Art. 8 Directive 2008/48; Arts. 18, 20 Directive 2014/17. See SWD (2020) 254 final, p. 61.

6. FINAL THOUGHTS

Both Directive 2008/48 and Directive 2014/17 aim to create an internal credit market and protect consumers, but in the first Directive the somewhat vaguely defined principle of responsible lending was seen as a stumbling block (too great a burden for the industry),[127] while the second was enacted when the economic and financial crisis had already erupted, as a consequence of which more emphasis was placed on sustainability in borrowing, for the benefit of both consumers and the financial system.[128] This required adopting new and rather more forceful measures to tackle the problem of over-indebtedness, although ultimately there are question marks over the usefulness of some of the measures, such as the need to supply a wealth of pre-contractual information that consumers do not understand anyway and establishing a period of reflection for offers, before which loans are not available, but that consumers can disregard anyway if national legislation provides for this.

According to one study, before the enactment of Directive 2008/48 – whose scope of application excludes mortgage credit – Member States rarely had legislation in place that obliged lenders to assess potential borrowers' ability to repay, and when they did it was not always effective as there was no provision for sanctioning infringements.[129] The reluctance with which Directive 2008/48 approached the problem is also in contrast to the legislature's firm commitment in Directive 2014/17. In accordance with the latter, lenders must not offer credit to consumers who are not in a position to pay it back, which is perfectly reasonable and necessary, not only to strengthen banks – the banking system in general – but also to protect borrowers' interests. Precisely because lenders cannot grant loans that are not suitable for consumers' needs or financial circumstances, it could be concluded that there is an implicit duty to advise them as to what is best for them, even though no directive expressly says so. The provisions of the Directive 2014/17 on the assessment of creditworthiness are also taken over by the new Directive 2025/2023 on consumer credits.

All in all, the creditworthiness provisions in the European credit directives are of paramount importance, because they are the main instrument for establishing whether the consumer deserves the loan they apply for, at what interest rate and within what limits. The aim is to avoid irresponsible granting of credit, both in the interest of the creditor (avoiding losses in case of default) and the consumer (providing affordable credit), although the directives tend to emphasise the latter, in order to prevent the creditor from basing their business

---

[127] P. Rott, above n. 63, p. 185.

[128] On the regulation's legal policy aims, see Recitals 2, 3, 5–6 Directive 2014/17. V. Mak, above n. 59, p. 413; G. Comparato, above n. 29, pp. 16–17.

[129] See European Commission, Directorate General for Employment, 'Towards a common operational European definition of over-indebtedness', Brussels 2008, pp. 67–68.

on the consumer's risk of default (e.g. in the form of high interest rates for those with a higher risk profile).[130]

In any event, it cannot be disregarded that private enforcement would be strengthened (and, therefore, also consumer protection) in the Member States if the banking supervisor's control allowed specialised entities to claim compensation directly from the bank or if lenders were encouraged to voluntarily join the consumer arbitration system – not to mention the possibility of making it mandatory –, which is not the case in Spain despite the provisions of Article 39 of Directive 2014/17.[131]

The notion of responsible lending goes hand-in-hand with responsible borrowing, but it is clear that the duty of prudence falls firstly on lenders, who have greater experience and more information than any creditor can have about their debtor. It is therefore logical that consumers can hold lenders liable when they grant credit over and above the advisable limits, although the directives once again remain silent on this point. The prohibition on granting credit cannot solve the problem of over-indebtedness once and for all, as its roots also lie in external causes (divorce, illness and unemployment), but will undoubtedly contribute to preventing unfair practices and to protecting the banking sector against its own excesses.

Directive 2014/17 needs to be revised, in compliance with Article 44, in order to continue to ensure an efficient and competitive internal market with a high and equivalent level of consumer protection. FinTech companies base their business on artificial intelligence, but the digitisation of financial services is also affecting traditional banking. Part of the mortgage lending process is already digitised, particularly in terms of online advertising and information, if not fully automated, thanks to credit scoring companies that profile and assess the creditworthiness of consumers.[132] The use of artificial intelligence presents challenges, which the legislator will have to take into account in the future reform of the Directive 2014/17. Consequently, it is certain that data protection will continue to play a decisive role in the responsible lending programme, ensuring the protection of the mortgage credit consumers following the path of the Consumer Credit Directive reform.

---

130 Recital 55 Directive 2014/17; Recital 54 and Art. 18.1 Directive 2023/2225.

131 Similar thoughts regarding Directive 2008/48, O. Cherednychenko and J. Meindertsma, 'Irresponsible Lending in the Post-Crisis Era: Is the EU Consumer Credit Directive Fit for Its Purpose?' (2019) 42 *Journal of Consumer Policy* 483, 510–511.

132 See Case C-634/21, *OQ v. Land Hessen/Schufa*, ECLI:EU:C:2023:957.

CHAPTER 7

BANK CODES OF CONDUCT AND EUROPEAN CONTRACT LAW

Moritz RENNER

1. INTRODUCTION: A REGULATORY PARADOX

The regulatory response to the financial crisis has had a paradoxical effect:[1] stricter public supervision of the financial sector has led to more private self-regulation.[2] So-called codes of conduct and codes of ethics, i.e. self-made rules of banks, banking groups and associations, have proliferated in recent years.[3]

---

1 For a systems-theory inspired analysis of the legal developments contributing to this situation see M. RENNER, 'Death By Complexity. The Financial Crisis and the Crisis of Law in World Society' in P.F. KJAER, G. TEUBNER and A. FEBBRAJO (eds.), *The Financial Crisis in Constitutional perspective: The Dark Side of Functional Differentiation*, Hart Publishing, Oxford 2011, p. 93.

2 The turn towards self-regulation in the financial sector clearly predates the financial crisis, for a political science analysis of this trend see T. BÜTHE and W. MATTLI, *The Global Rulers: The Privatization of Regulation in the World Economy*, Princeton University Press, Princeton NJ 2011. After the crisis, this trend has not been reversed, but even reinforced by regulatory interventions, as will be explained below, section 2.

3 Sector-wide conduct of business codes and standard contracts have a longstanding tradition, e.g. in the German banking sector, where the beginnings of this regulatory technique can be traced back well into the 19th century, cf. H.J. BUNTE and M. ARTZ, '§ 2. AGB-Banken (Allgemeiner Teil)' in J. ELLENBERGER and H.J. BUNTE (eds.), *Bankrechts-Handbuch. Band I*, 6th ed., C.H. Beck, München 2022, pp. 2–3.

They have grown in number, and they have often grown in length. But – have they also grown in importance? This will be the subject of this contribution, with a specific view to the doctrine and practice of European contract law.[4]

The contribution will proceed in three steps. As a first step, it will try to explain why and how the proliferation of private codes in the banking sector is a consequence of stricter public regulation (below section 2). The second step will be a brief look at a practical example of a conduct code in the banking sector (below section 3). The main focus will be on the third step. Here, the contribution aims to analyse the different ways in which codes of conduct might have legal effects on the relationship between the bank and its customers (below section 4). The contribution will then draw some conclusions, which might be relevant not only for the field of banking law, but for contract law more generally.

2. PUBLIC AND PRIVATE REGULATION AFTER THE CRISIS

Why are we talking about the role of conduct codes in the banking sector today? There is at least one very good reason: codes of conduct are a central building block in the regulatory response to the financial crisis, in Europe as well as in the US.

Why is that so? Let us reconsider the situation that regulators were facing after the crisis. The Dutch economist Dirk Schoenmaker has aptly described this situation as a regulatory trilemma.[5] The structure of our financial system relies on three conditions which are hard to reconcile: first, the financial system needs stability; second, the financial system is internationally integrated; and third, it is supervised by national authorities. It is all but impossible to create financial stability for a global financial market through national supervisory authorities.

The answer to this regulatory trilemma has been highly sophisticated. It is evidenced by the hundreds of pages of legislation on the European Banking

---

4 The role of competition law will not be dealt with extensively in this contribution. However, competition law can be a valuable enforcement mechanism for corporate codes of conduct especially in jurisdictions that foresee a private cause of action where provisions against unfair competition have been infringed. For an in-depth discussion of the interaction between codes of conduct and competition law see A. Beckers, 'The Regulation of Market Communication and Market Behaviour: Corporate Social Responsibility and the Directives on Unfair Commercial Practices and Unfair Contract Terms' (2017) 54 *Common Market Law Review* 475.

5 D. Schoenmaker, *Governance of International Banking*, Oxford University Press, Oxford 2013, pp. 18–33.

Union, and the CRD IV package[6] more specifically. One of the remarkable traits of this regulatory response is that it directly addresses the regulatory trilemma through a combination of public and private modes of enforcement. The corporate and group structures of global banks are employed for implementing the aims of supervisory regulation. For example, Articles 74–96 of the CRD IV Directive contain detailed obligations for banks to introduce internal compliance and risk management systems. These obligations must be fulfilled not only on an individual basis, but, according to Article 109(2) CRD IV Regulation, also by bank holding companies for the banking group as a whole, including its foreign subsidiaries. Consequently, the Deutsche Bank AG in Frankfurt/Germany, for example, is ultimately responsible for any non-compliance of its US subsidiaries with risk management requirements established by EU law.

A similar regulatory technique can be found in the governance rules of current capital markets regulation, e.g. in Article 16(3) MiFiD II,[7] which demands that investments firms 'shall maintain and operate effective organisational and administrative arrangements with a view to taking all reasonable steps designed to prevent conflicts of interest' and must 'maintain, operate and review a process for the approval of each financial instrument and significant adaptations of existing financial instruments before it is marketed or distributed to clients'. Here, the internal governance structures of banks and other financial institutions are exploited for implementing regulatory law.

Similar mechanisms of self-regulation are factually required by financial authorities who supervise the implementation of the European rules on banking regulation. The German financial markets authority, for instance, demands that banks must establish their own 'organisational guidelines' (MaRisk AT 5[8]) to fulfil regulatory compliance requirements. It is also in the banks' own interest to establish such codes: the global head office of an international bank, for example, will use group-wide codes of conduct to avoid (administrative as well as, potentially, civil) liability for wrongdoings of its foreign subsidiaries.

These mechanisms of public–private co-regulation allow national or supra-national regulators to implement financial stability rules with a global

---

6 Consisting of Directive 2013/36/EU of 26 June 2013 on access to the activity of credit institutions and the prudential supervision of credit institutions and investment firms, amending Directive 2002/87/EC and repealing Directives 2006/48/EC and 2006/49/EC [2013] OJ L 176/338 and Regulation (EU) No. 575/2013 of 26 June 2013 on prudential requirements for credit institutions and investment firms and amending Regulation (EU) No. 648/2012 [2013] OJ L 176/1.

7 Directive 2014/65/EU of 15 May 2014 on markets in financial instruments and amending Directive 2002/92/EC and Directive 2011/61/EU (recast) [2014] OJ L 173/349.

8 Bundesanstalt für Finanzdienstleistungsaufsicht, *Rundschreiben 09/2017 (BA) – Mindestanforderungen an das Risikomanagement – MaRisk*, available at: https://www.bafin.de/SharedDocs/Veroeffentlichungen/DE/Rundschreiben/2017/rs_1709_marisk_ba.html.

reach. They deliberately rely on the governance mechanism of banks. For one thing, they oblige financial institutions to establish certain internal structures and institutions, such as a group-wide compliance officer or a global risk management committee. Furthermore, they also make use of corporate codes of conduct with which banks bind themselves to a certain standard of behaviour *vis-à-vis* their customers and the public.

3. CODES OF CONDUCT IN THE BANKING SECTOR

Today, every major bank has its own code of conduct and ethics in place. In practice, such codes fulfil at least two purposes. First, they serve to satisfy regulatory requirements regarding compliance and risk management. Second, they also serve as a public relations tool.

This becomes apparent when we look, as a random example, at the 'Code of Conduct and Ethics' set in place by Swiss UBS.[9] The code not only looks like a PR brochure, but in large parts it also reads like one. It spells out rather vague principles such as 'client focus', 'agile innovation' and 'sustainable performance'.[10] But it also makes clear that the code 'applies to everything and everyone'.[11] And it refers to concrete legal obligations, specifically considering the bank's cross-border business.[12] With regard to the bank–client relationship, the code of ethics contains rather broadly formulated assertions ('We are committed to looking after our clients in the long term').[13] But it also makes clear that the bank will hold itself accountable for 'detecting, stopping and reporting money laundering matters', that it does 'not tolerate any form of corruption or bribery' and that it will 'not help … clients to evade taxes or misreport taxable income and gains'.[14] Furthermore, it makes a firm commitment to avoiding conflicts of interest 'by raising and addressing them immediately'.[15]

Given the multiple and overlapping purposes served by bank codes of conduct, their legal status is hard to determine. Are they legally binding at all? If so, do they bind the bank merely *vis-à-vis* regulatory authorities or also *vis-à-vis* customers, investors, or other private parties? And what are the legal instruments and avenues to enforce them? Do they give a cause of action that could be pursued in state courts? This contribution will try to answer these questions in the context of the bank-customer relationship. Here, the

---

9 Available at https://www.ubs.com/global/en/about_ubs/about_us/code_of_conduct.html.
10 UBS Code of Conduct and Ethics, pp. 3, 5.
11 UBS Code of Conduct and Ethics, p. 3.
12 UBS Code of Conduct and Ethics, p. 6.
13 UBS Code of Conduct and Ethics, p. 4.
14 UBS Code of Conduct and Ethics, p. 6.
15 UBS Code of Conduct and Ethics, p. 4.

contribution can draw on a growing discussion about the legal status of corporate codes of conduct in contract law.

4. CODES OF CONDUCT AND CONTRACT LAW

This growing discussion is currently being held in all European jurisdictions.[16] It starts from the observation that not only in the banking sector, but in the global economy generally, transnational corporations develop codes of conduct in order to improve working conditions, environmental impact and the respect for human rights in cross-border value chains.[17] The discussion is usually subsumed under the headline of 'corporate social responsibility', but in substance it is concerned with the legal consequences of corporate self-regulation. Most commentators agree that there are basically four ways in which corporate codes of conduct might have a direct impact on private law: (1) as a contractual duty; (2), as a quasi-contractual duty; (3) as a basis for non-contractual, i.e. mainly tort liability; and (4) as a unilateral obligation.

4.1. CODES OF CONDUCT AS CONTRACTUAL DUTIES

Let us consider the first alternative. Can codes of conduct cause enforceable contractual duties? Here, we can distinguish different scenarios. On the one hand, a code of conduct might be incorporated into a contract between the bank and its customers. On the other hand, the code might serve as a reference point for interpreting the contract.

The least problematic, but also very rare scenario would be a bank incorporating its code of conduct into a contract with a customer, by express reference in the contract itself or in standard terms. In this scenario it is clear in principle that the provisions of the code can have a binding effect, and this is

---

16 See e.g. for German law C. Glinski, *Die rechtliche Bedeutung der privaten Regulierung globaler Produktionsstandards*, Nomos, Baden-Baden 2011; for US and transnational law L.C. Backer, 'Economic Globalization and the Rise of Efficient Systems of Global Private Law Making: Wal-Mart as Global Legislator' (2007) 39 *Connecticut Law Review* 1739; for a comparative law perspective on English and German law A. Beckers, *Enforcing Corporate Social Responsibility Codes. On Global Self-Regulation and National Private Law*, Hart Publishing, Oxford 2015.

17 The legal-sociological underpinnings of this debate are masterfully described in G. Teubner, 'Global Private Regimes: Neo-spontaneous Law and Dual Constitution of Autonomous Sectors in World Society' in K. Ladeur (eds.), *Globalization and Public Governance*, Ashgate, Aldershot 2004, p. 71; G. Teubner, 'Self-Constitutionalizing TNCs? On the Linkage of "Private" and "Public" Corporate Codes of Conduct' (2011) 18 *Indiana Journal of Global Legal Studies* 617.

true for any jurisdiction.[18] However, it is highly uncommon for banks to make such incorporations. We may find incorporations of codes of conduct in other contexts, especially public procurements where public bodies bind a contractor to certain social and environmental standards. But this does not happen in the banking sector. Even financial institutions committed to ethical investments do not make their codes of conduct and ethics legally binding in this way.[19]

This leads to the more difficult question whether, in such constellations, codes of conduct and ethics might serve as a reference point for contractual interpretation. Specifically: can the general contractual duties of the bank towards its customers be read to include statements made in a code of conduct? And here, different European jurisdictions give very different answers. There is little common European ground to start from, apart from Article 2 of the Consumer Sales Directive,[20] which provides that the seller's public statements can determine the expected quality standard for the object of purchase. But the relevance of this provision is limited to consumer sales contracts.

English law takes a very cautious approach when it comes to interpreting a contract in the light of extra-contractual statements. Traditionally, the English law approach was that contractual interpretation had to be within the 'four corners' of the document. It was limited to the words of the agreement and their ordinary meaning.[21] In the last few decades, this strict approach has been somewhat relaxed to take into account the context in which a contract is concluded, its 'matrix of facts'.[22] But it remains a rule of interpretation that, in the words of Lord Hoffmann, 'the law excludes from the admissible background the previous negotiations of the parties and their declarations of subjective intent'.[23] As a consequence, evidence extrinsic to a contract, such as a code of conduct that was not incorporated into the contract, cannot generally be used for the interpretation of contractual terms.[24]

The remaining avenues for giving contractual effect to a code of conduct under English law are narrow. In certain circumstances, they might be seen

---

18 Cf. the comparative observations in A. Beckers, *Enforcing Corporate Social Responsibility Codes*, above n. 16, pp. 48–58.

19 E.g. the successful German GLS Bank, which relies on the standard terms and conditions of the German banking association, see GLS Bank, *Allgemeine Geschäftsbedingungen*, https://www.gls.de/privatkunden/agb/.

20 Directive 1999/44/EC of 25 May 1999 on certain aspects of the sale of consumer goods and associated guarantees [1999] OJ L 171/12.

21 E. McKendrick, *Contract Law*, 11th ed., Palgrave Macmillan, Basingstoke 2015, pp. 149–151 (meanwhile published in 15th edition).

22 Lord Hoffmann in *Investors Compensation Scheme Ltd. v. West Bromwich Building Society* [1998] 1 WLR 896, 912–913.

23 Lord Hoffmann in *Investors Compensation Scheme Ltd. v. West Bromwich Building Society* [1998] 1 WLR 896, 913.

24 A. Beckers, *Enforcing Corporate Social Responsibility Codes*, above n. 16, p. 71: 'only … under very exceptional circumstances'.

as so-called collateral contracts, but only if statements made in a code of conduct are decisive for the other party in entering into the contract.[25] In other instances, the provisions of a corporate code might be regarded as implied terms of the contract, as 'terms implied in fact'.[26] But according to English courts, the doctrine of implied terms should be only 'sparingly and cautiously used'.[27] In *Suriya and Douglas v. Midland Bank*, the Court of Appeal held that a bank's policy to advise clients on new banking facilities did not constitute an implied term in the bank's contracts with its customers.[28] Therefore, the bank's customers could not claim damages for breach of a duty of information.

In contrast to English law, German contract law is, in theory, much more open to considering the context of negotiations when interpreting a contract. Under German law, a contract between the bank and its customers must be interpreted according to the true intentions of the parties, with due attention paid to the circumstances of the contract, sections 133 and 157 *Bürgerliches Gesetzbuch*. So, even if a code of conduct is not expressly incorporated into a banking contract, it might be admissible evidence when it comes to interpreting the rights and duties set forth in the contract. However, especially in the case of written contracts which must satisfy mandatory form requirements – such as, for example, consumer loans – the threshold for admitting extrinsic evidence is very high. It is assumed that the written contract is conclusive as to the legal intentions of the parties.[29] Only in cases where the terms of the contract are ambiguous or incomplete, will extrinsic evidence play a considerable practical role.[30] In these constellations, codes of conduct and ethics are most likely to bear on the interpretation of a banking contract.

In French and Spanish law, the discussion largely resembles the debate in German doctrine. It is possible, but not common, that codes of conduct are 'contractualised' ('*contractualisées*'[31]) in the sense that they are incorporated into a contract by way of reference. An analysis of Spanish case law reveals that there have been at least nine cases in the past two decades where this was the case.[32] Beyond this kind of straight-forward incorporation, French doctrine seems especially open to interpreting the terms of a banking contract in the light of corporate codes of conduct. French courts seem to have a tendency

25 Ibid., pp. 71–72.

26 Ibid., pp. 72–77.

27 Lord Steyn in *Equitable Life Insurance Society v. Hyman* [2000] 1 AC 408, 459.

28 *Suriya and Douglas v. Midland Bank plc* [1999] 1 All ER (Comm.) 612.

29 E.g. BGH 05.07.2002, *NJW* 2002, 3164, 3165.

30 This holds true even in constellations where the wording of the contractual provision seems clear: BGH 08.12.1982, *NJW* 1983, 672.

31 For this notion see N. Apostolova, *Codes de bonne conduite et responsabilité dans le droit des marchés financiers*, Université Robert Schumann, Strasbourg 2003/2004, p. 16.

32 O. Soro Russell, 'Veinte años de resoluciones judiciales civiles y mercantiles españolas en materia de códigos de conducta: Una repercusión todavía muy limitada' [2010] *InDret. Revista para el Análisis del Derecho*.

to admit extrinsic statements in aid of contractual interpretation at least to the extent that they have been crucial for one of the parties' consent to the contract.[33] Some commentators rely on this tendency specifically with a view to corporate codes of conduct.[34] Moreover, French doctrine seems open to considering codes of conduct as trade usages which must be taken into account in contractual interpretation according to Article 1135 code civil. The problem with giving contractual effect to corporate codes of conduct is mostly seen in their nature as soft law or '*droit mou*'; that is, broadly worded provisions which seldom contain concrete and enforceable obligations of the corporation.

The interim conclusion of this contribution at this point is: Codes of conduct may be incorporated into contracts between a bank and its customers, but this is rarely the case. However, the relevance of corporate codes of conduct for contractual interpretation is widely acknowledged. English law is most restrictive in this respect; continental jurisdictions seem – at least in theory – more open to such an approach.

4.2. CODES OF CONDUCT AS QUASI-CONTRACTUAL DUTIES

To the extent that a code of conduct does not immediately bear on a contract and its interpretation, it seems at least conceivable that the code gives rise to pre-contractual or quasi-contractual duties.

Under English law, the doctrine of promissory estoppel recognises the existence of 'obligations to perform before contract'.[35] This could help give codes of conduct contractual effect, but it presupposes that the code can be seen as part of a bilateral agreement between the bank and its customer, specifically regarding the necessary consideration.[36] And, although the doctrine of consideration has undergone changes in recent decades, it still seems a major obstacle in the way of giving contractual effect to codes of conduct.

German law knows no such doctrine, and the regime of pre-contractual liability for negligence (*culpa in contrahendo*) might provide a basis for enforcing a bank's commitment in a code of conduct. German contract law foresees that the parties to a pre-contractual relationship have general duties

---

33 J. Ghestin, *La formation du contrat*, 3rd ed., LGDJ, Paris 1993, paras. 412–413.

34 E. Daoud and J. Ferrari, 'La RSE social: de l'engagement volontaire à l'obligation juridique' [2012] 39 *La Semaine Juridique – Edition Sociale*, pp. 13, 20.

35 *Combe v. Combe* [1951] 2 KB 215.

36 See *Baird Textile Holdings Ltd. v. Marks & Spencer plc* [2001] CLC 999, and the discussion of the problem in A. Beckers, *Enforcing Corporate Social Responsibility Codes*, above n. 16, pp. 101–102.

of care to respect the other party's rights and interests.[37] They do not, however, owe each other any kind of specific performance. It seems questionable whether obligations assumed in a corporate code of conduct can be seen as merely expressing general duties of care. It rather seems that if these codes are to have any impact of their own, they would need to have a more specific legal basis. The only viable way to establish *culpa in contrahendo* liability with regard to breach of a code of conduct would be to regard the code as a false statement made in the context of contractual negotiations and thus as a breach of the general duty to negotiate fairly.

In certain constellations, German courts have based the 'prospectus liability' of investment banks on this doctrine. And in several respects, the doctrine of prospectus liability seems an interesting blueprint for bank liability based on codes of conduct. Prospectus liability, too, is concerned with unilateral statements of a bank prior to the conclusion of a contract, specifically prior to the purchase of a financial product. Prospectus liability under German law now has a solid basis in a number of different financial market regulations.[38] The general idea of a bank's liability for misstatements in the prospectus of financial products, however, was first developed under the general doctrine of pre-contractual negligence,[39] and it continues to inform the broader concepts of bank liability, e.g. in view of the bank's pre-contractual duties to inform.[40] The most salient feature of the doctrine of prospectus liability is that it merely presupposes simple negligence on part of the bank for pre-contractual misstatements.[41]

Under French law, it has been discussed whether the subsidiary regime of quasi-contract under Article 1371 of the *code civil* might be an appropriate normative basis for giving effect to corporate codes.[42] This would presuppose that the code gives rise to legitimate expectations in the bank's customers

---

37 Ground-breaking for German doctrine before the codification of *culpa in contrahendo* liability was C. Canaris, *Die Vertrauenshaftung im deutschen Privatrecht*, C.H. Beck, München 1971.

38 Specifically the 2005 *Wertpapierprospektgesetz* (WpPG, BGBl. I p. 1698), the 2011 *Vermögenanlagengesetz* (VermAnlG, BGBl. I p. 2481) as well as the 2013 *Kapitalanlagengesetzbuch* (KAGB, BGBl. I p. 1981).

39 Now codified in sections 280 (1), 311 (2), 241 (2) *Bürgerliches Gesetzbuch*.

40 For examples see BGH 23.04.2012, *NZG* 2012, 744; BGH 23.04.2012, *NJW-RR* 2012, 1312; BGH 09.07.2013, *NZG* 2013, 980. This wider field of application for prospectus liability is usually subsumed under the term 'prospectus liability', for a brief overview see V. Emmerich, '§ 311 Rechtsgeschäftliche und rechtsgeschäftsähnliche Schuldverhältnisse' in F.J. Säcker, R. Rixecker, H. Oetker and B. Limberg (eds.), *Münchener Kommentar zum Bürgerlichen Gesetzbuch. Band 3*, 9th ed., C.H. Beck, München 2012, p. 185.

41 See D. Zimmer and C. Binder, 'Prospekthaftung von Experten? Kritik eines Gesetzesentwurfs' (2005) 59 *Wertpapier-Mitteilungen* 577.

42 B. Rolland, 'Le quasi-contrat au secours de la RSE?' [2015] *RISEO, Risques études et observations*, p. 4, http://riseo.fr/IMG/pdf/1-2015/16-LE-QUASI-CONTRAT-AU-SECOURS-DE-LA-RSE.pdf.

regarding a certain way of conduct. Most notably, the French regime of quasi-contract might even come into play where a code of conduct was not intended to bind the corporation for the benefit of its customers.[43] The legal consequences of quasi-contract under French law, however, seem to be disputed, with some pointing to contract law and others pointing to mere tort law liability.[44]

To sum up, French law does seem to offer a viable basis for legally enforcing obligations arising from a corporate code of conduct. Specifically, this regime seems to be able to adapt to the unique characteristics of codes of conduct which are made by unilateral acts of a self-binding nature rather than bilateral agreement. Pre-contractual liability under German law also appears open to this idea in view of the concept of prospectus liability that forms the basis of a far-reaching liability of banks for negligent misstatements more generally. The English regime of quasi-contractual liability, in contrast, seems to build very much on the model of a bilateral exchange contract and has more difficulties in accommodating the phenomenon of self-regulation by code.

4.3. CODES OF CONDUCT AND NON-CONTRACTUAL LIABILITY

Consequently, codes of conduct will in many cases and in many legal orders fall outside the regimes of contractual or quasi-contractual liability, and within the realm of mere tort law liability. In English law, it is possible that a code of conduct may cause liability for negligent misstatement.[45] English courts apply this doctrine only with regard to *factual* misstatements; it does not seem to be easily applicable to the normative provisions of a code of conduct.[46] However, a statement along the lines of 'We comply with regulation XY …' might well be read as a factual statement – and non-compliance penalised under tort law. And even with regard to factual statements, the threshold for assuming a negligent misstatement is very high. In *Caparo v. Dickman* the House of Lords ruled against the liability of a bank that had manipulated accounting figures of the target corporation in the context of a takeover battle.[47]

Under German law, it is theoretically conceivable that codes of conduct might have an impact on the standard of care that is used to define tort liability.

43 X. Pin and L. Devin, 'Quasi-contrat. Théorie générale' (2011) 39 *JurisClasseur Civil Code*, Art. 1370 and 1371, § 97.

44 See, on the one hand, X. Pin and L. Devin, 'Quasi-contrat. Théorie générale', *JurisClasseur Civil Code*, Arts. 1370 and 1371, (2011), § 113 and P. Le Tourneau, 'V Quasi-contrat': Encyclopédie Juridique Dalloz: Répertoire de Droit Civil 2014, § 33, on the other.

45 A. Beckers, *Enforcing Corporate Social Responsibility Codes*, above n. 16, pp. 157–162.

46 On a sceptical note A. Beckers, *Enforcing Corporate Social Responsibility Codes*, above n. 16, p. 158.

47 *Caparo Industries plc v Dickman* [1990] UKHL 2.

However, the standard of care is generally determined objectively; that is, with regard to the usages of the relevant market or industry.[48] This means that the code of conduct of an individual bank cannot establish a specific level of tort liability. Rather, it would be necessary that certain standards of behaviour are generally accepted in the banking sector, for example in the code of conduct of a banking association or a stock exchange. Yet the reach of tort liability in German law is very limited from the outset; most importantly it does not cover pure economic loss. Thus, tort liability under German law does not seem a particularly effective and attractive instrument for enforcing corporate codes.

Under French law, in contrast, tort law seems to be much more relevant for giving effect to corporate codes.[49] The *Cour de cassation* has expressly held that the infringement of a '*code de bonne conduite*' can cause tort liability if the code has effectively established a certain standard of behaviour.[50] The relevant decisions, however, are concerned not with individual codes of conduct, but with codes of conduct published by professional associations.

In sum, it seems that tort law in both French and German law may consider industry- or market-wide codes of conduct when it comes to determining the relevant standard of care. Individual codes of conduct, however, do not cause tortious liability. This may be different under English tort law, but only when it comes to factual statements made in such codes.

4.4. CODES OF CONDUCT AS UNILATERAL OBLIGATIONS

It can thus be observed that, in different legal orders, neither contract nor quasi-contract nor tort offers a firm basis for giving legal effect to corporate codes of conduct. But the apparent legal irrelevance of such codes seems hard to reconcile with their growing practical importance, especially in the banking sector. Given the rationale of current banking regulation and its turn to public-private co-regulation, this state of affairs seems rather unsatisfactory. Without going into detail at this point, it seems that there is a good case for strengthening private enforcement of such codes in order to improve both the stability of the financial system and the protection of individual customers. But how? Given the shortcomings of contractual, quasi-contractual and tortious liability the most promising instrument seems to be a specific liability for unilateral engagements. This form of liability would seem to be most adequate

---

48 G. Wagner, '§ 823 Schadensersatzpflicht' in F.J. Säcker, R. Rixecker, H. Oetker and B. Limperg (eds.), *Münchener Kommentar zum Bürgerlichen Gesetzbuch. Band 7*, 8th ed., C.H. Beck, München 2020, Rn. 38, 40.

49 N. Apostovola, *Codes de bonne conduite et responsabilité dans le droit des marchés financiers*, above n. 31, p. 17.

50 Cass. civ. 1ere, 18.03.1997, JCPéd. G 1997, II, n. 22829; Cass. com. 29.04.1997, D.1997, p. 459.

for reflecting the particular nature of codes of conduct, which are directed towards the general public, but at the same time promise to protect individual customers.

Under English law, the doctrine of equitable estoppel might provide a basis for such liability. So far, the case law of English courts limits the doctrine mostly to property law constellations.[51] Moreover, the Court of Appeal in *Baird Textile Holding v. Marks & Spencer* held that equitable estoppel should not be used for circumventing the general doctrine of consideration.[52] But some commentators have made the case for carefully developing equitable estoppel into a more general concept of liability for unilateral promises.[53] They rely on the general idea that liability for unilateral acts must be established, if it is inequitable to permit the promisor to avoid the legal consequences of his promise by insisting on his original legal rights.

In German doctrine, the idea of liability for unilateral acts has been discussed for several decades. In 1981, Köndgen published his magisterial book on self-commitment without contract.[54] He relies in large part on sociological theories of self-definition and self-representation for developing a doctrine of unilateral promises. This approach has been taken up by others, for example Bachmann in his 2006 work on private ordering.[55] Bachmann expressly discusses the binding nature of corporate codes as unilateral acts of private self-regulation.[56] And he points to a number of provisions in the German civil code that are concerned with the legal consequences of unilateral acts, such as section 661a *Bürgerliches Gesetzbuch* on prize notifications. So far, there is no established doctrine of unilateral promise in German contract law. However, the debate about corporate codes of conduct might well create the momentum for developing general principles in this direction.

For French and Spanish law, the state of the discussion seems largely comparable. Although there is no general principle either in the civil codes or in the case law, some commentators discuss the idea of an '*engagement unilatéral*' or '*declaración unilateral de voluntad*', especially in the context of corporate codes.[57]

---

51 A. Beckers, *Enforcing Corporate Social Responsibility Codes*, above n. 16, p. 101.

52 *Baird Textile Holdings Ltd v. Marks & Spencer plc* [2001] EWCA Civ 274.

53 Most notably A. Beckers, *Enforcing Corporate Social Responsibility Codes*, above n. 16, pp. 370–378.

54 J. Köndgen, *Selbstbindung ohne Vertrag. Zur Haftung aus geschäftsbezogenem Handeln*, Mohr Siebeck, Tübingen 1981.

55 G. Bachmann, *Private Ordnung. Grundlagen ziviler Regelsetzung*, Mohr Siebeck, Tübingen 2006.

56 Ibid., p. 298.

57 See E. Daoud and J. Ferrari, above n. 34, pp. 13, 20 and R. Illescas, 'La autorregulación, entre la quiebra de la relatividad y la obligatoriedad de la declaración unilateral de voluntad' (2003) 17 *Derecho privado y Constitución* 291, 291–306.

5. CONCLUSION: SELF-REGULATION AND SELF-BINDING

With this observation some conclusions can be drawn. Corporate codes of conduct test the traditional instruments of contract law doctrine in all European legal orders. There are two possible reactions to this state of affairs. One reaction would be to simply accept it. There are certainly good reasons why contract law doctrine does not provide general principles of liability for unilateral acts. European private law systems all centre around the idea of contract as an agreement between free and equal partners. It is their consent which legitimises the legal effects of the contract. And it is the parties' negotiations which procedurally guarantee the fairness and efficiency of the agreement. Against this background, the enforceability of unilateral promises appears as a rather exceptional situation. And it seems to be even less justifiable in the case of the vaguely formulated provisions of corporate codes, which are often clearly not intended to be legally binding.

However, there is a different possible reaction to the fact that the private law of most European jurisdictions recognises contractual liability for unilateral acts only in exceptional cases. This reaction would be to expand the scope of such liability by further developing existing doctrines, as seems to be the intention of Article I-103 DCFR. This might be a fruitful endeavour especially with a view to corporate codes of conduct in the banking sector, for two reasons.

The first reason is that the effectiveness of supervisory law is greatly enhanced by means of private enforcement. Supervisory requirements such as the rules on product governance in Article 16(3) and Article 24(2) MiFiD II might be transformed into directly applicable rules of private law if, for example, a code of conduct promises compliance with relevant supervisory law and the bank is then held accountable by customers who have incurred loss as a consequence of non-compliant investment practices. The relevant instruments of supervisory law expressly aim at protecting not only the stability of the financial market as a whole, but also individual investors and bank customers. This is evidenced by Recital 58 MiFiD II as well as by Recital 47 of the CRD IV Directive. National private law should be interpreted in conformity with this aim and with due regard to the principle of *effet utile*.

The second reason is that supervisory regulation has already transformed the banking sector in a way that makes traditional doctrines of contract law often seem inadequate. If traditional contract law rests upon the notion of a consensual agreement between equals, the very economic structure of the banking sector is far from an ideal market situation that is governed by such agreements. Quite to the contrary, current regulation of the banking sector embraces the idea of a highly concentrated industry which is controlled less by market forces than by a peculiar amalgam of public supervision and private co-regulation. European private law doctrine should seek to reflect this new reality by adapting its concepts and instruments, as it has always done when faced with economic and political change.

CHAPTER 8

INDIVIDUAL PROTECTION GOALS IN EU BANKING REGULATION – A PROCESS TOWARDS PRIVATE LAW ENFORCEMENT

Nikolai BADENHOOP*

* This contribution picks up on ideas developed by the author in 'Private Law Duties Deriving from EU Banking Regulation and its Individual Protection Goals' (2020) 16(2) *European Review of Contract Law* 233 and parts of the author's book *Europäische Bankenregulierung und private Haftung*, Mohr Siebeck, Tübingen 2020, available with open access, at: https://mohrsiebeck.com/buch/europaeische-bankenregulierung-und-private-haftung-9783161592065?no_cache=1.

1. INTRODUCTION

The effectiveness of EU law largely depends on national enforcement mechanisms. This concerns both national authorities executing EU administrative law and private parties enforcing EU law content. In EU banking regulation, most attention has been devoted to the administrative enforcement of regulatory goals at the national and EU levels. Private law has not played an important role in this context so far. This starkly contrasts with other areas of EU regulation where private law remedies have increasingly gained importance, namely competition law and capital markets regulation. In competition law, the ECJ first ruled in *Courage* that EU law required individual compensation rights for anybody negatively affected by a cartel and later specified conditions for cartel damages claims.[1] The EU legislator then introduced the Cartel Damages Directive.[2] In capital markets regulation, private law duties are sometimes explicitly codified in EU legislative acts and are sometimes the subject of discussion. The Transparency Directive and Prospectus Regulation provide for individual liability mechanisms.[3] In contrast, it is a matter of debate if and to

1 See below section 2.1.1.
2 See below section 2.1.2.
3 See below section 2.2.1.

what extent the MiFID II provisions on investment advice contain private law duties.[4] In any case, private enforcement has moved to the core of discussions on competition law and capital markets regulation.

At first sight, it seems that private enforcement has not yet reached banking regulation. This contribution uses the term 'EU banking regulation' with reference to both: (i) EU legal acts that set prudential standards for commercial banking, i.e. the Capital Requirements Directives (CRD IV,[5] CRD V[6] and CRD VI proposal[7]), the Capital Requirements Regulations (CRR I,[8] CRR II[9] and CRR III proposal[10]), the related tertiary law,[11] and transposition acts of

4 See below section 2.2.2.

5 Directive 2013/36/EU of the European Parliament and of the Council of 26 June 2013 on access to the activity of credit institutions and the prudential supervision of credit institutions and investment firms, amending Directive 2002/87/EC and repealing Directives 2006/48/EC and 2006/49/EC [2013] OJ L 176/338 (CRD IV).

6 Directive 2019/878/EU of the European Parliament and of the Council of 20 May 2019 amending Directive 2013/36/EU as regards exempted entities, financial holding companies, mixed financial holding companies, remuneration, supervisory measures and powers and capital conservation measures [2019] OJ L 150/253 (CRD V).

7 In December 2023, the European Parliament and Council reached a provisional agreement (PE757.234) resulting from interinstitutional negotiations on the European Commission's proposal for CRD VI (COM(2021) 663 final). Available at: https://eur-lex.europa.eu/legal-content/EN/TXT/PDF/?uri=CELEX:52021PC0663. On 24 April 2024, the European Parliament adopted its position at the first reading (T9-0362/2024), which is awaiting the Council's first reading position at the time of writing this contribution. While the final legislative act may well differ, the analysis in this contribution is based on this latest proposal adopted by the European Parliament (CRD VI proposal): https://www.europarl.europa.eu/doceo/document/TA-9-2024-0362_EN.html.

8 Regulation (EU) 575/2013 of the European Parliament and of the Council of 26 June 2013 on prudential requirements for credit institutions and investment firms and amending Regulation (EU) 648/2012 [2013] OJ L 176/1 (CRR I).

9 Regulation (EU) 2019/876 of the European Parliament and of the Council of 20 May 2019 amending Regulation (EU) 575/2013 as regards the leverage ratio, the net stable funding ratio, requirements for own funds and eligible liabilities, counterparty credit risk, market risk, exposures to central counterparties, exposures to collective investment undertakings, large exposures, reporting and disclosure requirements, and Regulation (EU) 648/2012 [2019] OJ L 150/1 (CRR II).

10 Concurrently with the CRD VI proposal (above n. 7), the EU co-legislators reached an interinstitutional agreement (PE757.233) on the European Commission's legislative proposal for CRR III (COM(2021) 664 final). Available at: https://eur-lex.europa.eu/resource.html?uri=cellar:14dcf18a-37cd-11ec-8daf-01aa75ed71a1.0001.02/DOC_1&format=PDF. While the final legislative act may well differ, this contribution refers to the latest proposal adopted by the European Parliament on 24 April 2024 (CRR III proposal) that is awaiting the Council's first reading position at the time of writing: https://www.europarl.europa.eu/doceo/document/TA-9-2024-0363_EN.html.

11 E.g. regulating technical standards, implementing technical standards as well as guidelines and recommendations issued by the European Banking Authority (EBA) according to Arts. 10–16 Regulation (EU) 1093/2010 of the European Parliament and of the Council of 24 November 2010 establishing a European Supervisory Authority (European Banking Authority), amending Decision 716/2009/EC and repealing Commission Decision 2009/78/EC [2010] OJ L 331/12 (EBA Regulation).

EU Member States; and (ii) EU legal acts stipulating the conduct-of-business rules with which commercial banks have to comply, especially in the area of consumer credit, e.g. the Consumer Credit Directive[12] and the Mortgage Credit Directive.[13]

The latest CRD VI and CRR III proposals ('Banking Package' as referred to by the European Commission) suggest tailored amendments to EU prudential banking regulation.[14] While the CRR III proposal introduces an 'output floor' for banks using internal models to calculate their capital requirements, the CRD VI proposal brings new rules, *inter alia*, for the acquisition or divestiture of a material holding and for providing cross-border core banking services to EU-based clients. The CRR III proposal is expected to start applying on 1 January 2025,[15] whereas the CRD VI proposal will have to be transposed into national law within 18 months from its entry into force.[16] Further, the Non-Performing Loans Directive (NPL Directive)[17] introduced an authorisation requirement and supervisory regime for credit servicers,[18] as well as rights and obligations of credit purchasers.[19] It also amended the Consumer Credit Directive and the Mortgage Credit Directive by strengthening information given to consumers in case of modification of the terms and conditions of a credit agreement, as well as regarding the exercise of reasonable forbearance before foreclosure proceedings are initiated.[20] The NPL Directive had to be transposed into national law by 29 December 2023.[21]

The EU legislators have traditionally refrained from introducing civil liability mechanisms because of differences in national private laws and private

---

12 Directive 2008/48/EC of the European Parliament and of the Council of 23 April 2008 on credit agreements for consumers and repealing Council Directive 87/102/EEC [2008] OJ L 133/66 (Consumer Credit Directive).

13 Directive 2014/17/EU of the European Parliament and of the Council of 4 February 2014 on credit agreements for consumers relating to residential immovable property and amending Directives 2008/48/EC and 2013/36/EU and Regulation (EU) 1093/2010 [2014] OJ L 60/34 (Mortgage Credit Directive).

14 For the European Commission's latest update regarding the banking package, see: https://finance.ec.europa.eu/news/latest-updates-banking-package-2023-12-14_en.

15 Art. 2 CRR III proposal.

16 Art. 2(1) CRD VI proposal.

17 Directive (EU) 2021/2167 of the European Parliament and of the Council of 24 November 2021 on credit servicers and credit purchasers and amending Directives 2008/48/EC and 2014/17/EU [2021] OJ L 438/1 (NPL Directive).

18 Arts. 4–15 NPL Directive.

19 Arts. 16–20 NPL Directive.

20 Arts. 27–28 NPL Directive.

21 Art. 32(1) NPL Directive. As of 3 May 2024, Czechia, Denmark, Germany, Ireland, Greece, France, Croatia, Latvia, Malta, Romania, Slovenia, and Sweden had transposed the NPL Directive, whereas Belgium, Bulgaria, Estonia, Spain, Italy, Cyprus, Lithuania, Luxembourg, Hungary, the Netherlands, Austria, Poland, Portugal, Slovakia, and Finland failed to meet the deadline, see:
https://eur-lex.europa.eu/legal-content/EN/NIM/?uri=celex:32021L2167.

enforcement cultures,[22] fears of excessive litigation and possible systemic risks arising from claims targeting systematically important financial institutions.[23] Yet, two points argue for an inclination in EU banking regulation towards private law remedies. First, the major relevant EU legislative acts, i.e. CRD IV/ CRD V/ CRD VI proposal and CRR I/ CRR II/ CRR III proposal, strongly promote depositor and investor protection as primary goals of EU banking regulation.[24] Second, and more explicitly, the EU legislators have formed the duty of responsible lending in the Consumer Credit Directive and the Mortgage Credit Directive. This duty has been transformed into a private law duty in some EU Member States, e.g. Germany.[25] Public enforcement by supervisory authorities generally aims to protect markets, not individuals. Therefore, individual protection goals are more likely to take shape in private law rights.[26] This contribution explores to what extent banking regulation can be more generally enforced via private law remedies *de lege lata*. It proceeds in three steps. First, it shows that private law enforcement emerges as a *leitmotiv* of EU regulation, especially in competition law and capital markets regulation (section 2.). Second, the current banking regulation framework is scrutinised concerning special reasons for private law enforcement. The regulatory goal of individual protection emerges as a key reason (section 3.). Third, the focus shifts towards using stronger private law enforcement under the existing EU law framework (section 4.). Against the backdrop of relevant ECJ judgments (4.1.), three reasons contend for stronger private law enforcement of banking regulation (4.2.): the structural and functional similarity to competition and capital markets regulation (4.2.1.), the comparability of the consumer creditworthiness assessment and client-related duties under CRD IV/ CRD V/ CRD VI proposal and CRR I/CRR II/CRR III proposal (4.2.2.), and the ECJ case law on 'individual rights' (4.2.3.). Finally, this contribution identifies contract interpretation, contract nullity, and damages as suitable remedies for the private law enforcement of prudential duties (4.3.).

---

22 F. Della Negra, 'The Regulatory Design and Goals of Civil Liability in EU Securities Regulation After the Global Financial Crisis: Trends and Perspectives' in O.O. Cherednychenko and M. Andenas (eds.), *Financial Regulation and Civil Liability in European Law*, Edward Elgar, Cheltenham 2020, p. 160; T. Tridimas, 'EU Financial Regulation: Federalization, Crisis Management and Law Reform' in P. Craig and G. De Burca (eds.), *The Evolution of EU Law*, 2nd ed., Oxford University Press, Oxford 2011, p. 794.

23 F. Della Negra, above n. 22, pp. 160, 178.

24 See below section 3.1.

25 See below section 3.2.

26 See below section 4.

2. PRIVATE LAW ENFORCEMENT AS A *LEITMOTIV* OF EU REGULATION

Enforcement of regulatory goals via private law remedies has become an overarching instrument of EU law.[27] While financial regulation consists of *ex ante* rules under public supervision and enforcement, private law typically provides for *ex post* remedies to compensate for losses.[28] At first glance, these two legal phenomena serve different purposes. However, private law concepts, such as civil liability, also promote the regulatory policy goals as they function as a deterrent against violations.[29] Whereas national private law rules seek to balance the rights and obligations of private parties, EU private law rules aim to achieve specific policy goals, e.g. protecting consumers or ensuring financial market efficiency.[30] A good example of a field of law that exploits this interplay is payment services law. In the Payment Services Directive (PSD II),[31] the EU legislators have chosen a combination of public and private law instruments, constituting 'the most striking example of the "private law" grammar in EU financial regulation'.[32] PSD II contains a special liability regime, e.g. for unauthorised payment transactions, under which payment service providers have to refund losses immediately,[33] while the payers only bear a very limited share of the loss.[34] Besides distributive justice and consumer protection concerns, this fosters the safety of payment systems as it incentivises technology improvements to avoid fraud and errors.[35]

Private enforcement plays a relatively bigger role in the United States, when compared to Europe.[36] Particularly in the field of capital markets law, US

---

27 F. Wilman, *Private Enforcement of EU Law Before National Courts*, Edward Elgar, Cheltenham 2015.

28 O.O. Cherednychenko, 'Financial Regulation and Civil Liability in European Law: Towards a More Coordinated Approach?' in O.O. Cherednychenko and M. Andenas (eds.), *Financial Regulation and Civil Liability in European Law*, Edward Elgar, Cheltenham 2020, p. 2.

29 O.O. Cherednychenko, above n. 28, p. 3., with references to CJEU case law.

30 F. Della Negra, *Financial Services Contracts in EU Law*, Oxford University Press, Oxford 2023, p. 32.

31 Directive (EU) 2015/2366 of the European Parliament and of the Council of 25 November 2015 on payment services in the internal market, amending Directives 2002/65/EC, 2009/110/EC and 2013/36/EU and Regulation (EU) No. 1093/2010, and repealing Directive 2007/64/EC [2015] OJ L 337/35 (PSD II).

32 O.O. Cherednychenko, above n. 28, p. 18.

33 Art. 73 PSD II.

34 Art. 74(1) PSD II (up to EUR 50).

35 A. Janczuk-Gorywoda, 'Enforcing Smart: Exploiting Complementarity of Public and Private Enforcement in the Payment Services Directive 2' in O.O. Cherednychenko and M. Andenas (eds.), *Financial Regulation and Civil Liability in European Law*, Edward Elgar, Cheltenham 2020, p. 119.

36 R. Veil, 'Sanctions' in R. Veil (ed.), *European Capital Markets Law*, 3rd ed., Hart Publishing, Oxford 2022, p. 178.

law considers private enforcement to be an essential element of enforcement against market abuse and violation of disclosure obligations.[37] Some suggest introducing a class action mechanism or other collective redress mechanisms to change the current situation in the EU.[38] A further obstacle to the effective and uniform application of harmonised EU financial law in private relationships is that national courts tend to reason from their domestic law doctrines upwards instead of applying common EU rules downwards.[39]

In the current legal framework, there are three different categories in terms of whether EU measures provide a private law remedy or not.[40] In the first category, a specific EU regulation remains silent by either (i) imposing an obligation or prescribing a standard without making any reference to rights,[41] or (ii) establishing a right without providing any remedy.[42] In the second category, the specific rule of EU law makes a general reference to national private law remedies.[43] Finally, the EU law rule may expressly introduce private law remedies.[44] The ECJ played an important role in fostering private law enforcement beyond sectoral boundaries. For example, in *Muñoz*,[45] the ECJ declared EU Regulations on the quality standards of fruit and vegetables to be directly applicable in civil proceedings between market participants as a result of the principle of effectiveness.[46] However, the areas most evidently reflecting private law enforcement are competition law (section 2.1.) and capital markets regulation (section 2.2.).

2.1. COMPETITION LAW

The prime example of EU regulation being enforced through private law remedies is competition law.[47] Neither primary nor secondary EU competition

---

37 R. Veil, above n. 36, p. 178.

38 R. Veil, above n. 36, p. 180.

39 M. Lamandini and D. Ramos-Muñoz, *Finance, Law, and the Courts*, Oxford University Press, Oxford 2023, p. 225.

40 T. Tridimas, 'Financial Regulation and Private Law Remedies: an EU Law Perspective' in O.O. Cherednychenko and M. Andenas (eds.), *Financial Regulation and Civil Liability in European Law*, Edward Elgar, Cheltenham 2020, pp. 51–56.

41 This is the default position of the EU founding treaties, which contain number of negative obligations for Member States without referring to any rights. T. Tridimas, above n. 40, p. 51.

42 E.g. the right of establishment or the principle of non-discrimination on grounds of nationality are directly effective and may be relied upon by individuals, but EU law does not provide the types of remedies that may be invoked in case of their breach. T. Tridimas, above n. 40, p. 51.

43 E.g. Art. 11(2) Prospectus Regulation, n. 97 below. T. Tridimas, above n. 40, p. 53.

44 E.g. Art. 101(2) TFEU. T. Tridimas, above n. 40, p. 54.

45 Case C-253/00, *Antonio Muñoz y Cia SA v. Frumar Ltd.*, ECLI:EU:C:2002:497.

46 Case C-253/00, *Muñoz*, paras. 30–32.

47 For early contributions see Th.M.J. Möllers and A. Heinemann (eds.), *The Enforcement of Competition Law in Europe*, Cambridge University Press, Cambridge 2008; A.P. Komninos, *EC Private Antitrust Enforcement – Decentralised Application of EC Competition Law by*

law initially prescribed private enforcement mechanisms. They were first established by the ECJ and then cemented by the EU legislator.[48] Article 101(2) TFEU and its predecessors create an immediate relationship with private law as it declares agreements and decisions which distort or restrict competition to be void. Since this provision is immediately applicable in the Member States,[49] it directly affects private law. However, the even stronger implication for private law results from cartel damages claims.

2.1.1. *ECJ in Courage and Manfredi*

In its landmark judgment *Courage*, of 20 September 2001, the ECJ paved the way for individuals to claim damages for losses they had suffered from a cartel.[50] According to English law, claimants could not rely on their own unlawful behaviour to substantiate damages claim. The referring English Court of Appeal wondered whether EU law overruled such a national provision.[51] The ECJ responded that the *effet utile* of EU law generally required national legal orders to provide for damages claims by 'any individual'[52] damaged by a cartel, even if they were party to that unlawful agreement:

> The full effectiveness of Article 85 of the Treaty and, in particular, the practical effect of the prohibition laid down in Article 85(1) would be put at risk if it were not open to any individual to claim damages for loss caused to him by a contract or by conduct liable to restrict or distort competition.[53]

However, given that EU law had not yet harmonised provisions on cartel damages claims, it was for the Member States to decide on the modalities of such claims as long as they respected the EU law principles of equivalence and effectiveness.[54] Equivalence implies that national rules regarding claims deriving from EU law have to be no less favourable than those governing domestic actions, while effectiveness requires that national rules do not render

National Courts, Hart Publishing, Oxford and Portland OR 2008; Ch. Gheur and N. Petit (eds.), *Alternative Enforcement techniques in EC competition law – Settlements, commitments and other novel instruments*, Bruylant, Brussels 2009.

48 W. Frenz, *Handbook of EU Competition Law*, Springer, Berlin and Heidelberg 2016, pp. 619–635.

49 Art. 1(1) Council Regulation EC No. 1/2003 of 16 December 2002 on the implementation of the rules on competition laid down in Articles 81 and 82 of the Treaty [2003] OJ L 1/1; see also Case C-10/69, *SA Portelange v. SA Smith Corona Marchant International*, ECLI:EU:C:1969:36, paras. 9–10.

50 Case C-453/99, *Courage Ltd. v. Bernard Crehan*, ECLI:EU:C:2001:465.

51 Case C-453/99, *Courage*, para. 16.

52 Case C-453/99, *Courage*, para. 24.

53 Case C-453/99, *Courage*, para. 26.

54 Case C-453/99, *Courage*, para. 29.

practically impossible or excessively difficult the exercise of rights conferred by EU law.[55] Within these boundaries, the national courts could prevent unjust enrichment by evaluating the respective bargaining power and conduct of the parties.[56] Hence, the ECJ created a general compensation right even for parties to a contract violating EU competition law.[57] National law could not bar the right to damages for the sole reason that the adversely affected person was party to a contract liable to restrict or distort competition.[58] Nevertheless, that person could be barred if they bore significant responsibility for the violation.[59]

This landmark judgment was followed by the judgment in *Manfredi* that specified the conditions of the new right to damages.[60] In *Manfredi*, the ECJ confirmed *Courage* and required a causal relationship between the competition law violation and the harm suffered by the claimant.[61] Since EU law had not harmonised procedural rules, they were a matter for the national law and courts, within the boundaries set by the principles of equivalence and effectiveness.[62] The same applied to the determination of the competent court, which was, in principle, a matter of national law.[63] As to the limitation period of compensation rights deriving from EU competition law, there was no EU harmonisation either, so that national courts could apply domestic rules provided they respected the equivalence and effectiveness principles.[64] The ECJ deemed a national rule starting the limitation period on the day of the cartel agreement likely to render the exercise of the compensation right practically impossible for a harmed individual later on.[65] Nevertheless, ultimately it left the decision to the national court.[66] The ECJ also answered the question whether EU competition law required national legal orders to grant punitive damages with reference to national autonomy within the boundaries of equivalence and effectiveness.[67] On the one hand, the principle of equivalence required national courts to grant punitive damages where national law did so.[68] On the other hand, the ECJ derived from the *effet utile* principle a wide scope of the

---

55 The Court refers to Case C-261/95, *Rosalba Palmisani v. Istituto Nazionale della Previdenza Sociale (INPS)*, ECLI:EU:C:1997:351, para. 27 which itself refers to Case C-6/90, *Andrea Francovich v. Italian Republic*, ECLI:EU:C:1991:428, paras. 41–43. Both judgments concerned state liability outside the realm of competition law.

56 Case C-453/99, *Courage*, paras. 30–32.

57 Case C-453/99, *Courage*, para. 36 answer 1.

58 Case C-453/99, *Courage*, para. 36 answer 2.

59 Case C-453/99, *Courage*, para. 36 answer 3.

60 Case C-295/04, *Vincenzo Manfredi v. Lloyd Adriatico Assicurazioni SpA*, ECLI:EU:C:2006:461.

61 Case C-295/04, *Manfredi*, para. 61.

62 Case C-295/04, *Manfredi*, paras. 62, 64.

63 Case C-295/04, *Manfredi*, paras. 70–72.

64 Case C-295/04, *Manfredi*, paras. 77–82.

65 Case C-295/04, *Manfredi*, paras. 78–79.

66 Case C-295/04, *Manfredi*, paras. 80–82.

67 Case C-295/04, *Manfredi*, para. 98.

68 Case C-295/04, *Manfredi*, para. 99.

compensation right, including not only compensation for actual loss (*damnum emergens*) but also for loss of profit (*lucrum cessans*).[69]

Legal scholars interpreted the protection goal of both judgments differently. According to some, the ECJ promoted the effectiveness of EU law with the sole aim to protect markets, which only indirectly caused the protection of individual interests.[70] Others underline the direct protective effect of individual compensation rights and divide 'effectiveness' into 'effective judicial protection', resulting in damages claims, and 'effective enforcement', focusing on market protection.[71]

2.1.2. *Cartel Damages Directive*

As appeared from *Manfredi*, the conditions of the compensation right depended a good deal on national law and, therefore, differed substantially between the Member States. In order to remedy this unlevel playing-field, the EU legislator accepted the judiciary's invitation to harmonise a new field of competition law and adopted the Cartel Damages Directive, based on Articles 103 and 114 TFEU.[72] The Commission's proposal of 2013 following the green paper of 2005[73] and the white book of 2008[74] followed the ECJ's rulings in *Courage* and *Manfredi*.[75] As to the goals of the legislation, it aimed both to optimise the interplay between public and private enforcement of competition law and to ensure effectively the full compensation of individuals suffering losses from cartels.[76] The recitals of the Cartel Damages Directive also emphasise the importance of individual protection, meaning the protection of 'subjective rights'.[77]

According to Article 3(1) Cartel Damages Directive, Member States shall ensure 'that any natural or legal person who has suffered harm caused

---

69 Case C-295/04, *Manfredi*, para. 100.

70 D. Poelzig, *Normdurchsetzung durch Privatrecht*, Mohr Siebeck, Tübingen 2012, pp. 143–144.

71 P. Nebbia, 'Damages actions for the infringement of EC competition law: compensation or deterrence?' (2008) 33(1) *European Law Review* 23, 28–36.

72 Directive 2014/104/EU of the European Parliament and of the Council of 26 November 2014 on certain rules governing actions for damages under national law for infringements of the competition law provisions of the Member States and of the European Union [3024] OJ L 349/1.

73 European Commission, Green Paper on Damages actions for breach of the EC antitrust rules of 19.12.2005, COM(2005) 672 final.

74 European Commission, White Paper on Damages actions for breach of the EC antitrust rules of 02.04.2008, COM(2008) 165 final.

75 European Commission, Proposal for a Directive of the European Parliament and of the Council on certain rules governing actions for damages under national law for infringements of the competition law provisions of the Member States and of the European Union of 11.06.2013, COM(2013) 404 final, p. 2.

76 COM(2013) 404 final, p. 3.

77 Recital 3 sentence 3 Cartel Damages Directive.

by an infringement of competition law is able to claim and to obtain full compensation for that harm'. The scope of application includes infringements of national and EU competition law, thereby synchronising both levels.[78] As to the extent of compensation, the Directive follows the ECJ in *Manfredi* and includes both actual losses and losses of profit, plus the payment of interest.[79] However, it explicitly rules out overcompensation, e.g. punitive or multiple damages.[80] The Directive further specifies the principles of effectiveness and equivalence.[81] Besides the provisions corresponding to previous ECJ judgments, the Directive contains material novelties. It introduces a limitation period of at least five years, which does not begin to run before the infringement has ceased and the claimant knows or can reasonably be expected to know of the violation, the harm it has caused and the identity of the infringer.[82] All infringers are jointly and severally liable unless they are privileged as small and medium enterprises.[83] The decisions of national competition authorities are binding upon national courts,[84] while the decisions of competition authorities of another Member State shall at least have the value of *prima facie* evidence.[85] As to the burden of proof, the Directive prescribes that it shall be presumed that cartel infringements cause harm.[86] The Directive further contains provisions regarding the passing on of overcharges[87] and the rights to compensation of indirect purchasers[88] and claimants from different levels in the supply chain.[89] From a procedural point of view, the Directive introduced detailed rules on the disclosure of evidence[90] and on consensual dispute resolution.[91]

2.2. CAPITAL MARKETS REGULATION

The second field of EU law that has seen an increasing use of private law mechanisms is capital markets regulation.[92] As opposed to competition law, there are no primary law provisions hinting at private law intervention.

---

78 Arts. 3(1), 2(1) Cartel Damages Directive.
79 Art. 3(2) Cartel Damages Directive.
80 Art. 3(3) Cartel Damages Directive.
81 Art. 4 Cartel Damages Directive.
82 Art. 10(2), (3) Cartel Damages Directive.
83 Art. 11 Cartel Damages Directive.
84 Art. 9(1) Cartel Damages Directive.
85 Art. 9(2) Cartel Damages Directive.
86 Art. 17(2) Cartel Damages Directive.
87 Arts. 12–13 Cartel Damages Directive.
88 Art. 14 Cartel Damages Directive.
89 Art. 15 Cartel Damages Directive.
90 Arts. 5–8 Cartel Damages Directive.
91 Arts. 18–19 Cartel Damages Directive.
92 R. Veil, 'Enforcement of Capital Markets Law in Europe – Observations from a Civil Law Country' (2010) 11 *European Business Organization Law Review* 409.

However, EU capital markets regulation contains a strong focus on investor protection both on the systemic and the individual levels.[93] The private law link is sometimes established by explicit private liability provisions of EU legislative acts. In other cases, the transformation of regulatory duties into private law duties is only implicit and, thus, subject to debate.

2.2.1. *Legislative Prescription of Personal Private Law Liability*

The EU legislative acts on securities prospectuses and general corporate transparency requirements exemplify EU legislation that directly creates private law duties.[94] It is noteworthy that in all cases the EU legislators based this private law enforcement on the internal market legislative competence under Article 95 TEC/Article 114 TFEU. The former Prospectus Directive[95] obliged the Member States to

> ensure that responsibility for the information given in a prospectus attaches at least to the issuer or its administrative, management or supervisory bodies, the offeror, the person asking for the admission to trading on a regulated market or the guarantor, as the case may be.[96]

The current Prospectus Regulation[97] includes the very same wording except that it expands the duty's scope to include statements in 'any supplement' of the prospectus.[98] The prospectus has to identify clearly the responsible persons and contain declarations that are correct to the best of their knowledge.[99] Another explicit personal liability rule results from the Transparency Directive,[100] which harmonised transparency requirements for securities issuers. It obliges Member

---

93 N. Moloney, *How to Protect Investors: Lessons from the UK and the EC*, Cambridge University Press, Cambridge 2010; M. Andenas and I.H.-Y. Chiu, *The Foundations and Future of Financial Regulation – Governance for Responsibility*, Routledge, London and New York 2014, pp. 135–139.

94 A. Hellgardt, 'Europarechtliche Vorgaben für die Kapitalmarktinformationshaftung – de lege lata und nach Inkrafttreten der Marktmissbrauchsverordnung' (2012) *Die Aktiengesellschaft* 154, 155.

95 Directive 2003/71/EC of the European Parliament and of the Council of 4 November 2003 on the prospectus to be published when securities are offered to the public or admitted to trading and amending Directive 2001/34/EC [2003] OJ L 345/64.

96 Art. 6(1) sentence 1 Prospectus Directive.

97 Regulation (EU) 2017/1129 of the European Parliament and of the Council of 14 June 2017 on the prospectus to be published when securities are offered to the public or admitted to trading on a regulated market, and repealing Directive 2003/71/EC [2017] OJ L 168/12.

98 Art. 11(1) sentence 1 Prospectus Regulation.

99 Art. 11(1) sentence 2 Prospectus Regulation; Art. 6(1) sentence 2 Prospectus Directive.

100 Directive 2004/109/EC of the European Parliament and of the Council of 15 December 2004 on the harmonisation of transparency requirements in relation to information about issuers whose securities are admitted to trading on a regulated market and amending Directive 2001/34/EC [2004] OJ L 390/38.

States to ensure that at least the issuer or its administrative, management or supervisory bodies are responsible and liable for the disclosure of annual and half-yearly financial reports as well as interim management statements and additional information.[101] While the Transparency Directive generally prescribes personal liability,[102] the Prospectus Regulation specifies that it requires civil liability.[103] In any case, the word 'liability' and the regulatory context are more likely to evoke private law than administrative law implementation.[104] As a matter of fact, the German legislator transposed the prospectus liability into private law duties.[105] And the Transparency Directive led the UK legislator to establish a specific private law compensation regime for misleading or dishonest information on the secondary market.[106] So in both cases, EU capital markets regulation induced private law liability. In addition, the Credit Rating Agencies Regulation[107] contains an explicit regime for civil liability according to which investors and issuers can claim damages from credit rating agencies under specific circumstances.[108]

Finally, three sectorial regulations on investment products marketed or sold only to retail clients that the EU adopted after the 2008 financial crisis include specific civil liability rules. Under the Packaged Retail and Insurance-based Investment Products Regulation (PRIIPS Regulation),[109] manufacturers of packaged retail and insurance-based investment products can be held liable for the losses suffered due to reliance on a key information document which does not satisfy the conditions laid down in the PRIIPS Regulation.[110] Similarly, under the European Long-Term Investment Funds Regulation (ELTIF Regulation),[111] managers of European long-term investment funds can be held liable in

---

101 Art. 7 Transparency Directive.

102 Art. 7 Transparency Directive.

103 Art. 11(1) sentence 2 Prospectus Regulation. For the national regimes implementing this duty see S. Mock (Germany), T. Bonneau (France), P. Giudici (Italy), J.R. Sánchez del Campo (Spain), J.P. Franx (the Netherlands), V. Hoffeld (Luxembourg) and G. McMeel (United Kingdom) in D. Busch, G. Ferrarini, J.P. Franx (eds.), *Prospectus Regulation and Prospectus Liability*, Oxford University Press, Oxford 2020, pp. 465–597.

104 The ECJ seems to have taken this view in Case C-174/12, *Alfred Hirmann v. Immofinanz*, ECLI:EU:C:2013:856, paras. 36–38.

105 Ss. 21–25 German Securities Prospectus Act (*Wertpapierprospektgesetz*).

106 The Financial Services and Markets Act 2000 (Liability of Issuers) Regulations 2010, (SI 2010/1192), amending s. 90A Financial Services and Markets Act 2000; see especially the Explanatory Memorandum thereto, paras. 4.1–4.4.

107 Regulation (EU) 462/2013 of the European Parliament and of the Council of 21 May 2013 amending Regulation (EC) 1060/2009 on credit rating agencies [2013] OJ L 146/1.

108 Art. 1(22) Credit Rating Agencies Regulation.

109 Regulation (EU) No. 1286/2014 of the European Parliament and of the Council of 26 November 2014 on key information documents for packaged retail and insurance-based investment products [2014] OJ L 352/1 (PRIIPS Regulation).

110 Art. 11(2) PRIIPS Regulation.

111 Regulation (EU) No. 2015/760 of the European Parliament and of the Council of 29 April 2015 on European long-term investment funds [2015] OJ L 123/98. (ELTIF Regulation)

accordance with Directive 2011/61/EU (AIFM Directive)[112] for loss or damage resulting from its non-compliance with the ELTIF Regulation.[113] Also, as per the pan-European Personal Pension Products Regulation (PEPP Regulation),[114] providers of pan-European personal pension products can be held liable for the losses of investors resulting from non-compliance in the switching process.[115]

2.2.2. Contentious Areas of Private Law Remedies

Other areas of EU capital markets regulation have caused debates on their private law aspect as they relate only implicitly to private law duties. Most prominently this concerns the duty to disclose inside information under the Market Abuse Regulation[116] (MAR) and the duty to provide investment advice in the best interest of the customer under the Market in Financial Instruments Directive II[117] (MiFID II). The EU legislator did not expressly connect the disclosure obligation under Article 17 MAR with civil sanctions. As a result, national laws treat civil liability and enforcement very differently.[118] The question has caused debate in legal doctrine. According to some, the Member States have leeway to decide whether they provide for civil compensation actions or not.[119] These commentators refer to the MAR provision on sanctions that is literally reduced to 'administrative sanctions and administrative measures'.[120] Others argue that the national legislators only have limited discretion to decide whether an EU norm has effects on national tort law.[121] Consequently, they focus on the regulatory

112 Directive 2011/61/EU of the European Parliament and of the Council of 8 June 2011 on Alternative Investment Fund Managers and amending Directives 2003/41/EC and 2009/65/EC and Regulations (EC) No. 1060/2009 and (EU) No. 1095/2010 [2011] OJ L 174/1 (AIFM Directive).

113 Art. 7(3) ELTIF Regulation.

114 Regulation (EU) No. 2019/1238 of the European Parliament and of the Council of 20 June 2019 on a pan-European Personal Pension Product [2019] OJ L 198/1 (PEPP Regulation).

115 Arts. 53, 55(1) PEPP Regulation; more in depth F. Della Negra, above n. 22, p. 175.

116 Regulation (EU) 596/2014 of the European Parliament and of the Council of 16 April 2014 on market abuse (market abuse regulation) and repealing Directive 2003/6/EC of the European Parliament and of the Council and Commission Directives 2003/124/EC, 2003/125/EC and 2004/72/EC [2014] OJ L 173/1 (MAR).

117 Directive 2014/65/EU of the European Parliament and of the Council of 15 May 2014 on markets in financial instruments and amending Directive 2002/92/EC and Directive 2011/61/EU [2014] OJ L 173/349.

118 M. Cless, *Unionsrechtliche Vorgaben für eine zivilrechtliche Haftung bei Marktmissbrauch*, Duncker & Humblot, Berlin 2018, pp. 42–44; R. Veil, above n.36, pp. 366–372.

119 D. Poelzig, 'Die Neuregelung der Offenlegungsvorschriften durch die Marktmissbrauchsverordnung' (2016) *Neue Zeitschrift für Gesellschaftsrecht* 761, 773; A. Pietrancosta, 'Article 17: Public Disclosure of inside information' in M. Ventoruzzo and S. Mock (eds.), *Market Abuse Regulation – Commentary and Annotated Guide*, 2nd ed., Oxford University Press, Oxford 2022, pp. 489–490, para. B.17.105.

120 Art. 30 MAR.

121 A. Hellgardt, above n. 94, 156–157; L. Klöhn, 'Art. 17 MAR' in L. Klöhn (ed.), *MAR Kommentar*, 2nd ed., C.H. Beck, Munich 2023, para. 589.

goals in EU law. MAR's recitals emphasise the goal of investor protection.[122] These can be read in the sense that investor protection requires private law sanctions in the shape of a subjective right to individual compensation.[123] Alternatively, some deduce the direct applicability of MAR in civil proceedings from its legal nature as an EU Regulation.[124] In *Quinn v. Irish Bank Resolution Corp.*, an Irish court held that a breach of the Irish laws transposing the then Market Abuse Directive 2003/6/EC did not render the contracts invalid.[125]

With regard to MiFID II, the discussions concerning civil liability are similar.[126] Article 24(1) MiFID II obliges a provider of investment services to act 'honestly, fairly and professionally in accordance with the best interests of its clients'. Although the European Commission's initial consultation paper aimed to introduce 'a principle of civil liability',[127] MiFID II was enacted without referring expressly to civil law obligations. The general provision on sanctions, Article 70(1) MiFID II, only addresses administrative sanctions. As a result, national provisions on civil liability are heterogeneous.[128] Therefore, again, the

---

122 Recital 8 sentences 7–8 MAR: 'The scope of this Regulation should therefore include financial instruments for which an application for admission to trading on an MTF has been made. This should improve investor protection, preserve the integrity of markets and ensure that market abuse of such instruments is clearly prohibited'. Recital 24 sentence 3 MAR: 'The question whether a person has infringed the prohibition on insider dealing or has attempted to commit insider dealing should be analysed in the light of the purpose of this Regulation, which is to protect the integrity of the financial market and to enhance investor confidence, which is based, in turn, on the assurance that investors will be placed on an equal footing and protected from the misuse of inside information'. Recital 49 sentence 1 MAR: 'The public disclosure of inside information by an issuer is essential to avoid insider dealing and ensure that investors are not misled'.

123 S. Grundmann, in C.-W. Canaris, M. Habersack and C. Schäfer (eds.), *Großkommentar HGB*, 5th ed., vol. 11/2, De Gruyter, Berlin and Boston MA 2018, 8th part, para. 257; A. Hellgardt, '§§ 97, 98 WpHG' in H.-D. Assmann, U.H. Schneider and P.O. Mülbert (eds.), *Wertpapierhandelsrecht*, 8th ed., Dr. Otto Schmidt, Cologne 2023, paras. 18–22.

124 As opposed to the Market Abuse Directive, V.D. Tountopoulos, 'Market Abuse and Private Enforcement' 2014 11(3) *European Company and Financial Law Review* 297.

125 *Quinn v. Irish Bank Resolution Corp.* [2015] IESC 29; M. Lamandini and D. Ramos-Muñoz, above n. 39, p. 300.

126 Comprehensively on this topic, see F. Della Negra, *MiFID II and Private Law – Enforcing EU Conduct of Business Rules*, Hart Publishing, Oxford 2019.

127 European Commission, *Public Consultation Review of the Markets in Financial Instruments Directive*, p. 63, para. 7.2.6 (liability of firms providing services): 'The Commission services regularly receive complaints, especially from retail investors, claiming that firms have violated conduct of business obligations. Introducing a principle of civil liability of investment services providers would be essential for ensuring an equal level of investor protection in the EU…'.

128 On France, the Netherlands and Germany Y. Svetiev and A. Ottow, 'Financial Supervision in the Interstices Between Private and Public Law' (2014) 10(4) *European Review of Contract Law* 496; on Finland, H. Marjosola, 'What Role for Courts in Protecting Investors in Europe – A View from Finland' (2014) 10(4) *European Review of Contract Law* 545, 552–569; on Italy and Spain F. Della Negra, 'The private enforcement of the MiFID conduct of business rules. An overview of the Italian and Spanish experiences' (2014) 10(4) *European Review of Contract Law* 571, 579–593.

question arises whether Member States are free to impose civil sanctions or not. The possibility to invoke a breach of the national law transposing MiFID II varies a lot between the Member States.[129] From an EU law perspective, the regulatory goals are central. Investor protection is ubiquitous in MiFID II regarding both the customer relationship and organisation duties.[130] The various positions on how to deal with this individual protection goal much resemble the discussions on MAR. Some argue that there is no specific EU law obligation to implement private law liability and thus argue in favour of mere public enforcement.[131] Others derive a private law obligation from the principle of effectiveness and the prominent investor protection goal of MiFID II.[132] More theoretically, it has been proposed to conceptualise the relationship between MiFID II duties and private law as either complementary or mutually integrative in order to foster both EU convergence and stronger cooperation between courts and supervisors.[133] The ECJ had the opportunity to decide this question in *Bankinter*[134] but did not take a clear position.[135]

3. INDIVIDUAL PROTECTION GOALS IN EU BANKING REGULATION

At the beginning, private law enforcement of competition law merely served the principle of effectiveness.[136] It now equally serves individual compensation interests, as appears from the Cartel Damages Directive.[137] In capital markets

---

129 As to MiFID I, see D. Busch, 'Why MiFID matters to private law – the example of MiFID's impact on an asset manager's civil liability' (2012) 7(4) *Capital Markets Law Journal* 386, 390–394, 404–406.

130 Recitals 7, 37, 42, 45, 54, 57, 58, 70, 74, 86, 87, 97, 133, 144, 154, 155, 164 MiFID II.

131 O.O. Chrednychenko, 'Public and Private Enforcement of European Private Law in the Financial Services Sector' (2015) 4 *European Review of Private Law* 621, 625; N. Moloney, 'Liability of asset managers: a comment' (2012) 7 *Capital Markets Law Journal* 414, 421–422; pointing at additional difficulty with horizontal application of directives N. Moloney, above n. 93, 445–446.

132 D. Busch, 'The Private Law Effect of MiFID the Genil Case and Beyond' (2017) 13(1) *European Review of Contract Law* 70, 74–75, 86 with reference to Art. 69(2) third paragraph MiFID II: 'Member States shall ensure that mechanisms are in place to ensure that compensation may be paid or other remedial action be taken in accordance with national law for any financial loss or damage suffered as a result of an infringement of this Directive or of Regulation (EU) No 600/2014'; F. Della Negra, above n. 127, pp. 22–26, 177–179, 201–206.

133 O.O. Chrednychenko, 'Contract Governance in the EU: Conceptualising the Relationship between Investor Protection Regulation and Private Law' (2015) 21(4) *European Law Journal* 500, 513–520.

134 Case C-604/11, *Genil 48 SL v. Bankinter SA*, ECLI:EU:C:2013:344.

135 See below section 4.1.1.

136 Case C-453/99 *Courage*, para. 26.

137 Recitals 3 and 4 Cartel Damages Directive (individual compensation); Recital 6 Cartel Damages Directive (effectiveness).

regulation, private law enforcement aims to foster investor protection both via compensation, as an individual goal,[138] and market stability, as a public goal.[139] Upon a closer look, the same applies to banking regulation (in a broader sense including both prudential standards and conduct-of-business rules),[140] which increasingly serves the individual protection of depositors, investors and consumer borrowers. CRD IV/ CRD V/ CRD VI proposal and CRR I/ CRR II/ CRR III proposal aim to protect depositors and investors (section 3.1.). The Consumer Credit Directive and the Mortgage Credit Directive introduced the principle of responsible lending, which safeguards consumer borrowers (section 3.2.).

3.1. DEPOSITOR AND INVESTOR PROTECTION GOALS IN CRD AND CRR

The main EU legislative acts of prudential banking regulation are CRD IV,[141] CRD V,[142] CRD VI proposal,[143] CRR I,[144] CRR II,[145] and CRR III proposal.[146] CRD IV/ CRD V/ CRD VI proposal and CRR I/ CRR II/ CRR III proposal pursue a twofold objective, as they aim to achieve both market stability and the individual protection of bank customers. This duality is apparent in both the recitals and normative provisions.

3.1.1. Recitals

Recital 47 sentence 1 CRD IV states that '[s]upervision of institutions on a consolidated basis aims to protect the interests of depositors and investors of institutions and to ensure the stability of the financial system'. While this is limited to supervision on a consolidated basis, Recital 7 sentence 1 CRR I makes clear that investor and depositor protection is a main goal of prudential regulation in general:

> This Regulation should, inter alia, contain the prudential requirements for institutions that relate strictly to the functioning of banking and financial services

138 E.g. Recitals 7, 37, 70, 97, 133, 154, 164 MiFID II; Recitals 8, 24, 49 MAR; Recitals 1, 2, 5, 7, 26, 27, 36, 41 Transparency Directive; Recitals 3, 4, 7, 27, 28 Prospectus Regulation.

139 E.g. Recitals 11, 68, 113, 164 MiFID II; Recitals 52, 73 MAR; Recital 1 Transparency Directive; Recitals 1, 7 Prospectus Regulation.

140 See above, section I.

141 See above n. 5.

142 See above n. 6.

143 See above n. 7.

144 See above n. 8.

145 See above n. 9.

146 See above n. 10.

> markets and are meant to ensure the financial stability of the operators on those markets as well as a high level of protection of investors and depositors.

Similarly to the information paradigm in capital markets regulation,[147] CRR I reinforces the idea that the prudential requirements serve to adequately inform depositors and investors:

> For the purposes of strengthening market discipline and enhancing financial stability it is necessary to introduce more detailed requirements for disclosure of the form and nature of regulatory capital and prudential adjustments made in order to ensure that investors and depositors are sufficiently well informed about the solvency of institutions.[148]

The EU legislator thereby approximates core prudential regulation (the bank's duty towards the regulator) to conduct-of-business regulation (the bank's duty towards the customer). Therefore, the prudential requirements on capital and liquidity in CRD IV and CRR I can be compared to the disclosure requirements under the Transparency Directive, the Prospectus Regulation, MAR and MiFID II. Furthermore, the protection of depositors and investors remains at the core of CRD V and CRR II. Recital 8 sentence 1 CRD V states that

> [c]lear, consistent and harmonised criteria for identifying those small institutions as well as low levels of variable remuneration are necessary to ensure supervisory convergence and to foster a level playing field for institutions and the adequate protection of depositors, investors and consumers across the Union.

Recitals 60 and 61 CRR II focus on investment in infrastructure and declare that CRR II aims to promote high-quality infrastructure projects and to reduce risks for investors. In addition, the Recitals of the CRD VI and CRR III proposals further hint at a closer tie between prudential banking regulation and private law enforcement. Recital 6 of the CRD VI proposal requires national laws to take into account the private law implications of the transposition of the directive and to make sure that clients' acquired rights under existing contracts are preserved. Also, according to Recital 19, the main *ratio legis* behind the novel classification of third-party branches that are authorised to accept retail deposits is the protection of the ability of the Member States' banking system to protect citizens' savings. Finally, Recital 2 CRR III indicates that the new 'output floor' mechanism, which is planned to be introduced as a mechanism

---

147 L. Klöhn, 'Wertpapierhandelsrecht diesseits und jenseits des Informationsparadigmas – Am Beispiel des "verständigen Anlegers" im Sinne des deutschen und europäischen Insiderrechts' (2013) 177 *Zeitschrift für das gesamte Handels- und Wirtschaftsrecht* 349.

148 Recital 76 CRR I.

to calculate capital requirements, must be reviewed by the Commission, which would assess whether it ensures an adequate level of depositor protection and safeguards financial stability in the Union.

From the recitals of CRD IV/ CRD V/ CRD VI proposal and CRR I/ CRR II/ CRR III proposal, it emerges that core elements of prudential regulation – such as the lessening of regulatory burdens for smaller institutions, low levels of variable remuneration of bankers and capital requirements more generally – aim to protect depositors and investors.

3.1.2. *Norm Provisions*

The objective of depositor and investor protection is embodied in the legislative provisions as well. For example, CRD IV allows for derogations from the general licence requirement only if the exempted activities 'are subject to regulations and controls intended to protect depositors and investors'.[149] Depositor protection is a relevant criterion for withdrawing the licence where a credit institution no longer meets capital and liquidity requirements or 'can no longer be relied on to fulfil its obligations towards its creditors, and, in particular, no longer provides security for the assets entrusted to it by its depositors'.[150] In cross-border banking emergency situations, the supervisory authorities of the host Member State may 'take any precautionary measures necessary to protect against financial instability that would seriously threaten the collective interests of depositors, investors and clients in the host Member State'.[151] These precautionary measures have to be 'proportionate to their purpose to protect against financial instability that would seriously threaten collective interests of depositors, investors and clients in the host Member State',[152] and can include a suspension of payment.[153] In any case, they 'shall not result in a preference for the creditors of the credit institution in the host Member State over creditors in other Member States'.[154] The same approach is visible in the CRD VI proposal where competent authorities may withdraw the authorisation of third-country branches if such a branch can no longer be relied on to fulfil its obligations towards its creditors and, in particular, no longer provides security for the assets entrusted to it by its depositors.[155]

149 Art. 9(2) CRD IV.
150 Art. 18(d) CRD IV; the quoted part was not affected by the amendment in Art. 1(8) CRD V.
151 Art. 43(1) CRD IV. The host Member State is a state where the institution has a branch or provides services, whereas the home Member State is where it is authorised: CRD IV, Art. 3(1)(39) and (40), and CRR II, Art. 4(1)(43) and (44).
152 Art. 43(2) sentence 1 CRD IV.
153 Art. 43(2) sentence 2 CRD IV.
154 Art. 43(2) sentence 3 CRD IV.
155 Art. 48d(2)(d) CRD VI proposal.

In a similar vein, cross-border collaboration of supervisory authorities serves the protection of depositors and investors. The authorities of the home Member State have to inform those of the host Member State on the liquidity situation and activities of branches of credit institutions 'to the extent that such information and findings are relevant to the protection of depositors or investors in the host Member State'.[156] In extreme situations like stark liquidity shortages, the host Member State authorities may 'take appropriate measures to prevent further breaches in order to protect the interests of depositors, investors and others to whom services are provided or to protect the stability of the financial system'.[157] In the context of structural measures to limit large exposures, CRR I puts the protection of depositors on the same level as the preservation of financial stability.[158] Also, the CRD IV provisos on manager remuneration hint at investor protection. When deciding on remuneration policies, the remuneration committee 'shall take into account the long-term interests of shareholders, investors and other stakeholders in the institution and the public interest'.[159] CRD V adds another aspect of depositor protection as it obliges branches of third-country credit institutions to report at least annually on the deposit protection arrangements available to depositors in the branch.[160] All in all, the protection of depositors, investors and clients emerges as a central regulatory goal of EU prudential regulation, as the wording of the provisions on licensing derogation and licence withdrawal, cross-border supervision, regulation of large exposures and manager remuneration has shown.

3.1.3. Individual vs. Collective Protection

The panoply of recitals and legislative provisions shows that the protection of depositors and investors is a core aim of CRD IV/ CRD V/ CRD VI proposal and CRR I/ CRR II/ CRR III proposal. However, what the protection of 'depositors' and 'investors' precisely entails is not established. It could be argued that the regulatory goal aims to safeguard the group as a whole (collective protection), which would come close to the objective of market stability. Yet, the wording could imply that prudential regulation protects each depositor and investor individually as long as he or she can be attributed to the protected group (individual protection). The latter reading presupposes that the group of depositors and investors can be individualised. In order to answer this question, the following analysis proceeds in three steps. First, it

156 Art. 50(2) CRD IV.
157 Art. 50(4) sentence 2 CRD IV.
158 Art. 395(6) sub-paragraph 1 CRR I.
159 Art. 95(2) sentence 4 CRD IV.
160 Art. 1(11)(a) CRD V inserting Art. 47(1a) in CRD IV.

undertakes a grammatical and plurilingual interpretation. Second, it scrutinises the systematic context of 'depositor and investor protection' in CRD IV/ CRD V/ CRD VI proposal and CRR I/ CRR II/ CRR III proposal. Third, it takes a look at the historical evolution of this goal in EU prudential regulation.

3.1.3.1. Grammatical and Plurilingual Interpretation

At first sight, the wording of 'depositor and investor protection' does not clearly indicate whether there ought to be individual or collective protection. On some occasions, CRD IV explicitly refers to the 'collective interests' of depositors and investors.[161] *Ex contrario*, this may mean that the other references to depositor and investor protection are not limited to collective interests, but rather include individual interests. An individualised meaning of depositors and investors is further supported by a plurilingual interpretation. The comparative analysis of the English, French, Italian, Spanish and German versions of CRD IV/ CRD V/ CRD VI proposal and CRR I/ CRR II/ CRR III proposal shows that they each refer to groups of persons that can be individualised. Instead of abstract references to deposits and investments as assets, CRD IV/ CRD V/ CRD VI proposal and CRR I/ CRR II/ CRR III proposal aim to protect 'depositors and investors', '*déposants et investisseurs*', '*investitori e depositanti*', '*inversores y depositantes*' and '*Einleger und Anleger*' as persons.[162] In this regard, depositor and investor protection differs from the CRD IV goal to 'protect savings', '*protéger l'épargne*', '*proteggere il risparmio*', '*proteger el ahorro*', which refers to the protection of savings as assets.[163] Only the German version of CRD IV refers to the individual savers ('*Schutz der Sparer*').[164] The individual protection goal of depositor and investor protection further becomes obvious from the different linguistic versions of the aim of supervision on a consolidated basis under CRD IV,[165] as well as the general aims of prudential regulation under

161 E.g. Art. 43(1), (2) sentence 1 CRD IV.

162 Recital 47, Arts. 9(2), 18(d) 43(1), (2), 50(2),(4), 95(2) CRD IV; Recital 8 CRD V (referring to 'depositors, investors and consumers'), Art. 1(8), (11)(a) CRD V (only referring to 'depositors'); Recital 19, Art. 1(13) CRD VI proposal inserting Art. 48d(2)(d) in CRD V, Art. 1(13) CRD VI proposal inserting Art. 48k(1)(c) in CRD V (only referring to 'depositors'), Recitals 7, 76, Art. 395(6) CRR I; Recitals 60 and 61 CRR II (only referring to 'investors'), Art. 1(3) CRR III proposal inserting Art. 5a(4)(f) in CRR II, Art. 1(251) CRR III proposal inserting Art. 506d(1) in CRR II (only referring to 'investors'), Recital 2(2), Art. 1(253) CRR III proposal inserting Art. 518(3) in CRR II (only referring to 'depositors').

163 See English, French, Italian and Spanish versions of Recital 12 sentence 1 CRD IV.

164 See German version of Recital 12 sentence 1 CRD IV.

165 Recital 47 sentence 1 CRD IV: 'Supervision of institutions on a consolidated basis aims to protect the interests of depositors and investors of institutions and to ensure the stability of the financial system'; '*La surveillance des établissements sur base consolidée vise à protéger l'intérêt des déposants et des investisseurs auprès des établissements et à assurer la stabilité du système financier*'; '*La vigilanza su base consolidata degli enti ha lo scopo di tutelare gli interessi di depositanti e investitori degli enti e di assicurare la stabilità del sistema finanziario*';

CRR I.[166] The plurilingual interpretation of CRD IV/ CRD V/ CRD VI proposal and CRR I/ CRR II/ CRR III proposal thus confirms that the goal is meant to protect individual depositors and investors.

3.1.3.2. Systematic Interpretation

As to the systematic context, CRD IV and CRR I often name investor and depositor protection in combination with market stability.[167] It could be argued that this conjunction unites the two goals in their pursuit of collective protection. This view could invoke the argument that the conjunction 'and' does not separate the two goals, but unifies them. However, from a systematic viewpoint, the explicit mention of investor and depositor protection tends to indicate the contrary. There appears to be no need for the EU legislator to specify two goals instead of one if they were in fact the same. Also, the juxtaposition of the two aims underlines that they each have a different meaning. The second reading reflects the general distinction in capital markets regulation between market protection and individual protection. It is well-established that individual protection does not contravene, but rather reinforces market protection.[168] Hence, it is probable that the EU legislator intends the duality of goals as market and individual protection. Recital 8 CRD V speaks in favour of this interpretation as it juxtaposes the three different aims of supervisory convergence, a level playing-field for institutions and adequate protection of depositors, investors and consumers, giving each aim equal weight. In that vein, Recital 19 CRD VI proposal addresses two adverse outcomes that could be caused by the failure of a third-country branch, which are (i) affecting highly vulnerable depositors, and (ii) a possible loss of confidence in the safety and soundness of the banking system of the Member State and its ability to protect citizens' savings.

'*La supervisión de las entidades en base consolidada tiene como objetivo proteger los intereses de los depositantes e inversores de entidades de crédito o de empresas de inversión y asegurar la estabilidad del sistema financiero*'; '*Die Beaufsichtigung von Instituten auf konsolidierter Basis zielt darauf ab, die Interessen von Einlegern und Anlegern zu schützen und die Stabilität des Finanzsystems sicherzustellen*'.

166 Recital 7 sentence 1 CRR I: 'a high level of protection of investors and depositors'; '*un niveau élevé de protection des investisseurs et des déposants*'; '*un elevato livello di protezione degli investitori e dei depositanti*'; '*un elevado grado de protección de los inversores y los depositantes*'; '*einen hohen Grad an Anleger- und Einlegerschutz*'.

167 E.g. Recital 47 sentence 1 CRD IV; Recital 7 sentence 1 CRR I.

168 K.J. Hopt, *Der Kapitalanlegerschutz im Recht der Banken – Gesellschafts-, bank- und börsenrechtliche Anforderungen an das Beratungs- und Verwaltungsverhalten der Kreditinstitute*, C.H. Beck, Munich 1975, pp. 51–52, 334–337; N. Moloney, above n. 93, pp. 45–67.

3.1.3.3. Historical Interpretation

The First Banking Directive[169] did not mention depositor and investor protection at all. Instead, the coordination of credit institutions was meant to protect savings and to create equal conditions of competition.[170] The regulatory goal of depositor and investor protection appeared for the first time in the Second Banking Directive[171] in provisions still present in the current framework. The derogation from the licence requirement already required the exempted activities to be otherwise 'subject to regulations and controls intended to protect depositors and investors and applicable to those cases'.[172] In cross-border banking activities, the host Member State supervisor was allowed to 'take any precautionary measures necessary to protect the interests of depositors, investors and others to whom services are provided'.[173] The ensuing Bank Solvency Directive[174] and Capital Adequacy Directive[175] focused on creating a common banking market and reducing distortions of competition.[176] Depositor and investor protection was not present in these legislative acts. However, it gained importance in the CRD I package consisting of a new Banking Directive[177] and a new Capital Adequacy Directive.[178] Since then, bank supervision on a consolidated basis aims specifically at 'protecting the interests of the depositors of credit institutions'[179] and capital requirements serve 'to ensure the continuity of institutions and to protect investors'.[180] This evolutionary process culminated in CRD IV/ CRD V/ CRD VI proposal and CRR I/ CRR II/ CRR III proposal, which articulate the aim of depositor and investor protection more strongly than did the previous legislative acts. Therefore, a historical interpretation of EU prudential regulation shows that

169 First Council Directive 77/780/EEC of 12 December 1977 on the coordination of laws, regulations and administrative provisions relating to the taking up and pursuit of the business of credit institutions [1977] OJ L 322/30.

170 Recital 4 First Banking Directive.

171 Second Council Directive 89/646/EEC of 15 December 1989 on the coordination of laws, regulations and administrative provisions relating to the taking up and pursuit of the business of credit institutions and amending Directive 77/780/EEC [1989] OJ L 386/1.

172 Art. 3 sentence 2 Second Banking Directive.

173 Art. 21(7) sentence 1 Second Banking Directive.

174 Council Directive 89/647/EEC of 18 December 1989 on a solvency ratio for credit institutions [1989] OJ L 386/14.

175 Council Directive 93/6/EEC of 15 March 1993 on the capital adequacy of investments firms and credit institutions [1993] OJ L 141/1.

176 Recital 4 Bank Solvency Directive; Recitals 9–10 Capital Adequacy Directive.

177 Directive 2006/48/EC of the European Parliament and of the Council of 14 June 2006 relating to the taking up and pursuit of the business of credit institutions (recast) [2006] OJ L 177/1.

178 Directive 2006/49/EC of the European Parliament and of the Council of 14 June 2006 on the capital adequacy of investment firms and credit institutions (recast) [2006] OJ L 177/201.

179 Recital 57 Banking Directive 2006/48/EC; reflected in Recital 47 sentence 1 CRD IV.

180 Recital 12 Capital Adequacy Directive 2006/49/EC; reflected in Recital 7 sentence 1 CRR I.

the regulatory goal of depositor and investor protection has increasingly gained importance. The legislative evolution further underlines the systematic interpretation according to which depositor and investor protection is meant in the opposite sense to the goal of market protection and therefore aims at individual protection.

3.2. CONSUMER CREDITWORTHINESS ASSESSMENT

Besides the core EU legislative acts of prudential regulation, individual protection has become the focus of EU consumer credit regulation. The increasing role of conduct-of-business duties can be seen in the evolution of the duty of responsible lending,[181] nowadays incorporated in the assessment of consumer creditworthiness.

3.2.1. Evolution up to the Consumer Credit Directive

The consumer creditworthiness assessment was still far away when the First Consumer Credit Directive[182] introduced the category of consumer borrowers. In 2002, the Commission proposed a new version containing the principle of 'responsible lending' as a partial exception to the otherwise dominant principle of borrower autonomy and personal responsibility.[183] It prescribed that

> [w]here the creditor concludes a credit agreement or surety agreement or increases the total amount of credit or the amount guaranteed, he is assumed to have previously assessed, by any means at his disposal, whether the consumer and, where appropriate, the guarantor can reasonably be expected to discharge their obligations under the agreement.[184]

---

181 Y.M. Atamer, 'Duty of Responsible Lending: Should the European Union Take Action?' in S. Grundmann and Y.M. Atamer (eds.), *The Failure of Contracting: Financial Crisis, Financial Services and General European Contract Law*, Wolters Kluwer, Alphen aan den Rijn 2011, pp. 179–202; V. Mak, 'What is Responsible Lending? The EU Consumer Mortgage Credit Directive in the UK and the Netherlands' (2015) 38 *Journal of Consumer Policy* 411.

182 Council Directive 87/102/EEC of 22 December 1986 for the approximation of the laws, regulations and administrative provisions of the Member States concerning consumer credit [1987] OJ L 42/48.

183 Art. 9 Proposal for a Directive of the European Parliament and of the Council on the harmonisation of the laws, regulations and administrative provisions of the Member States concerning credit for consumers (COM(2002) 443 final) [2002] OJ C 331 E/200.

184 Art. 9 COM(2002) 443 final.

According to the Commission's reasoning, this meant

> an obligation to consult centralised databases and to examine the replies provided by the consumer or the guarantor, to request the provision of sureties, to check the data supplied by credit intermediaries and to select the type of credit to be offered,

but was intended 'without prejudice to the obligation on the consumer to act with prudence when he looks for credit and to respect his contractual obligations'.[185] Since this proposal received manifold criticism,[186] it was finally dropped and the Consumer Credit Directive of 2008[187] instead introduced a less strict obligation to assess the creditworthiness of the consumer. According to this obligation,

> Member States shall ensure that, before the conclusion of the credit agreement, the creditor assesses the consumer's creditworthiness on the basis of sufficient information, where appropriate obtained from the consumer and, where necessary, on the basis of a consultation of the relevant database.[188]

The same duty applies before any significant increase in the total amount of credit.[189] This is less strict than the initial Commission proposal because it does not assume that the creditor's assessment is sufficient for the credit repayment to be reasonably predicted.

3.2.2. *Mortgage Credit Directive*

A similarly strong duty, however, was ratified for consumer mortgage credit. Pursuant to the Mortgage Credit Directive,[190] 'Member States shall ensure that, before concluding a credit agreement, the creditor makes a thorough assessment of the consumer's creditworthiness' which 'shall take appropriate account of factors relevant to verifying the prospect of the consumer to meet his obligations under the credit agreement'.[191] This assessment

> shall not rely predominantly on the value of the residential immovable property exceeding the amount of the credit or the assumption that the residential immovable

185 COM(2002) 443 final [2002] OJ C 331 E 200, p. 211.

186 See e.g. Draft Report of the EP Committee on Legal Affairs and the Internal Market of 23.09.2013 on COM(2002) 443 final, A5-0310/2003Rev1, pp. 6–7; Second Report of the EP Committee on Legal Affairs and the Internal Market of 02.04.2004 on COM(2002) 443 final, A5-0224/2004, pp. 15, 33–36, 69–70.

187 See above n. 12.

188 Art. 8(1) sentence 1 Consumer Credit Directive of 2008.

189 Art. 8(2) Consumer Credit Directive of 2008.

190 See above n. 13.

191 Art. 18(1) Mortgage Credit Directive.

property will increase in value unless the purpose of the credit agreement is to construct or renovate the residential immovable property.[192]

The creditor cannot cancel the credit agreement by arguing that the assessment was incorrectly conducted unless the consumer 'knowingly withheld or falsified the information'.[193] Furthermore,

> Member States shall ensure that the creditor only makes the credit available to the consumer where the result of the creditworthiness assessment indicates that the obligations resulting from the credit agreement are likely to be met in the manner required under that agreement.[194]

This provision comes close to the duty of responsible lending proposed initially, as it enters the realm of contractual lending responsibility.

3.2.3. The Individual Protection Aim According to the ECJ

Initially, it was not clear if the creditworthiness assessment under the Consumer Credit Directive aimed to protect consumers individually, especially regarding the effects it had on the contractual obligations. In *Le Crédit Lyonnais*,[195] the ECJ ruled that French law was incompatible with the Consumer Credit Directive for consumer protection reasons as, paradoxically, it granted a violating creditor higher interest rates than in case of compliance with the creditworthiness assessment.[196] When implementing the Mortgage Credit Directive, the French legislator also changed the relevant provisions regarding the general consumer creditworthiness assessment.[197] German scholars interpreted this ruling as confirming that the creditworthiness assessment aims to protect consumer borrowers individually.[198] In this sense, the ECJ judgment even induced the German legislator to complement the existing public law enforcement by introducing a fully-fledged private law

192 Art. 18(3) Mortgage Credit Directive.
193 Art. 18(4) Mortgage Credit Directive.
194 Art. 18(5)(a) Mortgage Credit Directive.
195 Case C-565/12, *LCL Le Crédit Lyonnais SA v. Fesih Kalhan*, ECLI:EU:C:2014:190.
196 Case C-565/12, *LCL Le Crédit Lyonnais*, paras. 43, 52–55.
197 Ordonnance n° 2016-301 of 14 March 2016 abolished Art. L. 311-48(2), (3) Code de la consommation and created Arts. L. 341-2 to L. 341-11 Code de la consummation.
198 S. Barta and U. Braune, 'Schadensersatz als Rechtsfolge der unzureichenden Prüfung der Kreditwürdigkeit des Verbrauchers – Konsequenzen aus der Entscheidung des EuGH in Sachen Le Crédit Lyonnais SA/Fesih Kalhan' (2014) *Zeitschrift für Bank- und Kapitalmarktrecht* 324, 329–330; P. Rott, 'Verbraucherschutz durch Prüfung der Kreditwürdigkeit' (2014) *Europäisches Wirtschafts- und Steuerrecht* 201, 202–203; D. Bartlitz, 'Anmerkung zu EuGH – Sanktionen bei mangelnder Bonitätsprüfung durch den Kreditgeber bei Verbraucherkrediten (LCL Le Crédit Lyonnais SA/Fesih Kalhan)' (2014) 27 *Neue Juristische Wochenschrift* 1944, 1945.

regime for the creditworthiness assessment both under the Consumer Credit Directive and the Mortgage Credit Directive.[199] Therefore, the current regime of sections 505a to 505d German Civil Code reflects the individual protection aim of the EU law requirement to conduct a creditworthiness assessment for consumer credit. In another decision fostering consumer protection, the ECJ ruled that Article 23 Consumer Credit Directive allows for national legislation rendering a consumer credit agreement free of charge and free of interest if it does not include minimum mandatory information, e.g. the annual interest rate, number and frequency of payments or the statement of notarial fees.[200]

4. STRONGER PRIVATE LAW REMEDIES TO ENFORCE BANKING REGULATION

So far, this contribution has shown that private law enforcement is a *leitmotiv* of EU regulation and that EU banking regulation aims to protect depositors, investors and consumer borrowers individually. This last section combines the previous two sections and investigates the extent to which the individual protection goal in EU banking regulation requires stronger enforcement by means of private law.[201] Therefore, it first looks at the ECJ's position on the issue in relevant judgments (section 4.1.). Second, it analyses the legal reasons for stronger private law enforcement of banking regulation (section 4.2.). One argument is that banking regulation is comparable to capital markets regulation and competition law from a structural and a functional point of view (4.2.1.). Another argument is that the creditworthiness assessment in consumer credit regulation represents a broader shift of banking regulation duties towards private law duties (4.2.2.). A third argument can be drawn from the ECJ case law on the effective enforcement of 'individual rights' (4.2.3.). Finally, the most promising private law remedies to enforce banking regulation are identified and illustrated with examples: contract interpretation, contract nullity and damages (section 4.3.).

---

199 Regierungsentwurf eines Gesetzes zur Umsetzung der Wohnimmobilienkreditrichtlinie vom 07.09.2015, BT-Drs. 18/5922, S. 97.

200 Case C-42/15, *Home Credit Slovakia v. Klára Bíróová*, ECLI:EU:C:2016:842, paras. 60–73.

201 On the European Banking Union shaping private law duties more generally, see S. Grundmann, 'The Banking Union Translated into (Private Law) Duties: Infrastructure and Rulebook' (2015) 16 *European Business Organization Law Review* 357, 370–379.

4.1. RELEVANT ECJ JUDGMENTS

The ECJ has not yet been asked to what extent the individual protection aim of prudential banking regulation requires enforcement via private law remedies. As to the Consumer Credit Directive, in *Le Crédit Lyonnais*, the ECJ acknowledged that it grants individual consumer protection with civil law repercussions.[202] The ECJ confirmed this ruling in *CA Consumer Finance* and further held that the burden of proof for the correct assessment of creditworthiness cannot be placed on the consumer.[203] Whether the duties arising from prudential banking regulation more generally require enforcement via private law remedies has not yet been decided upon. However, three cases give important hints in this context: *Parodi*, *Peter Paul* and *Bankinter*.

4.1.1. Parodi

In the period before the Second Banking Directive harmonised the mutual recognition of banking services (so-called 'EU passport'[204]), the ECJ created a similar regime based on the fundamental freedoms of EU law, in *Parodi*.[205] In this case, a French real estate company sought the annulment of a mortgage loan it had entered into with a Dutch bank and claimed the repayment of interests and contract charges on the grounds that the Dutch bank was not licensed in France.[206] Under French law, this was sufficient for the contract to be declared void. The French *Cour de Cassation* asked the ECJ if this requirement of French law infringed upon the freedom to provide services and the freedom of establishment.[207] The ECJ ruled that the freedom to provide services was contrary to such rules unless the licensing requirement applied to all banking activities in that state, and was furthermore justified on the grounds of public interest and was proportionate.[208] Although it was for the *Cour de Cassation* to decide whether the French rule respected these standards, the ECJ stated in an *obiter dictum* that the requirement of an establishment to be licensed under national law practically negates the freedom to provide cross-border

202 Case C-565/12, *LCL Le Crédit Lyonnais*, paras. 43, 52–55.

203 Case C-449/13, *CA Consumer Finance SA v. Ingrid Bakkaus*, ECLI:EU:C:2014:2464, paras. 20–32.

204 On the consequences of the UK leaving the EU in this context H. Berger and N. Badenhoop, 'Financial Services and Brexit – Navigating Towards Future Market Access' (2018) 19 *European Business Organization Law Review* 679.

205 Case C-222/95, *Société civile immobilière Parodi v. Banque H. Albert de Bary et Cie*, ECLI:EU:C:1997:345.

206 Case C-222/95, *Parodi*, paras. 2–3.

207 Cass. com., preliminary request of 13.06.1995, Bulletin IV no. 174, p. 161.

208 Case C-222/95, *Parodi*, para. 32.

banking services.[209] While the *Cour de Cassation* did not,[210] the *Cour d'Appel*, the ultimate arbiter, followed the ECJ and found that the French law violated the freedom to provide services.[211] In *Parodi*, the ECJ went beyond creating mutual recognition of banking services based on primary law. By explicitly accepting consumer protection as a justification to restrict the freedom to provide services,[212] the ECJ introduced consumer protection as a principle of EU banking regulation. With the licence requirement and the validity of loan contracts at stake, the ECJ furthermore decided a key case on the relationship between cross-border banking regulation and private law. After *Parodi*, it has been clear that EU law determines the effect that banking regulation has on private law. It can thus be interpreted in the sense that the ECJ is generally open to private law enforcement of banking regulation.

4.1.2. Peter Paul

In *Peter Paul*,[213] after being only partially reimbursed by the deposit guarantee scheme, depositors of an insolvent bank invoked state liability for defective supervision, claiming that the German provision reducing the goals of banking supervision to serving the public interest[214] violated EU law. The *Bundesgerichtshof* asked the ECJ if the EU legislation on prudential banking regulation conferred individual rights on savers and investors to supervisory action, granting them an individual right to compensation in case of defective supervision.[215] The ECJ answered that no such individual right derived either from the Deposit Guarantee Schemes Directive[216] or from the First and Second Banking Directives or the Own Funds Directive.[217] [218] Particularly interesting for this contribution, the ECJ ruled that those prudential rules serving the protection of depositors and investors did not intend to create an individual compensation right against the state.[219] While some argued that this generally

[209] Case C-222/95, *Parodi*, para. 31.

[210] Cass. com., judgment of 20.10.1998, Bulletin 1998 IV no. 246, p. 204.

[211] Cour d'appel de Paris, judgment of 14.06.2000, First Chamber, Section G, reported in Euredia 2000, 249.

[212] Case C-222/95 *Parodi*, para. 32.

[213] Case C-222/02, *Peter Paul, Cornelia Sonnen-Lütte and Christel Mörkens v. Bundesrepublik Deutschland*, ECLI:EU:C:2004:606.

[214] Formerly s. 6(4) German Banking Act (*Kreditwesengesetz*); now s. 4(4) Act Establishing the Federal Financial Supervisory Authority (*Finanzdienstleistungsaufsichtsgesetz*).

[215] *Bundesgerichtshof*, decision of 16.05.2002, III ZR 48/01, reported in (2002) *Neue Juristische Wochenschrift* 2464.

[216] Directive 94/19/EC of the European Parliament and of the Council of 30 May 1994 on deposit-guarantee schemes [1994] OJ L 135/5.

[217] Council Directive 89/299/EEC of 17 April 1989 on the own funds of credit institutions [1989] OJ L 124/16.

[218] Case C-222/02, *Peter Paul*, paras. 32, 47, 51.

[219] Case C-222/02, *Peter Paul*, paras. 40, 46.

precludes individual protection via private law enforcement,[220] it is important to clarify that the ECJ only addressed *state* liability, not the effect between banks and their customers. The preliminary question was limited to compensation claims against the state and the ECJ responded within this realm. Therefore, the *Peter Paul* judgment did not preclude general private law enforcement of the prudential aim of individual protection.

4.1.3. Bankinter

Even though the *Bankinter*[221] case concerned MiFID I, i.e. investment services, it is relevant for the present context of prudential banking regulation because it touched upon the transformation of regulatory duties into contractual duties. Two of the preliminary questions related to MiFID I conduct-of-business rules. They asked whether violations of the assessment duty regarding the appropriateness for the client of the offered service (Article 19(4) and (5) MiFID I) required the underlying contract to be void.[222] The ECJ replied cryptically in only three paragraphs.[223] It started by framing the question more broadly around the contractual consequences if the cited provisions were infringed.[224] Then, the ECJ cited Article 51 MiFID I and clarified that it only addressed administrative sanctions, and did not oblige Member States to provide for contractual consequences or prescribe what these consequences might be.[225] Since the EU has not harmonised this area, it is 'for the internal legal order of each Member State to determine the contractual consequences of non-compliance with those obligations, subject to observance of the principles of equivalence and effectiveness'.[226] As a result, the determination of the contractual consequences of non-compliance with MiFID I's conduct-of-business rules remains with the Member States, but has to respect the EU law boundaries of effectiveness and equivalence.[227] This judgment was differently interpreted among scholars and national courts, and two main interpretations emerged. First, *Bankinter* can be read as stating that MiFID does not regulate national private law and leaves the entire discretion with Member States to decide whether to provide for contractual sanctions or not. This reading is mostly popular among German

[220] C. Ohler, *Bankenaufsicht und Geldpolitik in der Währungsunion*, C.H. Beck, Munich 2015, § 5 para. 116; F. Möslein, 'Third Parties in the European Banking Union: Regulatory and Supervisory Effects on Private Law Relationships Between Banks and their Clients or Creditors' (2015) 16 *European Business Organization Law Review* 547, 552.

[221] Case C-604/11, *Genil 48 SL, Comercial Hostelera de Grandes Vinos SL v. Bankinter SA, Banco Bilbao Vizcaya Argentaria SA*, ECLI:EU:C:2013:344.

[222] Case C-604/11, *Bankinter*, para. 22 questions 2 and 3.

[223] Case C-604/11, *Bankinter*, paras. 56–58.

[224] Case C-604/11, *Bankinter*, para. 56.

[225] Case C-604/11, *Bankinter*, para. 57 sentence 1.

[226] Case C-604/11, *Bankinter*, para. 57 sentence 2.

[227] Case C-604/11, *Bankinter*, para. 58.

scholars[228] and was adopted by the *Bundesgerichtshof* as well.[229] Second, the judgment could mean that contractual sanctions are not made concrete by MiFID, but they still fall within the scope of application of EU law, as they are limited by the principles of effectiveness and equivalence. The latter reading is predominant among international scholars.[230] Some have specified that the ECJ implicitly acknowledged the MiFID conduct-of-business rules to be contractual but left the decision on modalities to the Member States.[231]

4.1.4. *Resulting ECJ Position on Private Enforcement of Banking Regulation*

From the three judgments, we can draw the following conclusions. In *Parodi*, the ECJ established consumer protection as an EU law principle allowing for restrictions on cross-border banking market access. Consumer protection was therefore raised to the level of primary law and can thus be assumed to be a principle of EU banking law more generally. The ECJ further showed openness towards individual protection. The *Peter Paul* judgment rejected claims for EU law-induced state liability for defective supervision. It is important to note that it only addressed state liability and not private law enforcement between private parties. Therefore, its relevance for the present question is limited. *Bankinter* concerned the private law impact of conduct-of-business rules regarding investment services. Nevertheless, it can be relevant for prudential banking regulation in so far as the latter affects the bank–client relationship in a fashion similar to conduct-of-business rules. It is not clear whether the ECJ excluded private law from MiFID's scope of application or whether the applicability of the effectiveness and equivalence principles in fact means that private law enforcement is within the scope of application, but not yet harmonised. The fact that the EU law principles of effectiveness and equivalence apply argues strongly in favour of the second interpretation. Were the private law sanctions outside the reach of EU law, these principles

---

228 J. Lieder, 'EuGH: Anlageberatung bei Zinsswaps' (2013) *LMK* 349–404; T. Bernau, 'Anlageberatung, Wertpapierdienstleistung, Wohlverhaltensregeln, MiFID, nationales Vertragsrecht' (2013) *Entscheidungen zum Wirtschaftsrecht* 629, 630; T.M.J. Möllers and M.C. Poppele, 'Paradigmenwechsel durch MiFID II: divergierende Anlegerleitbilder und neue Instrumentarien wie Qualitätskontrolle und Verbote' (2013) *Zeitschrift für Unternehmens- und Gesellschaftsrecht* 437, 468–469, 480.

229 *Bundesgerichtshof*, judgment of 17.09.2013, XI ZR 332/12, paras. 25–27, reported in (2013) *Wertpapier-Mitteilungen* 1983.

230 S. Grundmann, 'The Bankinter Case on MIFID Regulation and Contract Law' (2013) 9(3) *European Review of Contract Law* 267; O.O. Cherednychenko, 'Financial Consumer Protection in the EU Towards a Self-Sufficient European Contract Law for Consumer Financial Services' (2014) 10(4) *European Review of Contract Law* 476, 487–488; F. Della Negra, above n. 129, pp. 578–579; F. Möslein, above n. 221, p. 554; D. Busch, above n. 133, p. 86; C. Herresthal, 'Zu den Auswirkungen der MiFID auf das nationale Vertragsrecht' (2013) *Zeitschrift für Wirtschaftsrecht (ZIP)* 1420, 1420.

231 S. Grundmann, above n. 231, p. 278.

would not be applicable. Therefore, the ECJ was not indifferent to private law enforcement. Yet, the narrow question on contract annulment did not force the ECJ to take a position on whether Member States are allowed to exclude contractual sanctions altogether.[232] As long as the ECJ has not answered other, broader questions on the private law effect, *Bankinter* should not be interpreted as precluding any private law impact. It rather shows that – even in areas not yet harmonised – EU law applies in this domain via the principles of equivalence and effectiveness. This is the lesson to take away for private enforcement of prudential regulation. In the absence of EU law harmonisation, both principles need to be respected when it comes to the enforcement of EU regulatory duties.

4.2. REASONS FOR STRONGER PRIVATE LAW ENFORCEMENT

Now that the ECJ position has been addressed, it is necessary to explore the reasons for stronger private law enforcement of prudential banking regulation. Three reasons speak in favour of involving private law remedies on a larger scale in order to enforce regulatory duties deriving from CRD IV/ CRD V/ CRD VI proposal and CRR I/ CRR II/ CRR III proposal. First, banking regulation is structurally and functionally comparable to competition law and capital markets regulation, areas in which private law enforcement is already used (section 4.2.1.). Second, the privately enforceable obligation to assess the creditworthiness of consumers is similar to other prudential duties in CRD IV/ CRD V/ CRD VI proposal and CRR I/ CRR II/ CRR III proposal (section 4.2.2.). Third, it follows from ECJ case law that the effective enforcement of prudential norms protecting individuals ('individual rights') requires enforcement by means of private law if the individual protection is not ensured by the supervisory authorities (section 4.2.3.).

4.2.1. *Similarities of Banking, Capital Markets Regulation and Competition Law*

Banking regulation has a resemblance to both competition law and capital markets regulation as fields of EU regulation with private law enforcement. Competition law is meant to prevent distortions of competition and to create a market with equal conditions for competitors. This involves a clear cartel prohibition condemning any violating agreement to nullity. Although private law agreements are affected, the regulatory focus lies on their external effects on the market participants. Competition law aims primarily at market protection, but

---

232 S. Grundmann, above n. 231, pp. 275–278; O.O. Cherednychenko, above n. 134, p. 520.

also serves to protect individuals.[233] Prudential banking regulation concerns the corporate governance of banks, including capital and liquidity. At the same time, these provisions aim at mitigating the external effects *vis-à-vis* the bank's clients, i.e. debtors and creditors. The individual protection goals of both competition law and banking regulation act accordingly. Competition law protects clients from too high prices therefore granting individual rights to compensation through cartel damages.[234] The individual protection goal of banking regulation differs slightly because of the specific business model of banks. Since the bank's assets consist mainly of client debts, banking regulation aims to protect bank creditors, especially depositors and investors, from bank insolvencies. As competition law ought to prevent competition distortions, banking regulation ought to prevent insolvencies. Therefore, similarly to competition law protecting markets and market participants, the prevention of bank insolvencies by prudential regulation safeguards both markets and individual bank customers.

Banking regulation is even more similar to capital markets regulation from structural and functional perspectives. Both fields of law regulate financing structures and financial intermediaries. While banks take deposits, lend this money to borrowers and gain their profits from the interest spread between the deposits taken and the loans granted, capital markets serve direct financing of companies. Capital markets regulation is thus as much about information duties on the primary market[235] as on the secondary market.[236] While banks directly act as financing intermediaries by taking deposits and issuing loans, investment service providers do so indirectly when connecting the investor to the investee. However, from a functional perspective, bank depositors and capital market investors serve equally as creditors.[237] Therefore, the strong focus of capital markets regulation on investor protection and its private law enforcement can serve as a parameter for depositor and investor protection in prudential banking regulation. The conduct-of-business rules of capital markets regulation are functionally similar to the organisational requirements of prudential banking regulation. Capital markets regulation fights informational asymmetries, while banking regulation addresses 'organisational asymmetries'

---

233 T. Eilmansberger, 'The Green Paper on Damages Actions for Breach of the EC Antitrust Rules and Beyond: Reflections on the Utility and Feasibility of Stimulating Private Enforcement Through Legislative Action' (2007) 44 *Common Market Law Review* 431, 432; D. Poelzig, above n. 70, p. 133.

234 J. Drexl, 'The Interaction Between Private and Public Enforcement in European Competition Law' in H.-W. Micklitz and A. Wechsler (eds.), *The Transformation of Enforcement: European Economic Law in Global Perspective*, Hart Publishing, Oxford and Portland OR 2016, p. 135.

235 E.g. Prospectus Regulation.

236 E.g. know-your-customer under MiFID II, inside information under MAR and regular disclosure under Transparency Directive.

237 J.H. Dalhuisen, *Dalhuisen on Transnational Comparative, Commercial, Financial and Trade Law*, 5th ed., vol. 3, Hart Publishing, Oxford and Portland OR 2013, pp. 435–437.

between the bank and its depositors.[238] In light of this parallelism, private law remedies should not be restricted to capital markets regulation, but also extended to banking regulation.

4.2.2. Similarities of Prudential Duties and Consumer Creditworthiness Assessment

EU law explicitly formed private law enforcement of banking regulation with the consumer creditworthiness assessment.[239] Some see this as an exception to the general private/public law divide of banking regulation and banking private law.[240] However, if the obligation to assess the creditworthiness of consumers is structurally similar to other duties of prudential regulation, it can be argued that prudential regulation is open to private enforcement. The consumer creditworthiness assessment is a conduct-of-business rule protecting both the client from a debt that he/she cannot afford and the bank and the bank's creditors from a non-performing loan.[241] Individual protection of consumer borrowers and the general aim of market protection coalesce into a single prudential and conduct-of-business rule. As a result, the creditworthiness assessment aims to prevent systemic over-indebtedness.[242] Many CRD IV/ CRD V/ CRD VI proposal and CRR I/ CRR II/ CRR III proposal rules of an organisational character are structurally similar, insofar as they directly affect the bank-client relationship. Prudential rules on managerial behaviour can thus be considered to be conduct-of-business rules too if they have a direct impact on the depositors' deposits and the investors' investments. Such organisational and conduct-of-business rules directly affecting clients include the CRR I rules on large exposures[243] and the CRD IV rules on governance and remuneration.[244] In the first case, loan agreements are strongly shaped by regulation that clearly indicates how banks have to behave when lending large amounts of money. In the second case, the governance rules give strong guidance on how to manage deposits and investments. This directly affects depositors and investors. Thus, core prudential duties are comparable to the consumer creditworthiness assessment insofar as they affect the bank–client relationship.

---

238 Further on this point see below, section 4.3.3.

239 See above section 3.2.

240 J.-H. Binder, 'Vom offenen zum regulierten Markt: Finanzintermediation, EU-Wirtschaftsverfassung und der Individualschutz der Kapitalanbieter' (2017) *Zeitschrift für Europäisches Privatrecht* 569, 585–589.

241 S. Grundmann, above n. 202, p. 378.

242 Y.M. Atamer, above n. 182, pp. 185–200.

243 Arts. 387–403 CRR I.

244 Arts. 88–96 CRD IV.

4.2.3. *Effective Enforcement of 'Individual Rights' and Private Remedies*

As seen above, EU prudential banking regulation serves to protect depositors and investors individually.[245] Since the modalities for enforcing this individual protection goal are not clear from CRD IV/ CRD V/ CRD VI proposal and CRR I/ CRR II/ CRR III proposal, the ECJ requirements for enforcement of EU individual protection goals need a closer look. The ECJ has created the term 'individual rights' as a category of EU law beyond the sectoral boundaries of private or public law.[246] The notion is broad and not restricted to directly applicable provisions of primary EU law and regulations, but also extends to directives.[247] The ECJ has not set out clearly the conditions for 'individual rights' but rather follows a functional approach whereby legal positions and policy objectives qualify as 'individual rights' provided that they affect individual interests.[248] The prudential goal to protect depositors and investors individually as set out above clearly fulfils these requirements. With regard to the effective enforcement of EU law provisions in national law, the ECJ considers administrative, criminal and private law sanctions to be functionally equal.[249] When choosing between the different sanctions, Member States have to respect the principles of effectiveness and equivalence, and especially 'make the penalty effective, proportionate and dissuasive'.[250] This holds true for civil sanctions too.[251] As a result, it is for the Member States to decide whether they grant administrative or private law sanctions. But if they exclude the enforcement of EU law provisions by public means, they are obliged to grant enforcement via private law means.[252] As for Article 17 MAR, some argue that German law is obliged to grant private compensation rights because the

---

245 See above 3.1.

246 A. Hellgardt, *Regulierung und Privatrecht – Staatliche Verhaltenssteuerung mittels Privatrecht und ihre Bedeutung für die Rechtswissenschaft, Gesetzgebung und Rechtsanwendung*, Mohr Siebeck, Tübingen 2016, pp. 193–194; other scholars label such rights as 'implied rights' referring to the unexpressed nature of them. See: F. Della Negra, see above n. 30, p. 226; T. Tridimas, see above n. 40, p. 57.

247 Case C-29/84, *Commission of the European Communities v. Federal Republic of Germany*, ECLI:EU:C:1985:229, para. 23; M. Nettesheim, 'Subjektive Rechte im Unionsrecht' (2007) 132 *Archiv für öffentliches Recht* 333, 361–385; A. Hellgardt, above n. 247, pp. 186–187.

248 A. Hellgardt, above n. 247, pp. 185–186.

249 Case C-14/83, *Sabine von Colson and Elisabeth Kamann v. Land Nordrhein-Westfalen*, ECLI:EU:C:1984:153, para. 18; Case C-352/92, *Milchwerke Köln/Wuppertal eG v. Hauptzollamt Köln-Rheinau*, ECLI:EU:C:1994:294, para. 23; Case C-186/98, *Criminal proceedings against Maria Amélia Nunes and Evangelina de Matos*, ECLI:EU:C:1999:376, para. 14; Case C-230/01, *Intervention Board for Agricultural Produce v. Penycoed Farming Partnership*, ECLI:EU:C:2004:20, para. 37.

250 Case C-68/88, *Commission of the European Communities v. Hellenic Republic*, ECLI:EU:C:1989:339, paras. 23–24.

251 G. Wagner, 'Prävention und Verhaltenssteuerung durch Privatrecht – Anmaßung oder legitime Aufgabe?' (2006) 206 *Archiv für die civilistische Praxis* 352, 413.

252 A. Hellgardt, above n. 247, p. 197.

German legislator explicitly excluded public supervisory authorities from protecting individual interests in section 4(4) Act Establishing the Federal Financial Supervisory Authority.[253] This German provision is applicable to all supervisory fields of the Federal Financial Supervisory Authority (*Bundesanstalt für Finanzdienstleistungsaufsicht*), including the supervision of compliance with prudential banking regulation under CRR I/ CRR II/ CCR III proposal and the German Banking Act (*Kreditwesengesetz*) implementing CRD IV/ CRD V/ CRD VI proposal. Therefore, insofar as CRD IV/ CRD V/ CRD VI proposal and CRR I/ CRR II/ CRR III proposal contain individual protection of depositors and investors, the principle of effectiveness binds the German legal order to provide for private law remedies in order to achieve this individual protection goal.

4.3. PRIVATE LAW REMEDIES TO ENFORCE EU BANKING REGULATION *DE LEGE LATA*

This last section addresses the private law means that can foster the enforcement of EU banking regulation in accordance with the ECJ requirements of effective and equivalent enforcement. It is based on the view that the EU law regulatory goal to protect individual depositors and investors demands private law enforcement, especially where public enforcement does not safeguard individuals' interests. EU competition law and EU capital markets regulation are forceful illustrations of private law enforcement being a *leitmotiv* of EU regulation enforcement.[254] In both areas, private law enforcement plays a key role in achieving effective enforcement and to empower the protected party. This double aim of private law enforcement ensuring market and individual protection can be applied to banking regulation too. Three private law remedies are particularly suited to enforcing prudential regulation in the relationship between the bank and its customers: contract interpretation, contract nullity and damages.

4.3.1. Contract Interpretation

The first point of contact between regulation and private law is the interpretation of contracts.[255] Parties may disagree about whether a specific provision of a

253 A. Hellgardt, above n. 124, para. 20.

254 See above 2.

255 For a comparative analysis of enforcement before state courts and arbitral tribunals, see S. Clavel, 'The Challenges of Transnational Contractual Enforcement: The Relative Merits of Arbitration and State Courts Litigation' in H.-W. Micklitz and A. Wechsler (eds), *The Transformation of Enforcement: European Economic Law in Global Perspective*, Hart Publishing, Oxford 2016, pp. 303–317, 312–317.

contract is applicable to the facts (borderline problem) or the meaning of such clause.[256] When there is a pivotal problem, determining the meaning of a contract's wording requires a deep understanding of the contract's finality and principles, which draws analogies with interpreting a legal provision.[257] Where prudential duties concern a customer relationship, they can be assumed to shape the contract accordingly. In a landmark ruling on kick-back provisions under the German legislation implementing MiFID, the *Bundesgerichtshof* allowed for the transformation of regulatory duties on transparency into private law disclosure duties via extended contract interpretation.[258] Although this transformation was restricted to 'fundamental principles' of regulation,[259] the judgment can be seen as a step towards stronger recognition of regulatory duties in private law.[260] From an EU law point of view, Member States have to fulfil their obligation to implement the EU prudential regulation aim of protecting depositors and investors individually. This principle emerges from numerous indications and comprehensive treatment in the legislative acts of EU prudential banking regulation,[261] and can thus be considered to be a fundamental principle of EU banking regulation. The transformation of regulatory duties into contractual duties by way of contract interpretation is a private law remedy that can benefit bank customers. However, not all prudential duties can be meaningfully transformed into private law duties. Therefore, the transformation process should only be open to client-related duties of prudential regulation. The criterion of client-relatedness indicates the regulatory duty's impact on the bank–client relationship and circumscribes the possibility to unfold private law effects. A comparative analysis of the consumer creditworthiness assessment and other prudential duties supports this criterion because it shows that structural similarities become apparent insofar as the prudential duty is client-related.[262] Therefore, where public supervision does not protect individual depositors and investors at all (by law as in Germany) or not sufficiently (as might be the case elsewhere in the EU), client-related prudential duties deriving from EU law require transformation into contractual duties. A closer look at the scope of application reveals that capital, liquidity and organisational duties of CRD IV/ CRD V/ CRD VI proposal and CRR I/ CRR II/ CRR III proposal can

256 M. Lamandini and D. Ramos-Muñoz, above n. 39, p. 233.
257 M. Lamandini and D. Ramos-Muñoz, above n. 39, p. 233.
258 *Bundesgerichtshof*, judgment of 03.06.2014, reported in BGHZ 201, 310.
259 *Bundesgerichtshof*, judgment of 03.06.2014, XI ZR 147/12, reported in BGHZ 201, 310, para. 37 ('*Der Anleger kann (...) voraussetzen, dass die beratende Bank die tragenden Grundprinzipien des Aufsichtsrechts beachtet*').
260 P. Buck-Heeb, 'Aufklärung über Innenprovisionen, unvermeidbarer Rechtsirrtum und die Überlagerung durch Aufsichtsrecht – Zugleich Besprechung von BGH vom 3.6.2014 = WM 2014, 1382' (2014) *Wertpapier-Mitteilungen* 1601.
261 See above section 3.1.
262 See above section 4.2.3.

be client-related as they affect the bank's handling of deposits and investments. In this area, the individual protection goal of EU law thus obliges one to rethink the traditional public/private law divide. It is perfectly conceivable to include these fundamental principles of banking regulation in the extended contractual framework.

4.3.2. Contract Nullity

Contract nullity is the second private law remedy that can implement the individual protection goal of CRD IV/ CRD V/ CRD VI proposal and CRR I/ CRR II/ CRR III proposal. In comparison to contract interpretation, it is a drastic sanction and therefore needs to be treated with caution. Despite being a harsh sanction, nullity is deemed by the ECJ to be an appropriate remedy for harm suffered by individuals due to violation of capital markets regulations. Regarding company law, in its *Hirmann v. Immofinanz AG* decision, the ECJ upheld a national civil liability regime, under which an investor claimed the cancellation of a contract for the purchase of shares relying on wrong information contained in the prospectus,[263] and explicitly allowed the retroactive cancellation (contract nullity) of a contract for the purchase of shares as it did not annul the company pursuant to Articles 12 and 13 Directive 2009/201/ EC.[264] For foreign currency loans deemed unfair by national courts under the Unfair Contract Terms Directive,[265] there is a systemic dimension to creating a restitution regime for annulled mortgage loans issued in or indexed to foreign currencies that needs to balance fundamental principles of EU consumer law.[266] Notwithstanding serious concerns against an imbalanced decision for void B2C foreign currency loans,[267] the ECJ created a compensation regime that unilaterally benefits consumers while it penalises banks in *Arkadiusz Szcześniak v Bank M. SA.*[268] As a result, contract nullity can be carefully deployed where it serves the policy goals of EU private law or EU banking regulation. In the area

263 The ECJ found that the national civil liability regime transposing the Prospectus, Transparency and Market Abuse Directives did not violate Articles 12, 15, 16, 18, 19 and 42 Second Council Directive 77/91/EEC. Case C-174/12, *Hirmann v. Immofinanz AG*, paras. 22–45 (in particular 43–44).

264 Case C-174/12, *Hirmann v. Immofinanz AG*, paras. 49–63. Further on this case F. Della Negra, above n. 22, p. 175.

265 Council Directive 93/13/EEC of 5 April 1993 on unfair terms in consumer contracts [1993] OJ L 95/29.

266 S. Grundmann and N. Badenhoop 'Foreign Currency Loans and the Foundations of European Contract Law – A Case for Financial and Contractual Crisis?' (2023) 19(1) *European Review of Contract Law* 1, available with open access, at: https://doi.org/10.1515/ercl-2023-2002.

267 Ibid.

268 Case C-520/21, *Arkadiusz Szcześniak v. Bank M. SA*, ECLI:EU:C:2023:478; N. Badenhoop and S. Grundmann 'Restitutionsansprüche aus Fremdwährungskrediten bei AGB-Nichtigkeit' (2023) BKR - Zeitschrift für Bank- und Kapitalmarktrecht 530, 535.

of prudential regulation, again, client-relatedness is the appropriate criterion for identifying the transformable prudential duties. In the light of its strong legal effect, contract nullity can apply only where this is necessary to achieve the individual protection goal of the respective prudential duty. For example, the licence requirement for credit institutions is client-related and aims to protect depositors individually. If someone offers banking services without the necessary licence, the contracts should be considered void insofar as this protects the bank customers; the deposit contracts with depositors should not oblige them to wait until maturity and therefore ought to be deemed null by national contract law. The complete nullity of loan agreements, however, would unduly damage the borrowers of the unlicensed entity as they would have to pay back their loan immediately. Consequently, loan agreements of unlicensed credit institutions should be only partially void, i.e. to the detriment of the unlicensed lender. Furthermore, nullity can affect remuneration contracts exceeding the thresholds stipulated by CRD IV/ CRD V/ CRD VI proposal, CRR I/ CRR II/ CRR III proposal and national implementing acts. The remuneration rules relate to depositors and investors, given that they incentivise sound risk management and sustainable profitability to the benefit of depositors and investors as well.[269] In a similar vein, loan agreements infringing the large exposure rules under Articles 387–403 CRR are client-related, since they aim to protect the credit institution's depositors.[270] Therefore, violations of these rules should render the underlying loan agreements void.

4.3.3. *Damages*

The third private law remedy to transform regulatory duties into private law duties is a compensation right in the form of damages. In principle, administrative enforcement does not result in compensation for individual losses.[271] However, allowing individual private law claims against the banks can be a cost-effective way to ensure compensation as long as the claimant has the necessary information and the public authorities don't have it.[272] Contract and tort law addressing such cases varies between Member States to a large extent, especially penalising infringements of regulatory duties, which is treated very differently.[273] This does not preclude EU law from shaping damages under

[269] See Art. 95(2) sentence 4 CRD IV: 'When preparing such decisions, the remuneration committee shall take into account the long-term interests of shareholders, investors and other stakeholders in the institution and the public interest'.

[270] Art. 395(6) and (7)(b) CRR I.

[271] A. Janczuk-Gorywoda, above n. 35, p. 122.

[272] A. Janczuk-Gorywoda, above n. 35, pp. 121–122.

[273] R. Schulze (ed.), *Compensation of Private Losses – The Evolution of Torts in European Business Law*, Sellier, Munich 2011; W.H. van Boom, M. Lukas and C. Kissling (eds.), *Tort and Regulatory Law*, Springer, Vienna 2007.

contract and tort law in order to ensure its implementation. The individual protection goal of prudential regulation can result in private compensation rights where this is necessary to effectively achieve it. Damages claims are the core remedy to privately enforce competition and capital markets regulation.[274] In the light of clear structural and functional similarities to these regulatory areas,[275] this can be applied to banking regulation too. The comparability of the consumer creditworthiness assessment and other prudential duties also speaks in favour of applying damages as a sanctioning mechanism to ensure compliance.[276] At least, where national law does not sufficiently guarantee the individual protection of depositors and investors via public supervision,[277] damages claims are a forceful tool to ensure effective enforcement. Hence, EU law can require the domestic legal orders to grant compensation to depositors and investors when banks and their managers fail to comply with client-related regulatory duties intended to protect them individually. This is particularly relevant in the area of 'organisational asymmetry' between the bank and its depositors.[278] Similar to the informational asymmetry in investment services where investors rely on information provided by the issuer and the investment adviser, bank depositors are in a structural asymmetry towards the bank holding and managing their deposits. Depositors trust the sound organisation of the bank and rely on its future solvency but have little insight into the organisational arrangements within the bank and into how their deposits are reinvested. The term 'organisational asymmetry' reflects the depositors' particular information asymmetry *vis-à-vis* their banks. For this very reason, deposit guarantee schemes have been put in place.[279] However, their protection is limited to a certain value. Furthermore, they offer no direct compensation rights against bank managers who fail to comply with prudential duties. Facing depositors' damages claims would strongly incentivise bank managers to comply with the client-related prudential duties. Despite a general tendency to reduce depositor protection to a public goal,[280] it is the client-related governance duties under CRD IV/ CRD V/ CRD VI proposal and their national implementation that are able to protect depositors and investors from mismanagement of the deposits and investments the bank holds for them. This view is supported by CRR I, stating that it should

[274] See above section 2.

[275] See above section 4.1.1.

[276] See above section 4.1.2.

[277] See above section 4.1.3.

[278] See above section 4.1.1.

[279] Directive 2014/49/EU of the European Parliament and of the Council of 16 April 2014 on deposit guarantee schemes [2014] OJ L 173/149; more on deposit guarantee schemes under EU law see F. Barrière, in this book, Chapter 4.

[280] J.-H. Binder, 'The Banking Union and the Governance of Credit Institutions: A Legal Perspective' (2015) 16 *European Business Organization Law Review* 467, 477, 480.

> contain prudential requirements for institutions that relate strictly to the functioning of banking and financial services markets and are meant to ensure the financial stability of the operators on those markets as well as a high level of protection of investors and depositors.[281]

Prudential duties should therefore be enforced via damages claims where this is necessary to ensure individual depositor and investor protection.

5. CONCLUSIONS

This contribution has analysed private law enforcement as a general *leitmotiv* of EU regulation and illustrated it by the fields of competition law and capital markets regulation. It has then developed individual protection as a core principle of EU prudential banking regulation that aims to safeguard depositors, investors and consumer borrowers. Depositor and investor protection is strongly upheld in the core legislative acts on prudential regulation, CRD IV/ CRD V/ CRD VI proposal and CRR I/ CRR II/ CRR III proposal, which not only prescribe systemic, but also individual protection of these groups of individuals. The protection of consumer borrowers results from the Consumer Credit Directive and the Mortgage Credit Directive, chiefly from the obligation to assess consumers' creditworthiness. The comprehensive prudential principle of individual protection is not meant to remain a toothless legislative intention. Rather, the EU law requirement of effective enforcement connects the individual protection aim with private law remedies, thus creating a powerful legal remedy. Against the backdrop of the relevant ECJ judgments in *Parodi*, *Peter Paul* and *Bankinter*, this contribution has identified three reasons for stronger private law enforcement of banking regulation. First, banking regulation is structurally and functionally similar to competition law and capital markets regulation, being regulatory areas with strong private law enforcement. Second, the obligation to assess consumer creditworthiness gives not only an example of banking regulation shaping private law, but is also comparable to obligations under CRD IV/ CRD V/ CRD VI proposal and CRR I/ CRR II/ CRR III proposal. Third, the individual protection goal of prudential regulation creates 'individual rights', which require effective enforcement via private law if public supervision explicitly excludes the protection of individuals. Hence, duties deriving from EU prudential regulation necessitate private law enforcement via the remedies of contract interpretation, contract nullity and damages.

---

[281] Recital 7 sentence 1 CRR I.

This contribution has analysed the possibility to enforce EU banking regulatory duties by means of private law *de lege lata*. Besides, the EU legislators could foster private enforcement *de lege ferenda* by implementing private law sanctions when modifying the regulatory framework (e.g. CRD VI proposal or CRR III proposal) based on Article 114 TFEU, as they did in both the Cartel Damages Directive[282] and in legislative acts regulating capital markets and the financial services sector, such as the Prospectus Regulation, Transparency Directive and the Credit Rating Agencies Regulation.[283]

282 See above section 2.1.2.
283 See above section 2.2.1.

CHAPTER 9

ALTERNATIVE DISPUTE RESOLUTION SYSTEMS IN THE BANKING AND FINANCIAL MARKETS

Pietro SIRENA

1. THE SPREAD OF ADR BANKING AND FINANCIAL SYSTEMS IN EUROPE

Alternative Dispute Resolution mechanisms (ADR) have become increasingly widespread in Europe over the last two decades, being favoured by the laws of both the Member States and the Union, especially with regard to the trade of banking and investment services (and, to a lesser extent, insurance services as well).

Directive 2013/11/EU refined the general framework of ADR for consumer disputes in the Union's law,[1] which was further specified by the Regulation (EU) No. 524/2013 on Online Dispute Resolution for Consumer disputes (CODR).[2]

---

1 Directive (EU) 2013/11 of the European Parliament and of the Council of 21 May 2013 on alternative dispute resolution for consumer disputes and amending Regulation (EC) No. 2006/2004 and Directive 2009/22/EC [2013] OJ L 165/63.

2 Regulation (EU) 524/2013 of the European Parliament and of the Council of 21 May 2013 on online dispute resolution for consumer disputes and amending Regulation (EC) No. 2006/2004 and Directive 2009/22/EC [2013] OJ L 165/1. A series of articles dealing

The depiction of these mechanisms as 'alternative' means that they strive to settle disputes out of court, and it thus implies a neat opposition between them and the judicial systems of the Member States.[3] However, it is less appropriate than in the past to draw a line between these two realms of civil justice,[4] since on the one hand the boundary between them is becoming increasingly blurred, and on the other hand, ADR systems cannot be properly understood as (just) a means to address the shortcomings of the judicial process and to diminish the number of cases pending before the courts.

The nature of ADR systems is highly mutable, both in terms of their architecture and of the type of activity carried out in pursuing the settlement of disputes brought to them. In the banking and financial markets, particularly, the panoply of techniques used by ADR systems covers a broad array of services, ranging from a 'soft' facilitation of amicable solutions between the parties (mediation) to proper adjudication of cases by arbitrators, be they monocratic or sitting in a panel. Their decisions are mostly non-binding, as they do not prevent the applicants (and sometimes the opponents as well) from filing the same case at a court.

Frequently, either national administrations or (associations of) the banking or financial intermediaries set up an independent bureau, often named as an ombudsman, which is put in charge of settling disputes between the intermediaries themselves and their clients. Being of Swedish origin, the term of ombudsman is more familiar in the Nordic countries of Europe, but it

---

with the new ADR Directive and Regulation was published in (2016) 24 *European Review of Private Law*: M. Loos, 'Consumer ADR after Implementation of the ADR Directive: enforcing European consumer rights at the detriment of European consumer law', 61; J. Luzak, 'The ADR Directive: Designed to Fail? A Hole-Ridden Stairway to Consumer Justice', 81; E. Théocharidi, 'Effectiveness of the ADR Directive: Standard of Average Consumer and Exceptions', 103. For a wider account of European legislation on ADR systems and of national provisions implementing it, see the essays collected in: P. Cortés (ed.), *The New Regulatory Framework for Consumer Dispute Resolution*, Oxford University Press, Oxford 2016; M. Stürner, F. Gascón Inchausti and R. Caponi (eds.), *The Role of Consumer ADR in the Administration of Justice. New Trends in Access to Justice under EU Directive 2013/11*, Sellier, München 2015; F. Steffek, H. Unberath *et al.* (eds.), *Regulating Dispute Resolution: ADR and access to justice at the crossroads*, Hart Publishing, Oxford 2013; C. Hodges, I. Benöhr and N. Creutzfeldt-Banda (eds.), *Consumer ADR in Europe: Civil Justice Systems*, C.H. Beck/Hart Publishing/Nomos, Oxford 2012. For a comparative analysis, see G. Kardos, *Alternative Dispute Resolution für Verbraucherstreitigkeiten. Eine rechtsvergleichende Untersuchung zum englischen und deutschen Recht,* Mohr Siebeck, Tübingen 2023; D. Moura Vicente, E. Dias Oliveira and J. Gomes de Almeida, *Online Dispute Resolution,* Nomos, Baden-Baden 2022; X. Kramer, A. Biard, J. Hoevenaars and E. Themeli (eds.), *New Pathways to Civil Justice in Europe*, Springer, Cham 2021.

3 H. Eidenmüller and H. Grosserichter, 'Alternative Dispute Resolution' in J. Basedow, G. Rühl, F. Ferrari and P. de Miguel Asensio (eds.), *Encyclopedia of Private International Law*, Edward Elgar Publishing, Northampton 2017, p. 58.

4 S.P.J. Jänicke, 'Alternative Streitbeilegung und Mediation' in P. Derleder, K.-O. Knops, H.G. Bamberger (eds.), *Deutsches und europäisches Bank- und Kapitalmarktrecht*, 3. Auflage, Bd. 2, Springer, Berlin-Heidelberg 2017, Rd. 4, 1439.

has been widely adopted also by the rest of the continent, where it is now in widespread use.[5]

Despite a certain number of differences and peculiarities, ombudsmen may be depicted as ADR systems of an adjudicative nature. As already indicated, in some of the European countries banking or financial ombudsmen are mainly private bodies, and the participation of intermediaries in them is voluntary. This is the case in Germany, where several ombudsmen have been established, each of them being the outcome of an initiative freely taken by (an association) of intermediaries: banks (whether private, public, or cooperative), investment firms, and insurance companies. Some of these ADR systems are nonetheless recognised by the Federal Office of Justice (*Bundesamt für Justiz*).

In other European countries, ombudsmen are set up by parliaments or governments, as was the case in the UK with the establishment of the Financial Ombudsman Service (FOS) provided by the Financial Services and Markets Act 2000. In Italy, the 2005 *legge per la tutela del risparmio* (Protection of Savings Act) obliged all intermediaries operating within the national territory to participate in the *Arbitro Bancario Finanziario* (ABF) and entrusted the national supervisory authority (*Banca d'Italia*) with providing the logistical and organisational infrastructure necessary for the functioning of the three panels thereof, whose seats were initially located in Milan, Rome, and Naples.[6]

[5] For a comparative analysis, see M. Stella, *Lineamenti degli arbitri bancari e finanziari. In Italia e in Europa,* Giuffrè, Milan 2016), reviewed by G. Guizzi, 'Il valore delle decisioni dell'ABF (e dell'ACF) in un libro recente' (2016) 2 *Osservatorio del diritto civile e commerciale* 567.

[6] M.C. Paglietti, 'La riforma delle disposizioni ABF: una riflessione su legittimazione e giustizia procedurale degli ombudsmen nei mercati regolati' (2022) 75 *Banca borsa titoli di credito. Rivista di dottrina e giurisprudenza* 160; G. Fauceglia, 'L'esperienza dell'ABF: manifestazione di una "pedagogia"' (2021) 74 *Banca borsa titoli di credito* 857; A. Tucci, 'L'Arbitro Bancario Finanziario fra trasparenza bancaria e giurisdizione' (2019) 72 *Banca borsa titoli di credito* 623; R. Carleo, 'L'arbitro bancario-finanziario: anomalia felice o modello da replicare' (2017) *Rivista dell'arbitrato* 21; G. Marziale, 'L'Arbitro Bancario Finanziario: luci ed ombre' (2016) *I contratti* 49; E. Minervini, 'Gli strumenti di risoluzione stragiudiziale delle controversie in materia bancaria e finanziaria' in E. Capobianco (eds.), *I contratti bancari*, UTET, Turin 2016, and in P. Rescigno and E. Gabrielli (eds.), *Trattato dei contratti*, UTET, Turin 2016, p. 660; E. Lucchini Guastalla, 'Arbitro Bancario Finanziario' in *Annali dell'Enciclopedia del diritto*, VIII, Giuffrè, Milan 2015, p. 55; A. Pierucci, 'L'Arbitro bancario e finanziario: l'esperienza applicativa' (2014) *Giurisprudenza commerciale* 811; E. Minervini, *L'Arbitro bancario finanziario. Una nuova "forma" di ADR*, ESI, Naples 2014; A. Scarpa, 'Strumenti alternativi di risoluzione delle controversie bancarie e finanziarie' (2013) 29 *Contratto e impresa* 137; S. Delle Monache, 'Arbitro bancario finanziario' (2013) 66 *Banca borsa titoli di credito* 144; A. Berlinguer, 'L'ABF tra giudizio e media-conciliazione' (2013) *Rivista dell'arbitrato* 19; V. Sangiovanni, 'Regole procedurali e poteri decisori dell'Arbitro Bancario Finanziario' (2012) (8–9) *Le società* 953; E. Capobianco, 'Arbitro Bancario Finanziario' in N Abriani, E. Capobianco and F. Tesauro (eds.) *Digesto delle discipline privatistiche, Sezione Commerciale,* 6° aggiornamento, UTET, Turin 2012, p. 35; E. Capobianco, 'La risoluzione stragiudiziale delle controversie tra mediazione e procedura dinanzi all'Arbitro Bancario Finanziario'

The number of cases submitted to the ABF increased so rapidly that, in 2016, four new panels were added, placed in Turin, Bologna, Bari, and Palermo.

Similarly, according to a piece of legislation passed in 2015, the Italian supervisory authority on securities and exchange (CONSOB) was called on to establish of the *Arbitro per le Controversie Finanziarie* (ACF), which became operational in 2017.[7]

The English FOS and the Italian ABF and ACF are, therefore, hybrid bodies, which operate in the interstices between private law (in relation to fair dealing and transparency of contracts, especially when concluded with consumers) and public law (in relation to market regulation and supervisory standards).[8] They thus provide an overall private enforcement of market regulation, which transposes supervision standards into individual rights (of customers) and duties (of traders).[9] In the following, it will be assumed that ADR systems of

(2012) 8 *Obbligazioni e contratti* 571; E. Capobianco, 'Mediazione obbligatoria e Arbitro Bancario Finanziario' (2011) 16 *Contratto e impresa. Europa* 134; F. Capriglione and M. Pellegrini (eds.), *ABF e supervisione bancaria*, CEDAM, Padua 2011; M.S. Desario, 'Profili d'impatto delle decisioni dell'Arbitro Bancario Finanziario' (2011) 64 *Banca borsa titoli di credito* 492 et seq.; B. De Carolis, 'L'Arbitro Bancario Finanziario come strumento della trasparenza' in *Quaderni di ricerca giuridica della Banca d'Italia*, n. 70, Banca d'Italia, 2011; A. Scotti, 'ABF e rapporti finanziari' in N Abriani, E. Capobianco and F. Tesauro (eds.) *Digesto delle discipline privatistiche, Sezione Commerciale*, 6° aggiornamento, UTET, Turin 2012, p. 1; S. Ruperto, 'L'Arbitro Bancario Finanziario' (2010) 63 *Banca borsa titoli di credito* 325; E. Quadri, 'L'"Arbitro Bancario Finanziario" nel quadro dei sistemi di risoluzione stragiudiziale delle controversie' (2010) *Nuova giurisprudenza civile commentata* 305. A heated dispute about the desirability and effective usefulness of the ADR systems here concerned has been developed between F. Capriglione, 'La giustizia nei rapporti bancari e finanziari. La prospettiva dell'ADR' (2010) 63 *Banca borsa titoli di credito* 261 (against ABF) and G. Guizzi, 'Chi ha paura dell'ABF? (una breve risposta a *"La giustizia nei rapporti bancari finanziari. La prospettiva dell'ADR"*)' (2010) 63 *Banca borsa titoli di credito* 665 (in favour of ABF).

7 G. Percoco, 'Le procedure di *ADR (Alternative Dispute Resolution* – metodi alternativi per la risoluzione delle controversie) nel settore finanziario: dalla Camera di Conciliazione e Arbitrato presso la Consob all'Arbitro per le Controversie' (2017) *Rivista dell'arbitrato* 191; V. Mirra, 'I sistemi di *Alternative Dispute Resolution* trovano nuovo vigore: il recepimento della Direttiva ADR e l'introduzione del nuovo *Arbitro per le Controversie Finanziarie*' (2016) *Rivista dell'arbitrato* 693; N. Soldati, 'L'arbitro per le controversie finanziarie presso la CONSOB (ACF)' (2016) *I contratti* 1056; A. Dolmetta and U. Malvagna, 'Sul nuovo *ADR Consob*' (2016) 69 *Banca borsa titoli di credito* 251.

8 See E. Schmidt-Assmann, 'Öffentliches Recht und Privatrecht: ihre Funktionen als wechselseitige Auffangordnungen. Einleitende Problemskizze' in W. von Hoffman-Riem and E. Schmidt-Assmann (eds.), *Öffentliches Recht und Privatrecht als wechselseitige Auffangordnungen*, Nomos, Baden-Baden 1996, p. 41; N. Jansen and R. Michaels (eds.), *Beyond the State. Rethinking Private Law*, Mohr Siebeck, Tübingen 2008; C. Harlow, 'The 'Hidden Paw' of the State and the Publicisation of Private Law' in D. Dyzenhaus, M. Hunt and G. Huscroft (eds.), *A Simple Common Lawyer. Essays in Honour of Michael Taggart*, Hart, Oxford-Portland OR 2009, p. 75.

9 See S. Grundmann, 'The Banking Union Translated into (Private Law) Duties: Infrastructure and Rulebook' (2015) 16 *European Business Organization Law Review* 357.

this kind are capable of accruing a (quasi-)regulatory capacity, which plays a major role in the architecture of a bottom-up model of supervision.

In this context, it is important to mention an initiative taken by the European Union, which, while pursuing a general policy of promoting the development of Consumer Alternative Dispute Resolution (CADR), in 2001 created FIN-NET, a network of all the national organisations that are responsible for an ADR approach in the field of trade in financial services and are established in the European Economic Area (entailing Iceland, Liechtenstein, and Norway, in addition to the Union). FIN-NET enables mutual cooperation between its members and affiliates in addressing cross-border disputes, and it is committed to sharing with the European Commission any information thus gathered.

2. THE QUASI-REGULATORY FUNCTION OF ADR BANKING AND FINANCIAL SYSTEMS

In its origins, the trend in favour of ADR systems followed the lead of the 'access-to-justice approach' of the 1970s, which was aimed at empowering collective and fragmented interests of consumers and underpinned by a robust commitment to social justice.

Among the scholars who have contributed most in this direction, the name of Mauro Cappelletti comes to the fore, being one of the founding fathers of comparative law in Italy. Together with Bryant Garth, Cappelletti authored a famous 'Florence Access-to-Justice Project'.[10] More recently, a similar stance has been embraced by scholars advocating for the advent of a 'Justice 2.0'.[11]

In fact, the flourishing of ADR systems in contemporary societies, particularly in Europe, is fuelled by the dramatic crisis of national judicatures and the desperate quest for a cure to the shortcomings of civil justice rendered by courts, which is flawed by the unreasonable length of trials, exaggerated formalism of procedures, high costs borne by the parties, etc. Therefore, the willingness of states to support out-of-court civil justice is mostly due to the inefficiency and the downsides affecting national judiciaries.

However, this (mainstream) approach to ADR systems is not the most appropriate. Insofar as they are intended as a wonder drug to reduce the

---

10 G. Garth and M. Cappelletti, 'Access to Justice: The Newest Wave in the Worldwide Movement to Make Rights Effective' (1978) 28 *Buffalo Law Review* 1142.

11 See the essays collected in F. Francioni (ed.), *Access to Justice as a Human Right*, Oxford University Press, Oxford 2007. Furthermore, see K. Tuori, 'European Social Constitution: Between Solidarity and Access Justice' in K. Purnhagen and P. Rott (eds.), *Varieties of European Economic Law and Regulation. Liber Amicorum for Hans Micklitz*, Springer, Heidelberg-New York-Dordrecht-London 2014, p. 153.

number of cases pending at courts and to provide a smarter justice in civil matters, ADR systems run the risk of degenerating into snake oil.[12]

If compared to the judicature, in fact, ADR systems are less conversant with the rule of law and due process, thus potentially undermining the relevant constitutional clauses. From the viewpoint of economic analysis, furthermore, ADR systems may also run the risk of being cross-subsidised by consumers who are not involved in any dispute. The costs of ADR systems are generally borne not by the consumers who submit a complaint but by the traders who oppose it. Therefore, since traders naturally tend to pass on the costs of market regulation to the customers, all consumers in the banking and financial markets are going to foot the bill for ADR systems, including those who are not involved in any dispute with the intermediaries or are not interested in having it settled out of a court.[13]

Hence, for consumer redress as such, the judicature is still paramount for civil justice. However, in the banking and financial markets, where competition is not effective enough to drive the intermediaries' behaviour and to avoid the risk of market failure due to 'moral hazard' and adverse selection, the ultimate aim of ADR systems is to nudge the traders to comply with best practices and higher standards of fairness towards their clients, and transparency of contracts. For many a reason, ADR systems can better serve the purposes of affecting the intermediaries' conduct than enforcement of law through litigation in the courts, which tends to have a negligible impact on the market as a whole.[14]

In the light of the foregoing, the primary function of ADR systems in the banking and financial sector is to put pressure on traders, so that they improve their own systems and practices for handling clients' complaints. ADR systems in regulated markets can thus perform a quasi-regulatory rather than a quasi-judicial function, giving customers a voice, and hence a regulatory capacity.

Accordingly, the structure of the supervision over the intermediaries can be said to have grown to be three-sided: in addition to the two traditional actors therein, the regulator and the regulatees, who are at the end of a vertical relationship governed by public law, a third (collective) actor steps in, to wit the customer, whose complaints are fed into the overall supervisory mechanism through the ADR systems.

---

12 G. Wagner, 'Private Law Enforcement Through ADR: Wonder drug or snake oil?' (2014) 15 *Common Market Law Review* 165.

13 C. Hodges, 'Consumer Redress: Ideology and Empirism' in K. Purnhagen and P. Rott (eds.), *Varieties of European Economic Law and Regulation. Liber Amicorum for Hans Micklitz*, above n. 11, p. 793; D. Leczykiewicz, 'Regulatory Costs, the Consumer and the EU Constitutional Framework' in D. Leczykiewicz and S. Weatherhill (eds.), *The Images of the Consumer in EU Law. Legislation, Free Movement and Competition Law*, Bloomsbury, Oxford-Portland OR 2016, p. 257.

14 C. Hodges, *Law and Corporate Behaviour. Integrating Theories of Regulation, Enforcement, Compliance and Ethics*, Hart Publishing/C.H. Beck/Nomos, Oxford-Portland OR 2015.

In fact, the binary logic of 'command and control', which essentially guides prudential supervision, proves to be inconsequential in the field of banking supervision that is aimed at fostering traders' correctness towards clients and transparency of contracts. Banking supervision must here be driven by private enforcement mechanisms, designed to collect customers' complaints not handled by the intermediaries and churn all the information gathered from around the market, about which banks are misbehaving, what misconduct is becoming endemic, etc.

To put it differently, the functioning of ADR systems makes consumers less weak than they are usually assumed to be,[15] since their complaints may deeply affect the traders' conducts via a stringent interaction with the exercise of the supervisory powers by the competent authority. Thanks to this virtuous circle, consumers stand as co-regulators of the market.[16]

3. ADR SYSTEMS WITHIN THE FRAMEWORK OF THE BANKING UNION

In competitive markets, quality controls performed by firms in the course of pre-marketing and, above all, in post-marketing give voice to consumers, who can affect a retailer's conduct through the expression of visible opinions or, eventually, the choice to exit and move on to a competitor. In markets in which competition is ineffective, by contrast, there is a need for regulation and supervision and, accordingly, for the establishment of a system that can be used to scrutinise customers' complaints, especially those made by consumers. As mentioned above, this scrutiny is primarily aimed at protecting the individual rights of the applicants, but, at the same time, it amounts to a necessary driver of market regulation and supervisory standards, which are thus transposed into consistent forms of contract and business practices on the traders' side.

In the context of the European Banking Union,[17] Recital 28 of the Single Supervisory Mechanism Regulation stipulates that consumer protection as

15 For a critical overview of consumer weakness, see D. Leczykiewicz and S. Weatherhill, 'The Images of the Consumer EU Law' in D. Leczykiewicz and S. Weatherhill (eds.), *The Images of the Consumer in EU Law*, above n. 13, p. 1; H.-W. Micklitz, 'The Consumer: Marketised, Fragmentised, Constitutionalised', ibid., p. 21.

16 C. Hodges, 'The Consumer as Co Regulator' in D. Leczykiewicz and S. Weatherhill (eds.), *The Images of the Consumer in EU Law*, above n. 13, p. 245.

17 The Banking Union relies on four pillars, i.e. the Single Supervisory Mechanism (SSM), the Single Resolution Mechanism (SRM), the Deposit Guarantee Schemes and the Single Rule Book. For an overall account, see J.-H. Binder, C. Gortsos, K. Lackhoff and C. Ohler (eds.), European Banking Union, C.H. Beck/Hart Publishing/Nomos, München-Oxford-Baden-Baden 2022; D. Busch and F. Ferrarini (eds.), *European Banking Union*, 2nd ed., Oxford University Press, Oxford 2020; S. Grundmann and H.-W. Micklitz (eds.), *The European Banking Union and Constitution*, Hart Publishing, Oxford 2019; J.-H. Binder and

such is not a supervisory task of the European Central Bank, and it remains the responsibility of national authorities.[18] It is therefore with the competent authorities of the Member States, not with the European Central Bank as such, that ADR systems within banking systems have to cooperate.[19]

Pursuant to Article 3 of the SSM Regulation, however, national authorities conversely owe a duty to cooperate with the European Central Bank. *Inter alia*, the national authorities are thus required to provide the European Central Bank with ongoing feedback on market developments. In order to fulfil this task, the national supervision authorities must be regarded as obliged to actively promote and support ADR systems, which are the only mechanisms capable of collecting and aggregating all the relevant information on the market. It can therefore be assumed that, if national authorities do not promote ADR banking systems in their own country, they might fail to fulfil the aforementioned duty of co-operation with the European Central Bank.

For the same reasons, intermediaries should not be left free to participate or not in ADR systems; rather they must be obliged to do so. Indeed, for the sake of the quasi-regulatory functions of these systems, all the regulatees must participate in them.

C. Gortsos, *The European Banking Union. A Compendium*, C.H. Beck/Hart Publishing/Nomos, Baden-Baden 2016; L.M. Hinojosa Martínez and J.M. Beneyto Pérez (eds.), *European Banking Union*, Kluwer, Alphen aan den Rijn 2015. For an economic analysis, see F. Allen, E. Carletti and J. Gray (eds.), *The New Financial Architecture in the Eurozone*, European University Institute (EUI), San Domenico di Fiesole 2015.

18 It is dealt with by Council Regulation (EU) No. 1024/2013 of 15 October 2013 conferring specific tasks on the European Central Bank concerning policies relating to the prudential supervision of credit institutions (so-called SSM Mechanism), Recital 28 of which reads: 'Supervisory tasks not conferred on the ECB should remain with the national authorities. Those tasks should include the power to receive notifications from credit institutions in relation to the right of establishment and the free provision of services, to supervise bodies which are not covered by the definition of credit institutions under Union law but which are supervised as credit institutions under national law, to supervise credit institutions from third countries establishing a branch or providing cross-border services in the Union, to supervise payments services, to carry out day-to-day verifications of credit institutions, to carry out the function of competent authorities over credit institutions in relation to markets in financial instruments, the prevention of the use of the financial system for the purpose of money laundering and terrorist financing and consumer protection'.

19 In general, see C.V. Gortsos, 'Competence Sharing Between the ECB and the National Competent Supervisory Authorities Within the Single Supervisory Mechanism (SSM)' (2015) 16 *European Business Organization Law Review* 401.

4. PECULIARITIES OF ADR BANKING AND FINANCIAL SYSTEMS AS TO THEIR ORGANISATION

Contrary to a staple of arbitration *stricto sensu*, decisions taken by ADR systems in the banking and financial sector, as well as settlement agreements between the parties, should not be granted confidentiality. Quite the opposite, such decisions and agreements should be made easily accessible to intermediaries and customers (omitting the names of the parties and other personal data), in order to promote best market practices and to push towards their adoption. This way, the intermediaries will be enabled to further gauge their level of compliance, and the customers will be enabled to minimise the risk of adverse selection of traders.

The focus on a quasi-regulatory function of ADR systems in the banking and financial sector implies that access to them should not be restricted to consumers. All customers of the banks (except other banks) should be able to benefit from the advantages of these services and, conversely, contribute to their efficiency, by filing their complaints.

Finally, it is consequential that, in the banking and financial sector, the judgments of the ADR systems have to be backed up by the competent regulatory and supervisory authorities, which must be inclined to impose effective, proportionate and dissuasive sanctions on intermediaries who do not comply with those judgments. The general preference for reputational sanctions may be ineffective, where a 'shame culture' has not taken root significantly, and this is the case for supervisory sanctions.

Furthermore, the quasi-regulatory function of ADR systems implies that overall information collected on the market and its practices are fed back to the competent authorities, thereby triggering and driving the exercise of their own powers of market regulation and supervision.

5. PECULIARITIES OF LAW APPLIED BY ADR BANKING AND FINANCIAL SYSTEMS IN SETTLING DISPUTES

Given that ADR banking and financial systems are overwhelmingly aimed at achieving behavioural outcomes, the law they apply has inevitably to do with disincentives and incentives for the providers of banking services, particularly in the field of civil liability.

In most national jurisdictions in Europe, civil liability is designed to compensate a loss suffered by the victim of a wrong. In contrast to this understanding, however, in market regulation the rationale of damages is not centred on the claimant, but rather focuses on the respondent and the incentives faced by her or him. Hence, the function of civil liability operating in regulated markets must be conveniently "curved" to their own rationale.

It is undeniable that in most national jurisdictions (including Germany, France, and Italy) the award of punitive damages is deemed detrimental to the *ordre public* clause. However, the possibility that civil liability can carry out also a function of deterrence and disincentive is gradually gaining ground in Europe.[20] Moreover, Article 11 of the ADR Directive can be interpreted in the sense that ADR systems can legitimately derogate from any national law, except for mandatory provisions protecting consumers in the Member State in which they are habitually resident.[21]

Market regulation, including antitrust law and consumer protection, is a public good, damage to which affects not only the general interest as such, but also the myriad interests of individuals who lose the benefits of a social market economy. In a society based on private freedoms (a *Privatrechtsgesellschaft*,[22] according to one of the most recognisable claims of ordo-liberal thought) market regulation must not only trigger public sanctions (either administrative or criminal), but also be enforced through individual claims, which are aimed

---

20 Prominently, G. WAGNER, 'Prävention und Verhaltenssteuerung durch Privatrecht – Anmaßung oder legitime Aufgabe?' (2006) 206 *Archiv für die civilistische Praxis* 352.

21 Art. 11 (Legality) of Directive 2013/11/EU reads:
'1. Member States shall ensure that in ADR procedures which aim at resolving the dispute by imposing a solution on the consumer: (a) in a situation where there is no conflict of laws, the solution imposed shall not result in the consumer being deprived of the protection afforded to him by the provisions that cannot be derogated from by agreement by virtue of the law of the Member State where the consumer and the trader are habitually resident; (b) in a situation involving a conflict of laws, where the law applicable to the sales or service contract is determined in accordance with Article 6(1) and (2) of Regulation (EC) No. 593/2008, the solution imposed by the ADR entity shall not result in the consumer being deprived of the protection afforded to him by the provisions that cannot be derogated from by agreement by virtue of the law of the Member State in which he is habitually resident; (c) in a situation involving a conflict of laws, where the law applicable to the sales or service contract is determined in accordance with Article 5(1) to (3) of the Rome Convention of 19 June 1980 on the law applicable to contractual obligations, the solution imposed by the ADR entity shall not result in the consumer being deprived of the protection afforded to him by the mandatory rules of the law of the Member State in which he is habitually resident.
2. For the purposes of this Article, "habitual residence" shall be determined in accordance with Regulation (EC) No 593/2008'.

22 The concept was forged by F. BÖHM, 'Privatrechtsgesellschaft und Marktwirtschaft' (1966) 17 ORDO 75. Prominently, see as well C.-W. CANARIS, 'Verfassungs- und europarechtliche Aspekte der Vertragsfreiheit in der Privatrechtsgesellschaft' in P. BADURA and R. SCHOLZ (eds.) *Wege und Verfahren des Verfassungslebens. Festschrift für Peter Lerche zum 65. Geburtstag*, C.H. Beck, München 1993, p. 85 and the essays collected in K. RIESENHUBER, *Privatrechtsgesellschaft*, Mohr Siebeck, Tübingen 2007. About the history of the concept in private law, see S. GRUNDMANN, 'The Concept of the Private Law Society: After 50 Years of European and European Business Law' (2008) 16 *European Review of Private Law* 553; K. MEYER and J. SCHEINPFLUG, *Privatrechtsgesellschaft und die Europäische Union*, Mohr Siebeck, Tübingen 1996, pp. 11 et seq., 75 et seq.

at protecting the individual rights of citizens and, at the same time, at building a social order, i.e. the framework needed to put individual rights coherently together.[23]

'Translating' market regulation into individual rights and duties also means that, to a certain extent, the enforcement of market regulation can rely on the initiative of the individuals, and particularly of the customers who seek protection of their own rights against an allegedly 'rogue' trader. Historically, the forerunners of European market regulation have been the rulings of the European Court of Justice declaring as "not binding" those national measures which were found to be inconsistent with the Founding Treaties. By adjudicating single cases, therefore, the European Court of Justice has not only protected the individual rights of the plaintiff, but also gradually removed the inconsistencies and filled in the lacunae of European market regulation.

This interaction between judge-made law and market regulation would not be possible, had the European Court of Justice not rendered the decision in the *van Gend & Loos* case,[24] which has a major constitutional dimension.[25] It was thus established by the ECJ that an individual, by pleading for the judicial protection of her or his own interests, is entitled to challenge the Member States' compliance with the founding Treaties.[26] Therefore, litigation between the parties overlaps with the non-compliance of the market regulation and, particularly, with the protection of fundamental freedoms that is the underlying principle of all market regulation.[27]

---

23 C. Hodges and N. Creutzfeldt, 'Transformation in Public and Private Enforcement' in H.-W. Micklitz and A. Wechsler (eds.), *The Transformation of Enforcement. European Economic Law in Global Perspective*, Hart Publishing, Oxford-Portland OR 2016, p. 115; J. Drexl, 'The Interaction Between Private and Public Enforcement in European Competition Law', ibid., 135.

24 Case 26-62 *NV Algemene Transport- en Expeditie Onderneming van Gend & Loos v. Netherlands Inland Revenue Administration* ECLI:EU:C:1963:1.

25 Incidentally, the judgment was a major achievement by an Italian judge of the European Court, namely Alberto Trabucchi, one of the most prominent scholars of private law of the time. He was able to overcome the opposing and traditional opinion of his colleagues at the Court, to convince them to abandon the view of the Founding Treaties merely as an international settlement of relationships between the Member States, and to understand them also as the source of individuals' entitlement to fundamental freedoms. After that decision, the way was paved for the flourishing of a new *ius honorarium* (see A. Trabucchi, 'Il nuovo diritto onorario' (1963) *Rivista di diritto civile* 259), through which the Court of Justice has arisen as the most powerful and effective agent of Europeanisation of the Member States' economies and laws.

26 S. Perner, *Grundfreiheiten, Grundrechte-Charta und Privatrecht*, Mohr Siebeck, Tübingen 2013, pp. 46 et seq.; G. Bachmann, 'Nationales Privatrecht im Spannungsfeld der Grundfreiheiten' (2010) 210 *Archiv für die civilistische Praxis* 430.

27 Regarding the issue of direct or indirect applicability of European directives in national law, see C.-W. Canaris, 'Drittwirkung der gemeinschaftsrechtlichen Grundfreiheiten' in H. Bauer *et al.* (eds.), *Umwelt, Wirtschaft und Recht. Wissenschaftliches Symposium aus Anlaß des 65. Geburtstages von Reiner Schmidt, 16./17. November 2001*, Mohr Siebeck, Tübingen 2002, p. 29; A. Hartkamp, 'The Effect on the EC Treaty in Private Law: On Direct

Obviously, the legislature cannot be prevented from separating public regulation pertaining to vertical relations (between the regulators and the regulatees) and private law pertaining to horizontal relations (between the regulatees and their customers), and this is generally justified when measures of a purely technical nature impinge exclusively on the inner organisation of the regulatees, and not on their relations towards other actors in the market. Yet, there should be a general assumption that market regulation flows into private law, unless its enforcement invariably involves the appraisal of factual circumstances and ultimately requires a technical decision that can be taken only by an independent authority (or an akin agency).[28] It means that regulatory measures can be applied to horizontal relations between banks and their clients not only in the event that these subjects, or groups thereof, are purportedly protected by the regulator,[29] but also if this aim can be inferred from the normative content of the regulation concerned, via interpretation of its provisions, recitals, etc.[30] Conversely, regulatory measures cannot be applied to horizontal relations between banks and their clients if they exclusively pursue the general interest to maximise the common good, without seeking enforcement of any individual interest.[31]

A good example may be found in responsible lending, which, although traditionally a matter for banking supervision, is explicitly addressed by the 2008 Consumer Credit Directive,[32] i.e. a piece of (European) legislation which governs the rights and duties of the parties to contract for the provision of credit.[33]

Particularly, Recital (26) of the aforementioned directive expressly stipulates that 'Member States should take appropriate measures to promote responsible

---

and Indirect Horizontal Effects on Primary Law' (2010) 18 *European Review of Private Law* 527. For a similar debate regarding fundamental rights, see A. Gentili, 'Diritti fondamentali e rapporti contrattuali. Sulla efficacia orizzontale della Convenzione europea dei diritti dell'uomo' (2016) *La Nuova giurisprudenza civile e commerciale* 183; V. Trstenjak, 'General Report: The Influence of Human Rights and Basic Rights in Private Law' in V. Trsteniak and P. Weingerl (eds.), *The Influence of Human Rights and Basic Rights in Private Law*, Springer, Heidelberg-New York-Dordrecht-London 2016, p. 3.

28 S. Grundmann, 'Privatrecht und Regulierung' in M. Auer, H.C. Grigoleit, J. Hager *et al.* (eds.), *Privatrechtsdogmatik im 21. Jahrhundert. Festschrift für Claus-Wilhelm Canaris zum 80. Geburtstag*, de Gruyter, Berlin 2017, p. 907, at p. 934.

29 S. Grundmann, ibid.

30 S. Grundmann, 'Privatrecht und Regulierung', above n. 28, at 944–945.

31 S. Grundmann, ibid.

32 Directive 2008/48/EC of the European Parliament and of the Council of 23 April 2008 on credit agreements for consumers and repealing Council Directive 87/102/EEC [2008] OJ L 133/66.

33 In general, see Y.M. Atamer, 'Duty of Responsible Lending: Should the European Union Take Action?' in S. Grundmann and Y.M. Atamer (eds.), *Financial Services, Financial Crisis and General European Contract Law. Failure and challenges of contracting*, Kluwer, Alphen aan den Rijn 2011, p. 179; O. Osuji, 'Responsible Lending: Consumer protection and prudential regulation perspectives' in K. Fairweather, P. O'Shea and R. Grantham (eds.), *Credit, Consumers and the Law. After the global storm*, Routledge, New York 2016, p. 62.

practice during all phases of the credit relationship, taking into account the specific features of their credit market'. And also that 'Member States should carry out the necessary supervision to avoid such behaviour [i.e., irresponsible lending] and should determine the necessary means to sanction creditors in the event of their doing so'.

In cases of over-indebtedness of consumers, particularly when they have been financed many times, it is possible that the pre-contractual obligation of financial advice has been violated by intermediaries, because they have given credit beyond the financial possibilities of that particular client.

Therefore, a standard of supervision by competent authorities is directly 'translated' into individual rights and duties of the contracting parties. Consequently, litigation about a possible violation of the client's right (to a proper financial advice service) overlaps with non-compliance of the intermediary with market regulation (practices of irresponsible lending). It also means that adjudication of relevant cases shall trigger the improved exercise of the powers of supervision by competent authorities.

In a regulated market, therefore, ADR systems constitute necessary infrastructure of an ordo-liberal architecture of law and society and should be taken into consideration more seriously within the discourse on the scope and the content of a 'regulatory private law', which stands at the forefront of European legal developments.[34]

---

[34] See H.-W. Micklitz, 'The Visible Hand of European Regulatory Private Law-The Transformation of European Private Law from Autonomy to Functionalism in Competition and Regulation' (2009) 28 *Yearbook of European Law* 3; G. Comparato, H.-W. Micklitz and Y. Svetiev, 'The regulatory character of European private law' in C. Twigg-Flessner, *Research Handbook on EU Consumer and Contract Law*, Edward Elgar Publishing, Northampton 2016, p. 35. See also P. Hacker, *Verhaltensökonomik and Normativität*, Mohr Siebeck, Tübingen 2016; A. Hellgarth, *Regulierung und Privatrecht – Staatliche Verhaltenssteuerung mittels Privatrecht und ihre Bedeutung für Rechtswissenschaft, Gesetzgebung und Rechtsanwendung*, Mohr Siebeck, Tübingen 2016; D. Poelzig, *Normdurchsetzung durch Privatrecht*, Mohr Siebeck, Tübingen, 2015. Furthermore, see C. Hadjemmanuil, 'The Banking Union and Its Implications for Private Law: A Comment' (2015) 16 *European Business Organization Law Review* 383; F. Mezzanotte, 'Regulation of Business-Clients Relationships Through "Organisational Law"' (2017) 13 *European Review of Contract Law* 1; F. Mezzanotte, 'L'appartenenza come tecnica di regolazione (a proposito di *"Regulatory Property Rights"*)' (2016) 34 *Rivista critica di diritto privato* 635; F. Möslein, 'Third Parties in the European Banking Union: Regulatory and Supervisory Effects on Private Law Relationships Between Banks and their Clients or Creditors' (2015) 16 *European Business Organization Law Review* 547; P. Sirena, 'L'Unione bancaria e il suo impatto sul rapporto tra intermediari e consumatori!2016) (1) *Economia e diritto del terziario* 41; Y. Svetiev, 'European Regulatory Privat Law: From Conflicts to Platforms' in K. Purnhagen and P. Rott (eds.), *Varieties of European Economic Law and Regulation. Liber Amicorum for Hans Micklitz*, above n. 11, p. 153, as well as the essays collected in H.-W. Micklitz and Y. Svetiev (eds.), *A Self-sufficient European Private Law: a viable concept?*, in EUI Working Papers Law, No. 2012/31, and in H.-W. Micklitz, Y. Svetiev and G. Comparato (eds.), *European Regulatory Private Law – The Paradigm Tested*, in EUI Working Papers Law, No. 2014/04.

CHAPTER 10

FOREIGN CURRENCY LOANS UNDER POLISH LAW*

Piotr Tereszkiewicz

1. INTRODUCTION

The legal assessment of foreign currency loans under the Unfair Contract Terms Directive has recently become a topic of major importance in the scholarship on European private law.[1] Litigation regarding foreign currency mortgage loans in several Member States of the European Union, mostly in Central and Eastern Europe, led to dozens of judgments by the Court of Justice

---

* This research was written within the framework of a research project funded by the Polish National Science Centre (NCN), grant no. 2018/29/B/HS5/01281.

1 See E. Mišćenić, 'Currency Clauses in CHF Credit Agreements: A "Small Wheel" in the Swiss Loans' Mechanism' (2020) (6) *Journal of European Consumer and Market Law (EuCML)* 226; M. Farina, 'Unfair Terms and Supplementation of the Contact' (2021) 3 *European Review of Private Law* 441; F. Esposito, 'Loans and the Unfair Contract Terms Directive after C-472/20 Lombad – Where Are We Now?' (2022) (6) *EuCML* 223; J. Sladič, 'La réception de la jurisprudence de la Cour de justice relative aux clauses abusives dans les prêts en devises étrangères dans les États membres' in M. Combet (ed.), *Le droit européen de la consommation au XXIe siècle: état des lieux et perspectives*, Bruylant, Brussels 2022, p. 345.

of the European Union (subsequently CJEU).[2] This contribution gives a brief account of the Polish experience with foreign currency loans.[3] It focuses on the CJEU jurisprudence inspired by requests for preliminary rulings by Polish courts and its implications for the jurisprudence of Polish courts. The chapter advances the claim that a national legal system which provides no significant regulatory intervention of its own to remedy the consequences of foreign currency lending is far more susceptible to the influence of CJEU law-making than legal systems offering national solutions.

Poland is one of the countries most affected by the legal and economic consequences of foreign currency lending. Early in the 2000s, as interest rates were much lower in Switzerland than in Central and Eastern European countries, the Swiss franc emerged as an attractive currency index for mortgage loans. In 2010 around 64 per cent mortgage loans in Poland were indexed in foreign currency (mostly CHF) with the total value of 40 billion euro.[4] Yet, the value of the Swiss franc began to drop, from around 2.1–2.3 francs per PLN in 2006–2007, towards 3.5 or close to 4 francs per PLN in 2014 to finally exceed 4 francs per PLN in the last few years. This dramatic shift of currency exchange

---

2 See, in particular, Case C-26/13, *Árpád Kásler and Hajnalka Káslerné Rábai v. OTP Jelzálogbank Zrt*, ECLI:EU:C:2014:282; Case C-143/13, *Bogdan Matei and Ioana Ofelia Matei v. SC Volksbank România SA*, ECLI:EU:C:2015:127; Case C-186/16, *Ruxandra Paula Andriciuc and Others v. Banca Românească SA*, ECLI:EU:C:2017:703; Case C-51/17, *OTP Bank Nyrt. and OTP Faktoring Követeléskezelő Zrt. v. Teréz Ilyés, Emil Kiss*, ECLI:EU:C:2018:750; Case C-118/17, *Zsuzsanna Dunai v. ERSTE Bank Hungary Zrt*, ECLI:EU:C:2019:207; Case C-260/18, *Kamil Dziubak and Justyna Dziubak v. Raiffeisen Bank International AG*, ECLI:EU:C:2019:819; Case C-125/18, *Marc Gómez del Moral Guasch v. Bankia SA*, ECLI: EU:C:2020:138; Case C-269/19, *Banca B. SA v. A.A.A.*, ECLI:EU:C:2020:954; Case C-19/20, *I.W., R.W. v. Bank BPH S.A.*, ECLI:EU:C:2021:341; Case C-609/19, *BNP Paribas Personal Finance SA v. VE*, ECLI: EU:C:2021:469; Case C-932/19, *JZ v. OTP Jelzálogbank Zrt.*, ECLI:EU:C:2021:673; Case C-212/20, *M.P. and B.P. v. 'A.' prowadzący działalność za pośrednictwem 'A.' S.A.*, ECLI:EU:C:2021:934; Case C-472/20, *Lombard Pénzügyi és Lízing Zrt. v. PN*, ECLI: EU:C:2022:242. Further CJEU judgments are quoted below. See, e.g., R. Manko, 'Unfair terms in Swiss franc loans: Overview of European Court of Justice Case Law' European Parliamentary Research Service (Briefing PE 689.361, March 2021).

3 This chapter builds upon my prior research on foreign currency loans, including: 'Fremdwährungskredite als Frage des Verbraucherschutzes Eine Zwischenbilanz' in B. Heiderhoff and R. Shulze (eds.), *Verbraucherrecht und Verbraucherverhalten,* Nomos, Baden-Baden 2016, p. 83; 'Complex Mortgage Loans as a Case Study for Consumer Law and Economics' in K. Mathis and A. Tor (eds.), *Consumer Law and Economics*, Springer, Cham 2021, p. 19 (with M.J. Golecki); 'Foreign Currency Loans and Directive 93/13: The CJEU as a Legal Architect' in P. Tereszkiewicz and M. Golecki (eds.), *Protecting Financial Consumers in Europe*, Brill Nijhoff, Leiden and Boston 2023, p. 229.

4 See the position of the Polish Financial Market Supervision Authority (*Urząd Komisji Nadzoru Finansowego*), 02.03.2021, on the impact of foreign currency lending on the Polish banking system, available at: https://www.knf.gov.pl. For data on foreign currency loans in Poland up to 2015 see P. Tereszkiewicz, 'Neutral Third-Party Counselling as Nudge Toward Safer Financial Products? The Case of Risky Mortgage Loan Contracts' in K. Mathis and A. Tor (eds.), *Nudging – Possibilities, Limitations and Applications in European Law and Economics*, Springer, Cham 2016, p. 169, p. 170.

rates had a huge impact on the extent of the monthly credit instalments in foreign currency indexed loans which increased automatically.[5]

In 2011, an amendment to the provisions on loan contracts was passed to take account of broadly available foreign currency loan products. The Law of 29 July 2011[6] laid down an amendment to the Banking Law Act[7] regarding the mandatory information that has to be included in a loan contract. Under the newly introduced Article 69(2)(4a) of the Banking Law Act, the loan agreement must specify, in particular,

> in the case of a loan agreement denominated in, or indexed to, a currency other than the Polish currency, detailed rules laying down the methods for, and dates of, determination of the exchange rate on the basis of which, in particular, the amount of the loan, its instalments, and capital and interest payments are calculated as well as the rules for converting amounts into the currency in which the loan was disbursed or is being repaid.

Additionally, the newly introduced provision of Article 69(3) of the Banking Law Act provided:

> In the case of a loan agreement denominated in, or indexed to, a currency other than the Polish currency, the borrower may make capital and interest payments and repay the loan early, in full or in part, directly in that currency. In this case, the loan agreement shall also set out the provisions for opening and maintaining the account in which funds intended for the payment of the loan are accumulated and the provisions for making payments using that account.

While these provisions offered a slight improvement of the position of borrowers, they did not address the question of whether contract terms dealing with foreign currency indexation in loans already concluded had been transparent or fair. These questions became subject to legal analysis several years later after Polish courts followed their counterparts from other Central and Eastern European countries in requesting preliminary rulings from the CJEU on the interpretation of the Unfair Contract Terms Directive.

---

5 A. Fischer and Y. Pinar, 'Foreign currency loan conversions and currency mismatches' *Swiss National Bank Working Paper* 4/19, 2019.

6 The Law amending the Banking Law Act of 29 July 2011 (Dz. U. 2011, No. 165, item 984).

7 The Banking Law Act of 29 August 1997 (Dz. U. 1997, No. 140, item 939).

2. CJEU JUDGMENTS IN CASES INVOLVING REQUESTS FROM POLISH COURTS

2.1. *DZIUBAK*

In *Dziubak*[8] the referring court asked the CJEU whether it is possible to uphold a contract following the deletion of an unfair term that is inextricably linked with other terms defining the principal obligation of the contract.[9] In particular, the Polish court asked whether it is possible for the loan contract to continue in existence without terms relating to indexation to the foreign currency of the amount due under the contract, as this would amount to performing a different type of contract than the one concluded by the parties. If a contract term regarding the 'exchange difference' between the currencies were to be found unfair and did not apply, that would result in transforming the loan contract from one indexed to CHF and subject to the interest rate of CHF to one expressed in PLN, but still subject to the (initial) lower interest rate of the CHF that was deployed as an index currency.[10] The facts of *Dziubak* demonstrate that once the core terms of the contract relating to the currency conversion are removed, it may be impossible for a court to determine a correct exchange rate applicable to the loan and thus keep this contract in force. Drawing on its settled case law, the CJEU reiterates that the purpose of Article 6 of the Unfair Contract Terms Directive is to substitute for the formal balance established by the contract between the rights and obligations of the parties real balance re-establishing equality between them, it being specified that the contract at issue must continue in existence, in principle without any amendment other than that resulting from the deletion of unfair terms. When the latter condition is fulfilled, the contract may be continued as long as, in accordance with the rules of national law, such a continuity of the contract is legally possible without the unfair terms.[11] Arguably, the most important part of the Court's ruling in *Dziubak* concerns the question of where the criteria governing the

---

8 I draw here on my account of P. Tereszkiewicz, 'Foreign Currency Loans and Directive 93/13: The CJEU as a Legal Architect', n. 3 above. On Case C-260/18 *Dziubak v. Raiffeisen Bank International AG*, n. 2 above, see also F. Esposito, '*Dziubak* is a Fundamentally Wrong Decision: Superficial Reasoning, Disrespectful of National Courts, Lowers the Level of Consumer Protection' (2020) 16(4) *European Review of Contract Law* 538; A. Wiewiórowska-Domagalska, 'Unfair Contract Terms in CHF Mortgage Loans Case C-260/18 *Dziubak* – Where Do We Go From Here?' (2020) 9(5) *EuCML* 206.

9 Case C-260/18, *Dziubak*, ECLI:EU:C:2019:819, paras. 26–27.

10 Raised by the Polish court in the request for a preliminary ruling and rightly pointed out in the Opinion of Advocate General Pitruzzella, Case C-260/18, *Dziubak*, ECLI:EU:C:2019:405, para. 41.

11 Case C-260/18, *Dziubak*, ECLI:EU:C:2019:819, para. 44, quoting Case C-118/17, *Zsuzsanna Dunai v. ERSTE Bank Hungary Zrt.*, ECLI:EU:C:2019:207, paras. 40 and 51; re-affirmed in Case C-472/20, *Lombard Pénzügyi*, ECLI:EU:C:2022:242, paras. 58–60.

legal continuity of the contract should be derived from – EU law or national law? Article 6 Unfair Contract Terms Directive, as the Court emphasises, does not specify the criteria governing the possibility of a contract continuing in existence without unfair terms, but rather leaves it to the national legal order to determine those criteria in a manner consistent with EU law. Consequently, the CJEU takes the view that Article 6 of the Unfair Contract Terms Directive does not in principle preclude a contract from being annulled where a national court considers that it is impossible under the relevant provisions of national law to uphold that contract without the unfair terms which it contains.[12] In *Dziubak*,[13] the CJEU held that the possibility of substituting unfair contract terms with supplementary provisions established by the *Kásler* judgment[14] is restricted to supplementary provisions of national law or those applicable in the event of agreement by the parties, and is based, *inter alia*, on the ground that those provisions are presumed not to contain unfair terms. As the CJEU explains, those provisions are presumed to reflect the balance that the national legislature wished to establish between the rights and obligations as a whole of parties to certain contracts, in cases where the parties did not depart from a standard rule laid down by the national legislature for the contracts concerned or expressly chose the applicability of a rule established by the national legislature for that purpose.[15] At the same time, in *Dziubak* the CJEU holds that general provisions of national law, such as Article 56 of the Polish Civil Code (CC) on supplementing the effects of the contract, do not appear to have been specifically assessed by the legislature with a view to establishing that balance, and accordingly they do not benefit from the presumption that they are not unfair.[16] As a result, the CJEU authorises national courts to fill gaps in a contract caused by the removal of the unfair terms only on the basis of supplementary provisions of national law or provisions applicable where the parties to the contract so agree.[17] It is worthwhile to note that a subsequent judgment in *Gómez del Moral Guasch* extends the position taken in *Dziubak* beyond foreign currency loans. There, the

---

12 Case C-118/17, *Dunai*, ECLI:EU:C:2019:207, para. 53; Case C-260/18, *Dziubak*, ECLI:EU:C:2019:405, para. 58; re-affirmed in Case C-472/20, *Lombard Pénzügyi*, ECLI:EU:C:2022:242, para. 60.

13 Case C-260/18, *Dziubak*, ECLI:EU:C:2019:405, was the first of three handed down by the CJEU in response to requests for a preliminary ruling from Polish courts. The others are Case C-19/20, *Bank BPH*, ECLI:EU:C:2021:341 and Case C-212/20, *M.P. and B.P. v 'A.' prowadzący działalność za pośrednictwem 'A.' SA*, ECLI: EU:C:2021:934.

14 See n. 2 above.

15 Case C-260/18, *Dziubak*, ECLI:EU:C:2019:819, para. 60.

16 Case C-260/18, *Dziubak*, ECLI:EU:C:2019:819, para. 61.

17 Case C-260/18, *Dziubak*, ECLI:EU:C:2019:819, para. 62.

CJEU ruled that a replacement index provided for under national law should apply instead of an unfair contract term.[18]

Undoubtedly, the CJEU position in *Dziubak* appears debatable. Defending *Dziubak*, this author suggested that denying the possibility of substituting unfair terms by means of applying open-ended general provisions of national law may be justified by the Court's concern that extending the *prima facie* presumption of fairness to all national law provisions would threaten the objective of a high degree of consumer protection.[19] The CJEU takes into account the possibility that national law provisions that refer to vague notions, such as 'equity' or 'established customs', when applied to specific cases involving consumers (borrowers), could yield results unfavourable to them.[20] More significantly, giving national courts *carte blanche* to fill contract gaps with any provisions of national law they deem fit under particular circumstances certainly threatens the objective of the uniformity and predictability of consumer protection in the EU, which Directive 93/13/EEC also pursues. Were the CJEU to grant national courts such a high degree of judicial discretion, it could contribute to a de-centralisation of consumer protection in the EU. In his opinion in *Dziubak*, Advocate General Pitruzzella rightly cautioned that the use of a contractual term which reflects a general provision (such as 'equity') would constitute 'creative' intervention by courts, capable of altering the balance of interests sought by the parties.[21] Such an outcome would not be consistent with the long-standing jurisprudence of the CJEU on the Unfair Contract Terms Directive.

2.2. *BANK BPH*

In *Bank BPH*[22] the CJEU considered the question of validity of a loan contract which cannot continue to bind due to the absence of terms that had been found unfair under the Unfair Contract Terms Directive. The CJEU clarified that the consequences of a judicial finding that a term of a contract concluded between a seller (lender) and a consumer is unfair are covered by national

[18] Case C-125/18, *Marc Gómez del Moral Guasch v. Bankia SA*, ECLI:EU:C:2020:138, paras. 65–66. In para. 66 CJEU also re-states its position on replacing unfair terms with supplementary provisions of national law.

[19] See P. Tereszkiewicz, above n. 3, pp. 242–243.

[20] Advocate General Pitruzzella emphasises this consideration in his opinion in Case C-260/18, *Dziubak*, para. 78: 'if the court had to have recourse to a general clause, it would be called on to make an assessment of the content of the general clause and the application thereof within the contract'.

[21] The Opinion of Advocate General Pitruzzella, Case C-260/18, *Dziubak*, para. 74.

[22] Case C-19/20, *I.W., R.W. v. Bank BPH SA*, *ECLI:*EU:C:2021:341.

law.[23] Whereas the Court affirmed that Article 6 of the Unfair Contract Terms Directive does not in principle preclude the invalidation of the contract, the invalidation 'cannot depend on an express request to that effect by consumers but is a matter of objective application by the national court of the criteria established under national law'.[24] This and the question of continuity of the contract should be assessed by a national court of its own motion, in accordance with an objective approach, on the basis of those provisions of national law.

Further, the CJEU held that Articles 6(1) and 7(1) of the Unfair Contract Terms Directive do not preclude the national court from removing only the unfair element of a term in a contract concluded between a seller/supplier and a consumer where the deterrent objective pursued by the Directive is ensured by national legislative provisions governing the use of that term, provided that that element consists of a separate contractual obligation, capable of being subject to an individual examination of its unfair nature. Second, those provisions of the Directive preclude the referring court from removing only the unfair element of a term in a contract concluded between a seller/supplier and a consumer where such removal would amount to revising the content of that term by altering its substance, which is for a national court to determine.[25]

Assessing the effects of the Polish Act of 2011 in the light of the Unfair Contract Terms Directive, the CJEU emphasised that the fact that a contractual term was, on the basis of national legislation, declared unfair and void and replaced by a new term cannot have the result of weakening the protection guaranteed to consumers under the Directive.[26] It follows that the adoption by the legislature of provisions governing the use of a contractual term which contribute to ensuring the deterrent effect pursued by the Directive as regards the conduct of sellers or suppliers is without prejudice to the rights conferred on the consumer by that directive.

2.3. *M.P., B.P.*

The reference for a preliminary ruling in *M.P., B.P.* concerned the question of whether the unfairness of a contract term can be remedied by means of judicial interpretation of that term. Bearing in mind that the CJEU already found a judicial revision of an unfair term inadmissible in *Bank BPH*, this request for a preliminary ruling offered an opportunity to the Court to consolidate its jurisprudence on the powers of national courts when a contract term is

---

23 Case C-19/20, *I.W., R.W. v. Bank BPH SA*, *ECLI*:EU:C:2021:341, para. 84.

24 Case C-19/20, *I.W., R.W. v. Bank BPH SA*, *ECLI*:EU:C:2021:341, paras. 86–89.

25 Case C-19/20, *I.W., R.W. v. Bank BPH SA*, ECLI:EU:C:2021:341, para. 80.

26 Case C-19/20, *I.W., R.W. v. Bank BPH SA*, ECLI:EU:C:2021:341, paras. 54 and 78, citing Case C-118/17, *Dunai*, EU:C:2019:207, para. 43.

found unfair. Unsurprisingly, the CJEU held that Articles 5 and 6 of the Unfair Contract Terms Directive must be interpreted as precluding the national court that has found that a term of a contract concluded between a seller (lender) and a consumer (borrower) is unfair – within the meaning of Article 3(1) of the Unfair Contract Terms Directive – from interpreting that term so as to remedy its unfairness, even if that interpretation would correspond to the common intention of the parties to that contract. In the CJEU's view, the Directive excludes the application of Article 65(2) CC under which 'contracts should be interpreted from the point of view of the parties' common intention and the purpose of the contract rather than relying on the literal wording of the contract'. Referring to the *Dziubak*-test for assessing what can be regarded as 'a supplementary provision of national law', the CJEU considered Article 65(2) CC to contain a general rule of interpretation.

The CJEU judgments analysed above – *Dziubak, BPH* and *M.P., B.P.*, appear to demonstrate that the CJEU refused to endorse policing unfair terms in foreign currency loans by means of general provisions of the Polish Civil Code. Yet, in its judgments the CJEU laid down specific provisions by means of interpreting Article 6(1) of the Unfair Contract Terms Directive.

3. THE IMPLICATIONS OF *DZIUBAK* IN THE JURISPRUDENCE OF POLISH COURTS

In the aftermath of *Dziubak*, Polish courts took the view that the inclusion of foreign currency conversion clauses, which were considered unfair and thus unlawful, results in the nullity of the loan agreement in its entirety. The effects of nullity arise by law and operate *ex tunc* (retrospectively), which means that all services, i.e., payments, provided in the performance of the loan contract must be reimbursed pursuant to Article 405 of the Civil Code, read in conjunction with Article 410 § 1 of that Code.[27]

The jurisprudence of the Supreme Court gradually clarified the position of the parties when a loan agreement is found invalid as a result of containing unfair terms. This implied clarifying how provisions about unjust enrichment should be interpreted with respect to mutual claims for reimbursement

[27] Under Article 405 CC, 'Whoever without legal grounds has gained a material benefit at the expense of another person shall be obliged to return that benefit in kind and, if that is impossible, to return its value'. Under Article 410 CC: '§ 1. The provisions of the preceding paragraphs shall be applicable in particular to an undue performance.
§ 2. A performance shall be undue if he who made it would have no obligation at all, or would have no obligation to the person to whom he made the performance, or if the grounds for the performance had ceased to exist, or the intended purpose of the performance had not been attained, or the act in law which obliged him to make the performance was null and void and did not become valid after the making of the performance'.

following the nullity of a loan agreement. Under the two claims theory, the restitutionary claims of the parties, i.e., the bank's claim for reimbursement of the loan amount paid out and the consumer borrower's claim for reimbursement of the loan instalments paid are considered legally separate and independent. By contrast, according to the competing *Saldo* theory (from the German law of unjust enrichment) one should assume that the balance of the value of the benefits incurred by the two parties is decisive and the restitutionary claim is only available to the party who has received less than it has paid itself, and is limited to reimbursement of the value exceeding the party's own benefit.[28]

In a judgment of 16 February 2021, the Supreme Court[29] held that a party (i.e., a borrower) who has repaid a loan in performance of an invalid loan agreement is entitled to a claim for restitution of the repaid funds as an undue benefit, pursuant to Article 410 § 1 in connection with Article 405 of the Civil Code, irrespective of whether and to what extent this party remains the bank's debtor in respect of the duty to reimburse the capital loan received without a legal basis. The Supreme Court explained that where a loan agreement is invalid, the payments made by the putative borrower, which are to constitute repayment of the loan used, are deemed 'undue benefits' to the lender, just as the payment of money by the bank in such a situation is an undue benefit to the borrower. Pursuant to Article 410 § 1 in conjunction with Article 405 of the Civil Code, undue benefits are subject to reimbursement. A straightforward application of this rule, so the Supreme Court ruled, leads to the conclusion that two distinct restitutionary claims arise between the bank and the putative borrower: the claim of the putative borrower to return the money used and the claim of the bank to return the payments made.[30] The provisions of Articles 410 et seq. of the Civil Code do not contain any specific legal basis that would indicate a connection (proximity) between these two claims. Further, the Supreme Court held that restitutionary claims arising out of the nullity of a loan agreement due to it containing unfair terms are subject to generally applicable provisions.

Invoking the CJEU position expressed in *Dziubak*,[31] the Supreme Court clarified the important question of when the limitation period for the bank's claim for restitution begins to run. Given that the consumer borrower has the choice as to whether to uphold and 'cure' the unfair term (and thus avoid the

---

28 P. Mostowik, in A. Olejniczak (ed.), *Prawo zobowiązań – część ogólna. System Prawa Prywatnego*, 3rd ed., vol. 6, C.H. Beck, Warsaw 2018, pp. 213 et seq. M. Gutowski, *Wadliwość umów kredytów frankowych*, C.H. Beck, Warsaw 2022; M. Szymański, 'Eliminacja abuzywnej klauzuli waloryzacyjnej umowy kredytu indeksowanego do franka szwajcarskiego' (2020) 2 *Monitor Prawniczy* 107.

29 The judgment of the Supreme Court of 16.02.2021, case III CZP 11/20.

30 See also Supreme Court of 11.12.2019, case V CSK 382/18, Glosa 2020, Issue 4.

31 Case C-260/18, *Dziubak*, paras. 55, 67; also to that effect Supreme Court of 11.12.2019, case V CSK 382/18, Glosa 2020, Issue 4.

consequences of the invalidity of the contract) or to invoke the nullity of the entire contract even where a contract could be upheld by replacing an unfair term with a relevant provision, it should be recognised that, as a general rule, the limitation period for claims for the repayment of benefits unduly provided can only begin to run once the consumer borrower has made a binding (conscious, express and free) decision in this regard. For it is only then that the lack of a legal basis for the performance of an obligation can be assumed to have become definite, and the parties can effectively demand the return of the undue performance under Article 120 § 1 of the Civil Code.[32]

This standpoint was confirmed in the Supreme Court's resolution on 7 May 2021[33] regarding the effects of nullity of a loan contract on mutual claims between the parties with a view to the application of the provisions on unjust enrichment. The decision, which was handed down in response to a request by the Financial Ombudsman to provide a uniform interpretation of law, is significant for clarifying two questions. First, the Supreme Court held that, pursuant to Article 385[1] § 1 of the Civil Code, an unfair contract term is by law ineffective 'in favour of the consumer', which means that the consumer may give subsequent 'informed, explicit and free consent' to this term and thus restore its legal effect retroactively.[34] Should the consumer elect not to subsequently 'revive' the contract term, it remains invalid and produces no effect between the parties. A court deciding a dispute has to take into account *ex officio* that an unfair term does not produce any legal effect.[35] Furthermore, Article 385[1] § 2 of the Civil Code – whereby where an unfair contract term does not bind the consumer, the parties shall nevertheless be bound by the remaining provisions of that contract – takes precedence over general provisions on partial nullity of a contract.[36] This is how the Supreme

---

[32] The Supreme Court notes the similarity of this case to the established requirement of *condictio causa finita*.

[33] The resolution of the Supreme Court of 07.052021, case III CZP 6/21.

[34] The Supreme Court explains that a consumer may express their consent before a court or out-of-court provided they have been comprehensively informed about the right to give consent to the contract term but also about the consequences of permanent ineffectiveness of the contract.

[35] The Supreme Court cites an extensive case law which arose mostly before foreign currency loans litigation: Supreme Court resolution of 29.062007 r., III CZP 62/07, OSNC 2008, Issue 7–8, item 87 and resolution of a panel of seven judges of the Supreme Court of 20.062018, III CZP 29/17, OSNC 2019, No. 1, item 2; Supreme Court of 30.05.2014, III CSK 204/13, 'Monitor Prawa Bankowego' 2015, No. 1, p. 22; Supreme Court of 01.03.2017, IV CSK 285/16; Supreme Court of 14.07.2017, II CSK 803/16, OSNC 2018, Nos. 7–8, item 79; Supreme Court of 04.04.2019, III CSK 159/17, OSP 2019, no. 12, item 115; Supreme Court of 30.06.2020, III CSK 343/17, OSNC 2021, no. 2, item 13.

[36] Under Article 58(3) CC, 'Where only part of a legal act is invalid, the act shall remain valid as regards the remaining parts, unless it follows from the circumstances that without the invalid provisions the act would not have been concluded'. If one disapplies Article 58(3)

Court implements the CJEU case-law on Article 6 of the Unfair Contract Terms Directive under the Polish Civil Code.

Second, in explicitly approving the previous judgment of 16 February 2021, the Supreme Court took the view that where a loan agreement cannot continue to bind the parties without an invalid provision, both parties, the consumer borrower and the lender, have separate claims for the return of monies paid in respect of performance of that contract under Article 410 § 1 in conjunction with Article 405 of the Civil Code. Further, the lender may demand the reimbursement of the performance from the moment at where the loan agreement became permanently ineffective (invalid). In justifying its position, the Supreme Court drew heavily on the CJEU jurisprudence on unfair terms in consumer contracts. It is clear in the light of the CJEU case law, the Supreme Court underscored, that the payments made by the consumer on the basis of an invalid contract term are, in principle, subject to restitution. This principle also appears to be fully applicable where, as a result of the removal of unfair terms, the entire loan contract is rendered permanently ineffective (invalid) because it cannot continue to bind without the invalid term. When this obtains, the consumer may have a duty to provide reimbursement to the lender. Thus the Supreme Court reiterates the concern expressed by the CJEU that finding a contract invalid may put the consumer at a disadvantage, given that the lender may acquire a claim for a full reimbursement of the amount extended to the consumer.[37] Interestingly, the Supreme Court observes that whichever of two competing theories of restitutionary claims were to be applied under Polish law to the bank–consumer borrower reimbursement claims, their application would not be inconsistent with the consumer protection model under the Unfair Contract Terms Directive.

Most recently, the Supreme Court consolidated its jurisprudence and clarified its position on certain questions regarding foreign currency loan agreements in the full Private Law Chamber resolution of 25 April 2024.[38] The resolution addressed five questions referred to the Court by the Supreme Court President in view of discrepancies in the jurisprudence. The Supreme Court held the following. First, as the law stands now, where a provision in a foreign currency loan agreement relating to the manner of determining the foreign currency exchange rate constitutes an unfair contract term and is not binding,

CC, it thus becomes irrelevant whether the parties would have concluded the contract without an unfair term in it, see Supreme Court judgments of 09.052019, case I CSK 242/18; of 11.12.2019, case V CSK 382/18, and of 30.06.2020, case III CSK 343/17.

37 See Case C-260/18, *Dziubak*, para. 55.

38 The resolution of the Supreme Court of 25.04.2024, case III CZP 25/22, sitting in the full Private Law Chamber. Several government or consumer protection bodies, including the Attorney General, the Ombudsman, the President of the National Central Bank, the Financial Ombudsman, the Financial Supervision, submitted their positions on the case to the Supreme Court.

it cannot be assumed that a different manner of determining the foreign currency exchange rate, resulting from the law or customs, applies. Second, where it is impossible to determine a foreign currency exchange rate binding for the parties in a foreign currency loan agreement, the agreement shall not be binding in the remaining scope. Third, where, in the course of performing a loan agreement that is not binding due to the unfair character of its terms, the bank has paid out all or part of the loan amount to the borrower, and the borrower has made repayments, separate claims for the reimbursement of the undue performances shall arise in favour of each party to the contract. Fourth, where a loan agreement is not binding due to the unfair nature of its terms, the statute of limitations applicable to the bank's claim for the reimbursement of amounts paid out under the loan agreement shall, in principle, begin to run from the day following the day on which the borrower challenged vis-à-vis the bank the binding force of the agreement. Fifth, where a loan agreement is not binding due to the unfair character of its terms, there shall be no legal basis for either party to claim interest or other remuneration for the use of its funds during the period between the time when the undue benefit was made available and the time when the repayment of that performance becomes delayed.

4. THE CJEU JUDGMENT IN *BANK M.*

The CJEU jurisprudence discussed above concerned the question of policing and supplementing the content of foreign currency loan contracts under the Unfair Contract Terms Directive. What is largely missing in the account provided above is the question of the bank's liability towards a consumer borrower in damages. The most recent request for a preliminary ruling from a Polish court in *Bank M.* extended to the question of liability. Specifically, the request to the CJEU for a preliminary ruling from the District Court in Warsaw concerned whether Articles 6(1) and 7(1) of the Unfair Contract Terms Directive and the principles of effectiveness, legal certainty and proportionality preclude:

a) a judicial interpretation of national law, according to which the consumer is entitled to seek compensation going beyond reimbursement of the monthly instalments paid and the expenses paid in respect of the contract; or

b) a judicial interpretation of national law according to which the credit institution is entitled to seek compensation from the consumer going beyond the reimbursement of the capital paid in respect of the performance of the contact, together with the payment of default interest at the statutory rate.

Significantly, as Advocate General Collins pointed out, the referring court did not ask the CJEU to provide guidance on the national provisions governing the consumers' or the banks' claims, to which the order for reference related, but rather to indicate whether the Unfair Contract Terms Directive and the principles of EU law allow such claims as above to be advanced.[39] These questions have not been clarified in the jurisprudence of Polish courts.[40] Further, the requirements for the bank's liability towards a borrower have not been developed under Polish law to the extent shown by German or French law.

In *Bank M.*, closely following the Opinion of the Advocate General, the CJEU affirmed the right of the borrower to seek reimbursement compensation, while it found that the bank has no right to seek compensation going beyond the reimbursement of the amounts as defined in (a) and (b) above.

In replying to the first question as to the consumer's right to seek compensation, the Court of Justice set out by recognising that the Unfair Contract Terms Directive does not govern the consequences of the invalidity of a contract concluded between a seller and a consumer after the removal of the unfair terms in that contract.[41] But, while it is for the Member States to determine the consequences of the invalidity, the rules which Member States lay down must be compatible both with EU law in general and specifically with the objectives of the Unfair Contract Terms Directive. In this regard, drawing on *Gutiérrez Naranjo and Others*,[42] the CJEU in *Bank M.* stated that national rules on the consequences of invalidity of a mortgage loan agreement such as the one in question should make it possible to restore the situation to that in which the consumer would have been if there had been no unfair terms in the contract. National rules should also not undermine the aim of the Unfair Contract Terms Directive, which is to deter sellers (here: lenders) from placing consumers (borrowers) at a disadvantage in an unfair manner. Crucially, the Court of Justice took the view that the possibility for the consumer borrower to assert claims that go beyond reimbursement between the parties (of the monthly instalments paid and the expenses paid in respect of the performance of that contract together with – where applicable – payment of default interest at the statutory rate from the date on which notice is served), does not undermine the objectives of the Unfair Contract Terms Directive, which is to restore the situation the consumer would have been in had the contract not been concluded.[43] It is for the national courts, which decide on the merits of the dispute, to assess whether and to what extent upholding the

39 Opinion of Advocate General Collins, Case C-520/21, *Arkadiusz Szcześniak v. Bank M. SA*, ECLI:EU:C:2023:120, para. 35.

40 For an analysis of the lender's liability under Polish law from a comparative perspective, see P. Tereszkiewicz, *Obowiązki informacyjne w umowach o usługi finansowe*, Lex Wolters Kluwer, Warsaw 2015.

41 Case C-520/21, *Bank M.*, ECLI:EU:C:2023:120, para. 64.

42 Joined Cases C-154/15, C-307/15 and C-308/15, *Gutiérrez Naranjo v. Cajasur Banco S.A.U. and Others*, ECLI:EU:C:2016:980. Paragraphs cited in C-520/21, *Bank M.*, include paras. 61–65.

43 C-520/21, *Bank M.*, para. 68.

borrower's claim is a proportionate means of achieving the objectives of the Unfair Contract Terms Directive, in particular the objective of deterring sellers or suppliers from using unfair terms in their contracts.[44]

Having affirmed the consumer's right to seek compensation, in the second and much shorter part of the judgment the Court of Justice rejected the bank's right to seek compensation from the borrower in powerful terms. To begin, referring to *Banco Español de Crédito*,[45] the Court took the view that granting such a right to lenders would contribute to eliminating the deterrent effect on lenders of the annulment of the mortgage loan agreement.[46] Specifically, an interpretation under which lenders had a right to seek compensation from borrowers might result in a situation in which it would be more advantageous for the consumer to continue the performance of the contract containing an unfair term than to exercise their rights under the Unfair Contract Terms Directive. Further, in order to counter Bank M.'s argument that – in the absence of the lender's right to seek compensation going beyond reimbursement of the capital paid and the default interest – a consumer would obtain a loan 'free of charge', the Court invoked the principle of '*nemo auditor propriam turpitudinem allegans*', which means that a party cannot be allowed to derive economic advantages from its unlawful conduct or to be compensated for the disadvantages caused by such conduct.[47] Drawing on the Advocate General's Opinion, the Court held that any annulment of the mortgage loan agreement is a consequence of the bank's use of unfair terms. This means that the bank cannot be compensated for the loss of a profit similar to that which it hoped to derive from the contract (paragraph 82).

Second, the CJEU, speaking in very clear terms, refused to be drawn not only into evaluating but even considering the impact of its judgment on the stability of the financial system.[48] The argument that the stability of the financial markets would be threatened if banks were not allowed to seek compensation from consumers going beyond reimbursement of the capital paid and the default interest had been raised by Bank M. but also by the Chair of the Board of the Financial Supervision Authority in Poland. As the Court held, the argument relating to the stability of the financial markets is not relevant in the context of the interpretation of the Unfair Contract Terms Directive, which is intended to protect consumers (borrowers). The objectives of the

---

44 C-520/21, *Bank M.*, para. 73.

45 C-618/10, *Banco Español de Crédito SA v. Joaquin Calderòn Camino*, EU:C:2012:349, para. 69.

46 C-520/21, *Bank M.*, paras. 77–78.

47 C-520/21, *Bank M.*, para. 81; on this aspect see E. Mišćenić, 'Unfair Treatment of Banks in Croatian Collective Redress Proceedings on Swiss Franc Loans'. Case Note on ECtHR decision in *OTP banka d. d. and Others v. Croatia*, (2023) 12(3) *Journal of European Consumer and Market Law* 118.

48 C-520/21, *Bank M.*, para 83.

Directive cannot be circumvented on the ground of preserving the stability of the financial markets. It is for banking institutions to organise their affairs in compliance with the Directive.

Analysed from the perspective of the Member States' degree of autonomy in regulating bank–consumer borrower relationships involving foreign currency loans, there is a clear lesson to be drawn from both *Bank M.* and previous judgments: numerous Member States concerned which, unlike Hungary, have not (yet) enacted specific provisions aimed at re-shaping legal relations emerging from foreign currency loan contracts, should accept that the final shape of those legal matters will be determined by the Court's jurisprudence. Hungary was the first Member States to pass a statute regulating the repayment of foreign currency loans in 2014 (the Act imposed the retroactive application of a single exchange rate fixed by the National Bank of Hungary without invalidating loan agreements in their entirety).[49] Regardless of whether one approves of the Hungarian solution or not, the balance of power between the banks and consumer borrowers was shaped at the national level; the Hungarian provisions have so far stood the test of judicial review by the Court of Justice and would have most likely provided an answer to the question arising in *Bank M.*

5. CONCLUSION

There is no doubt that the CJEU jurisprudence on foreign currency mortgage loans has strengthened the position of the consumer borrower in relation to the lender. I would argue that the CJEU's jurisprudence has been consistently moving toward establishing a right for the consumer to a transparent and fair loan contract. The view underlying the CJEU's reasoning appears to be as follows: the banking institution as a lender has a duty to provide a transparent loan contract without any unfair clauses in it. If the contract does contain unfair clauses, the lender may be penalised for it; remedies applicable under national law should put the consumer in the position they would have been in if the contract had not been concluded. This may entail claiming compensation going beyond mere reimbursement of the loan instalments paid and other payments made to the bank. I have long espoused the view – expressed decades ago by *Johannes Köndgen*[50] – that the bank loan contract entails the bank's duty

[49] For an account of Hungarian law on foreign currency loans see A. Pomeisl, 'Foreign Currency Loans in Hungary' in P. Tereszkiewicz and M. Golecki (eds.), *Protecting Financial Consumers in Europe*, Brill Nijhoff, Leiden and Boston 2023, p. 105.

[50] In Köndgen's view, a loan contract entails an element of 'managing somebody else's affairs' [*Interessenwahrung*], J. Köndgen, 'Bankhaftung – Strukturen und Tendenzen' in J. Köndgen (eds.), *Neue Entwicklungen im Bank- und haftungsrecht*, RWS Verlag, Köln 1987, p. 156; J. Köndgen, 'Die Entwicklung des privaten Bankrechts in den Jahren 1999–2003' (2004) *Neue Juristische Wochenschrift* 1288 et seq.

to take into account the borrower's best interest, placing serious limits on an unrestricted exercise of self-interest by the lender in offering complex and one-sided loan products to consumer borrowers. The CJEU's *Bank M.* judgment is a powerful endorsement of that view of the banker-consumer borrower relationship in the light of the Unfair Contract Terms Directive. While the remedial potential of the Unfair Contract Terms Directive has already been discovered, its spillover effect may help establish general requirements for banks' liability under private law in Poland.

INDEX

EUROPEAN CONTRACT LAW AND THEORY SERIES

1. *Rules and Principles in European Contract Law*, Jacobien Rutgers and Pietro Sirena (eds.)
2. *European Contract Law and the Charter of Fundamental Rights*, Hugh Collins (ed.)
3. *European Contract Law in the Digital Age*, Stefan Grundmann (ed.)
4. *European Contract Law in a Changed Banking and Financial Architecture*, Stefan Grundmann and Pietro Sirena (eds.)
5. *European Contract Law and the Creation of Norms*, Stefan Grundmann and Mateusz Grochowski (eds.)
6. *From Formal to Material Equality: Comparative Perspectives from History, Plurality of Disciplines and Theory*, Stefan Grundmann and Jan Thiessen (eds.)
7. *European Sales Law, Challenges in the 21st century*, Stefan Grundmann and Yesim Atamer (eds.)

www.ingramcontent.com/pod-product-compliance
Ingram Content Group UK Ltd.
Pitfield, Milton Keynes, MK11 3LW, UK
UKHW051926100926
8556IPUK00022B/1404

9 781780 686622